GUITAR CHORD MASTER™

POWER CHORDS

The Missing Method
An imprint of
Tenterhook Books, LLC
Akron, Ohio

CHRISTIAN J. TRIOLA

The Missing Method

Discover what you've been missing.

Copyright ©2019 Christian J. Triola, Amy Joy Triola
All Rights Reserved.

Except as permitted under the U.S. Copyright Act of 1976, no part of this publication may be reproduced, distributed, or transmitted, in whole or in part, in any form or by any means, or stored in any form of retrieval system, without prior written consent of the author. For permissions and bulk sales inquiries, contact the author at info@themissingmethod.com.

Cover and Book Design by Amy Joy Triola, ©2019 Amy Joy Triola

The Missing Methed™ for Guitar is an imprint of Tenterhook Books, LLC. The Missing Method name and logos are property of Tenterhook Books, LLC.

First Edition 2019, Tenterhook Books, LLC. Akron, Ohio
ISBN-13: 978-1677693153

Table of Contents

About the Author • i

Introduction • 1

Rhythm Review • 3

Chord Theory: Power Chords • 5

Lesson 1: Open Power Chords • 6

Lesson 2: Root 6 Power Chords • 9

Lesson 3: Root 5 Power Chords • 23

Lesson 4: Root 5 and Root 6 Combined • 41

Lesson 5: Palm Muting • 60

Lesson 6: Three Note Power Chords • 68

Lesson 7: Root 4 Power Chords • 83

Lesson 8: Inverted Power Chords • 104

Lesson 9: Three-Note Inverted Power Chords • 129

Lesson 10: Review All Power Chords • 137

Lesson 11: Drop D Power Chords • 150

Chord Reference • 173

Resources to Take Your Playing Further • 179

Welcome to
The Missing Method for Guitar community!

We're dedicated to helping you master your instrument. To that end, there are a couple of resources we want to make sure you are aware of:

The Missing Method for Guitar YouTube channel.

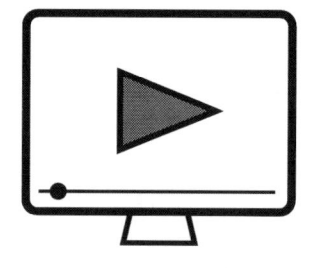

Here you'll find free weekly lessons we know you'll find useful as you work your way through this book, including tutorials on how to play your favorite songs. Find it at: https://bit.ly/Missing-Method-YouTube.

The Missing Method for Guitar Monthly Newsletter.

We only send out one a month, and you won't want to miss the updates on new resources, discount promotions, and more. Plus, when you sign up, we'll send you a free ebook full of exercises to help improve your playing. Sign up at https://themissingmethod.com/newsletter/.

About the Author

Over the past 20 years, Christian J. Triola has taught hundreds of students to play guitar and authored over two dozen popular guitar method books. He holds a Master's Degree in Education and a Bachelor's Degree in Music (Jazz Studies), and has played in a variety of bands in addition to his many solo performances.

What is the Missing Method?

The Missing Method™ is an imprint of Tenterhook Books, LLC, owned and operated by Christian J. Triola and his wife, Amy Joy Triola. The imprint began in 2013 in an effort to bring method books that didn't exist to Christian's guitar students. Today, we have expanded that mission to create high quality instructional materials to inspire and empower guitar players around the world.

The Missing Method™ now spans many series of guitar books, addressing topics from chords, to note reading, practice strategies, playing techniques and much more. Find them all at TheMissingMethod.com.

Introduction

How this book works

Guitar Chord Master 3: Power Chords is designed to teach you how to play power chords anywhere on the neck. In the previous book in the series, we extended the chords, adding more notes to simple major and minor sounds. In this book, we will be doing the opposite. We are throwing out major and minor and simply focusing on the chord sound that defined rock music: the power chord. It should be noted, however, that power chords are good to learn even if you don't play rock. They help you find your way around the neck of the guitar faster, so as you move up the guitar's neck, you'll start to understand the logic behind how the guitar works even better. They also help build up your finger strength so when you learn barre chords in the next book, your fingers will be ready to tackle them.

Keep in mind that this book assumes that you've already finished at least *Guitar Chord Master 1: Basic Chords*, and possibly *Guitar Chord Master 2: Beyond Basic Chords* and are now ready for more. Or at the very least, that you know some open chords, have a desire to learn power chords, and want to become proficient with them as quickly as possible.

What you will learn

Guitar Chord Master 3: Power Chords starts you off by learning basic, open-voiced power chords. Then it moves on to teaching you how to play any power chord anywhere on the neck, starting with chords whose roots can be found on the sixth string, and later, chords whose roots are found on strings 5, 4, and 3. Along the way, you'll learn palm muting, accenting, and have plenty of practice with different time signatures and full songs!

Guitar Chord Master 3: Power Chords is in many ways a definitive guide to learning and playing power chords, and as such includes a section on how to play power chords in popular drop "D" tuning as well. By the time you finish this book, you'll be able to play all the most commonly used power chords, from the basics, to drop "D", to everything else in between.

Good luck and enjoy!

Access the audio files

Audio files are available for each exercise and song. Access these via The Missing Method website: https://themissingmethod.com/audio-files/.

Rhythm Review

Rhythm is essentially the idea of how long or how short you hold a chord or note. In this book, and in many other guitar publications, you will find guitar chords written as a chord symbol with slash-notation to show you how each chord is to be played. It should be noted that plenty of publications, including most fake books, leave the strum pattern entirely up to you. Therefore, it is helpful to have several strum patterns learned and at your disposal.

In books one and two of *Guitar Chord Master*, several different rhythms were covered. Below is a summary of these rhythms.

Basic Rhythms

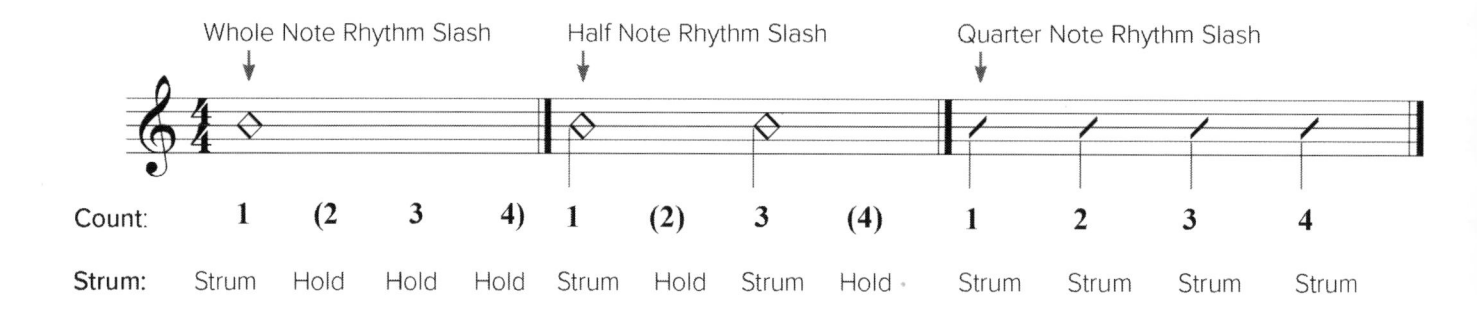

	Whole Note Rhythm Slash				Half Note Rhythm Slash				Quarter Note Rhythm Slash			
Count:	1	(2	3	4)	1	(2)	3	(4)	1	2	3	4
Strum:	Strum	Hold	Hold	Hold	Strum	Hold	Strum	Hold	Strum	Strum	Strum	Strum

Divided Rhythms

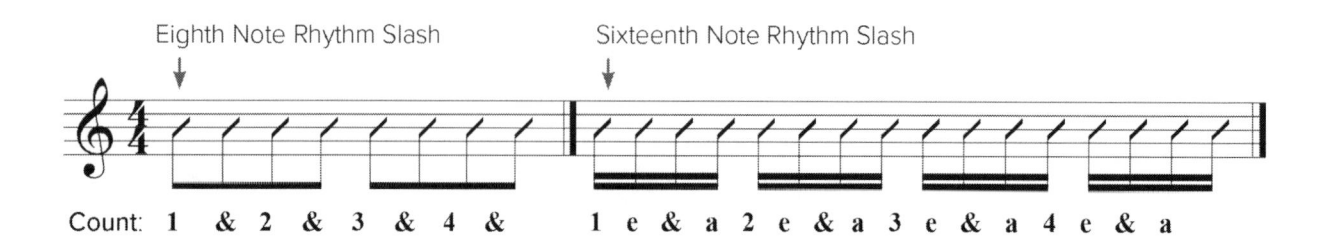

Eighth Note Rhythm Slash

Sixteenth Note Rhythm Slash

Count: 1 & 2 & 3 & 4 &   1 e & a 2 e & a 3 e & a 4 e & a

Sixteenth Note Variation Rhythms

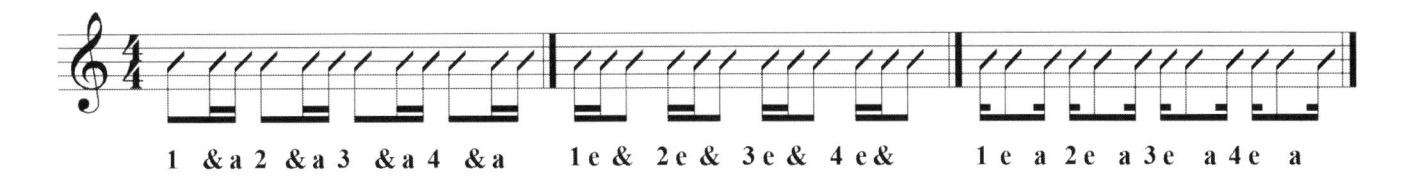

1 &a 2 &a 3 &a 4 &a   1 e & 2 e & 3 e & 4 e &   1 e a 2 e a 3 e a 4 e a

Dotted Rhythms

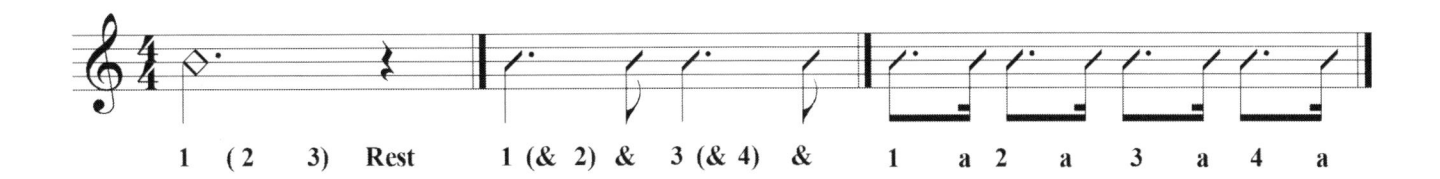

1 (2 3) Rest   1 (& 2) & 3 (& 4) &   1 a 2 a 3 a 4 a

Rests

Whole Note Rest   Half Note Rest   Quarter Note Rests   Eighth Note Rests   Sixteenth Note Rests

6/8 Time

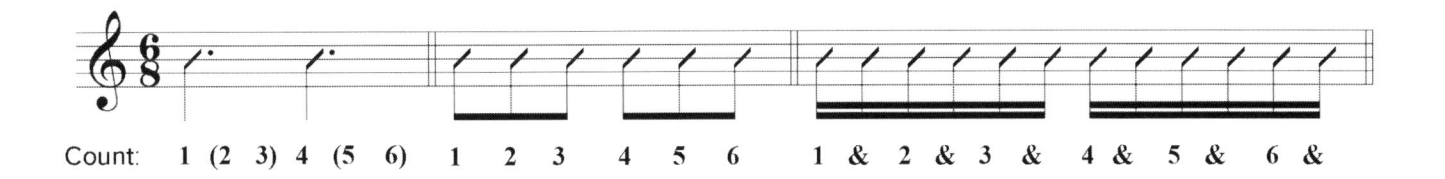

Count: 1 (2 3) 4 (5 6)   1 2 3 4 5 6   1 & 2 & 3 & 4 & 5 & 6 &

Chord Theory: Power Chords

Power chords, also known as "rock chords", are two to three note chords whose tonalities are neither major nor minor. A major chord, for example, contains three main notes: a root, a major third, and a fifth. The chord C major is made up of the root C, the major third E, and the fifth G. The chord C minor contains the notes C, the minor third Eb, and the fifth G. So as you can see, it is the third of the chord that determines whether or not chord has a major or minor sound.

A power chord only contains two of these notes: the root and the fifth (meaning of course, a note five notes away from the root).

Example: C D E F G

Therefore, the chord symbol representing the power chord will be shown like this: C5. This means that the chord is a C chord, but the only other note included is the fifth of the chord.

Using only two notes, power chords can be voiced in a variety of ways. First, they can be played with the root as the lowest note, followed by the fifth, which is the most common voicing. Second, the root's octave can be added to help fill out the sound. Third, the two notes can be inverted so that the fifth of the chord is the lowest note, leaving the root a fourth higher.

One of the nice things about learning power chords is that they are moveable shapes. This means that you learn where to place your fingers to get the chord, but then you can move that shape all over the neck and achieve the same sound at different pitch levels. In other words, you are learning one chord that can be moved up and down the strings, so instead of focusing on where to place your fingers, your focus is on which fret will produce the right chord. As a result, learning power chords helps you learn your neck faster.

Since they are only made up of two primary notes, and since those notes are fairly far apart, they are perfect for adding effects to, like distortion. If you add distortion to a regular major or minor chord, the result is often a muddy, indistinct sound. However, the power chord does not have this issue. In fact, effects often help the chord to sound fuller.

Lesson 1: Open Power Chords

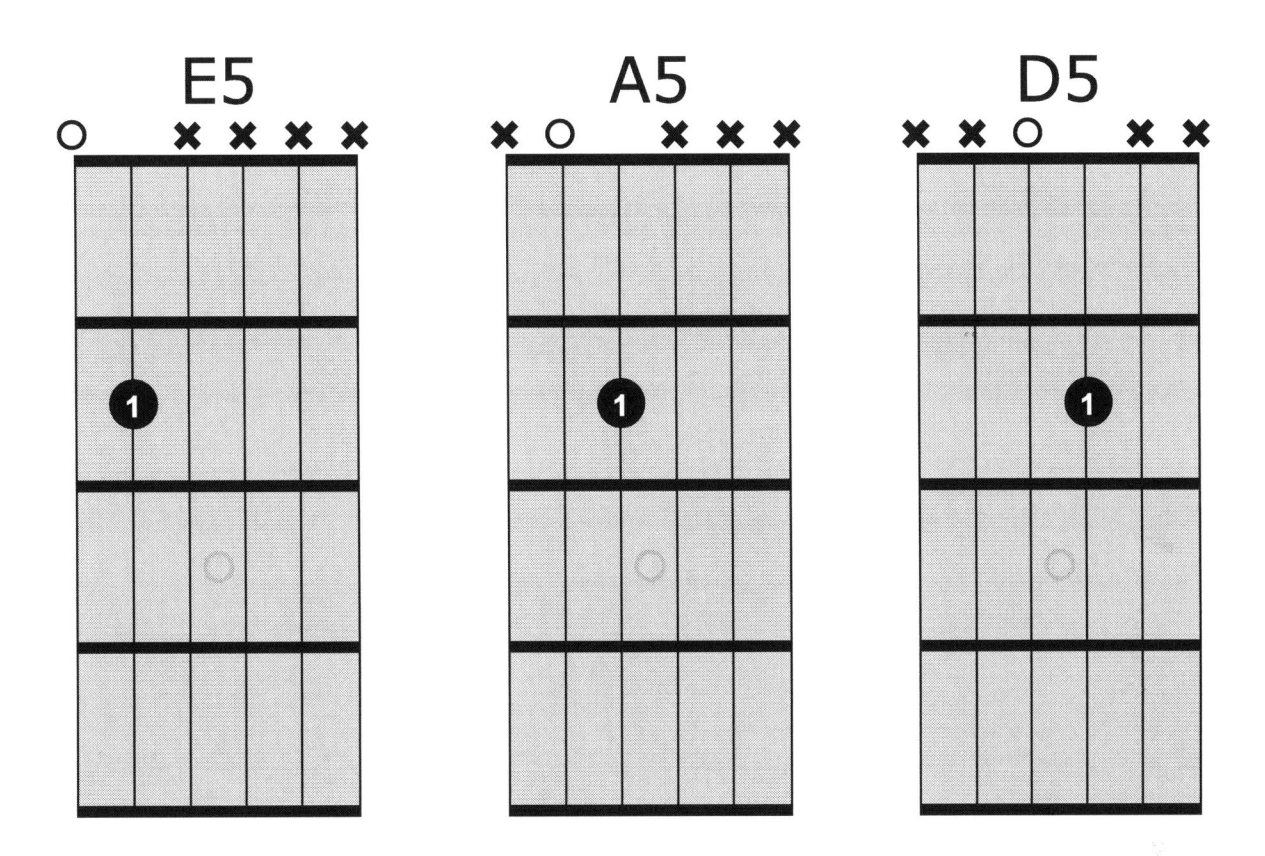

E5 **A5** **D5**

Try it: Practice strumming the two-note, open power chords below. Be sure to only strum the two strings indicated in the above charts.

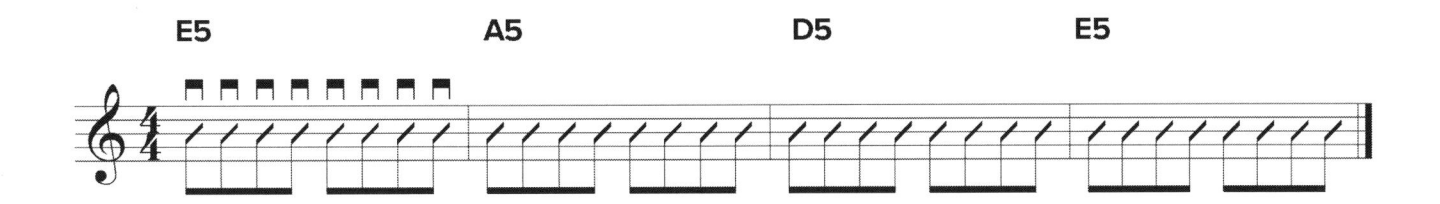

E5   A5   D5   E5

Practicing Open Power Chords

Exercise 1

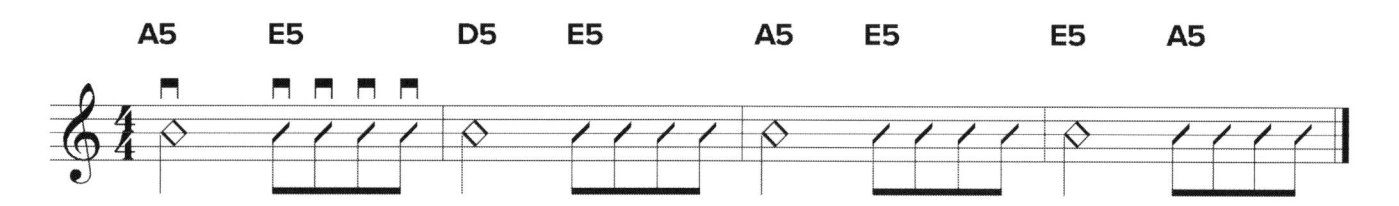

Exercise 2

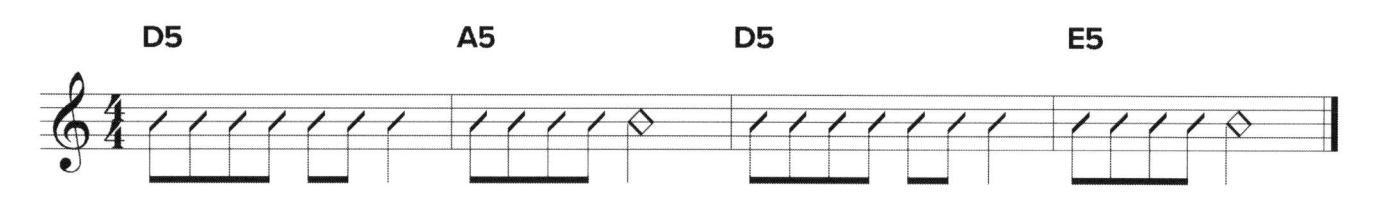

Exercise 3

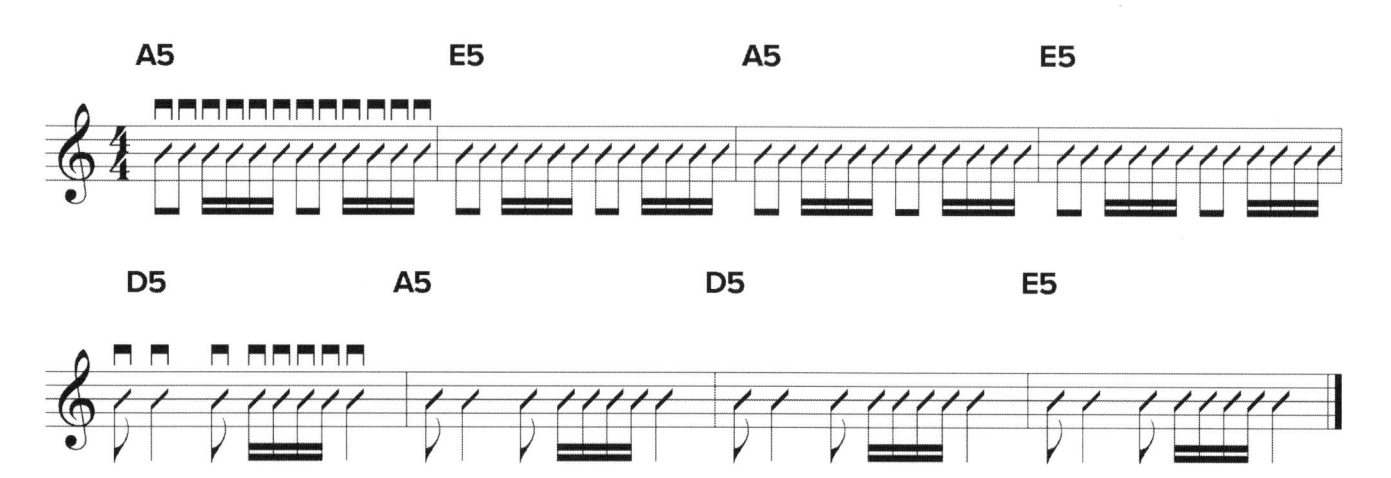

Exercise 4

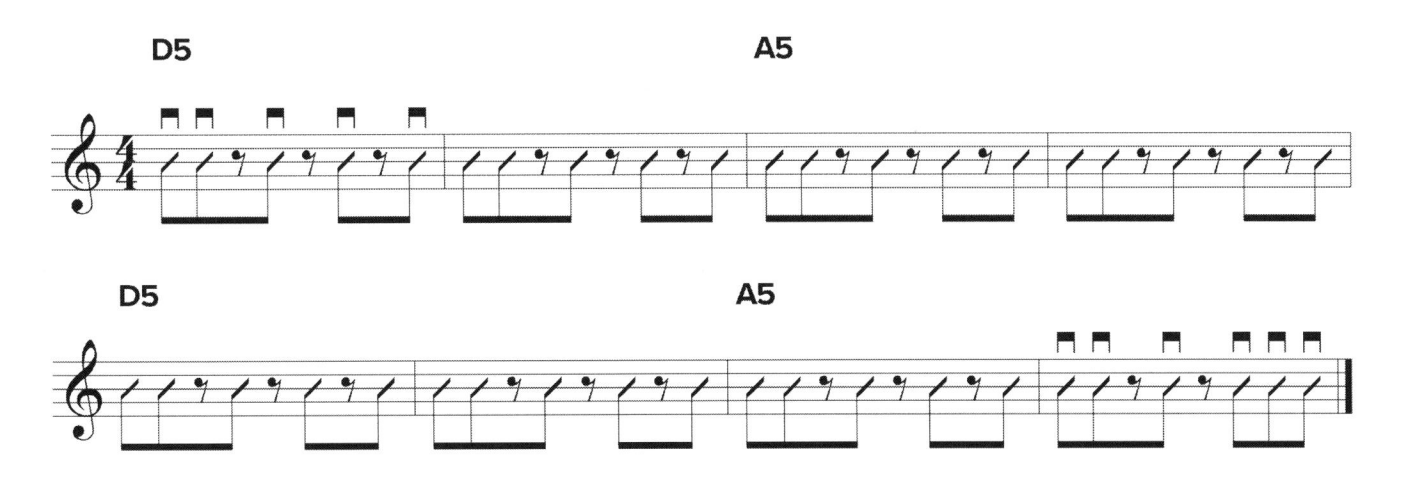

D5   **A5**

D5   **A5**

Exercise 5

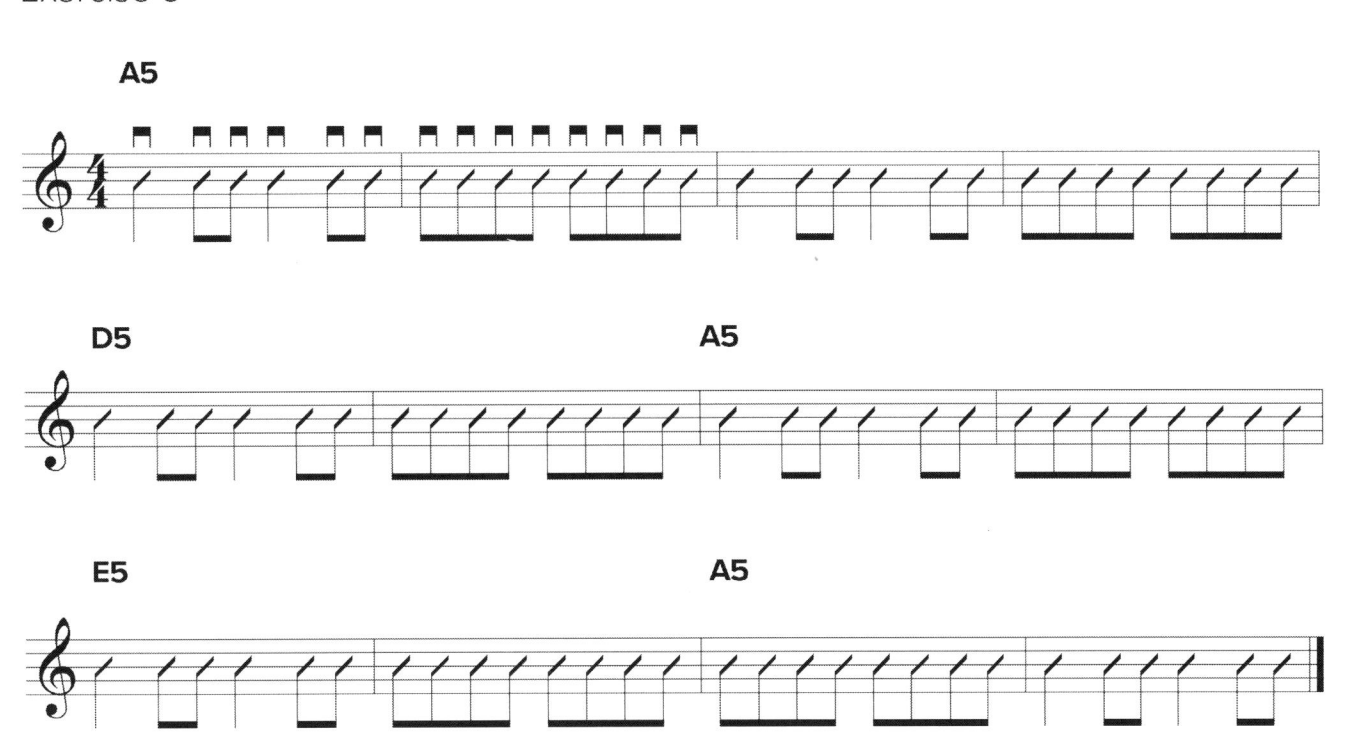

A5

D5   **A5**

E5   **A5**

Lesson 2: Root 6 Power Chords

Since power chords only consist of two notes, it becomes possible to play these chords easily all over the neck. To do so, take an E5 power chord. Then move the note on the second fret up by a half step. Next, place your index finger on the first fret of the last string. This chord shape is the F5 power chord. This shape can be moved up the string. As you move, each new place on the neck will become a new power chord. The chart below shows you the natural notes on the sixth string, which are the root notes of the power chords. Therefore, if you take the F5 shape (shown below) and move it up to the third fret, the resulting chord is a G5 power chord.

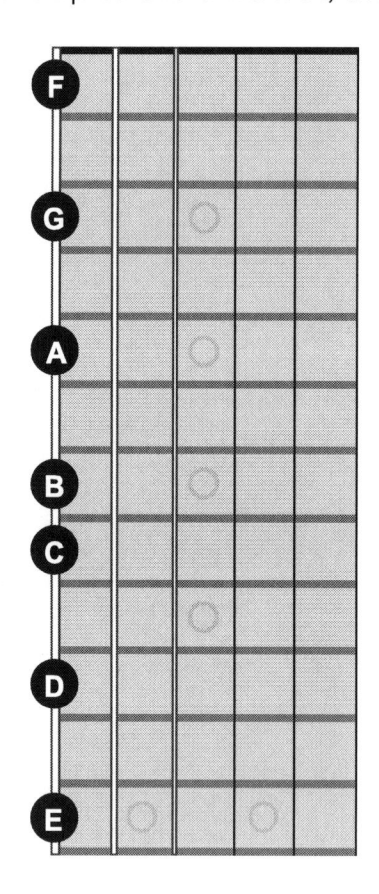

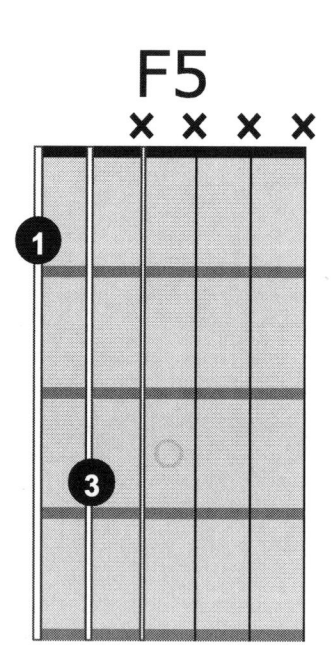

Try it: Practice strumming the two-note, root 6 power chords below. Be sure to only strum the two strings indicated in the above chart.

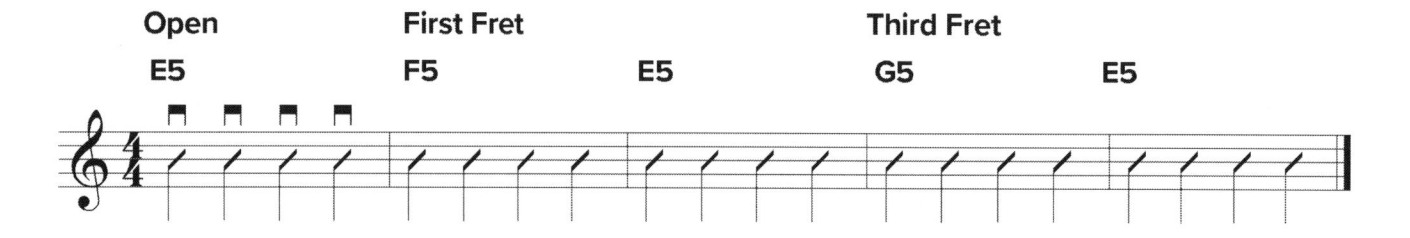

Open	First Fret		Third Fret	
E5	F5	E5	G5	E5

Practicing Root 6 Power Chords

Exercise 1

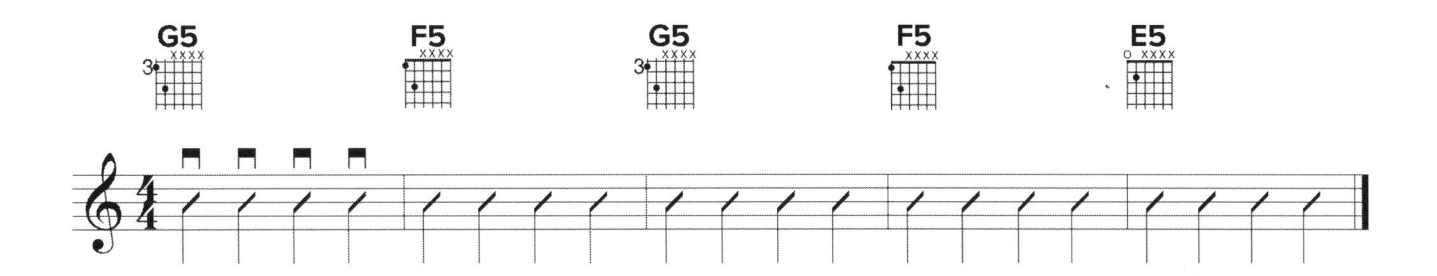

G5   **F5**   **G5**   **F5**   **E5**

Exercise 2

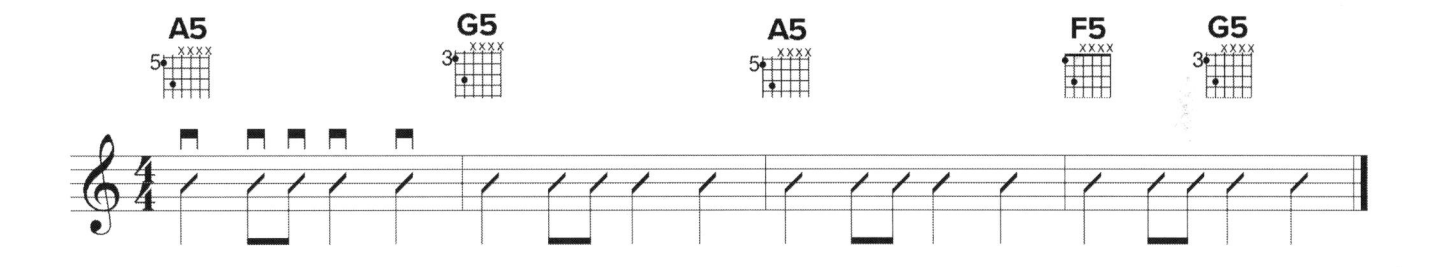

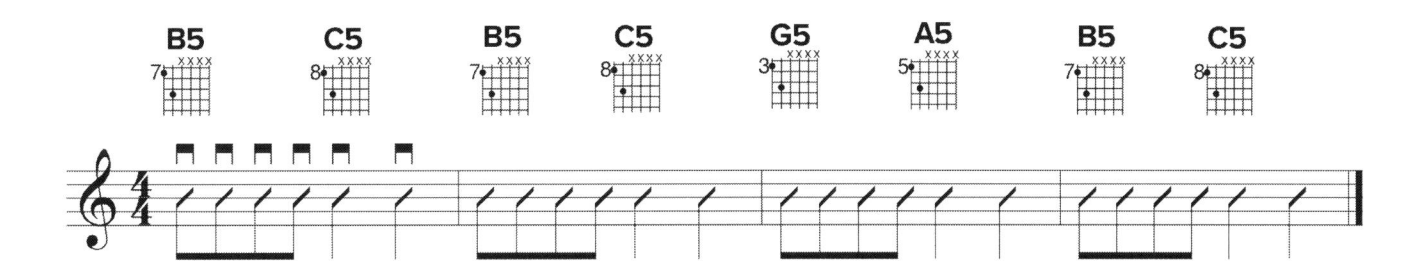

A5   **G5**   **A5**   **F5**   **G5**

Exercise 3

B5   **C5**   **B5**   **C5**   **G5**   **A5**   **B5**   **C5**

Exercise 4

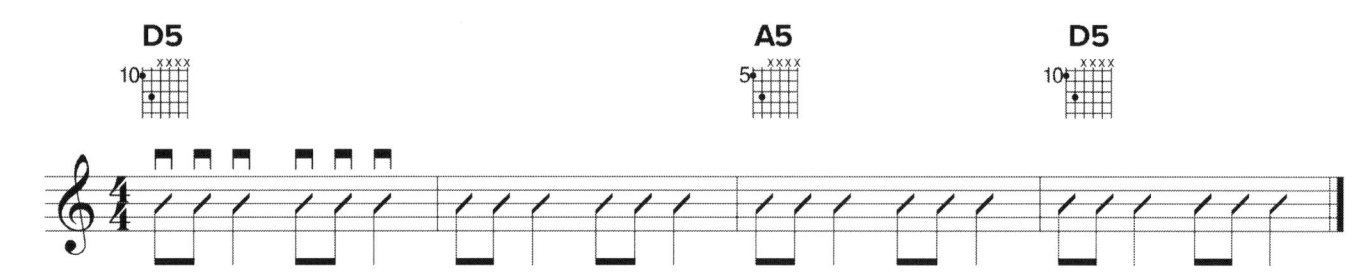

Exercise 5

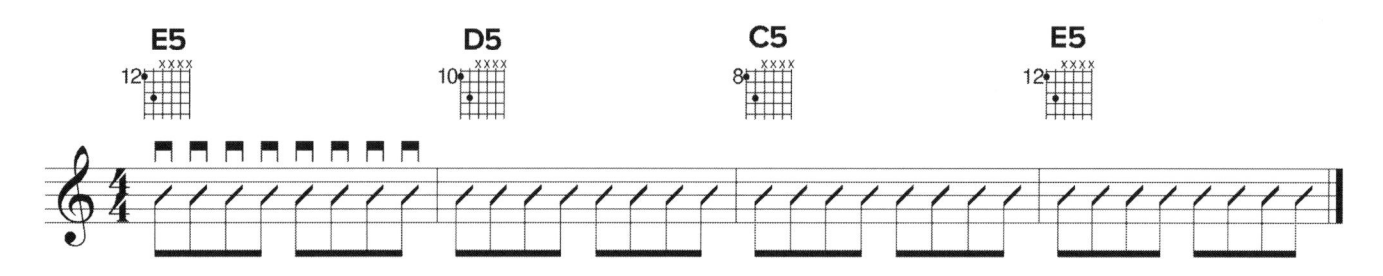

Exercise 6

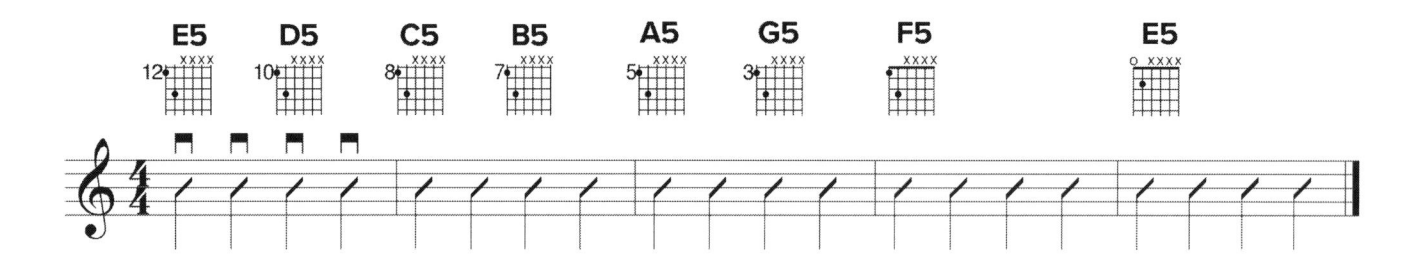

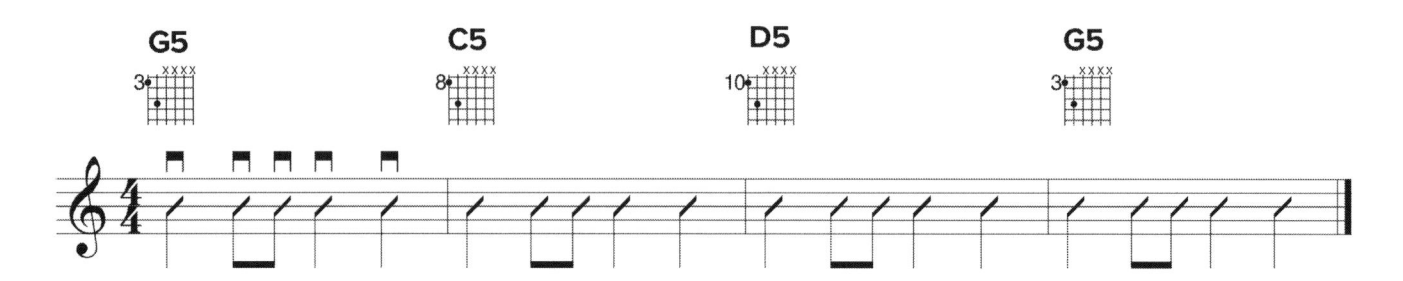

Exercise 7

Exercise 8

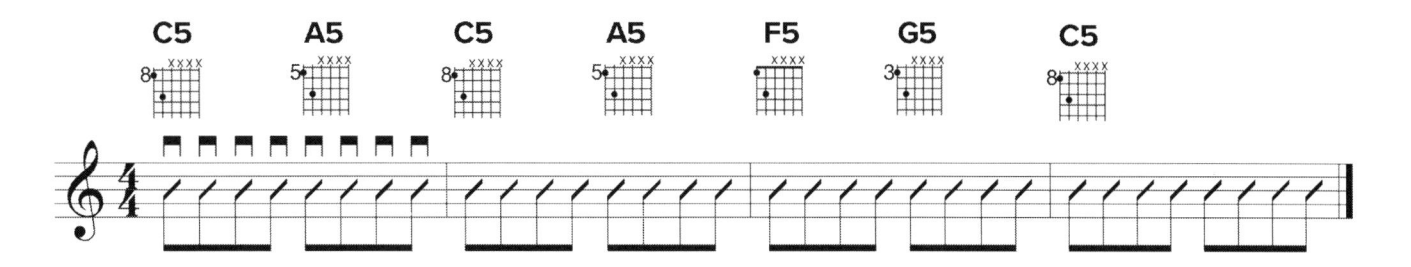

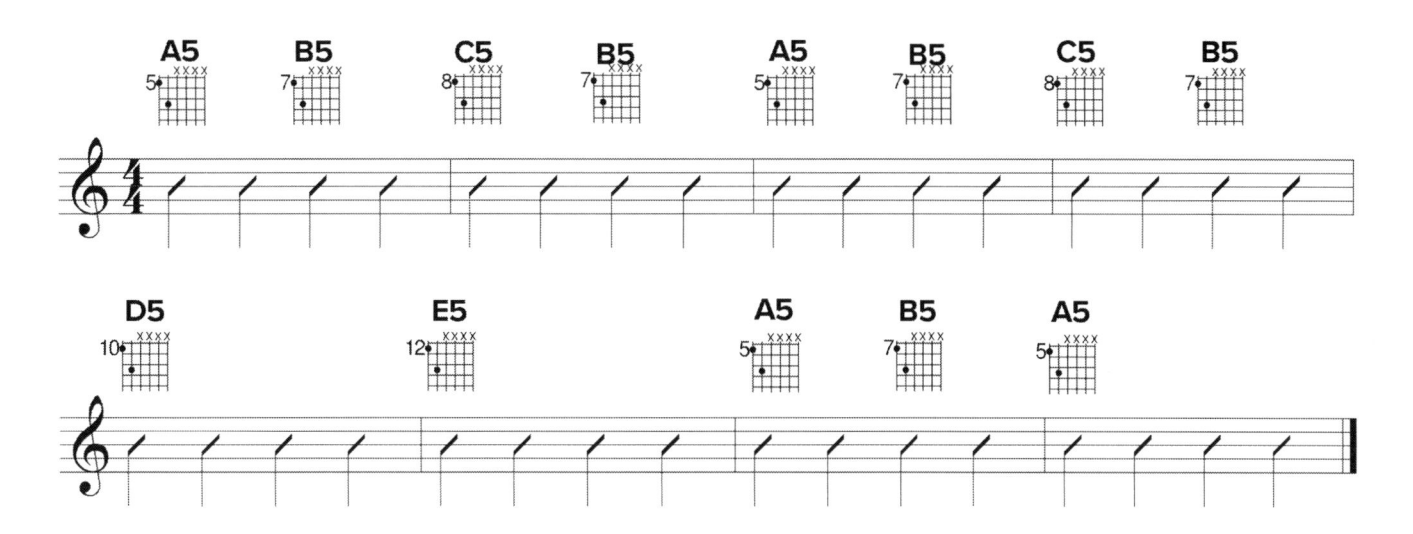

Radical Roots

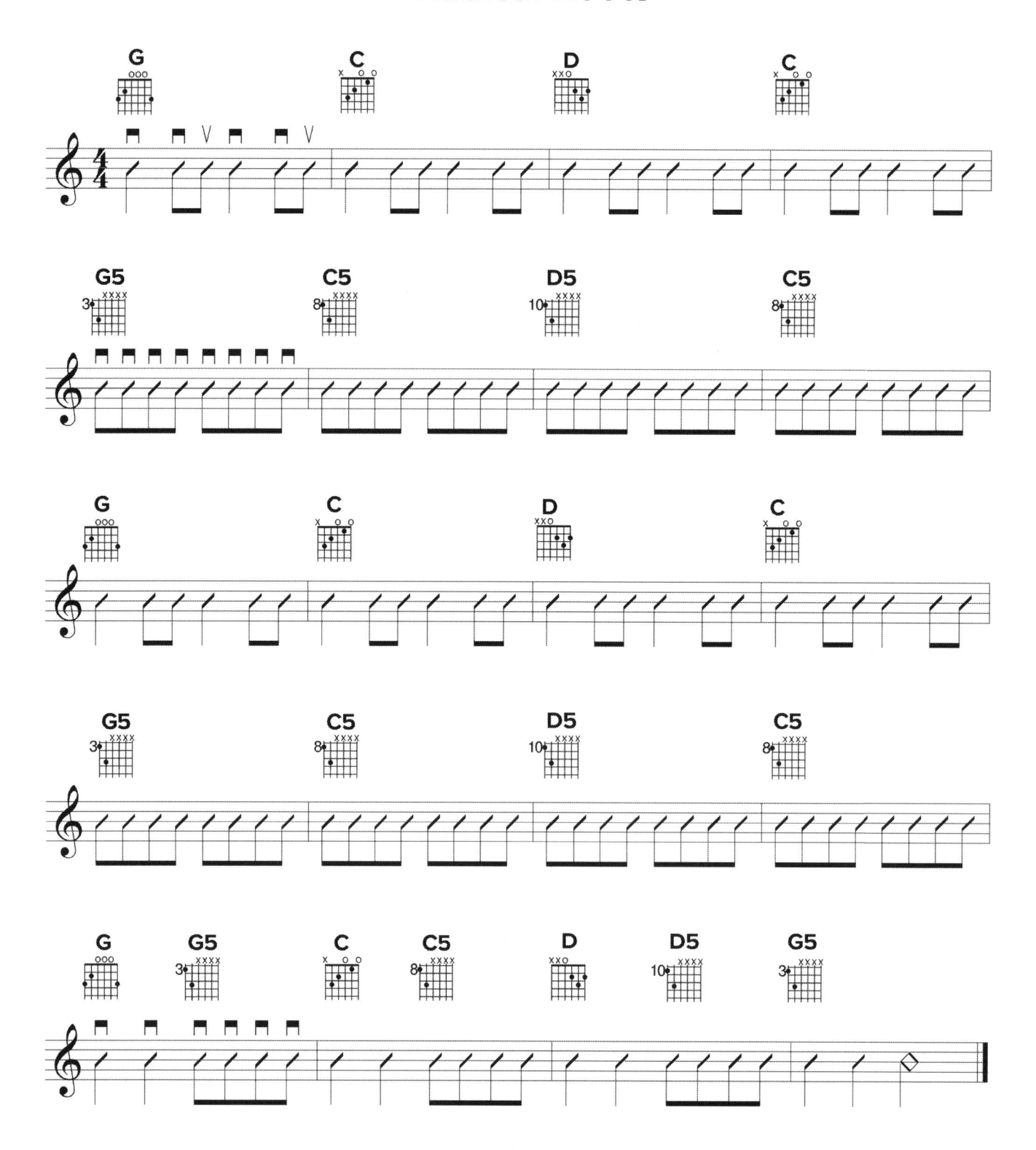

So far, we've only played power chords whose roots are natural notes, or in other words, A, B, C, D, E, F, and G. In the chart below, you can see the names of the sharp and flat notes found on the sixth string that are the roots of their corresponding power chord. However, since these are sharps and flats, that means each has an enharmonic equivalent. See below.

Enharmonic Equivalents

F#=Gb
G#=Ab
Bb=A#
C#=Db
D#=Eb

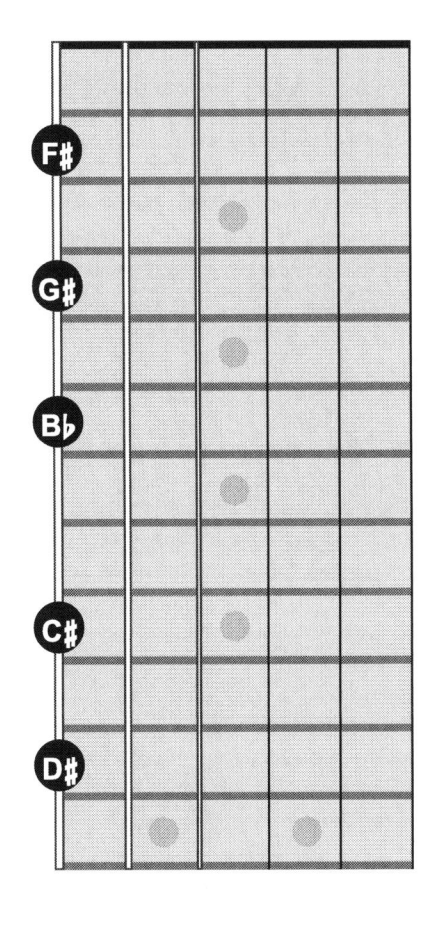

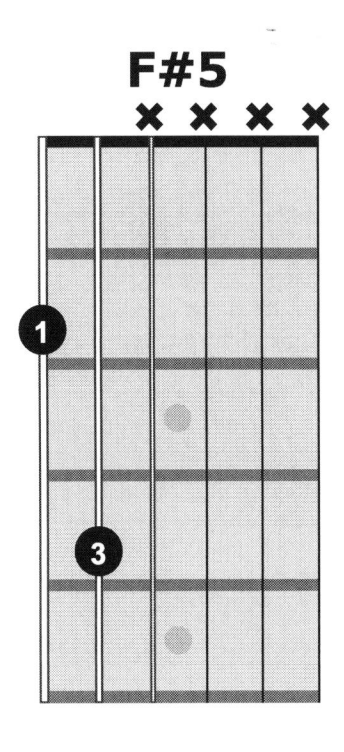

Exercise 10

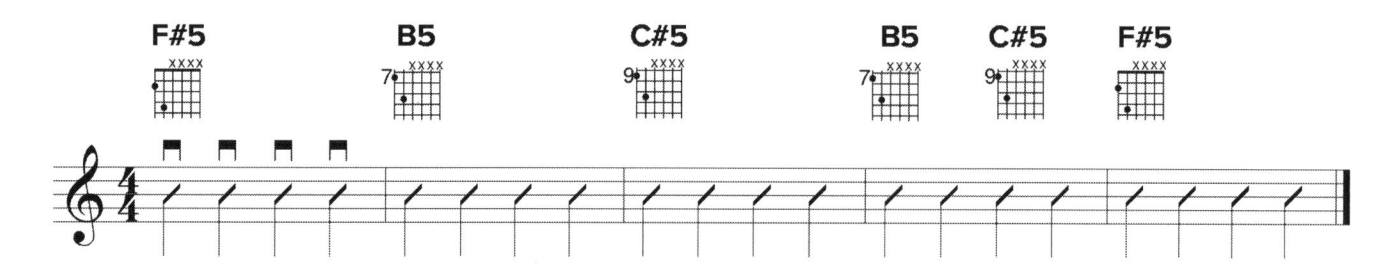

F#5   **B5**   **C#5**   **B5**   **C#5**   **F#5**

Exercise 11

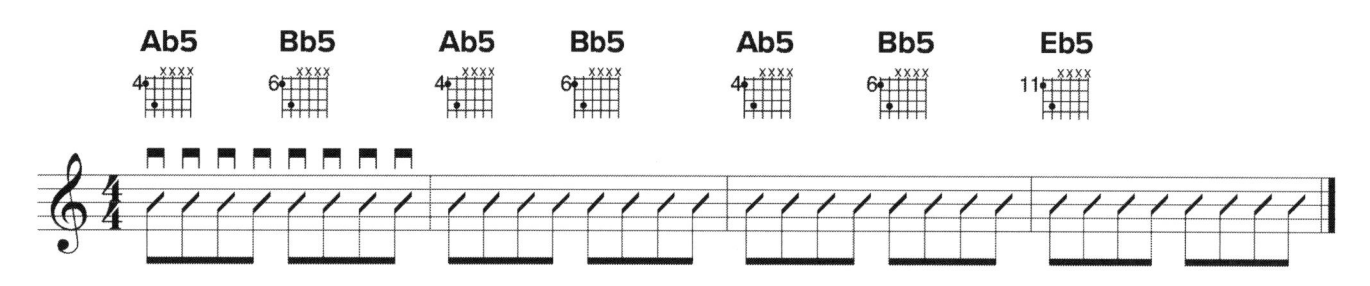

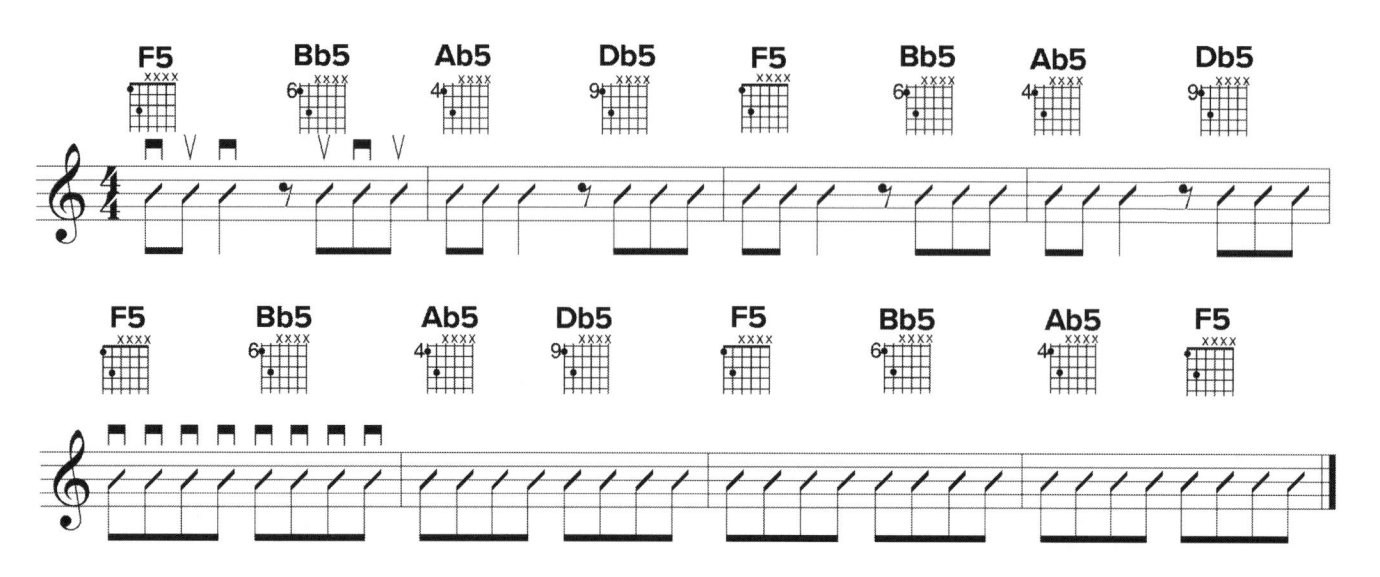

Ab5   **Bb5**   **Ab5**   **Bb5**   **Ab5**   **Bb5**   **Eb5**

Exercise 12

F5   **Bb5**   **Ab5**   **Db5**   **F5**   **Bb5**   **Ab5**   **Db5**

F5   **Bb5**   **Ab5**   **Db5**   **F5**   **Bb5**   **Ab5**   **F5**

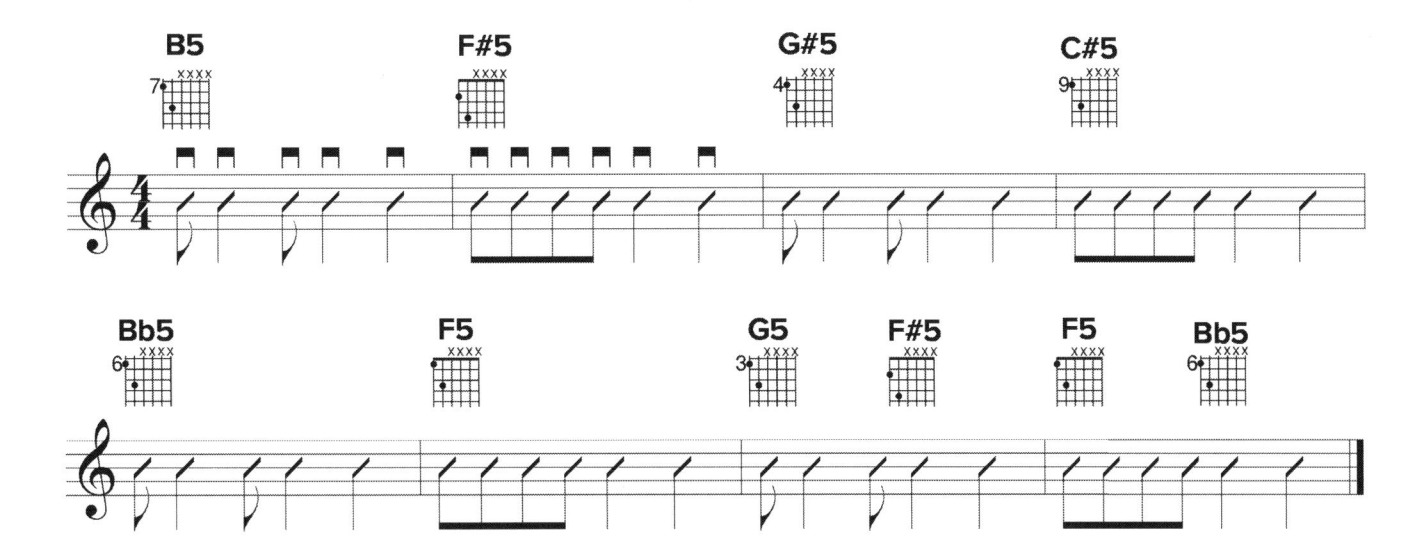

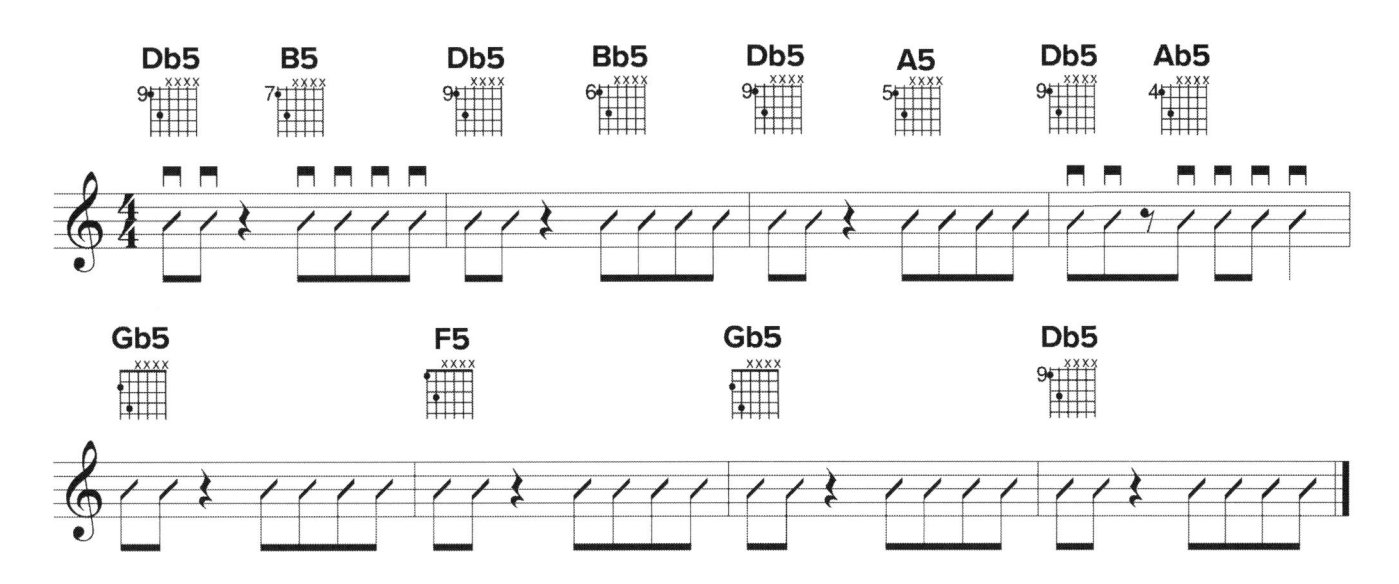

Exercise 13

Exercise 15: Now try to play the power chords without the aid of the chord boxes.

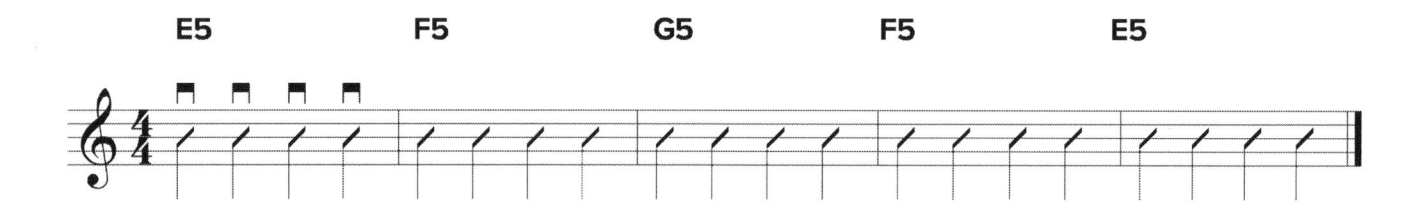

| E5 | F5 | G5 | F5 | E5 |

Exercise 16

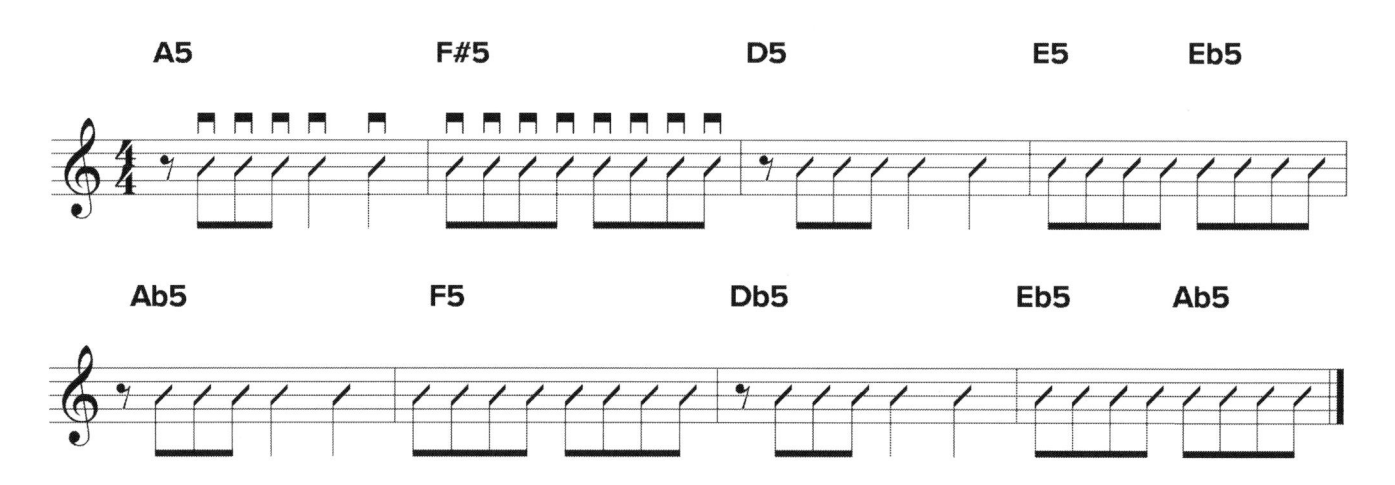

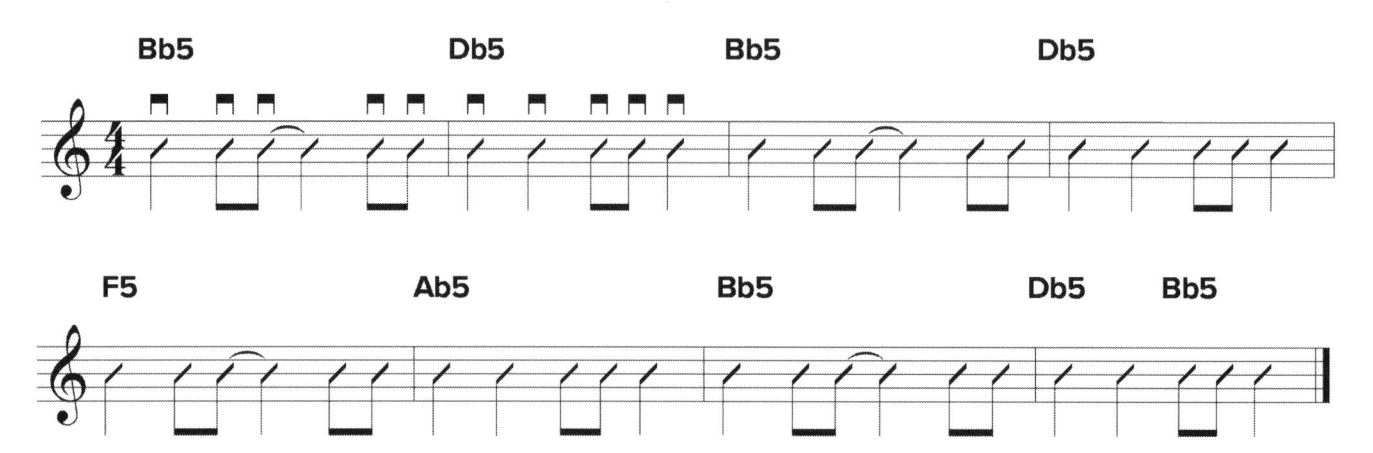

| A5 | F#5 | D5 | E5 | Eb5 |
| Ab5 | F5 | Db5 | Eb5 | Ab5 |

Exercise 17

| Bb5 | Db5 | Bb5 | Db5 |
| F5 | Ab5 | Bb5 | Db5 | Bb5 |

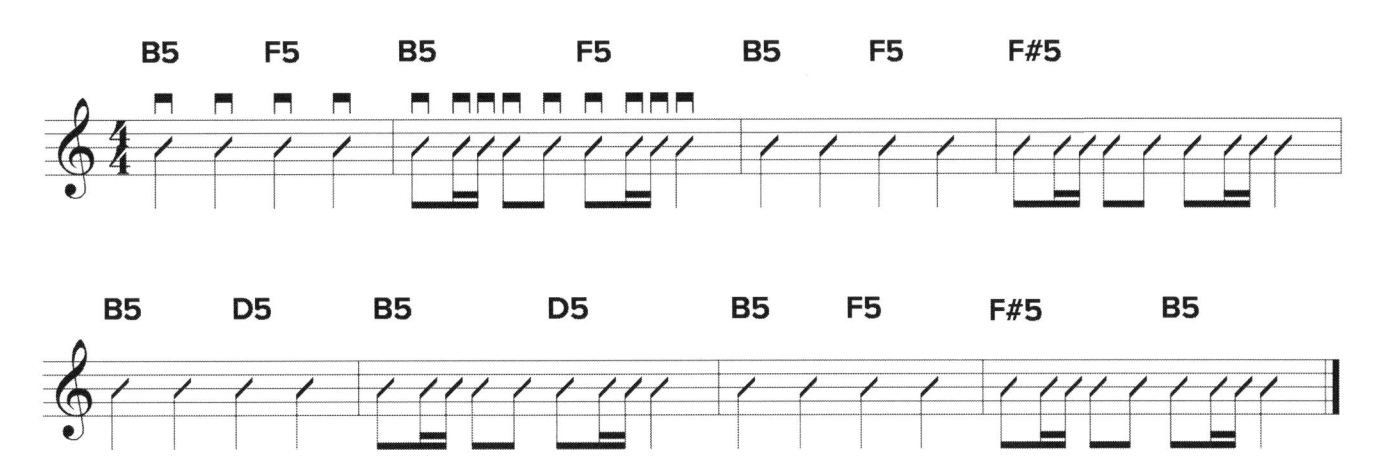

Exercise 18

Overpowered

Be sure to note the use of three-four time, as well as the open chords in the chorus section.

Intro

Verse

Chorus

Verse

Chorus

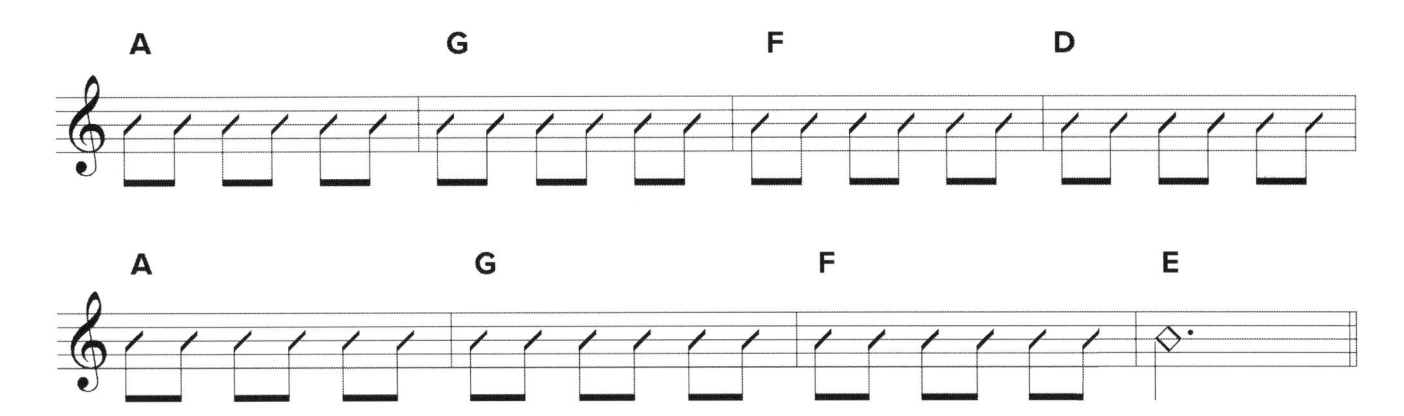

A	G	F	D
/ / / /	/ / / /	/ / / /	/ / / /

A	G	F	E
/ / / /	/ / / /	/ / / /	◇.

Outro

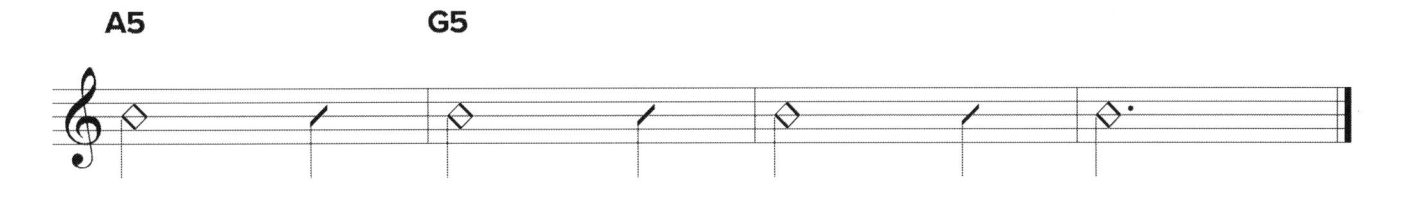

A5	G5		
◇ /	◇ /	◇ /	◇.

The Long Road Trip

Intro

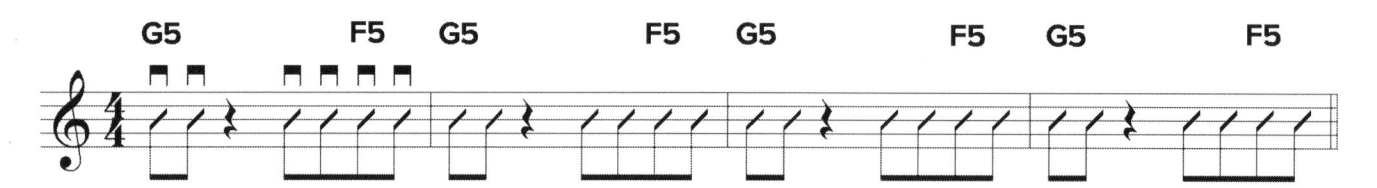

| G5 | F5 | G5 | F5 | G5 | F5 | G5 | F5 |

Verse

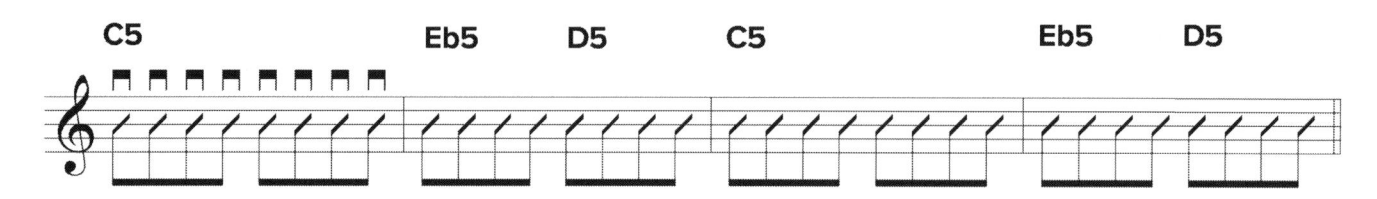

| C5 | Eb5 | D5 | C5 | Eb5 | D5 |

Chorus

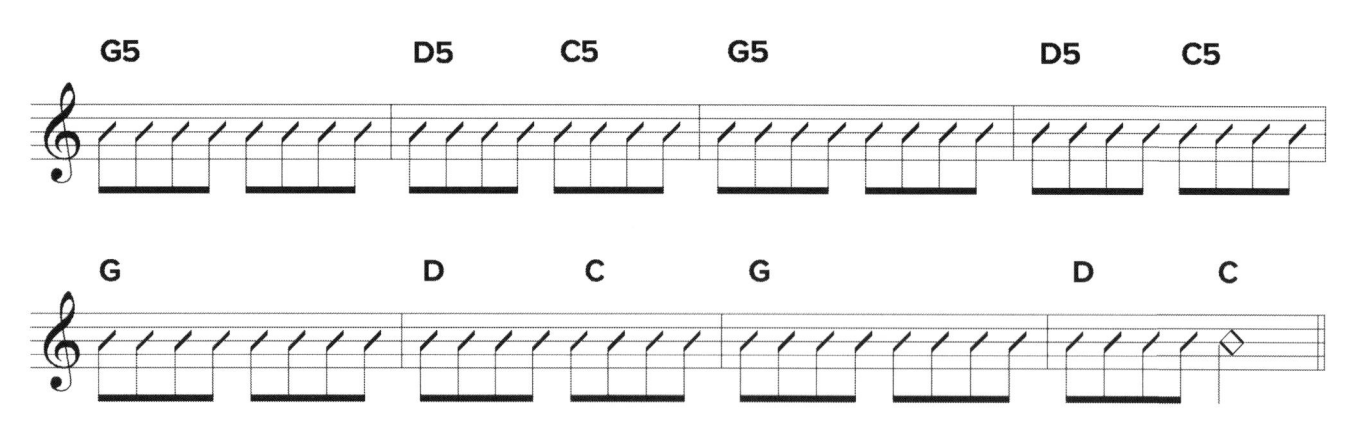

| G5 | D5 | C5 | G5 | D5 | C5 |

| G | D | C | G | D | C |

Bridge

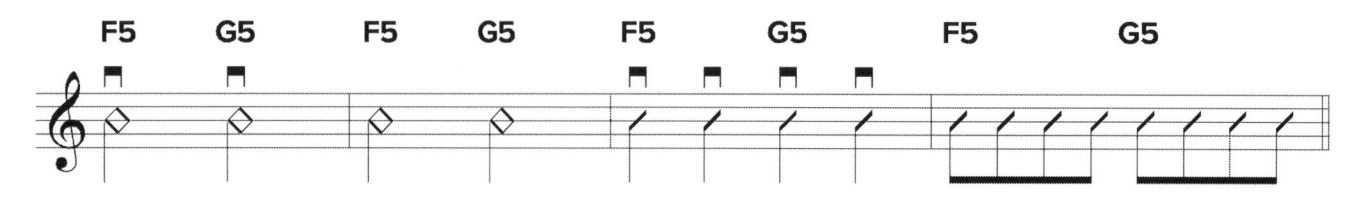

| F5 | G5 | F5 | G5 | F5 | G5 | F5 | G5 |

Verse

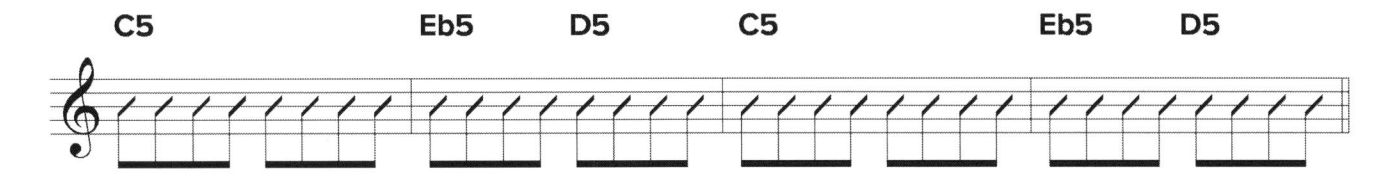

| C5 | Eb5 | D5 | C5 | Eb5 | D5 |

Chorus

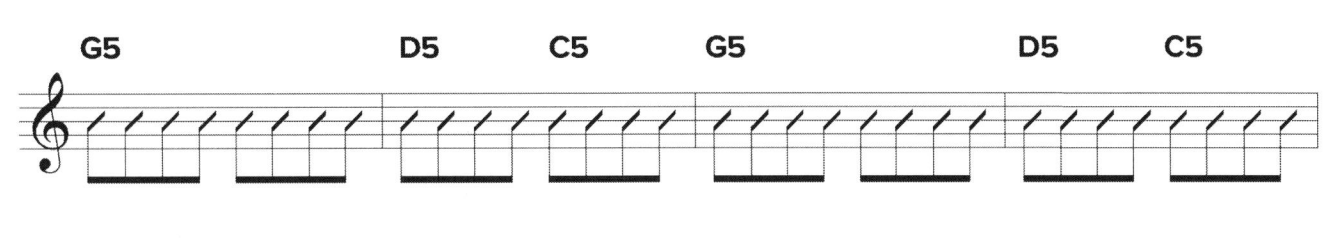

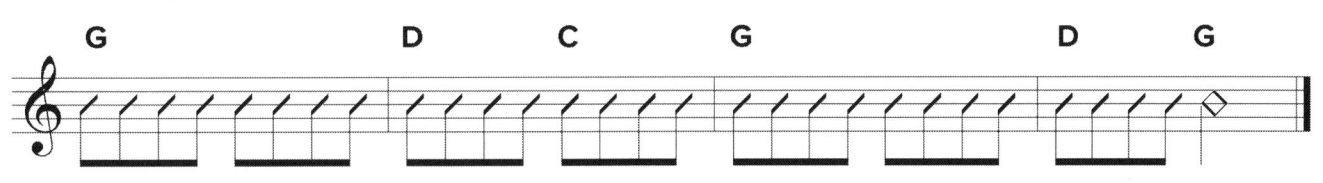

| G5 | D5 | C5 | G5 | D5 | C5 |

| G | D | C | G | D | G |

Lesson 3:
Root 5 Power Chords

Root 5 power chords work in the same manner as the root 6. However, with this set of chords, since the root of the chord is on the fifth string, the sixth string is not played. Also note that the first natural note on this string is the B natural, found on the second fret of the fifth string.

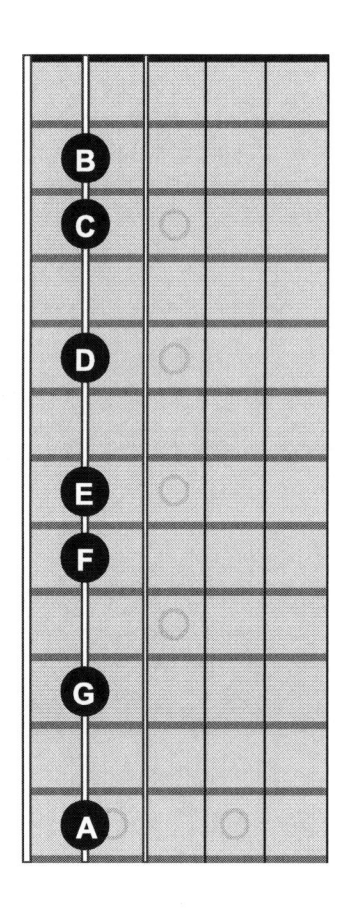

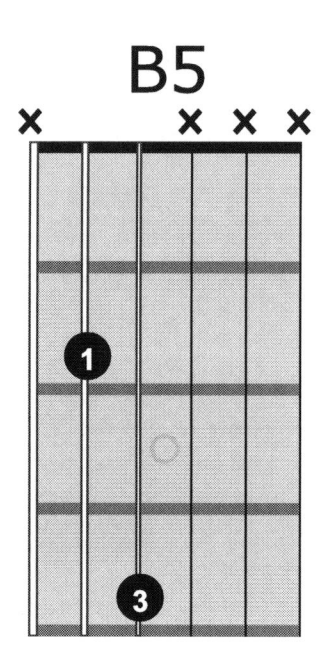

Practicing Root 5 Power Chords

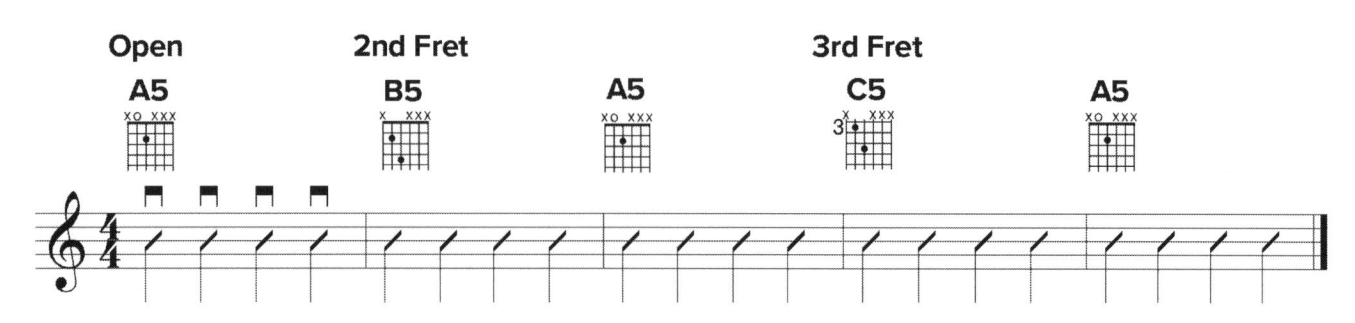

Exercise 1

Open	2nd Fret		3rd Fret	
A5	B5	A5	C5	A5

Exercise 2

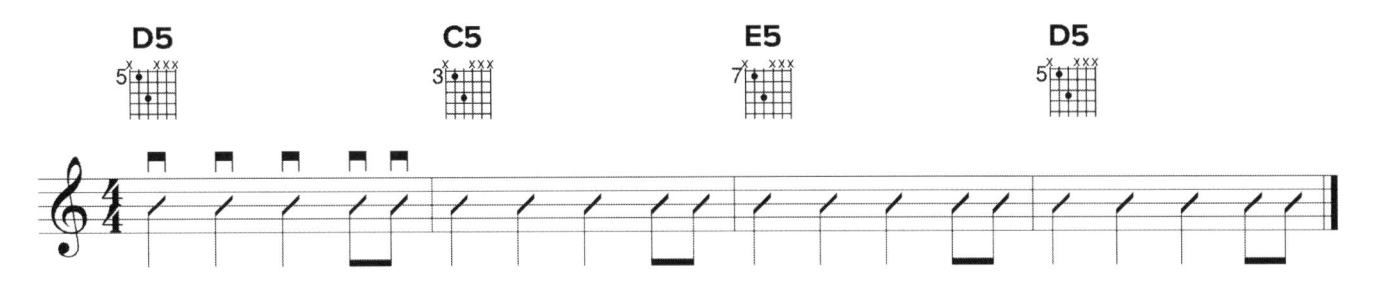

D5 (5th fret)   **C5** (3rd fret)   **E5** (7th fret)   **D5** (5th fret)

4/4 time

Exercise 3

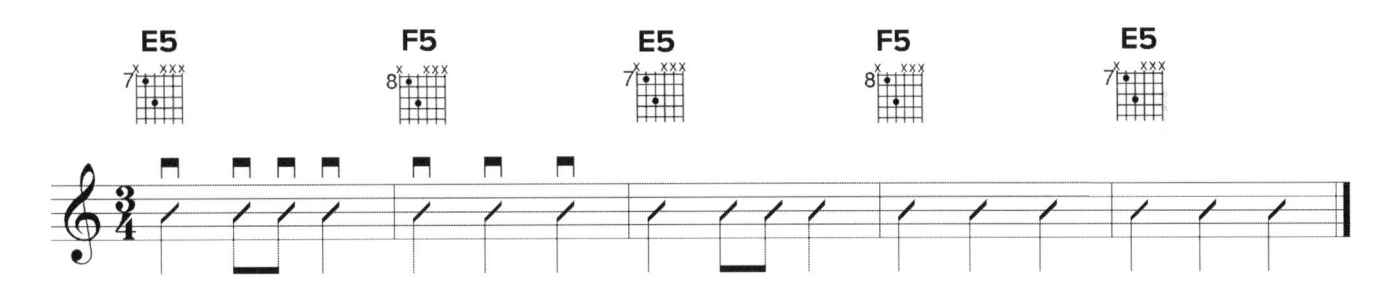

E5 (7th fret)   **F5** (8th fret)   **E5** (7th fret)   **F5** (8th fret)   **E5** (7th fret)

3/4 time

Exercise 4

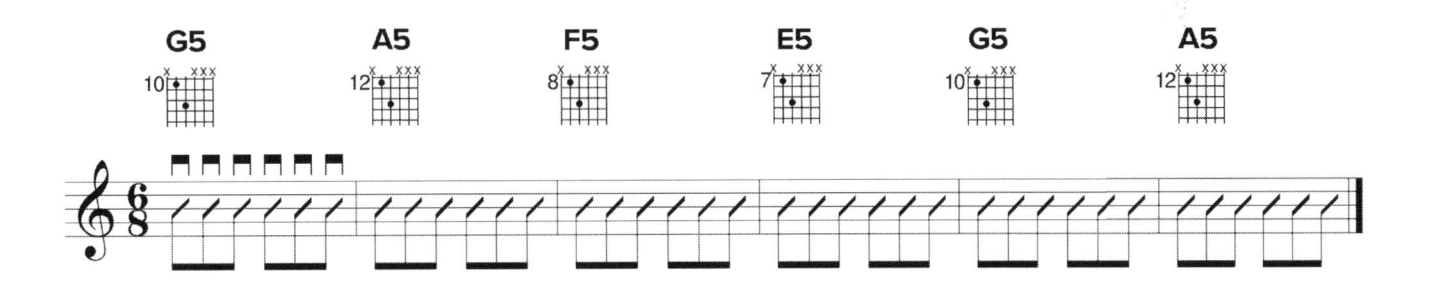

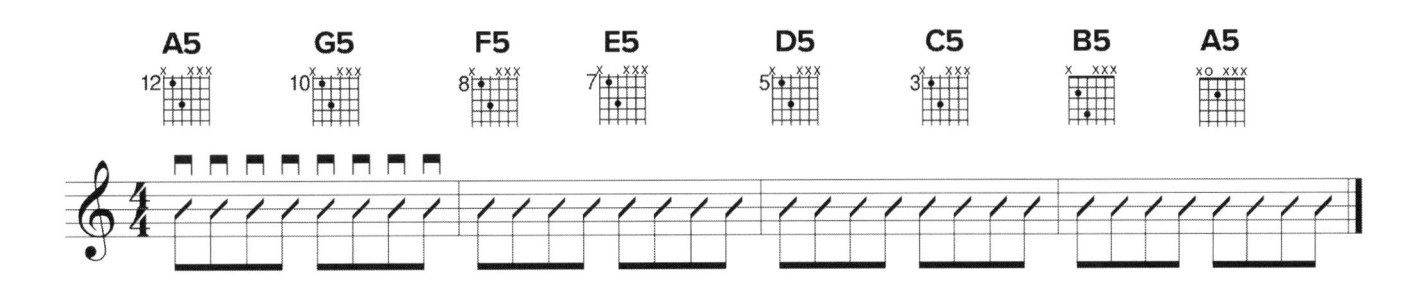

G5 (10th fret)   **A5** (12th fret)   **F5** (8th fret)   **E5** (7th fret)   **G5** (10th fret)   **A5** (12th fret)

6/8 time

Exercise 5

A5 (12th fret)   **G5** (10th fret)   **F5** (8th fret)   **E5** (7th fret)   **D5** (5th fret)   **C5** (3rd fret)   **B5**   **A5**

4/4 time

Exercise 6

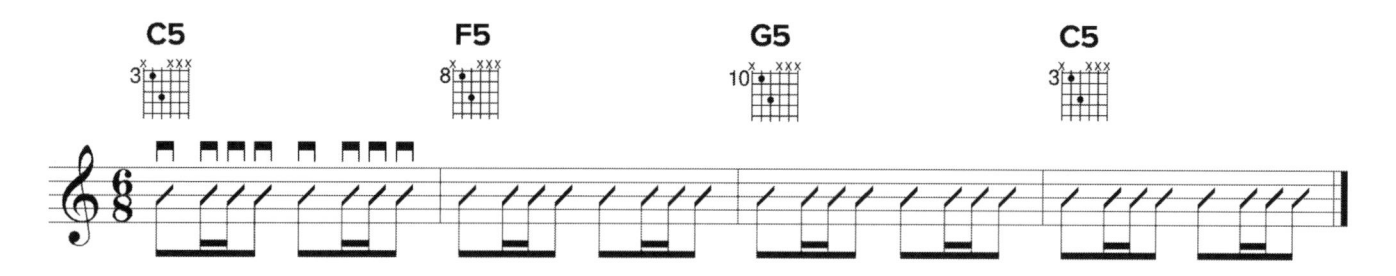

Exercise 7

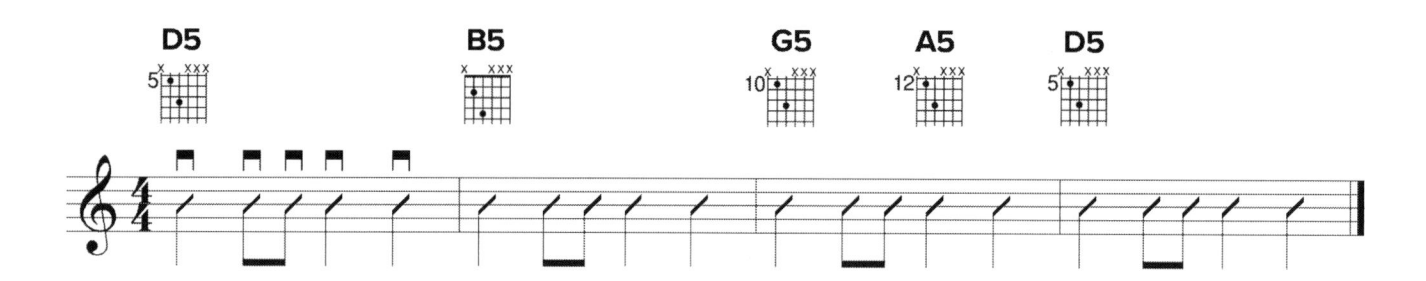

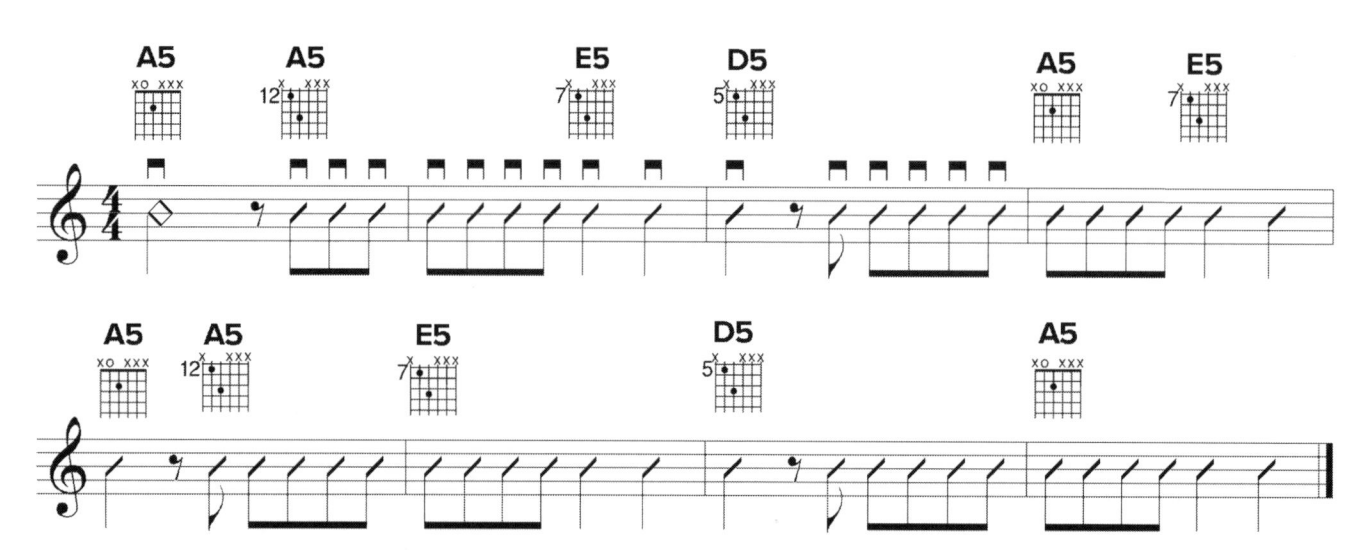

Exercise 8

Exercise 9

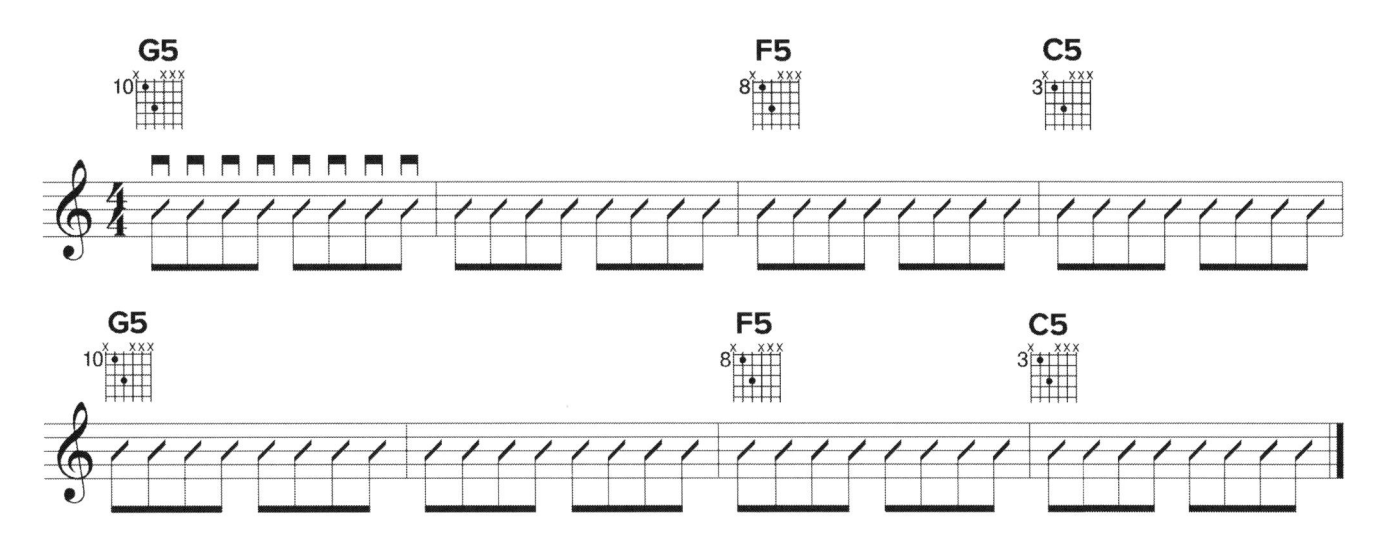

Exercise 10

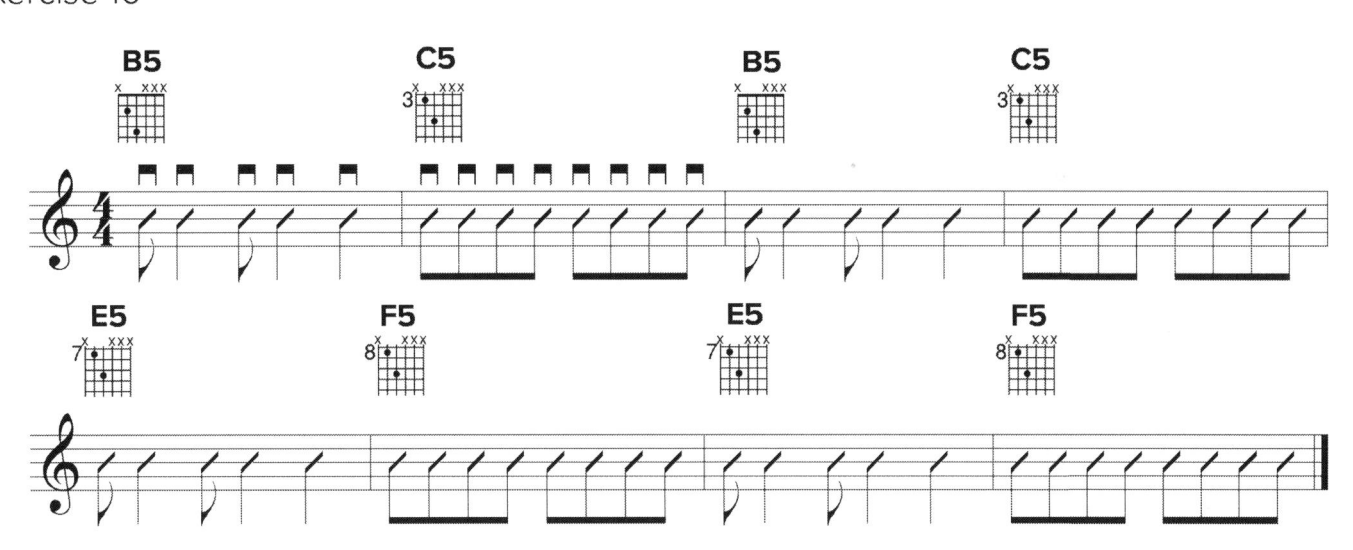

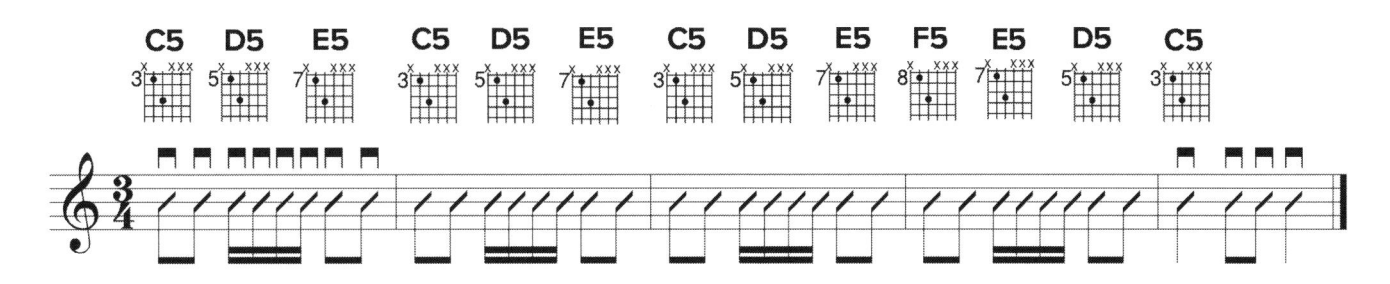

Exercise 11

Masks

Intro
Dm   Am   G

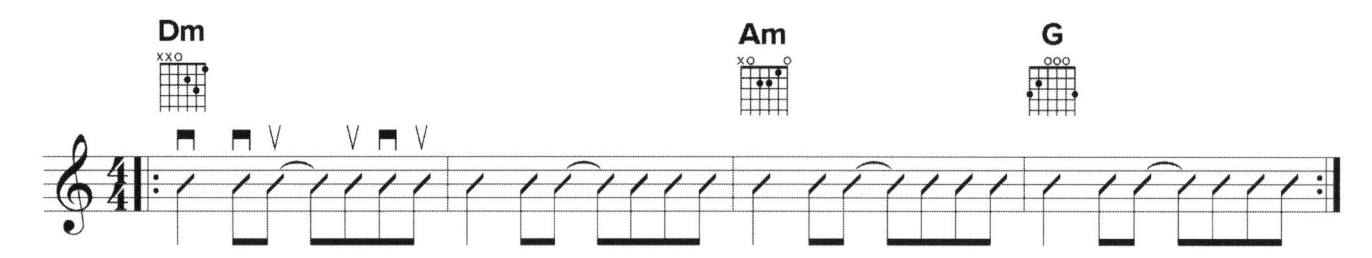

Verse
D5 F5 E5 D5 A5 C5

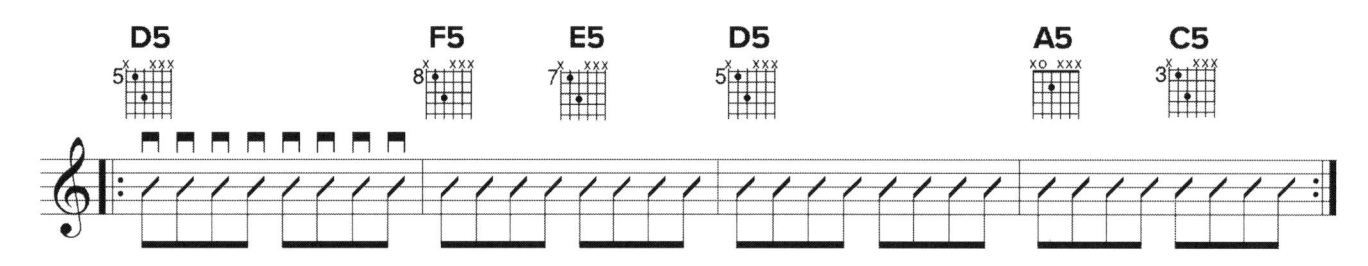

Chorus
Dm G Am G

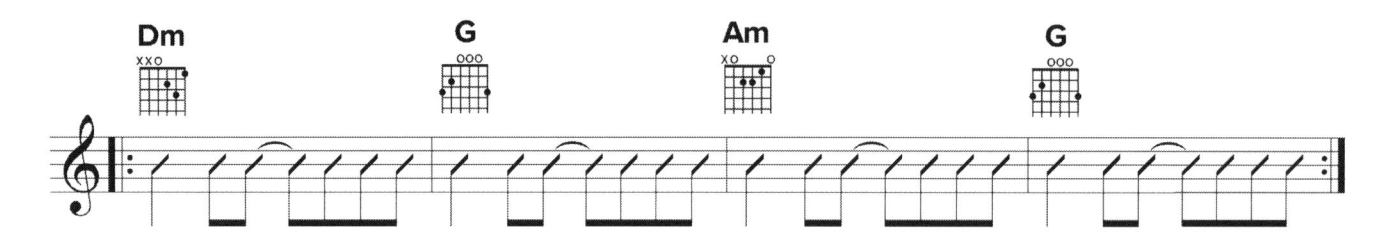

Verse
D5 F5 E5 D5 A5 C5

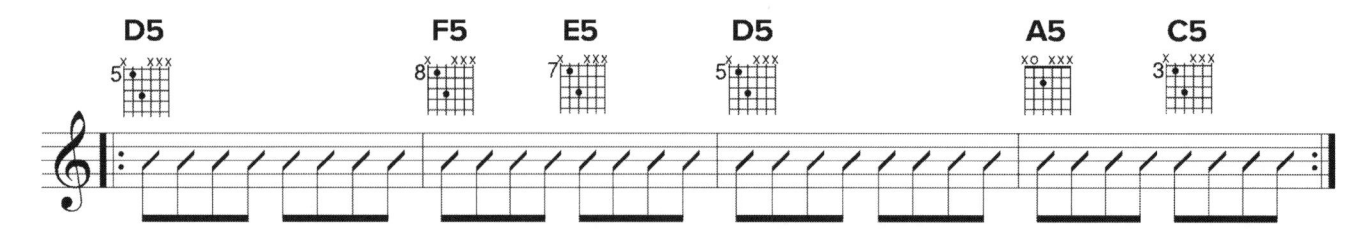

Chorus

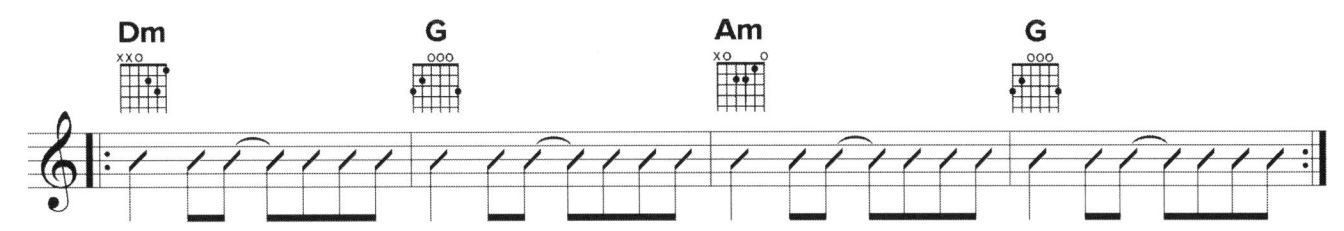

| Dm | G | Am | G |

Outro

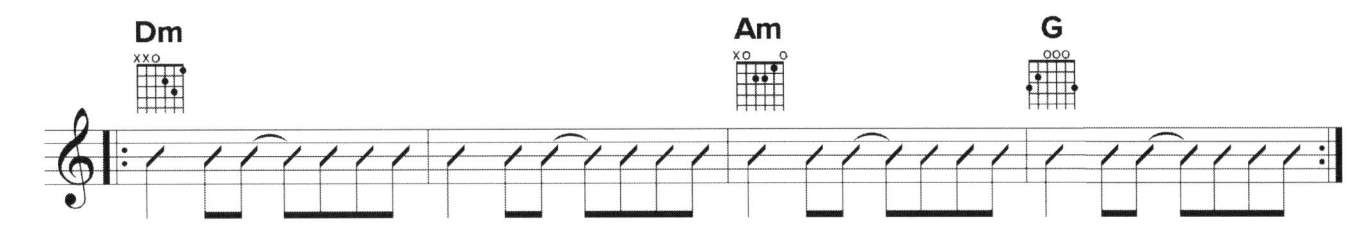

| Dm | | Am | G |

Much like the previous unit, so far, we've only played power chords whose roots are natural notes, A, B, C, D, E, F, and G. In the chart below, you can see the names of the sharp and flat notes found on the fifth string that are the roots of their corresponding power chord. However, since these are sharps and flats, that means each has an enharmonic equivalent. See below.

Enharmonic Equivalents

Bb=A#
C#=Db
D#=Eb
F#=Gb
G#=Ab

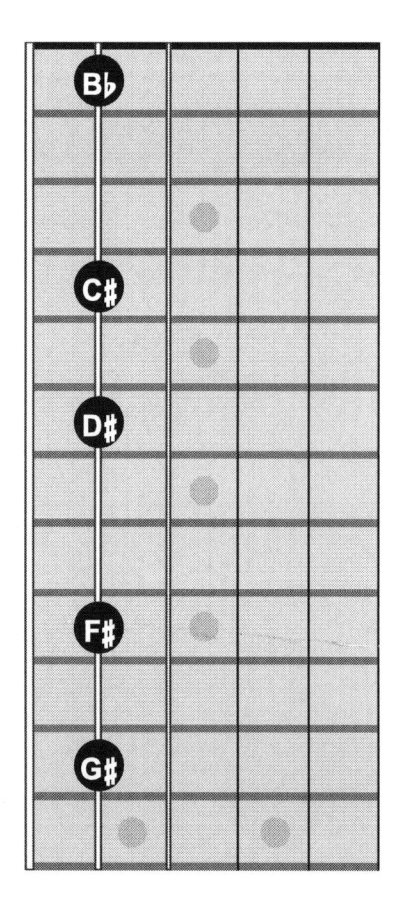

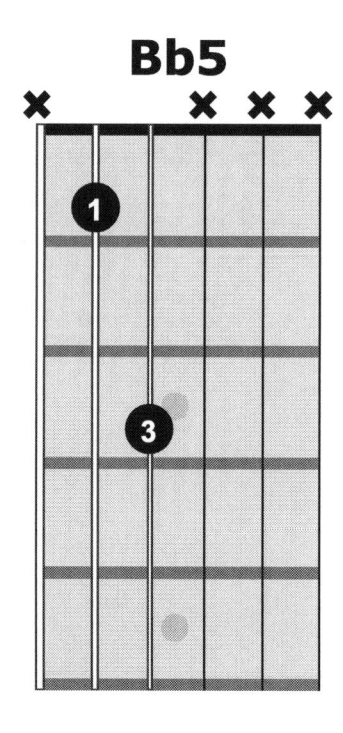

Bb5

Exercise 12

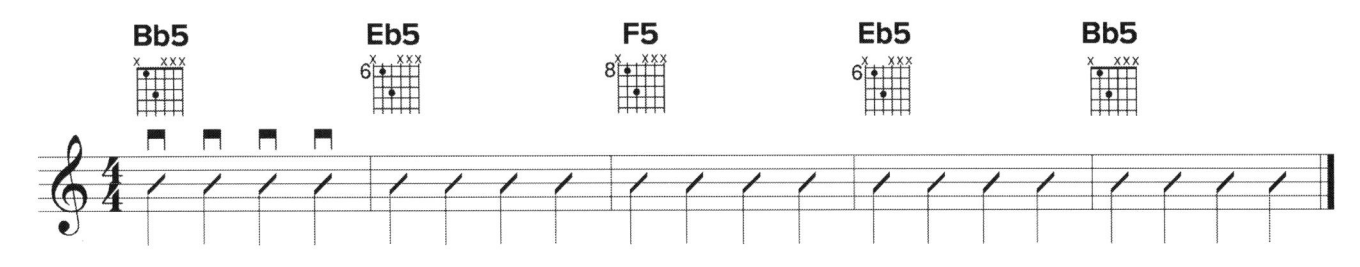

Exercise 13

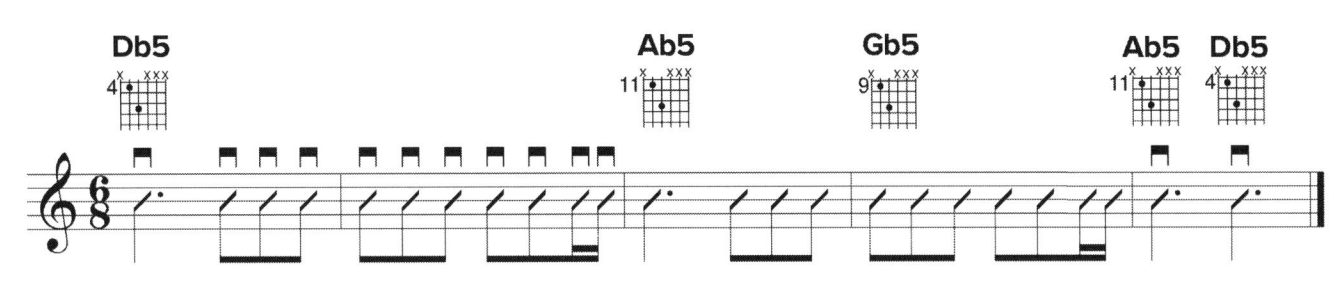

Exercise 14

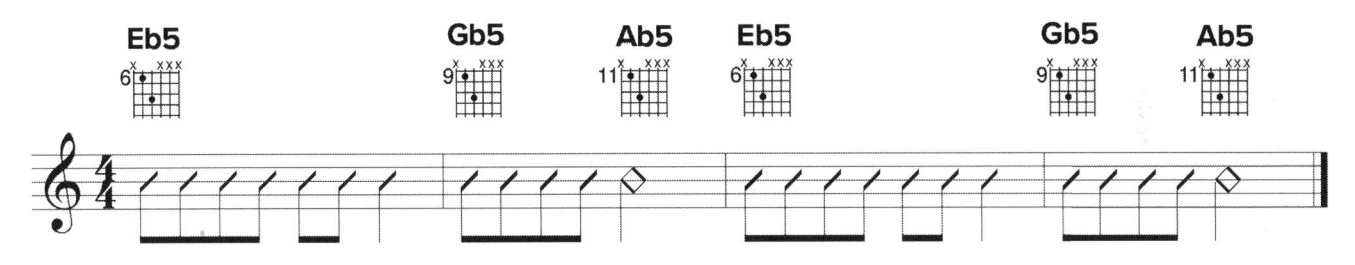

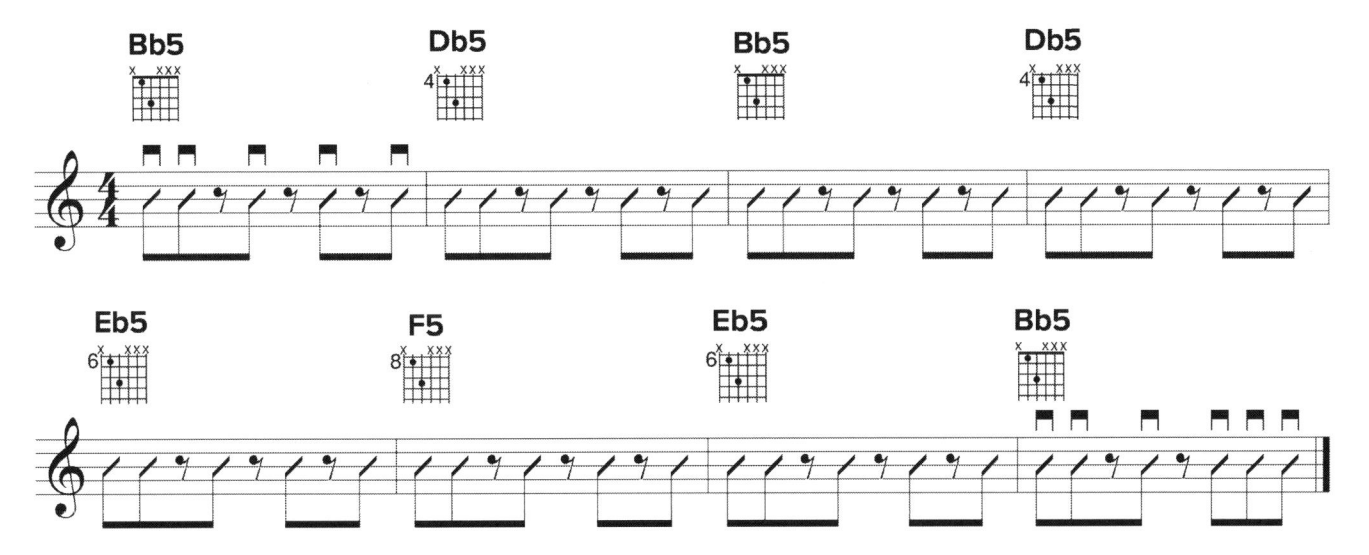

Exercise 15

Exercise 16

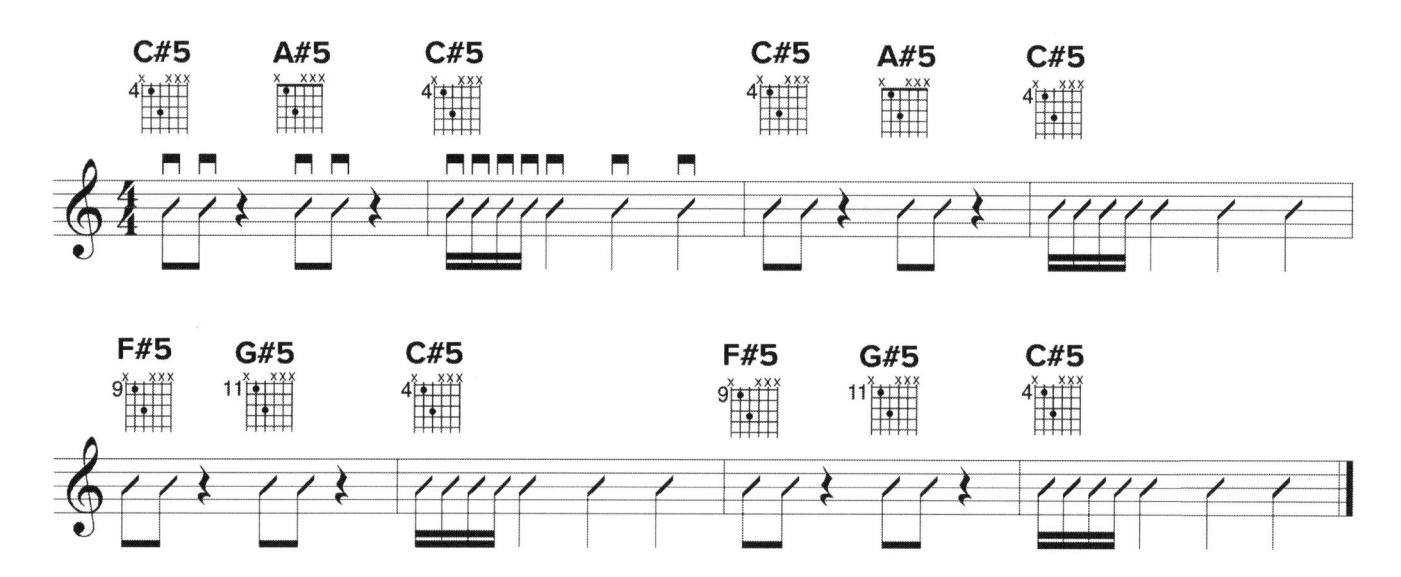

Exercise 17

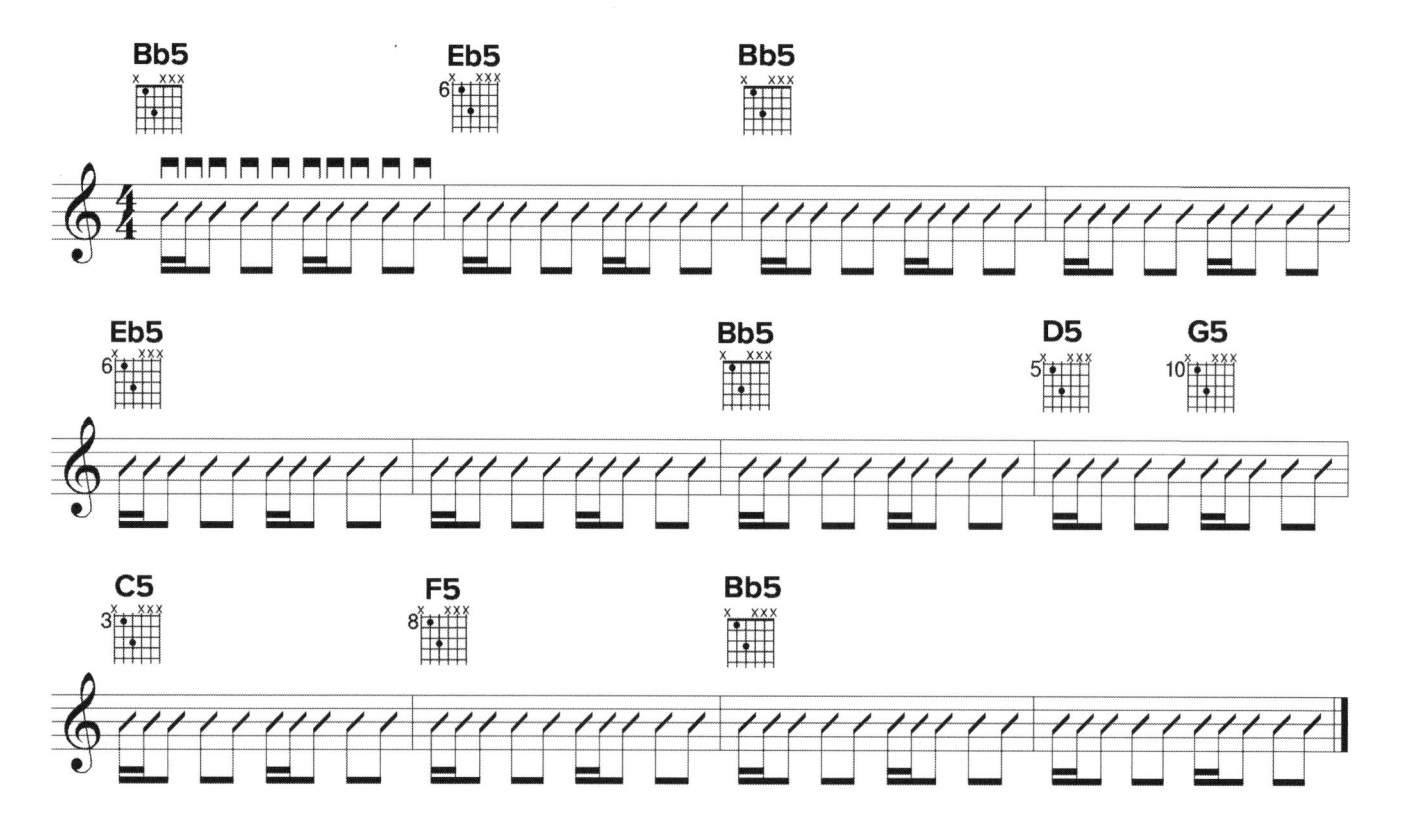

In exercises 18-23, the chord boxes have been omitted to test your memory.

Exercise 18

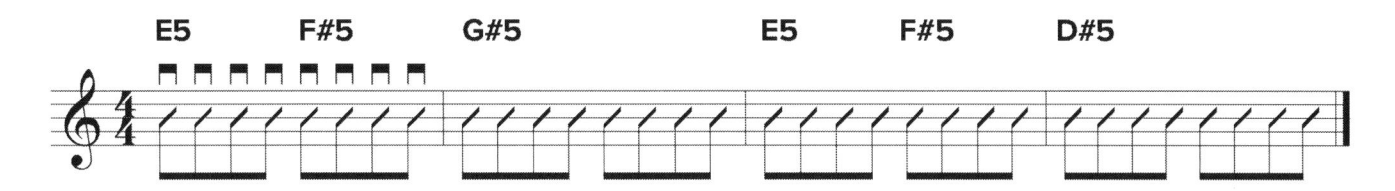

Exercise 19

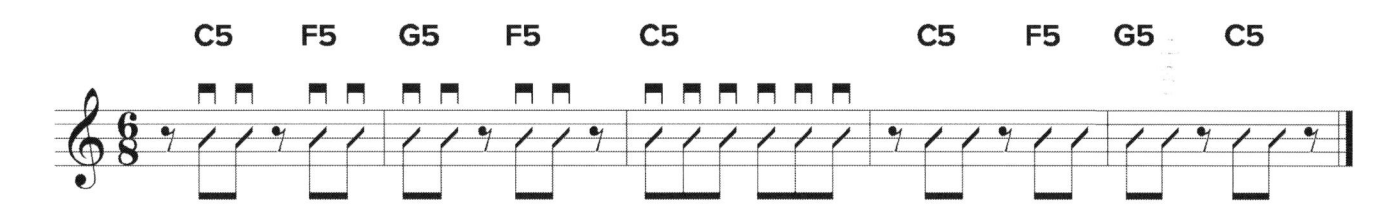

Exercise 20

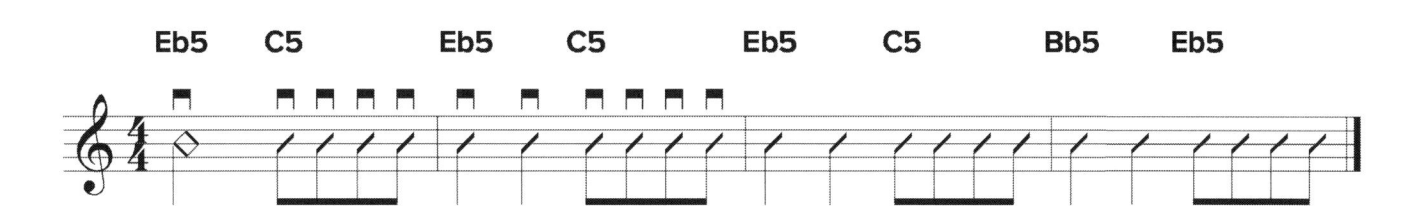

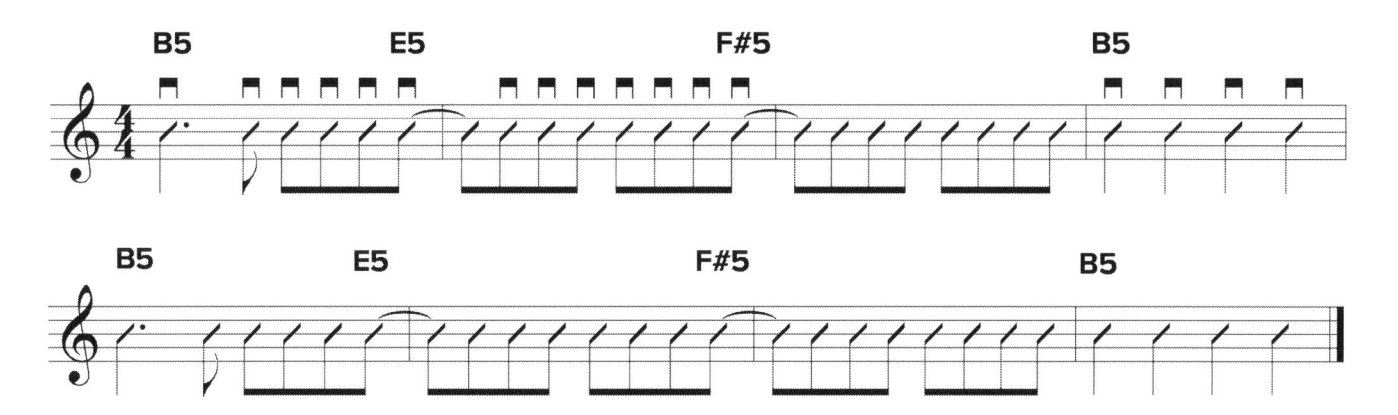

Exercise 21

Exercise 22

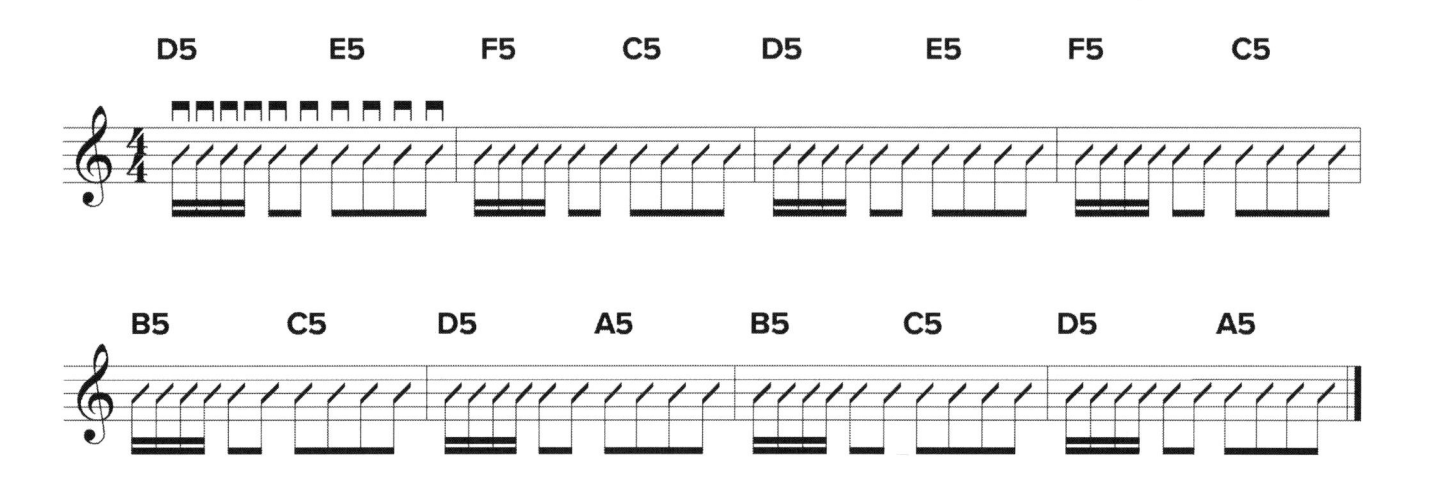

D5   E5   F5   C5   D5   E5   F5   C5

B5   C5   D5   A5   B5   C5   D5   A5

Exercise 23

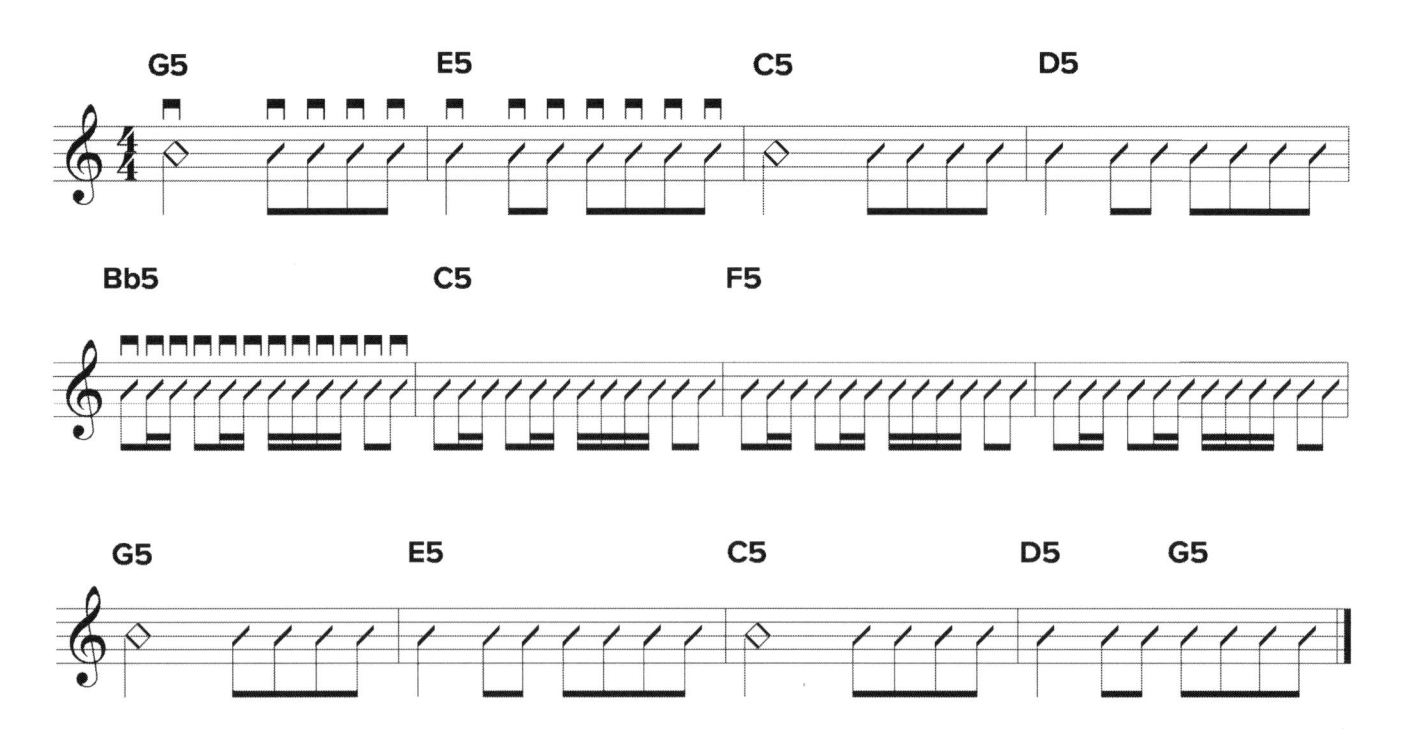

G5   E5   C5   D5

Bb5   C5   F5

G5   E5   C5   D5   G5

The Waterless Flood

Intro

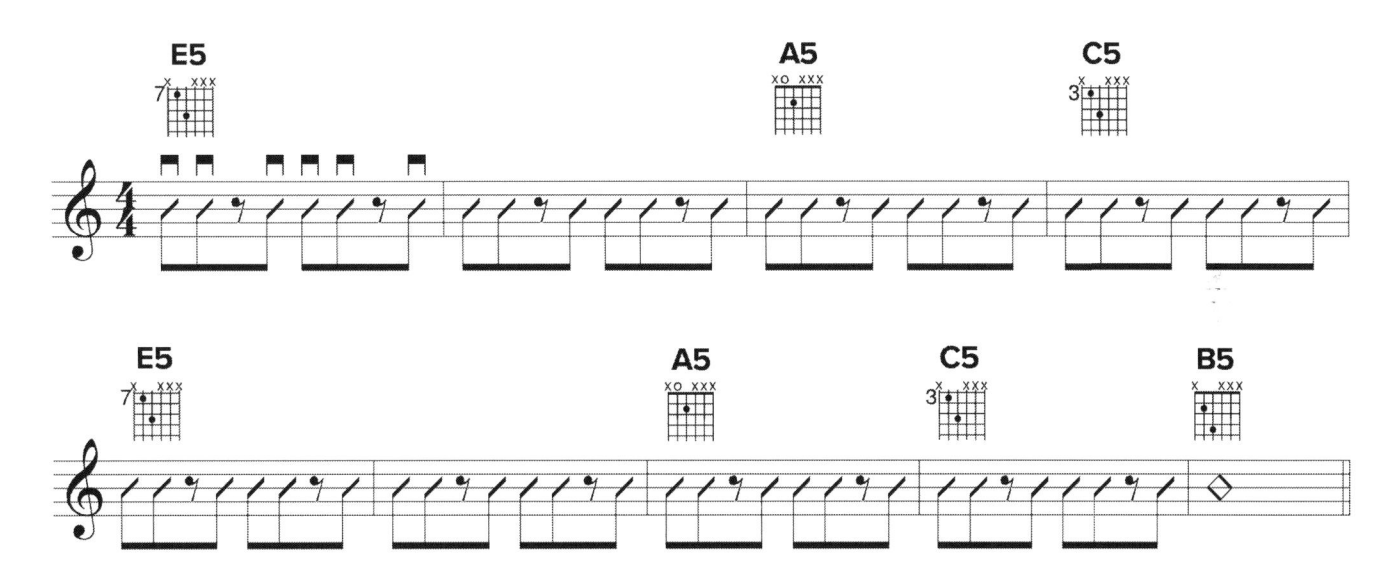

| E5 | | A5 | C5 |

| E5 | | A5 | C5 | B5 |

Verse

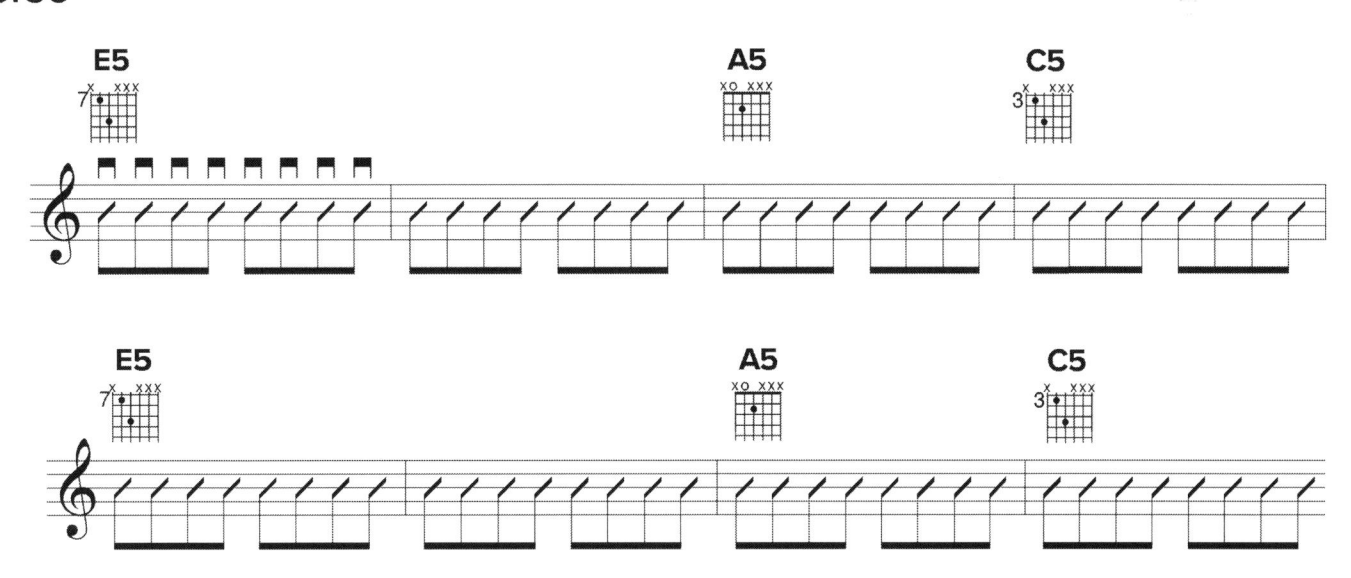

| E5 | | A5 | C5 |

| E5 | | A5 | C5 |

Chorus

Bridge

Verse

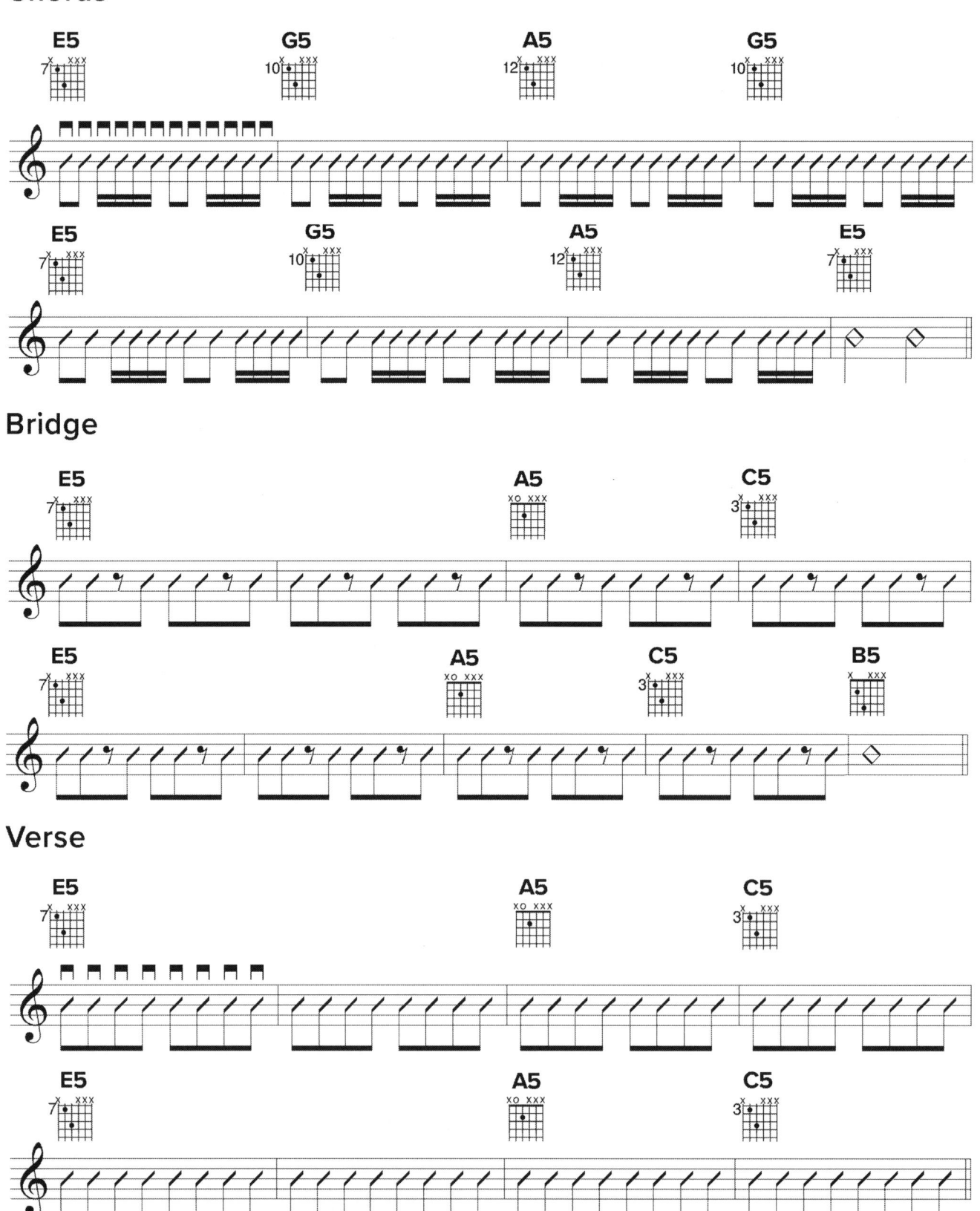

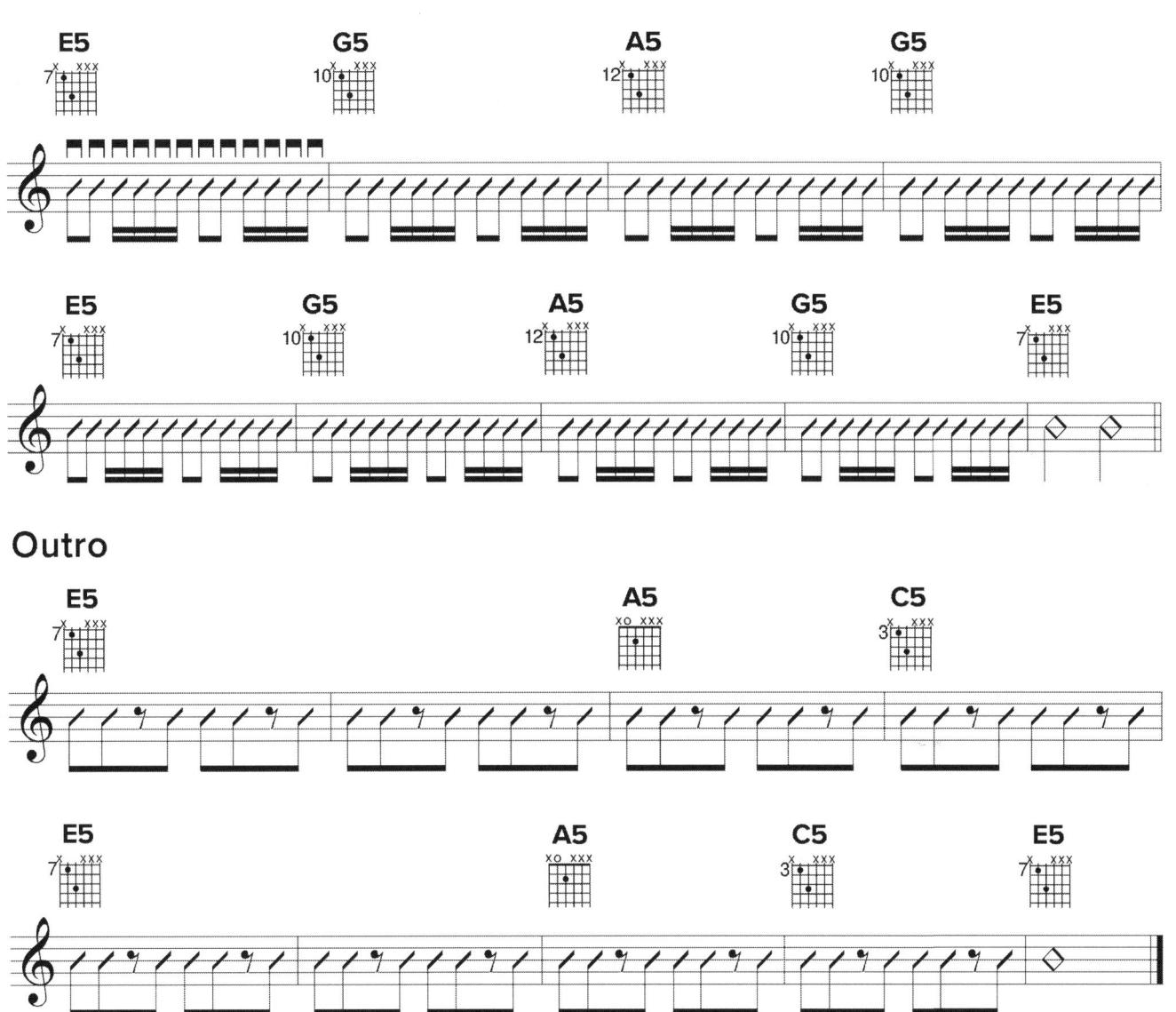

Chorus

Outro

July Justice

Intro

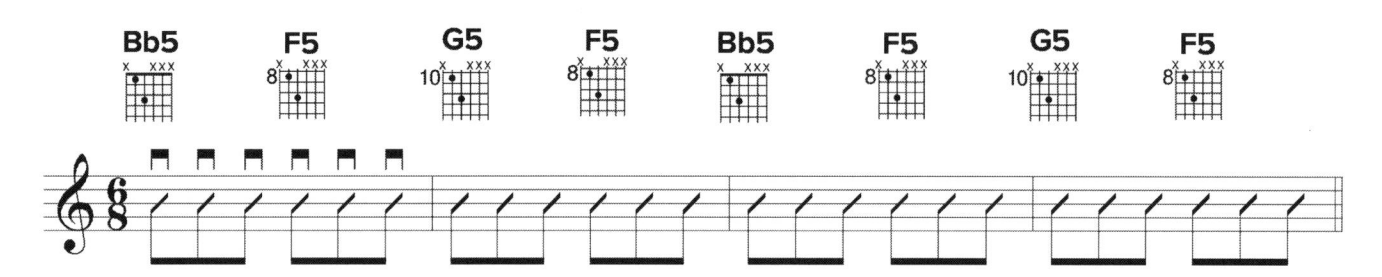

| Bb5 | F5 | G5 | F5 | Bb5 | F5 | G5 | F5 |

(6/8 time)

Verse

| Bb5 | F5 | G5 | F5 |

| Bb5 | F5 | G5 | F5 |

(changes to 4/4)

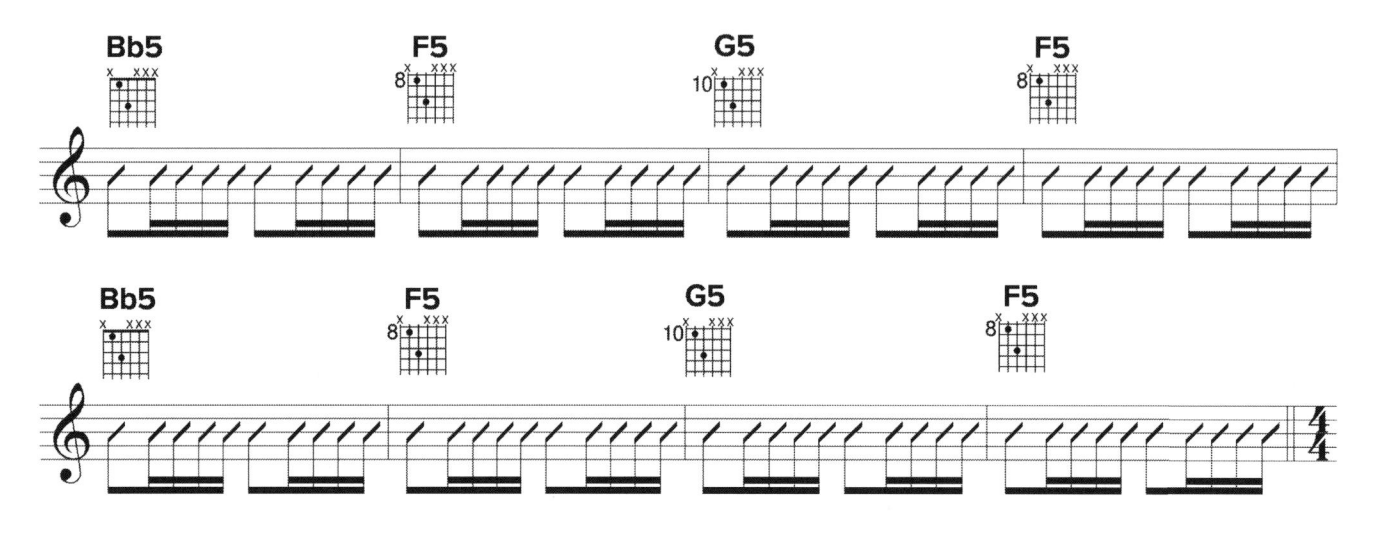

Chorus

| C5 | Eb5 | F5 |

| C5 | Eb5 | F5 |

(changes to 6/8)

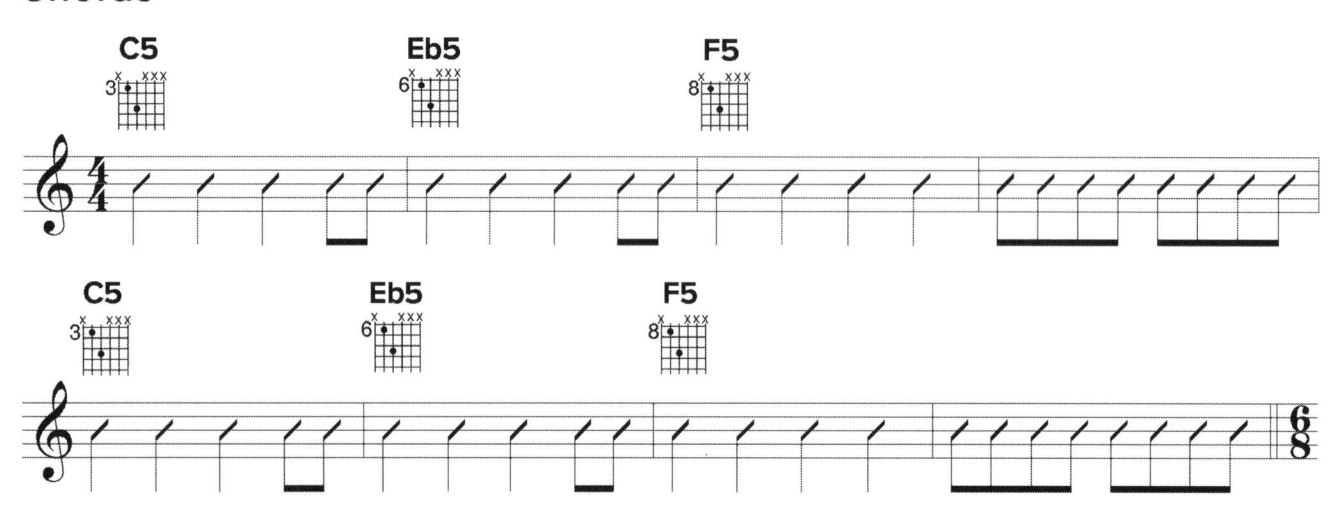

Verse

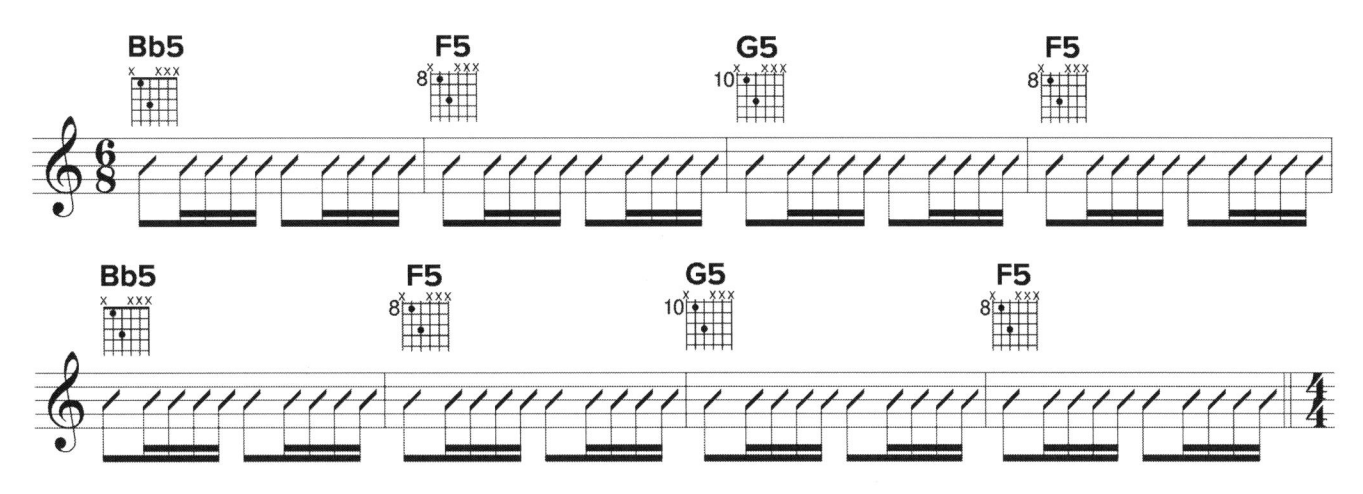

| Bb5 | F5 | G5 | F5 |
| Bb5 | F5 | G5 | F5 |

Chorus

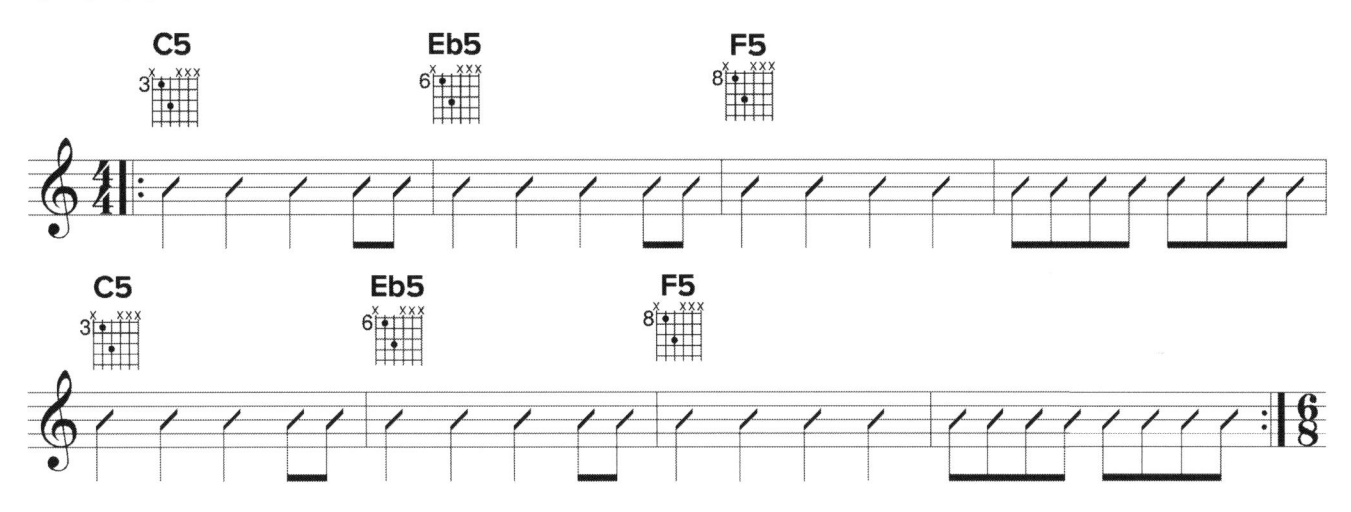

| C5 | Eb5 | F5 |
| C5 | Eb5 | F5 |

Outro

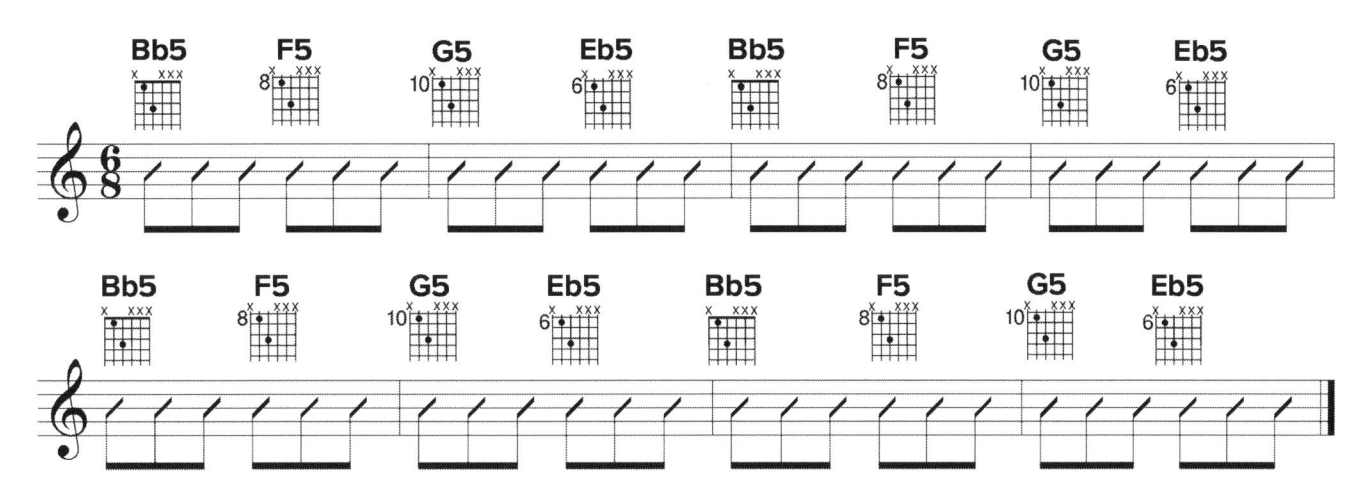

| Bb5 | F5 | G5 | Eb5 | Bb5 | F5 | G5 | Eb5 |
| Bb5 | F5 | G5 | Eb5 | Bb5 | F5 | G5 | Eb5 |

Sometimes

Honey Dew Blues

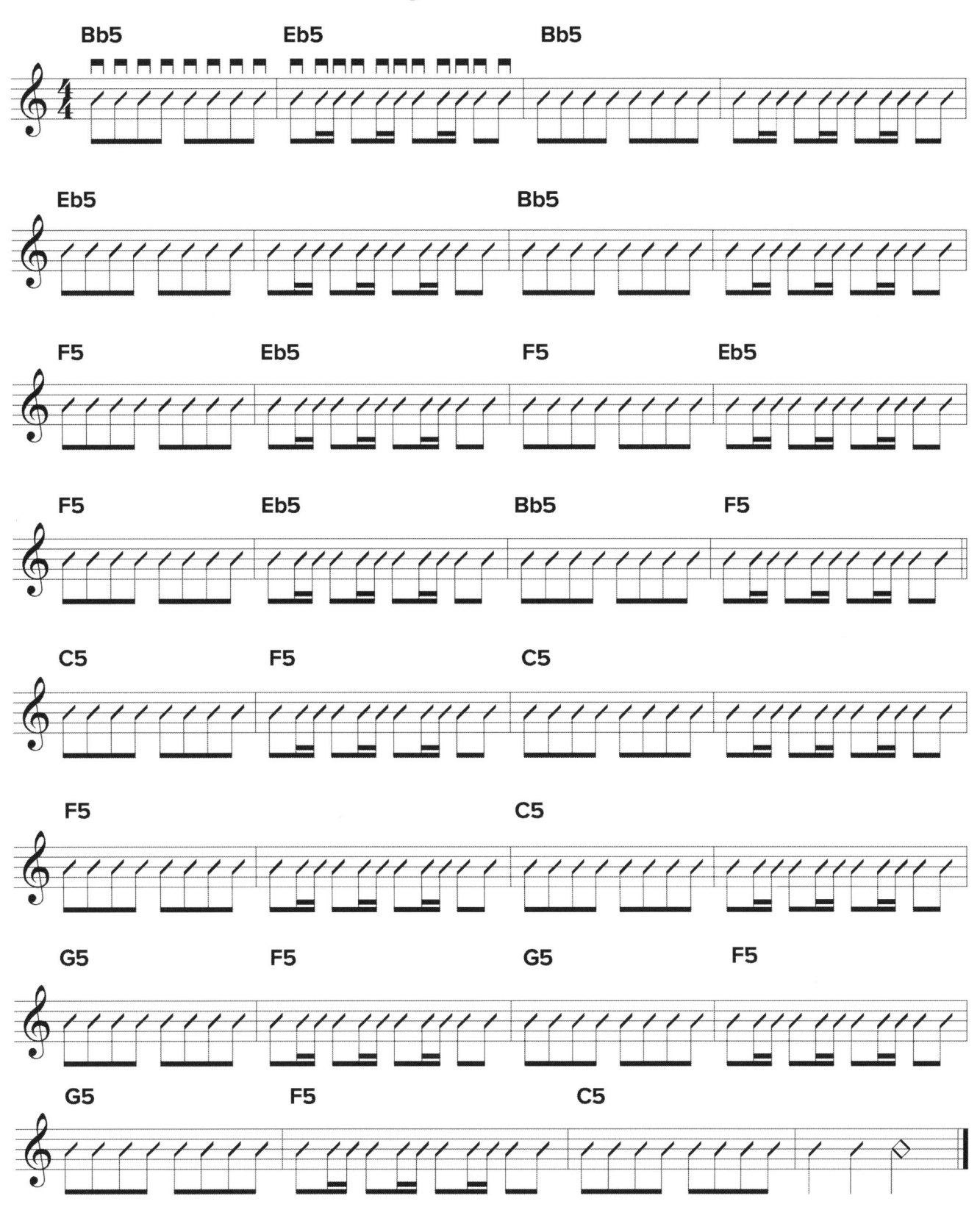

Lesson 4:
Root 5 and Root 6 Combined

In this lesson, will we be practicing playing power chords in a more practical manner by switching between strings rather than staying on one string like we have in the two previous lessons. This is by far the more common way of playing power chords. Since there are now so many options for playing the same thing, a general rule you'll want to follow is this: ask yourself what version of the chord is closest to where you are now? Then move to that chord. For example, if you were to play a root 6 G5 chord and wanted to play C5 power chord next, you would simply move from the G5 on the last string third fret to the fifth string third fret C5 power chord rather than skipping all the way up to the eighth fret on the sixth string.

Exercise 1

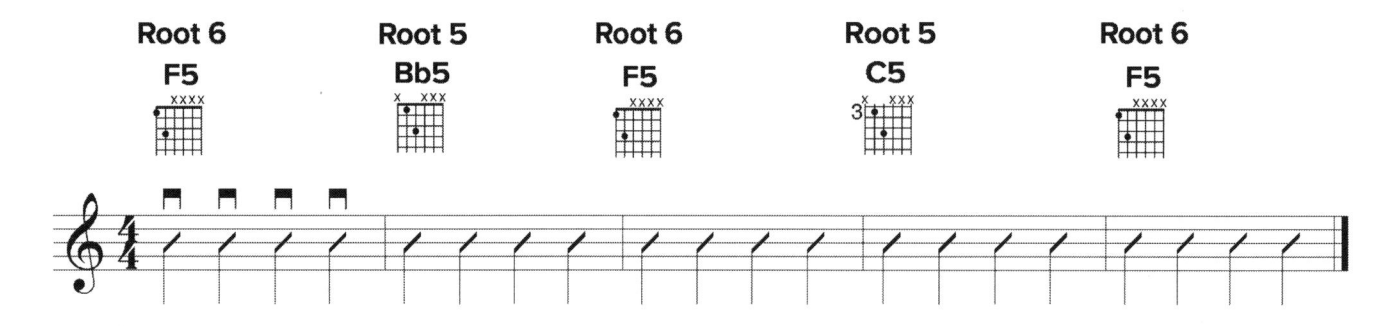

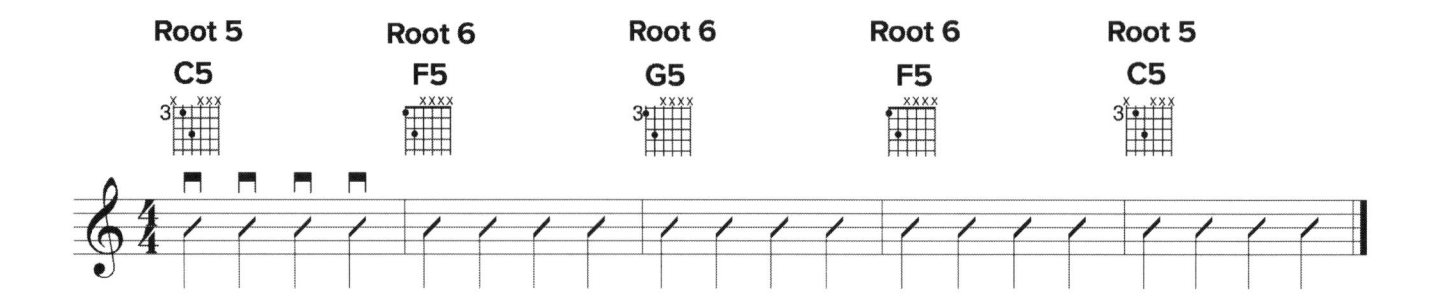

Root 6	Root 5	Root 6	Root 5	Root 6
F5	Bb5	F5	C5	F5

Exercise 2

Root 5	Root 6	Root 6	Root 6	Root 5
C5	F5	G5	F5	C5

Exercise 3

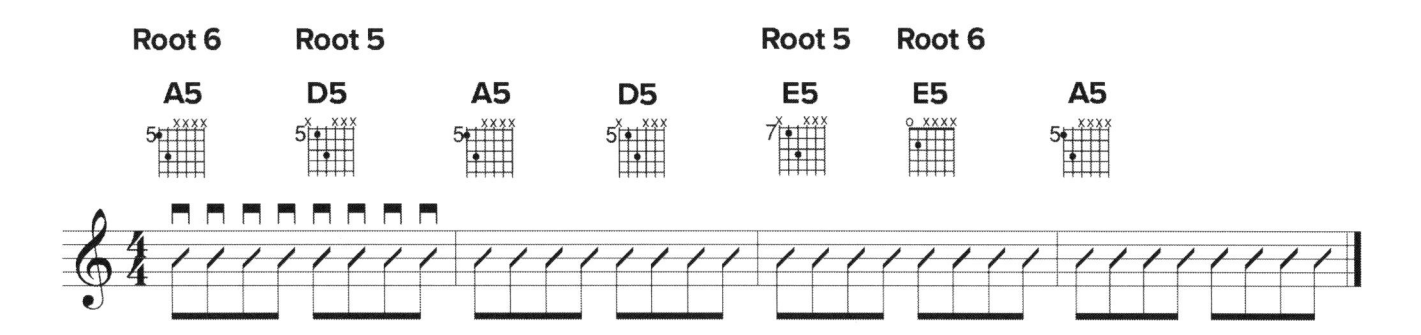

Root 6	Root 5			Root 5	Root 6	
A5	D5	A5	D5	E5	E5	A5

Exercise 4

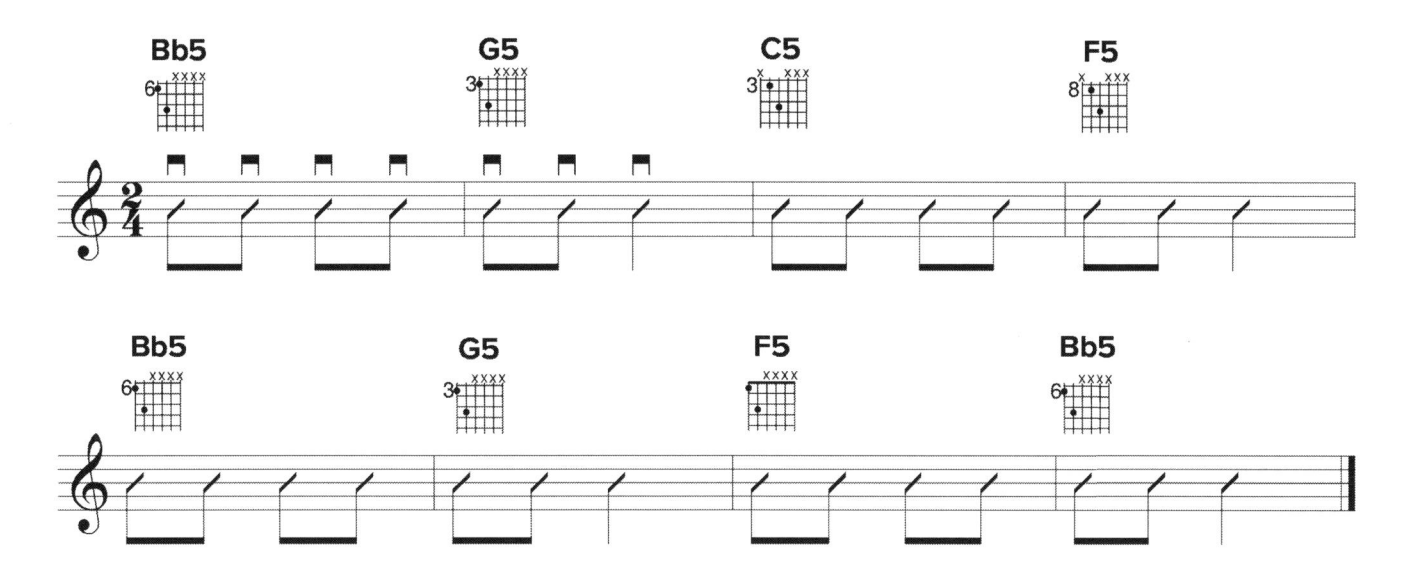

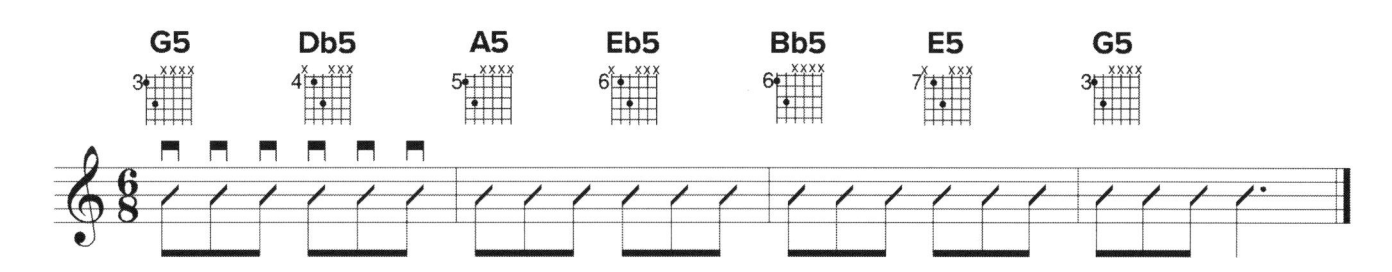

Bb5   G5   C5   F5

Bb5   G5   F5   Bb5

Exercise 5

G5   Db5   A5   Eb5   Bb5   E5   G5

Exercise 6

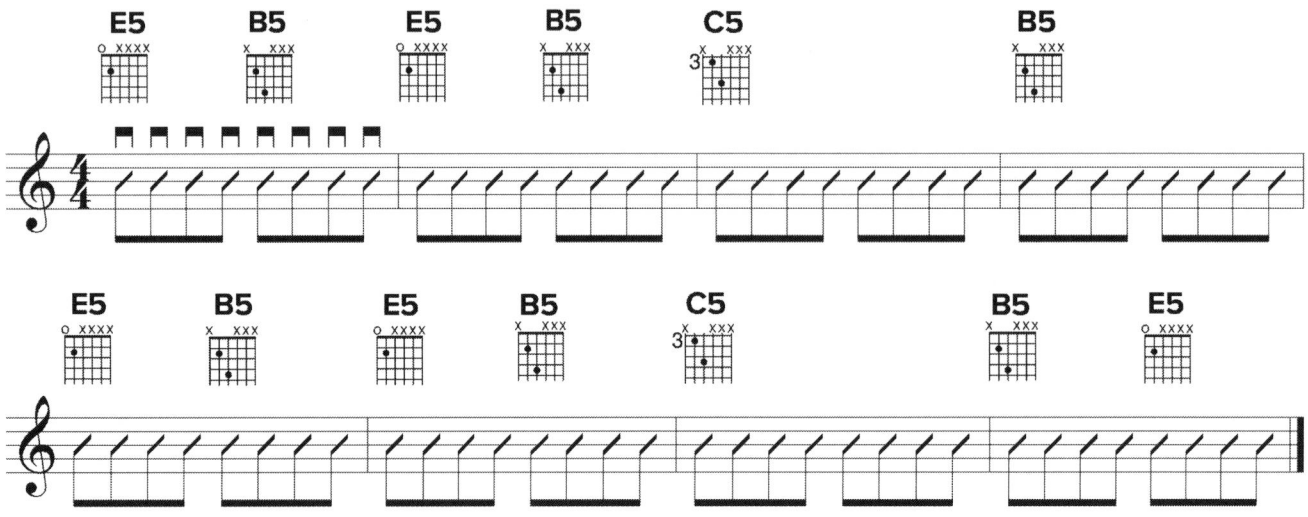

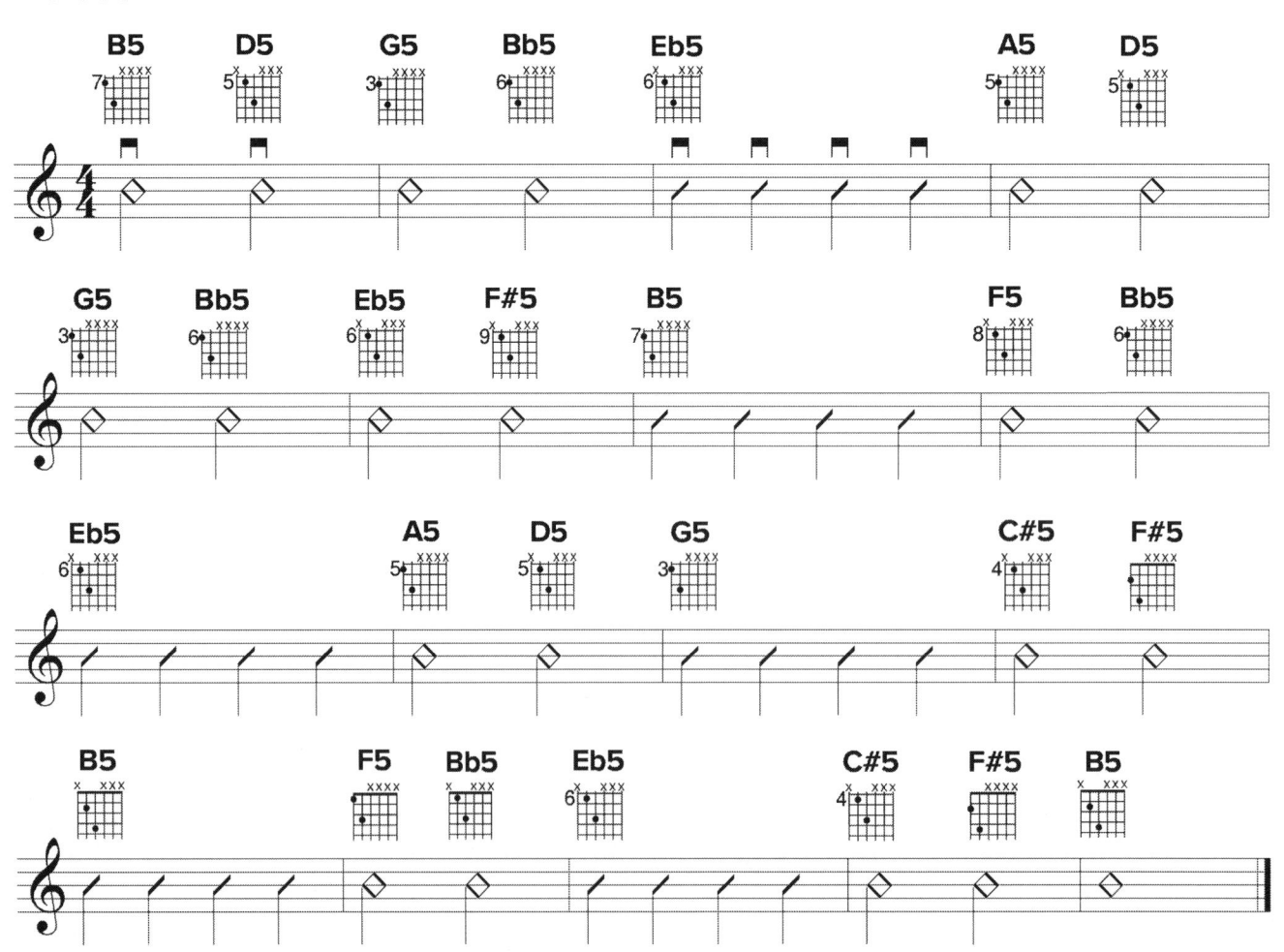

Exercise 7

Exercise 8

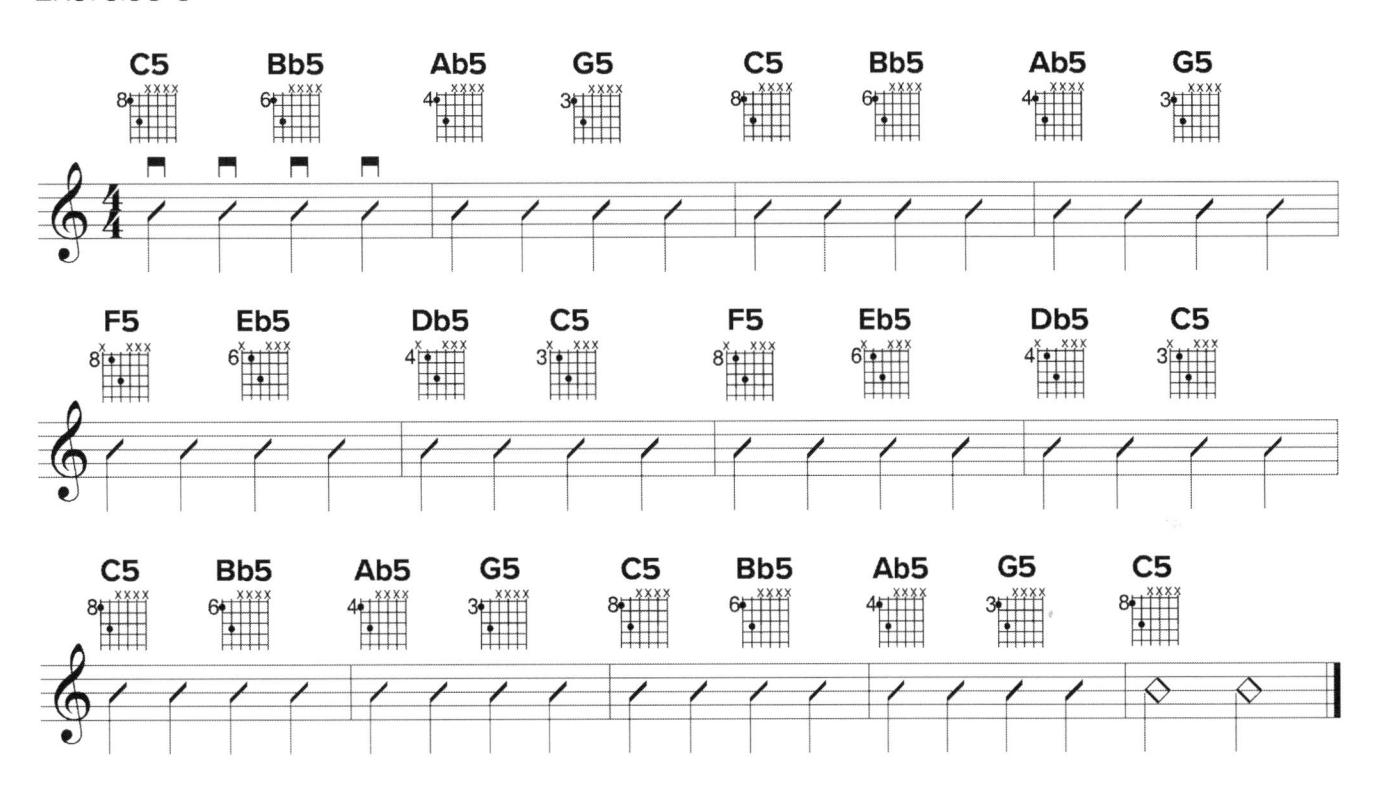

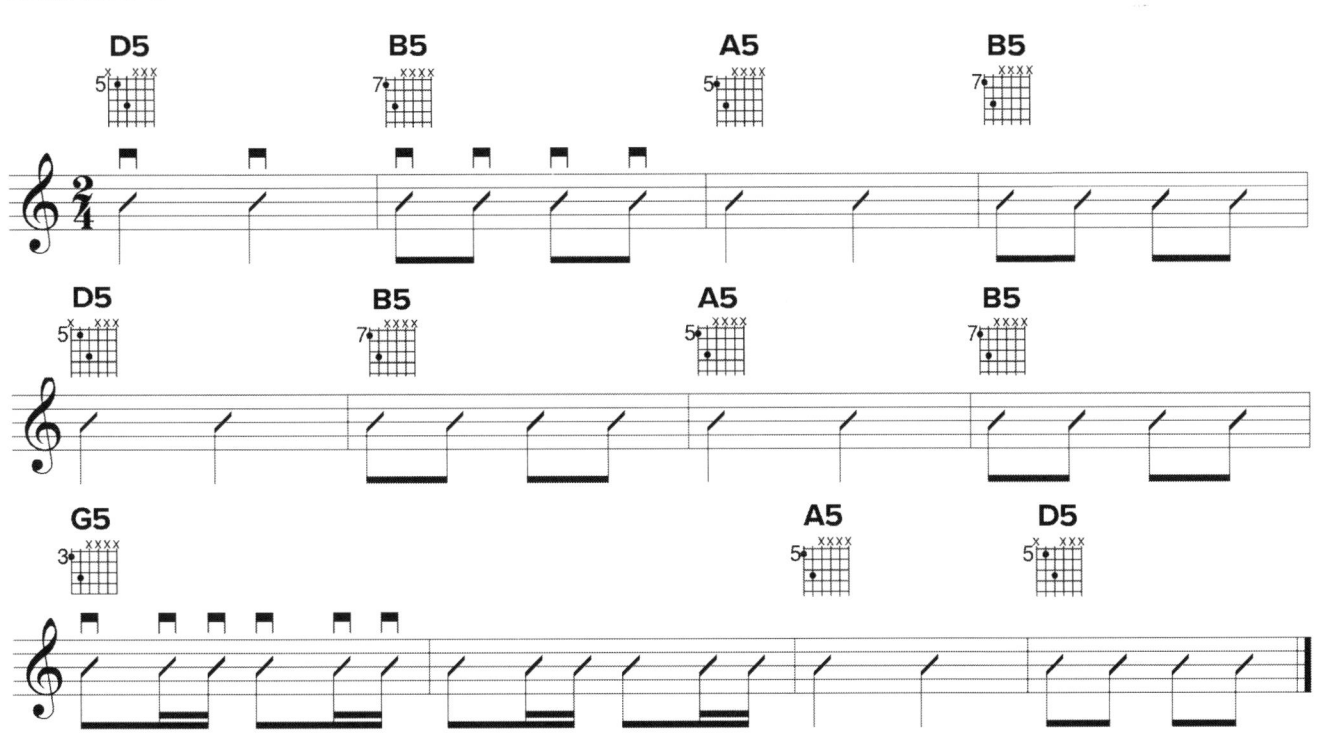

| C5 | Bb5 | Ab5 | G5 | C5 | Bb5 | Ab5 | G5 |

| F5 | Eb5 | Db5 | C5 | F5 | Eb5 | Db5 | C5 |

| C5 | Bb5 | Ab5 | G5 | C5 | Bb5 | Ab5 | G5 | C5 |

Exercise 9

| D5 | B5 | A5 | B5 |

| D5 | B5 | A5 | B5 |

| G5 | A5 | D5 |

Exercise 10

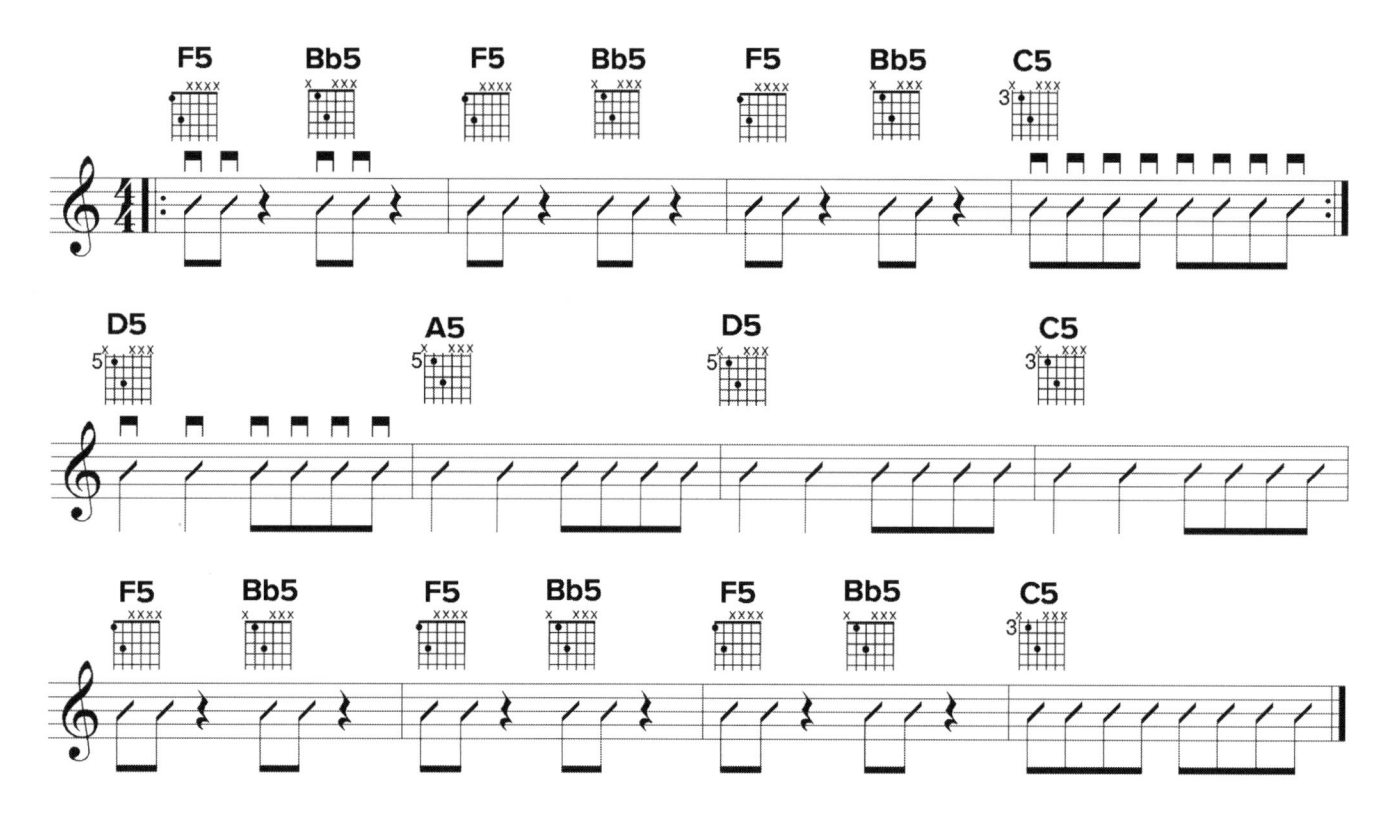

Exercise 11

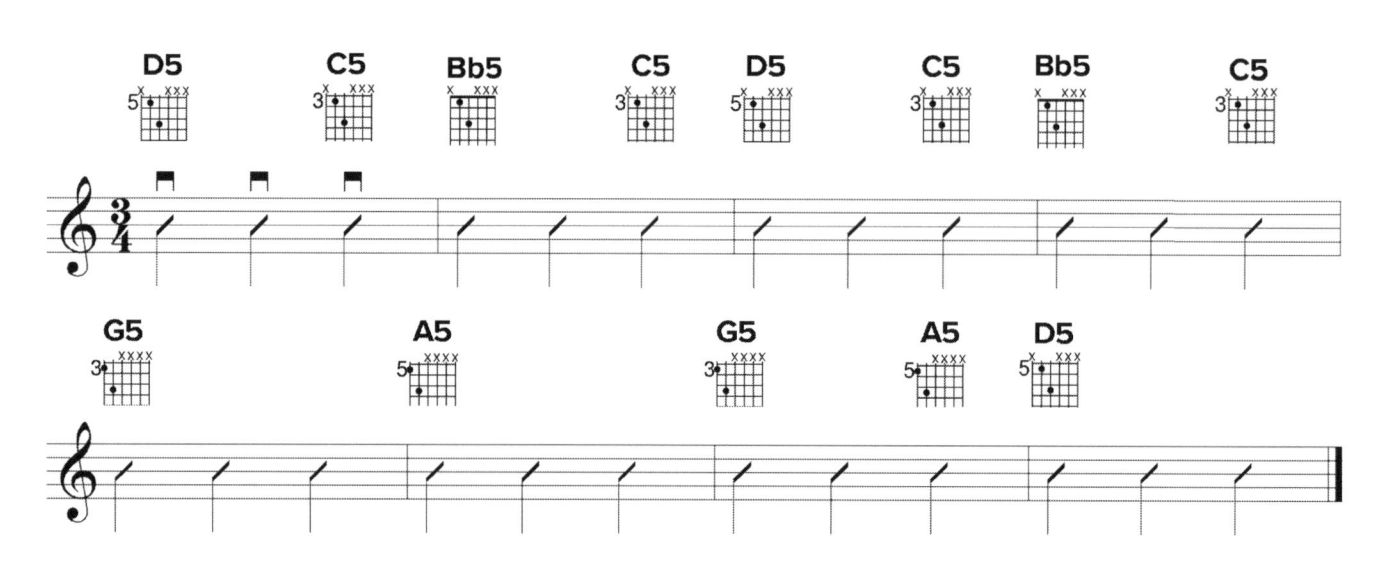

Exercise 12

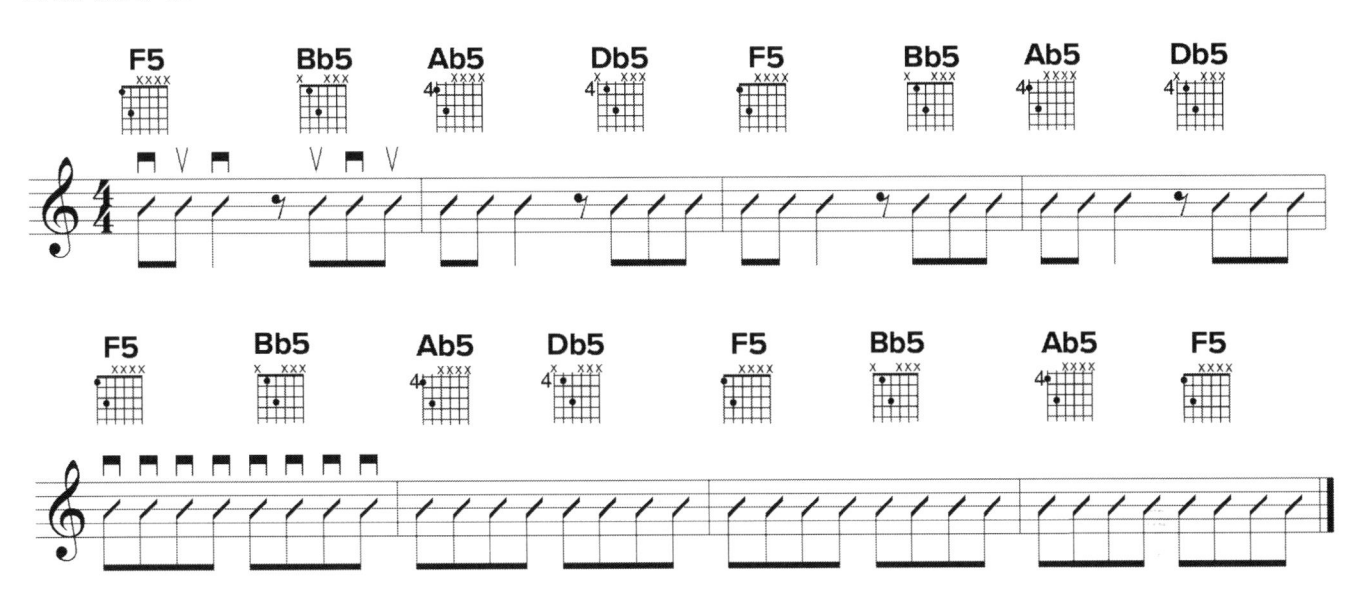

Exercise 13

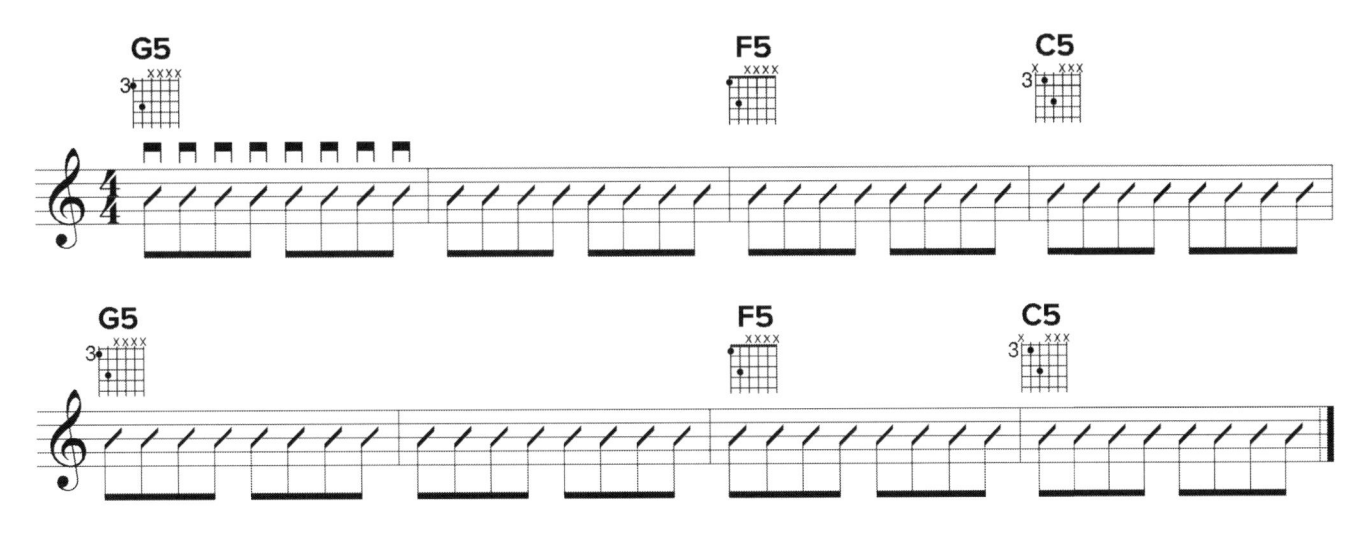

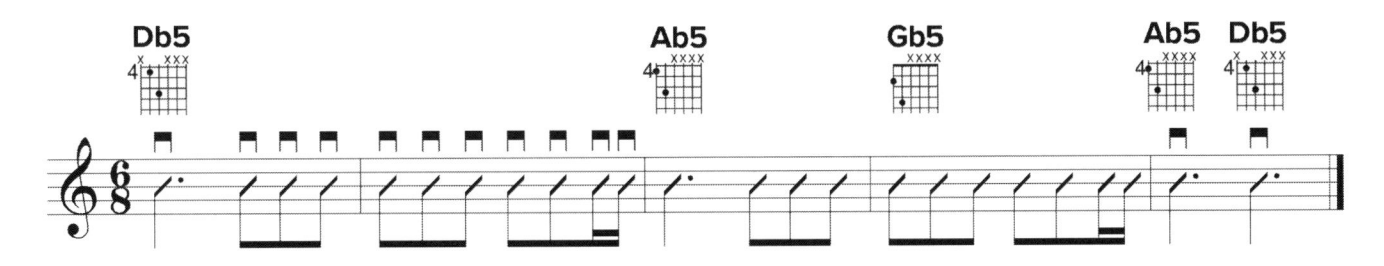

Exercise 14

In the following exercises, no chord locations are given. Therefore, it is up to you to figure out the best way to play each exercise. There is no wrong way to do this as long as you play any version of the listed chord.

Exercise 15

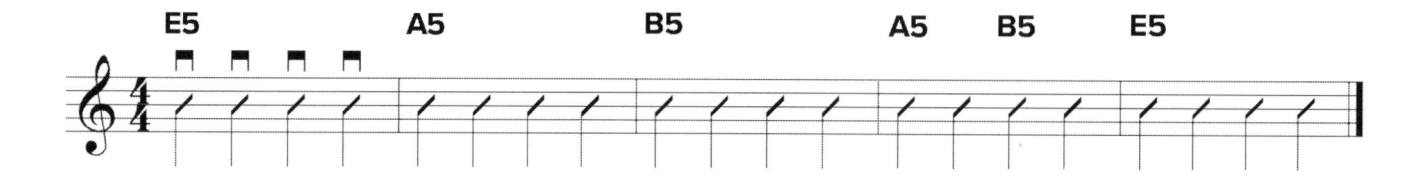

Exercise 16

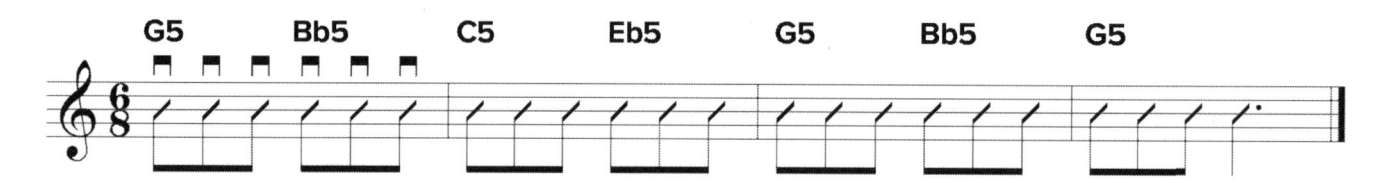

Exercise 17

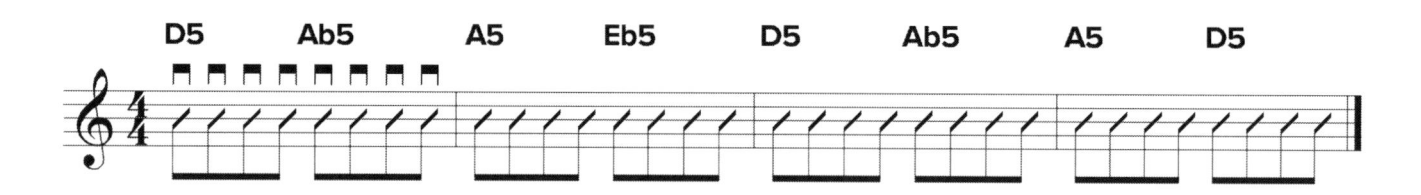

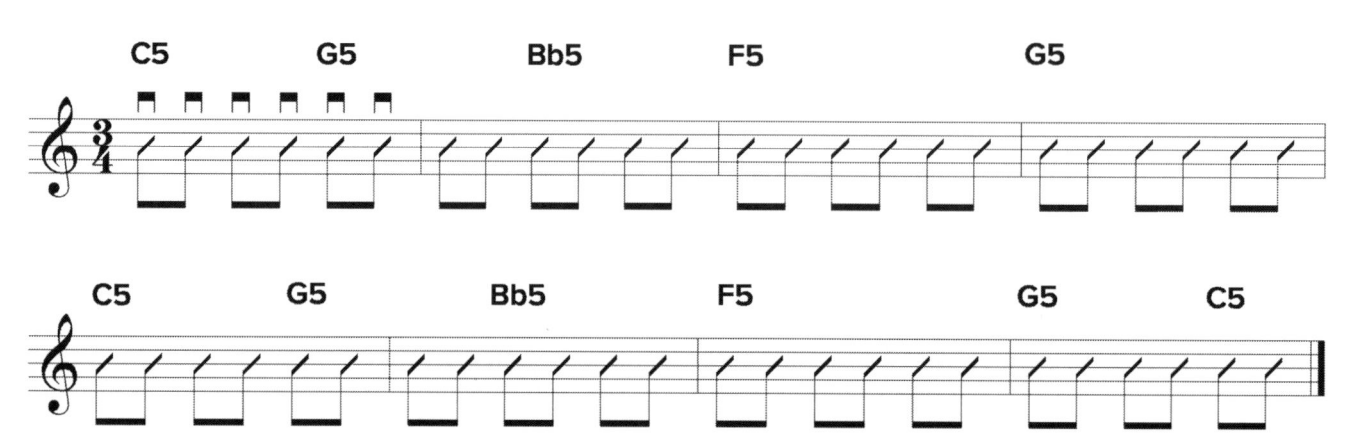

Exercise 18

M C Squared

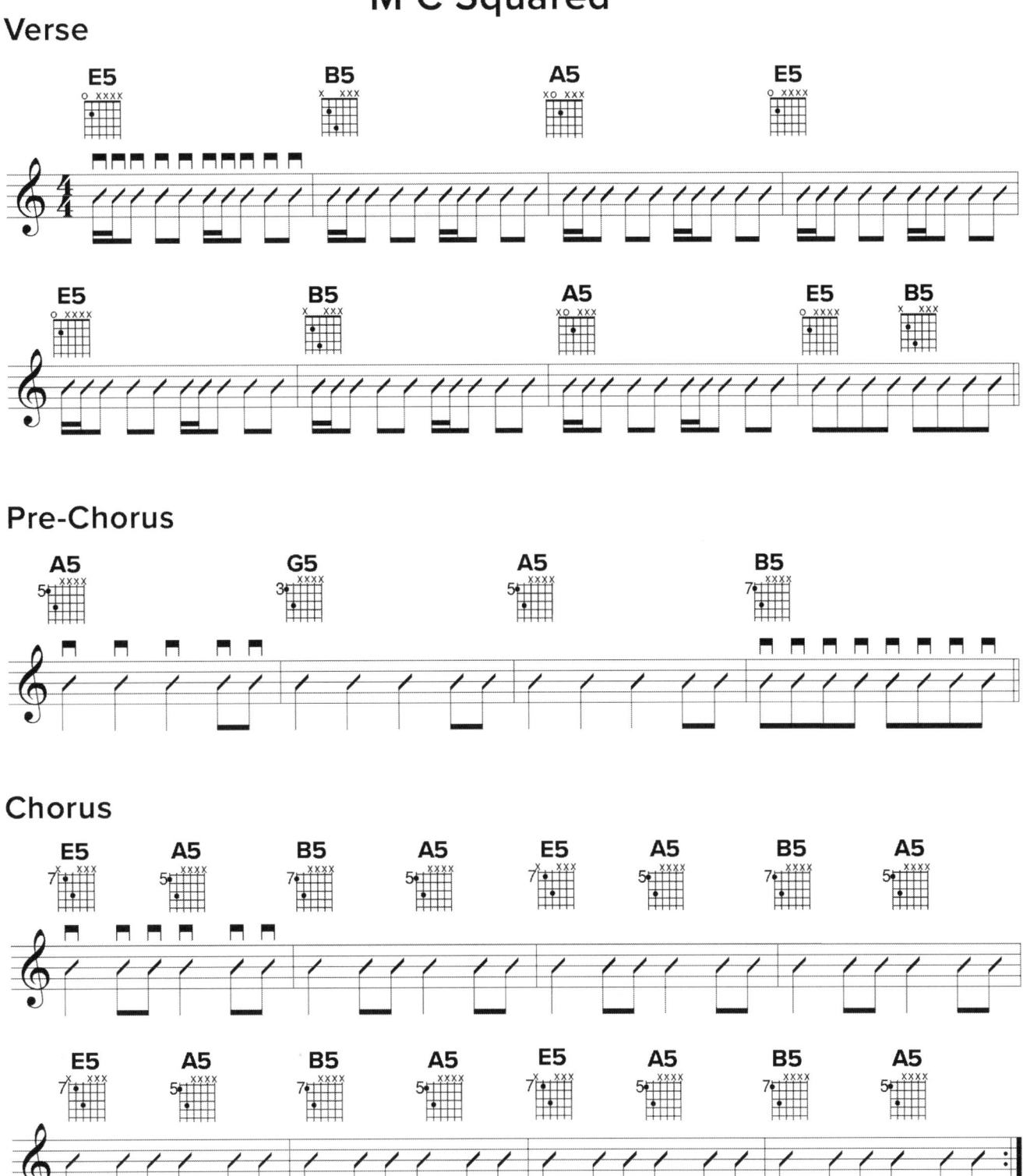

Verse

| E5 | B5 | A5 | E5 |

| E5 | B5 | A5 | E5 | B5 |

Pre-Chorus

| A5 | G5 | A5 | B5 |

Chorus

| E5 A5 | B5 A5 | E5 A5 | B5 A5 |

| E5 A5 | B5 A5 | E5 A5 | B5 A5 |

Verse

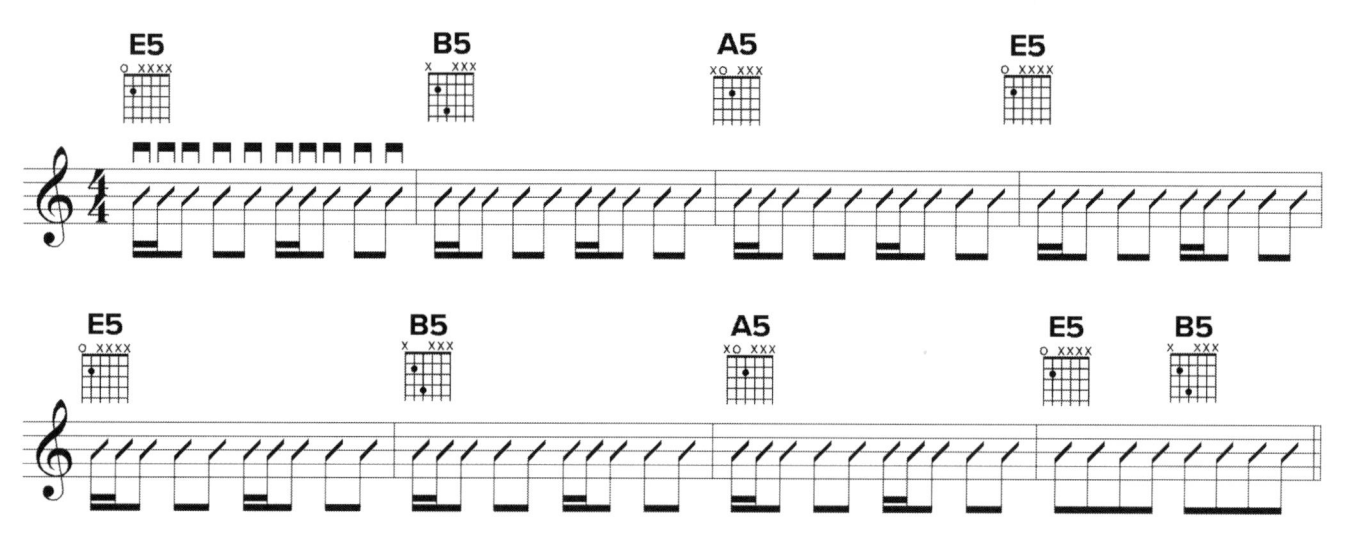

E5 | **B5** | **A5** | **E5**

E5 | **B5** | **A5** | **E5** **B5**

Pre-Chorus

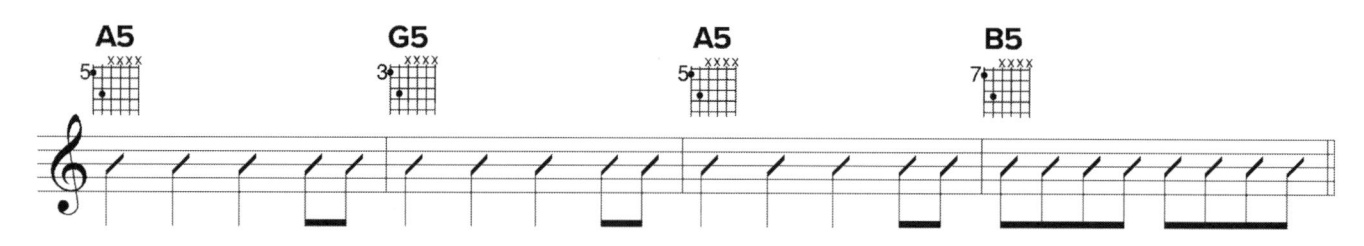

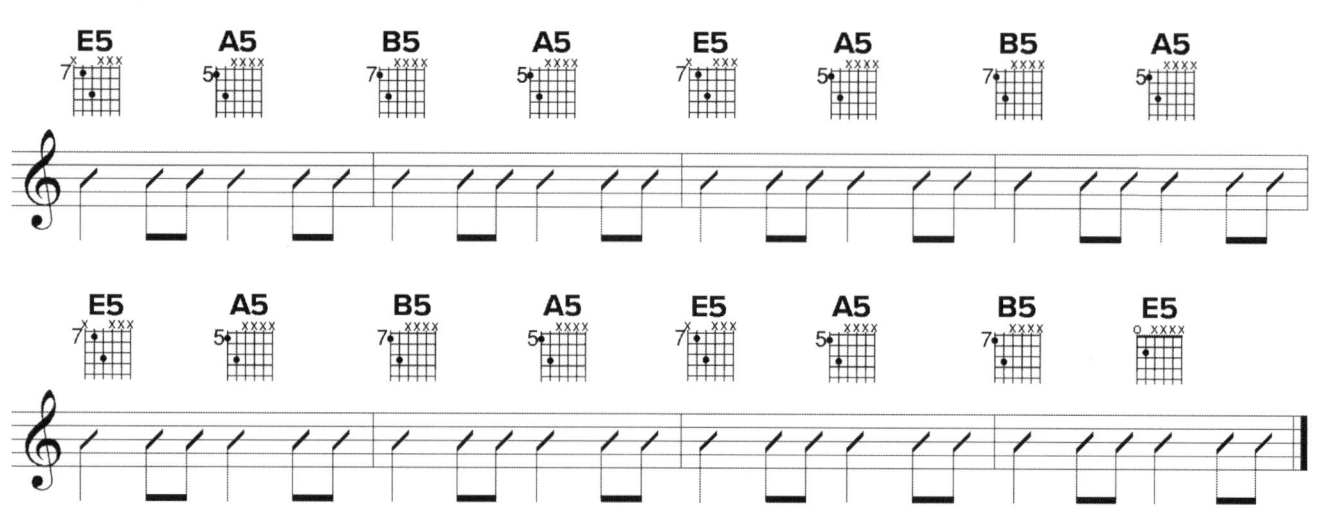

A5 | **G5** | **A5** | **B5**

Chorus

E5 **A5** | **B5** **A5** | **E5** **A5** | **B5** **A5**

E5 **A5** | **B5** **A5** | **E5** **A5** | **B5** **E5**

New City Rock n' Roll

Intro

E5			
A5		E5	

Verse

| A5 | D5 E5 | A5 | D5 E5 |
| A5 | D5 E5 | A5 | D5 E5 |

Chorus

| D5 | | A5 | D5 A5 |
| D5 | | B5 | D5 E5 |

Verse

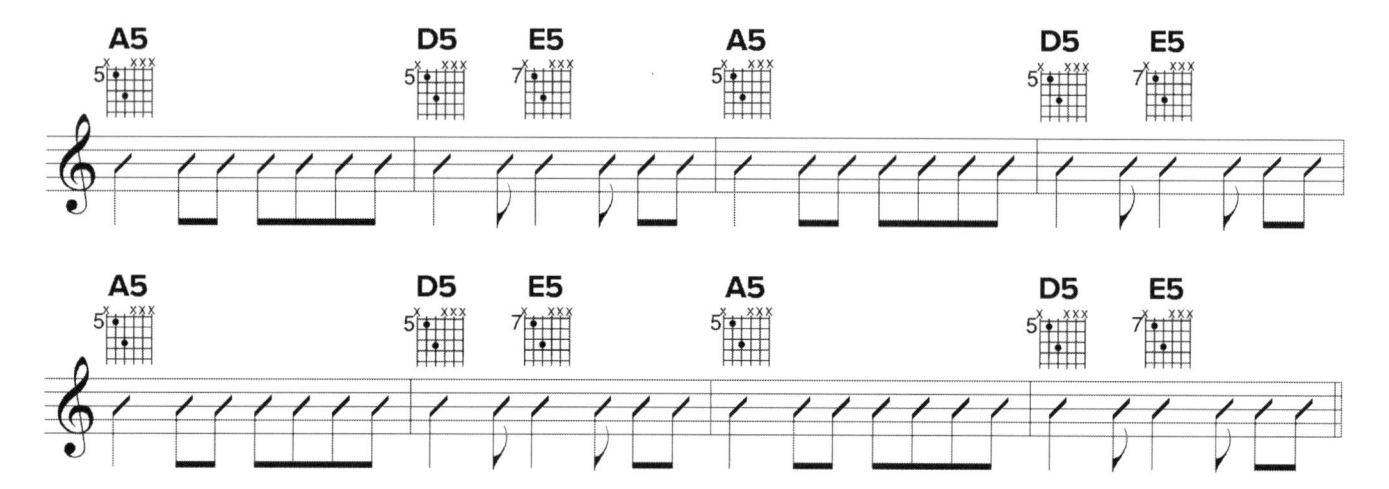

Chorus

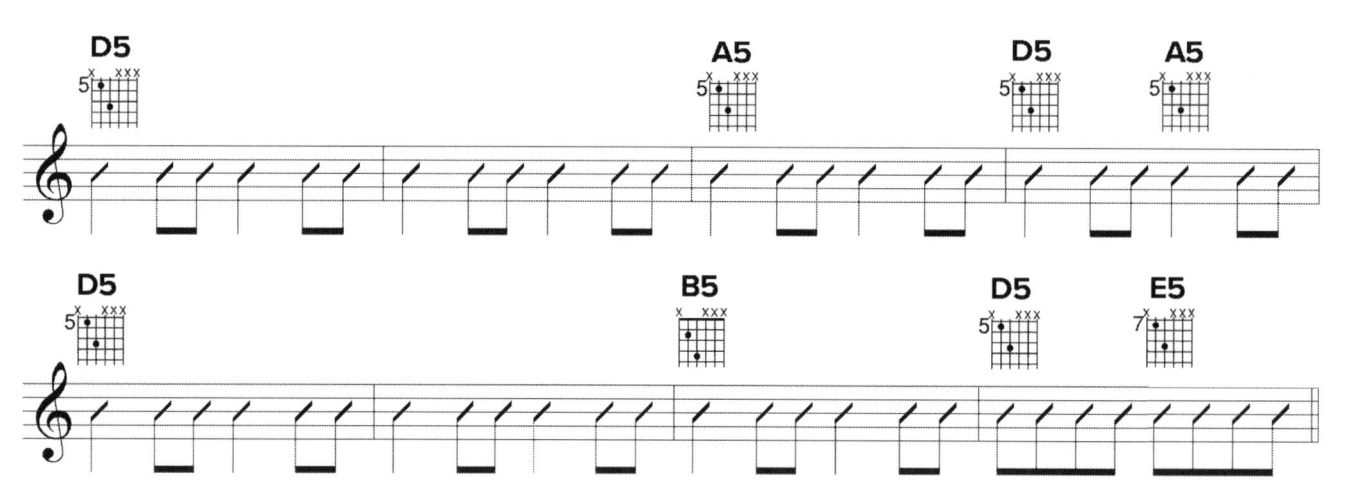

Bridge

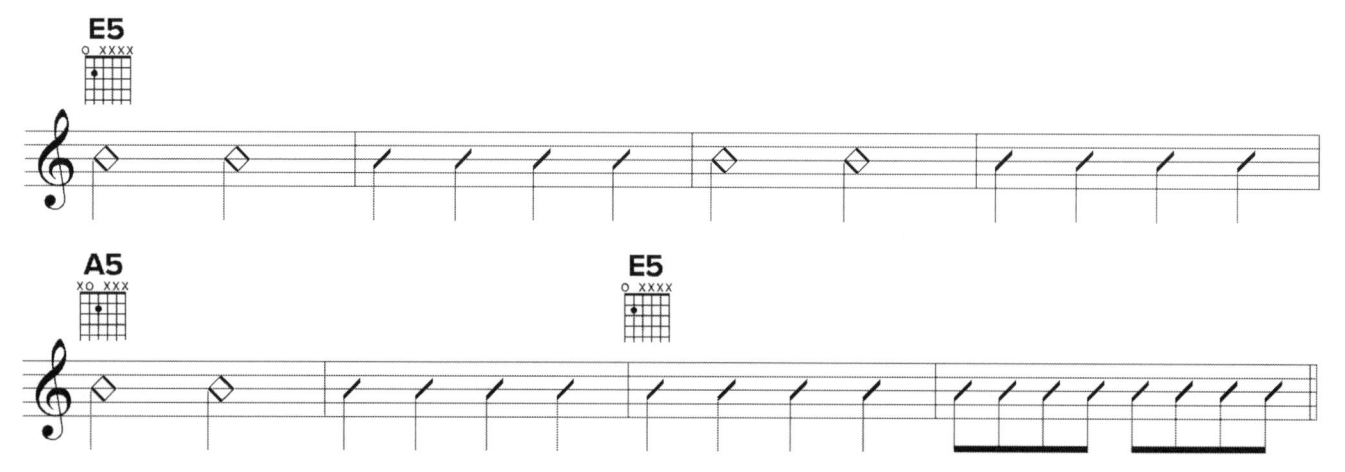

Chorus

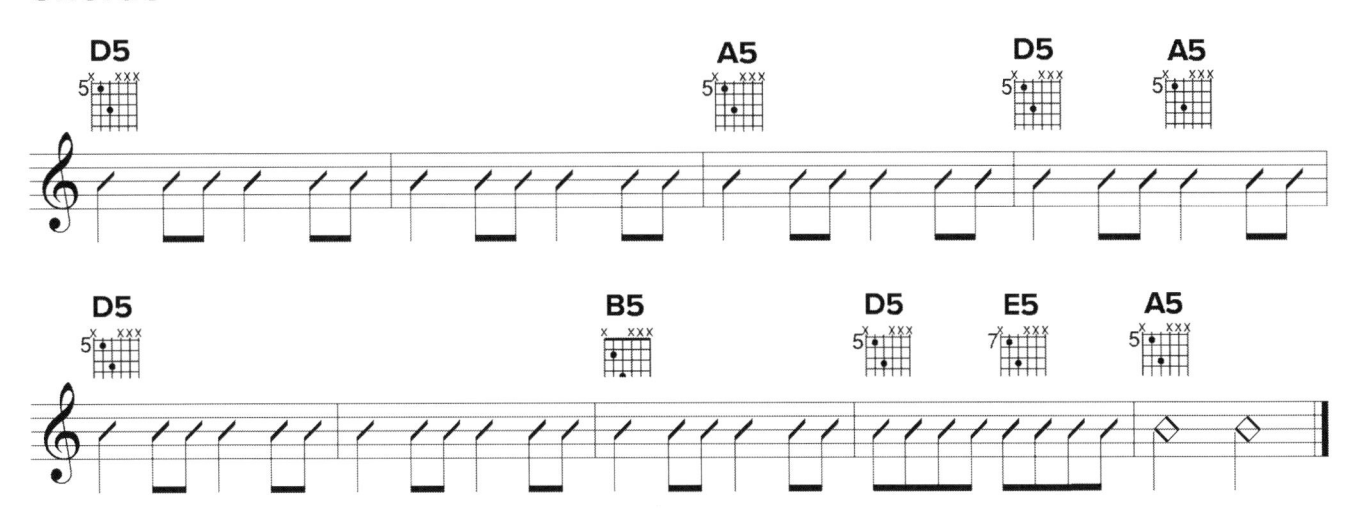

Walking to Beverly Hills

Intro

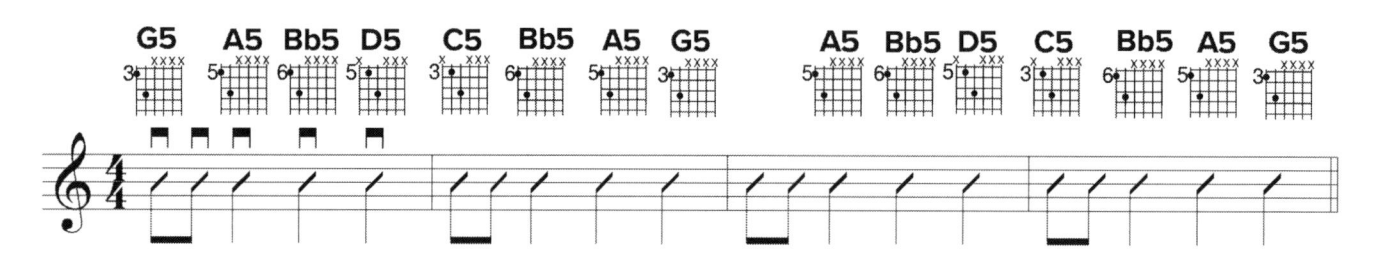

| G5 | A5 | Bb5 | D5 | C5 | Bb5 | A5 | G5 | A5 | Bb5 | D5 | C5 | Bb5 | A5 | G5 |

Verse

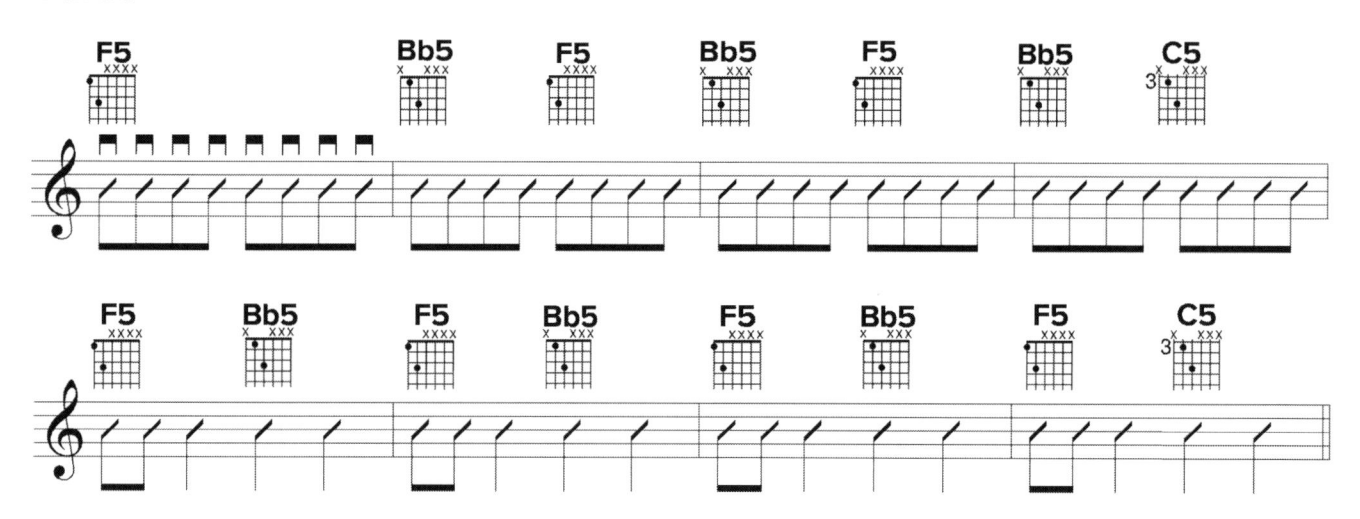

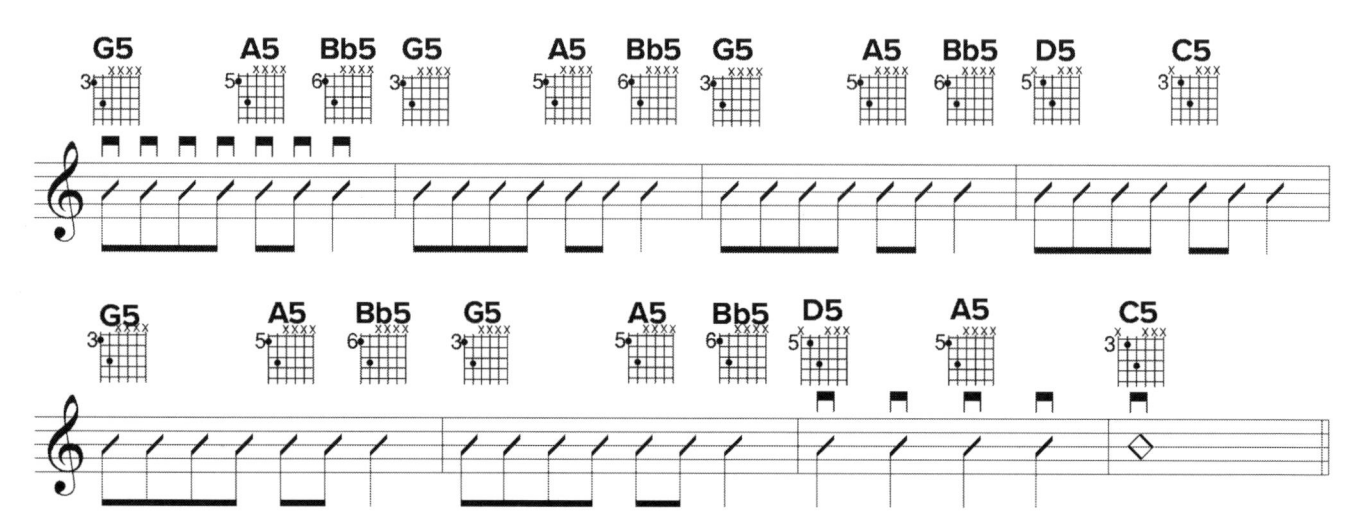

| F5 | | | | Bb5 | F5 | Bb5 | F5 | Bb5 | C5 |

| F5 | Bb5 | F5 | Bb5 | F5 | Bb5 | F5 | C5 |

Chorus

| G5 | A5 | Bb5 | G5 | A5 | Bb5 | G5 | A5 | Bb5 | D5 | C5 |

| G5 | A5 | Bb5 | G5 | A5 | Bb5 | D5 | A5 | C5 |

Verse

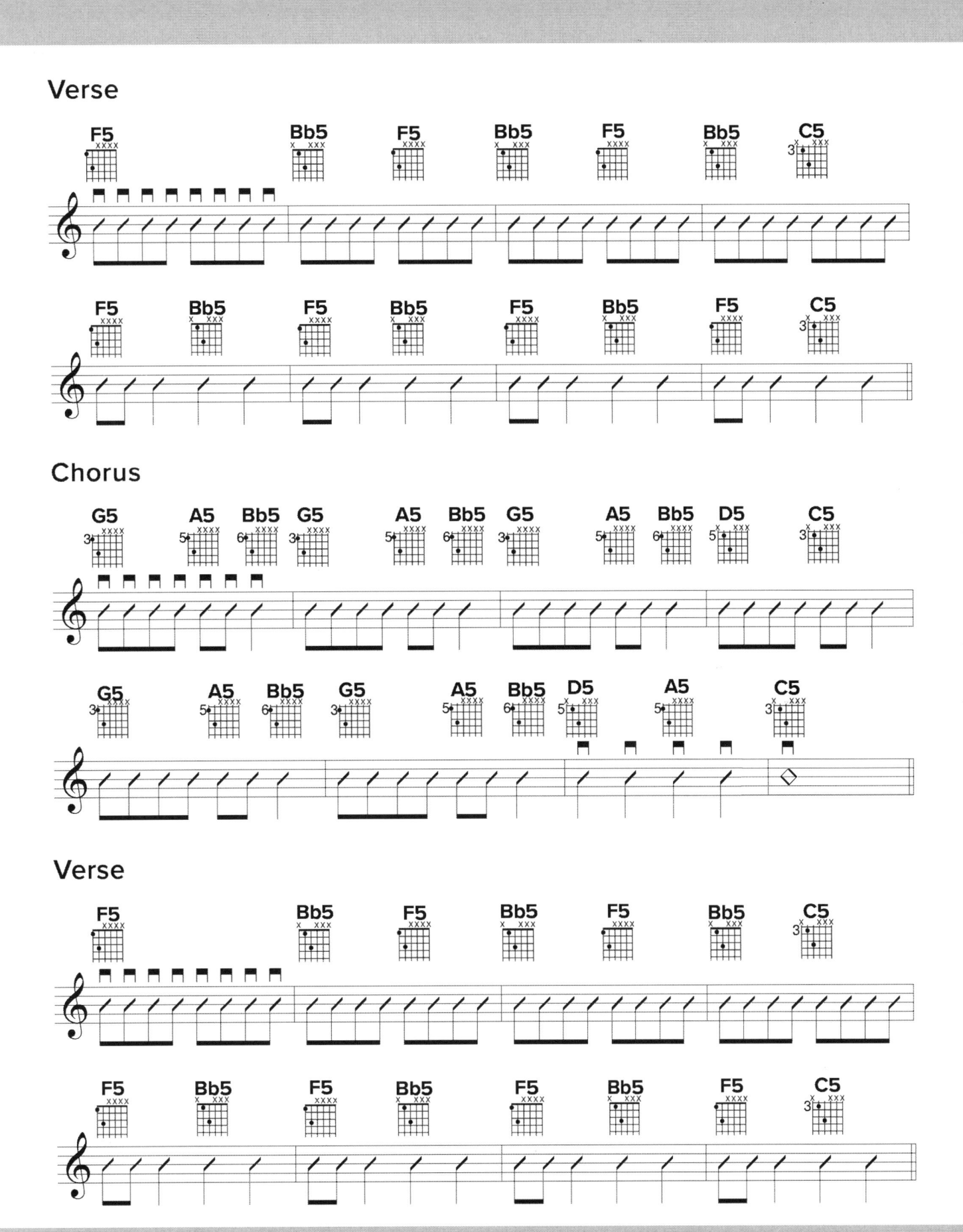

Chorus

Verse

Chorus

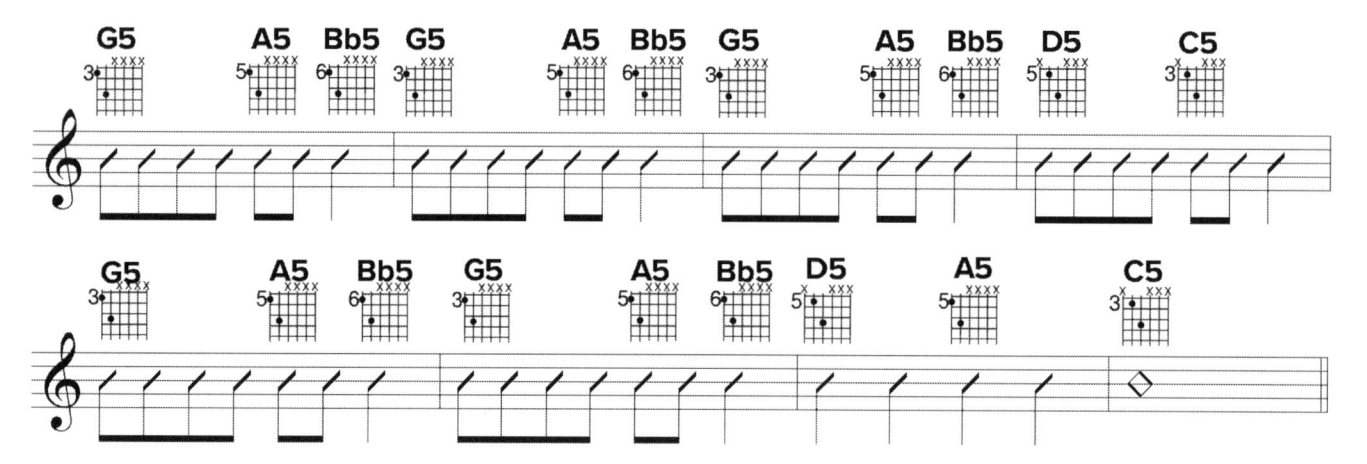

Outro

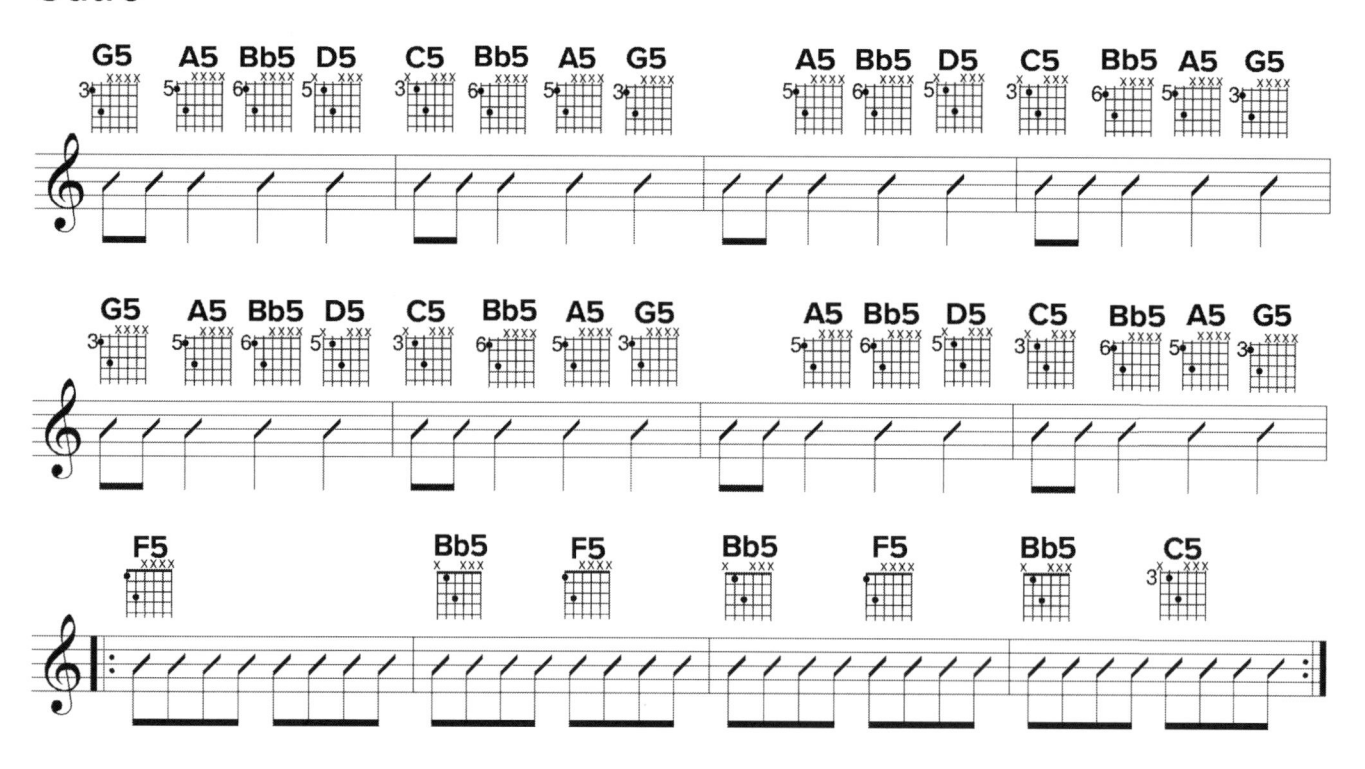

UFO Rock n' Roll

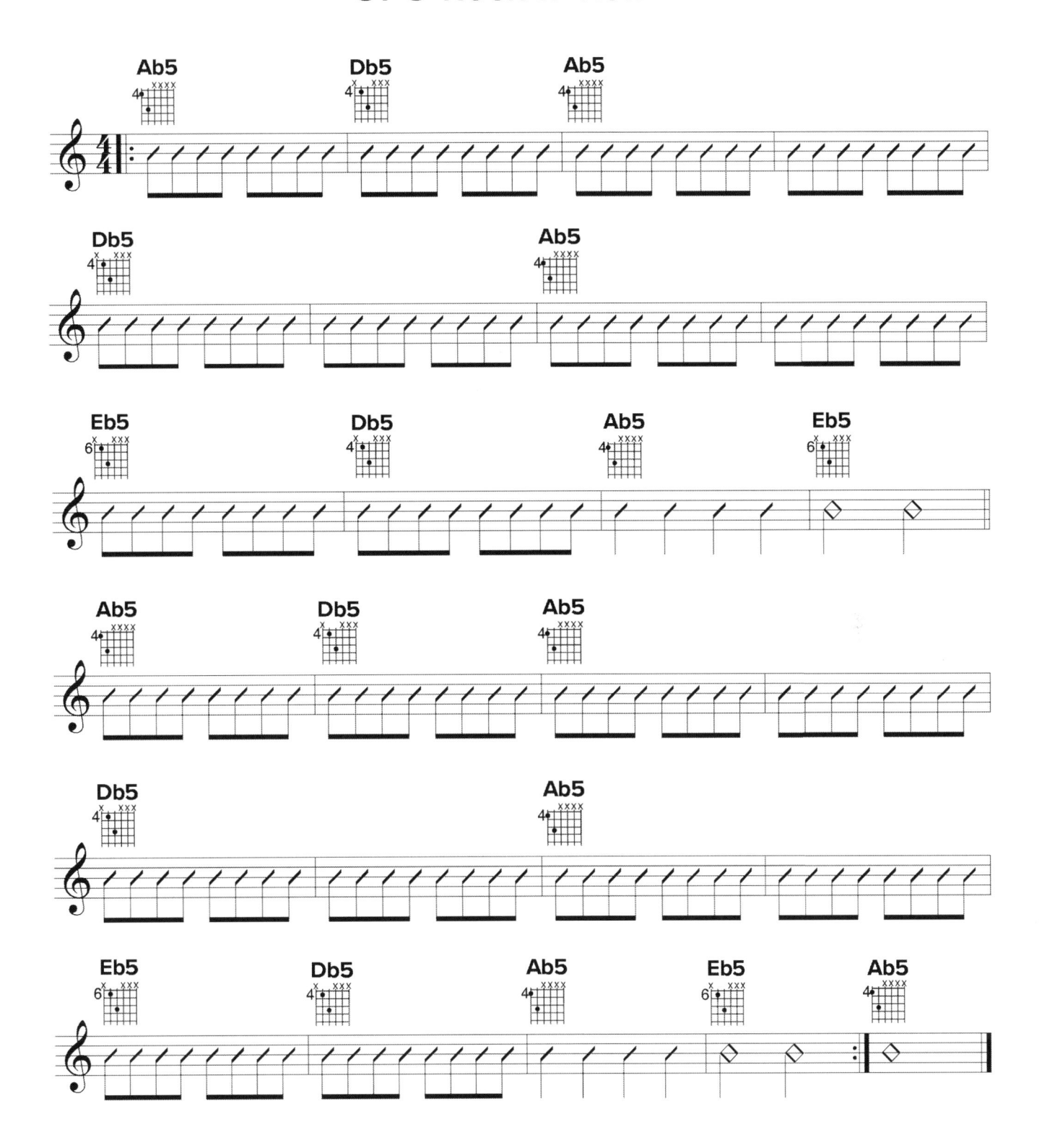

Lost Lane

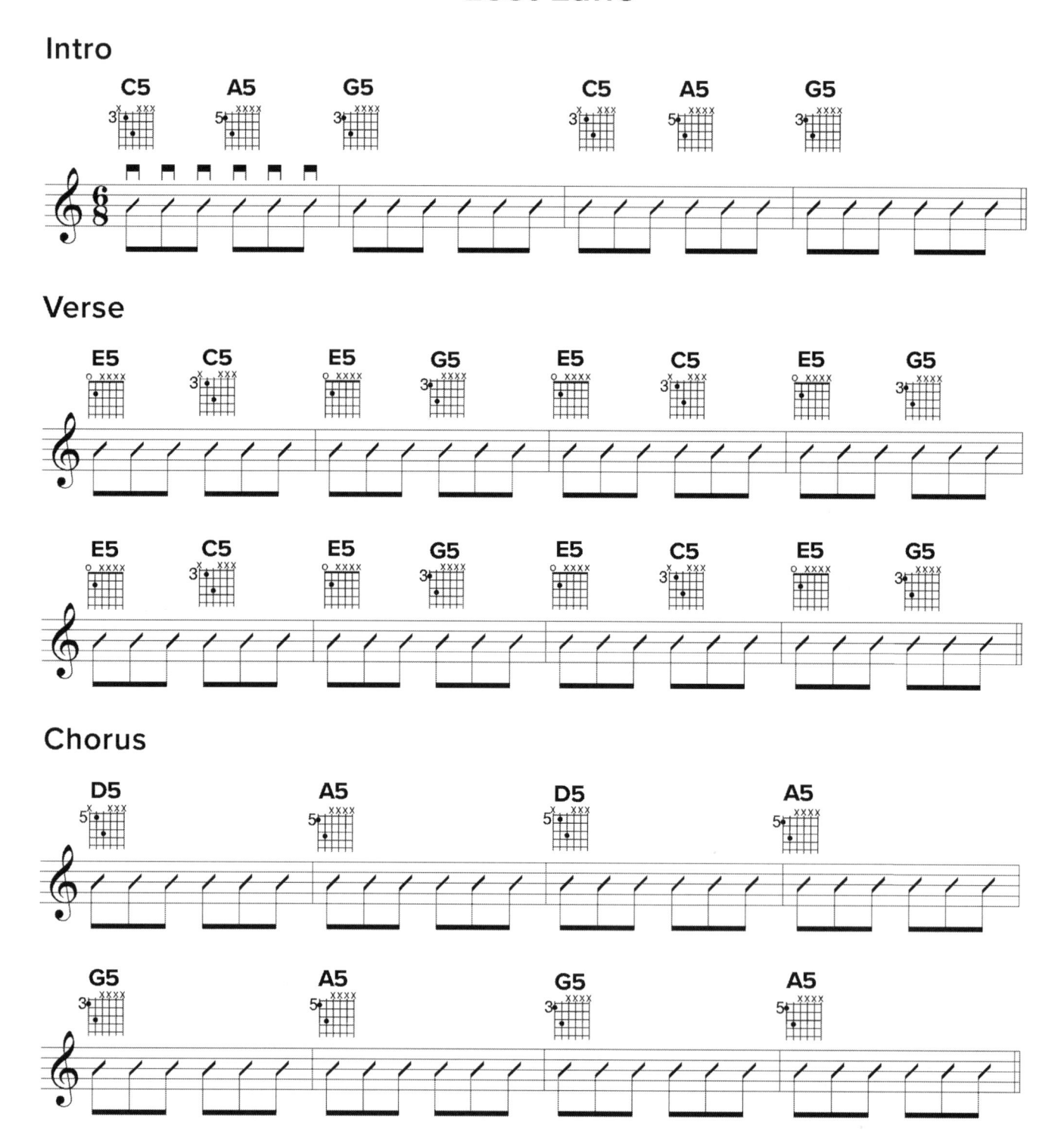

Intro

| C5 | A5 | G5 | | C5 | A5 | G5 |

Verse

| E5 | C5 | E5 | G5 | E5 | C5 | E5 | G5 |

| E5 | C5 | E5 | G5 | E5 | C5 | E5 | G5 |

Chorus

| D5 | A5 | D5 | A5 |

| G5 | A5 | G5 | A5 |

Verse

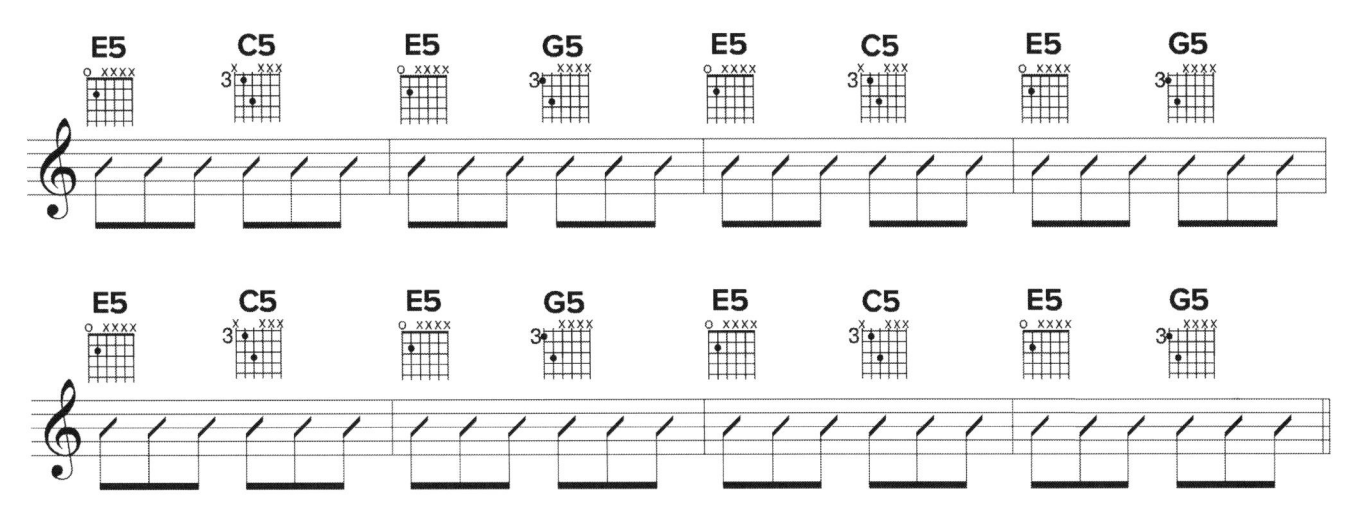

| E5 | C5 | E5 | G5 | E5 | C5 | E5 | G5 |

| E5 | C5 | E5 | G5 | E5 | C5 | E5 | G5 |

Chorus

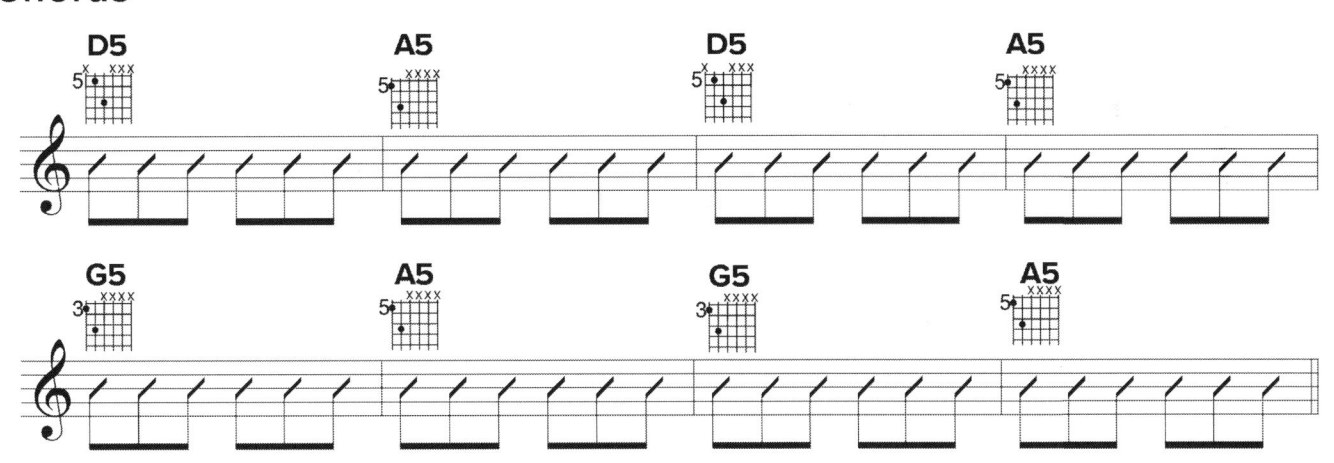

| D5 | A5 | D5 | A5 |

| G5 | A5 | G5 | A5 |

Bridge

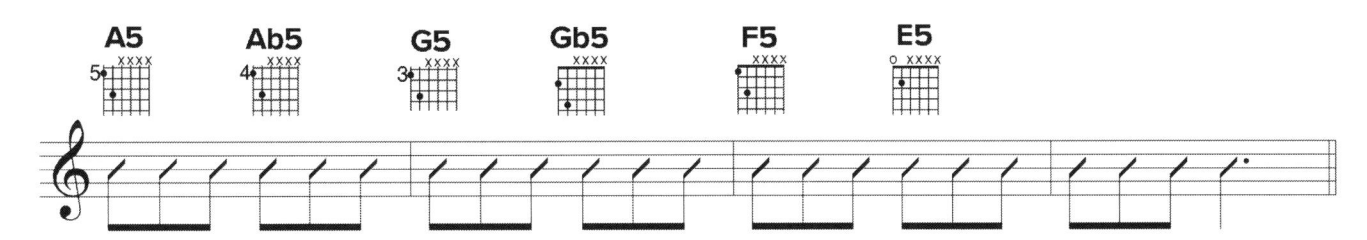

| A5 | Ab5 | G5 | Gb5 | F5 | E5 |

Verse

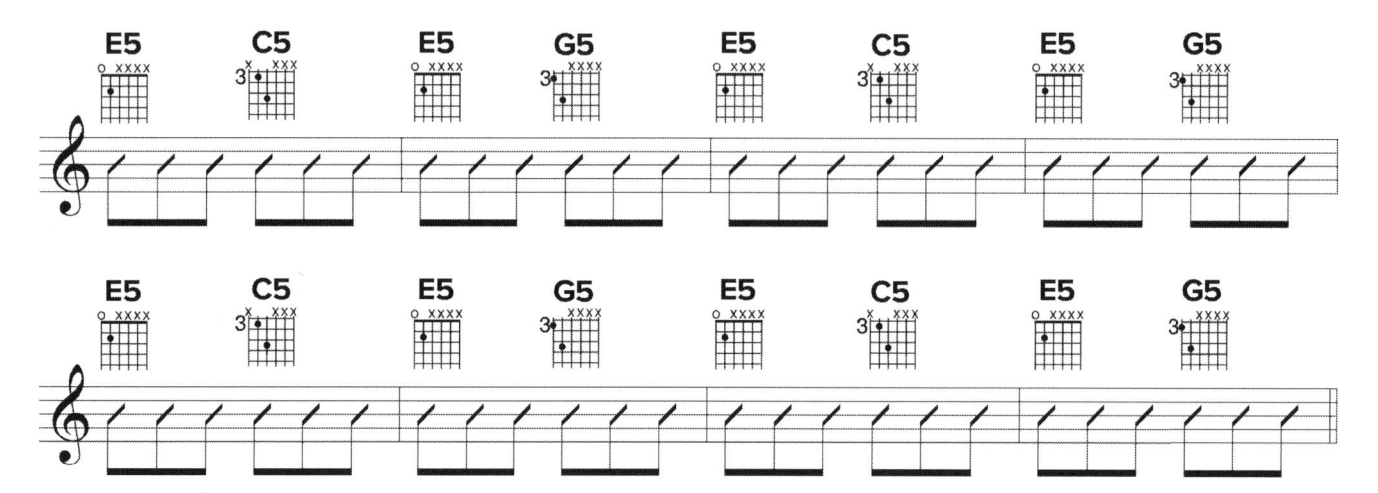

| E5 | C5 | E5 | G5 | E5 | C5 | E5 | G5 |

| E5 | C5 | E5 | G5 | E5 | C5 | E5 | G5 |

Outro

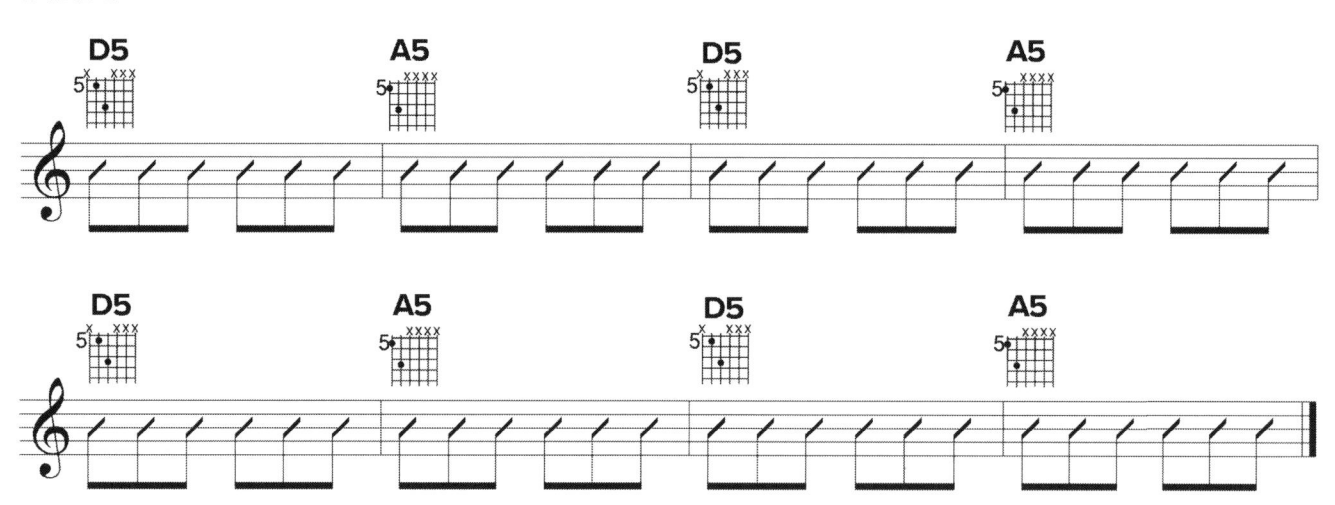

| D5 | A5 | D5 | A5 |

| D5 | A5 | D5 | A5 |

Lesson 5: Palm Muting

When playing power chords, one technique that is often used to add variety is palm muting. Use the following directions in order to properly perform a palm mute:

1. Though it is called a palm mute, use the side of your palm, not the flat part of your hand.

2. Bring your hand back to the bridge of the guitar. Rest the side of your palm against the strings so that part of your hand is on the strings and part is on the bridge. Don't press down. Just let your hand rest on the strings and bridge.

3. Keeping your hand on the strings, play any power chord. The resulting sound should still have a tone, but it will be muffled.

In the sheet music, you will see the abbreviation "p.m." followed by a dashed line. This tells you that the palm mute is to be played for as long as the dashed line is present. No dashed line means that you should release the palm mute. See examples 1 and 2.

Example 1

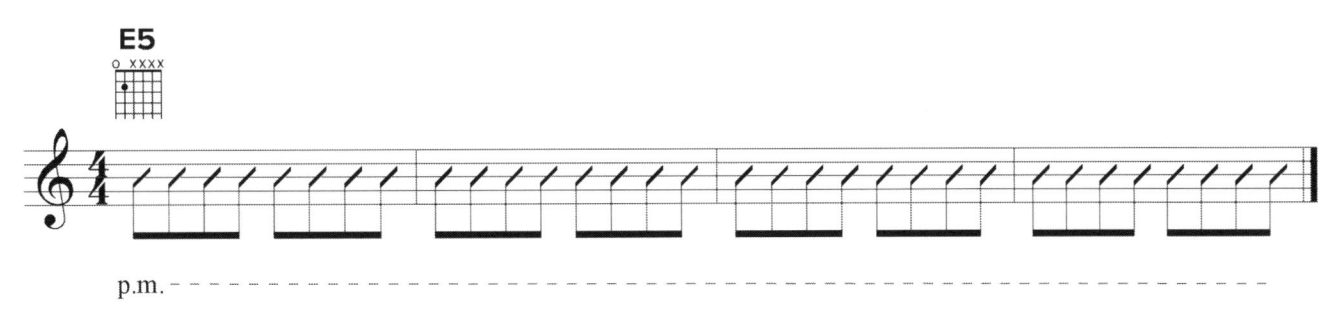

Example 2

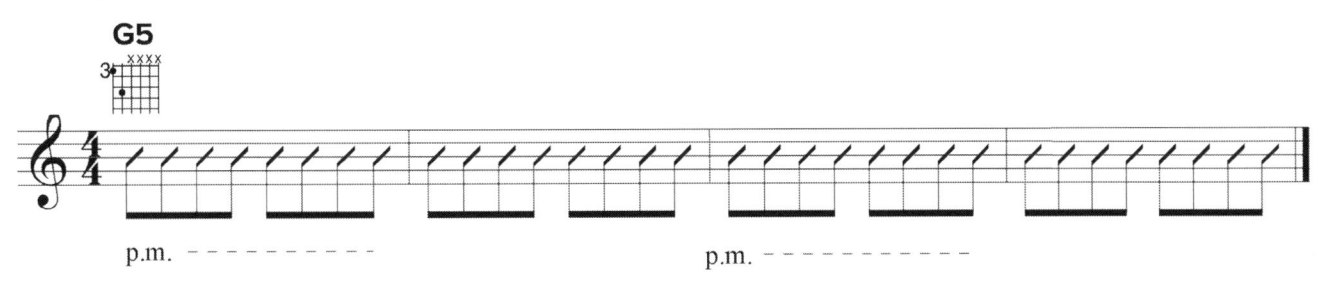

Exercise 1

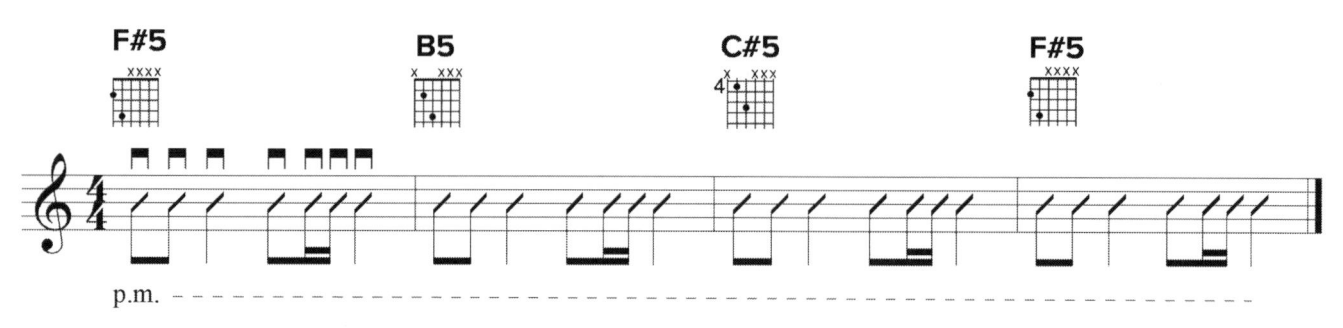

Exercise 2

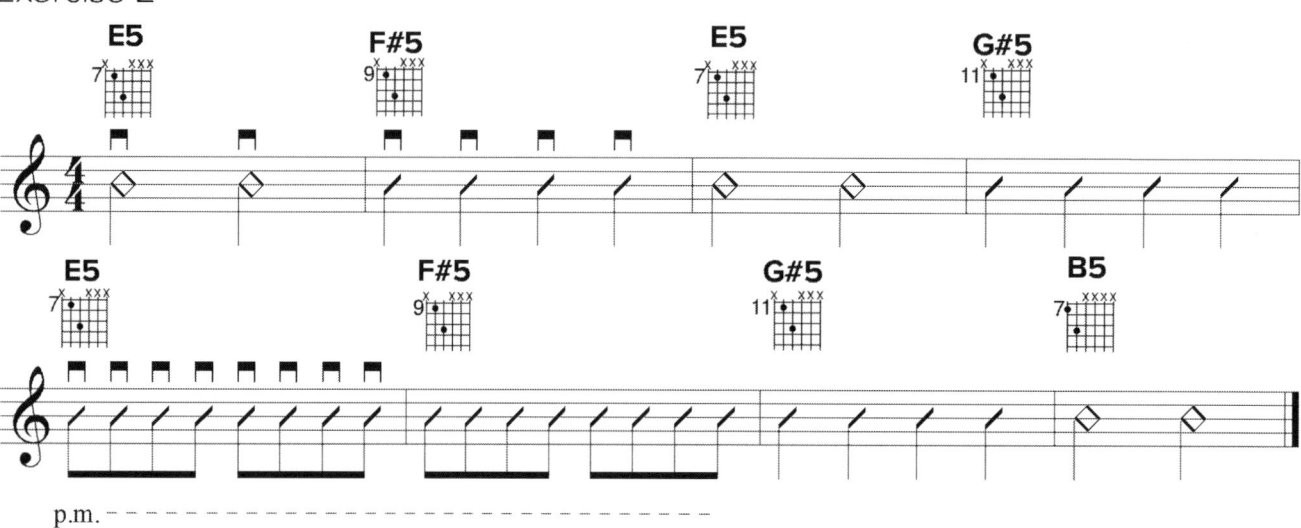

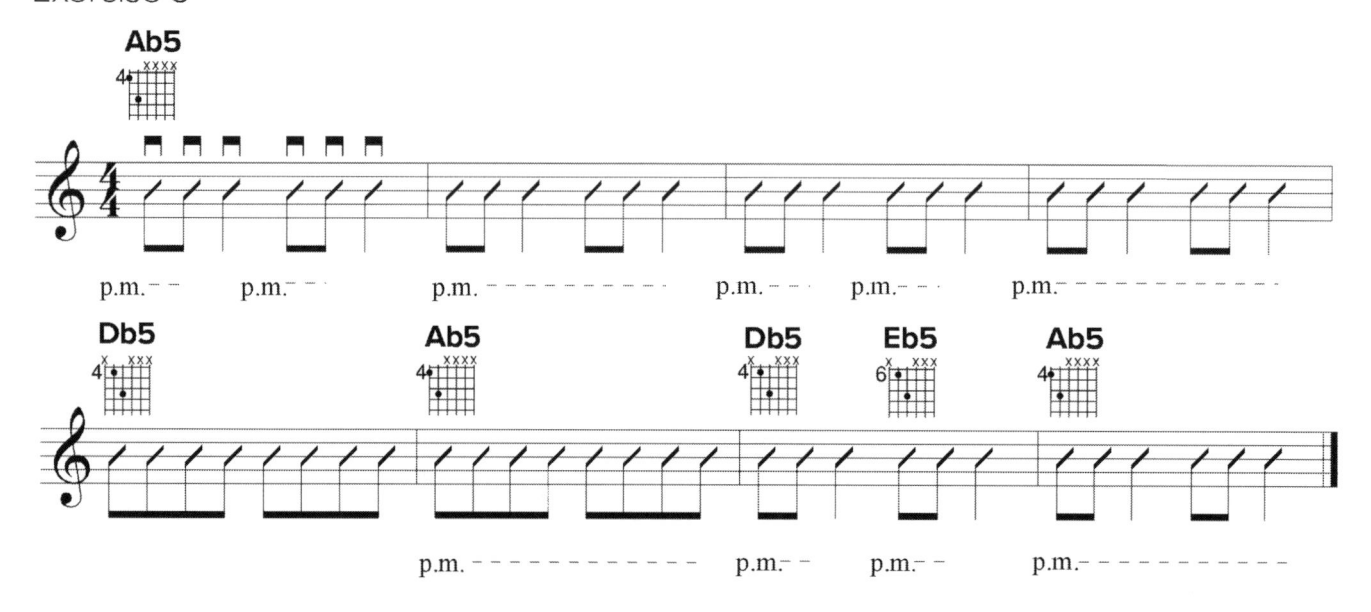

Exercise 3

Exercise 4

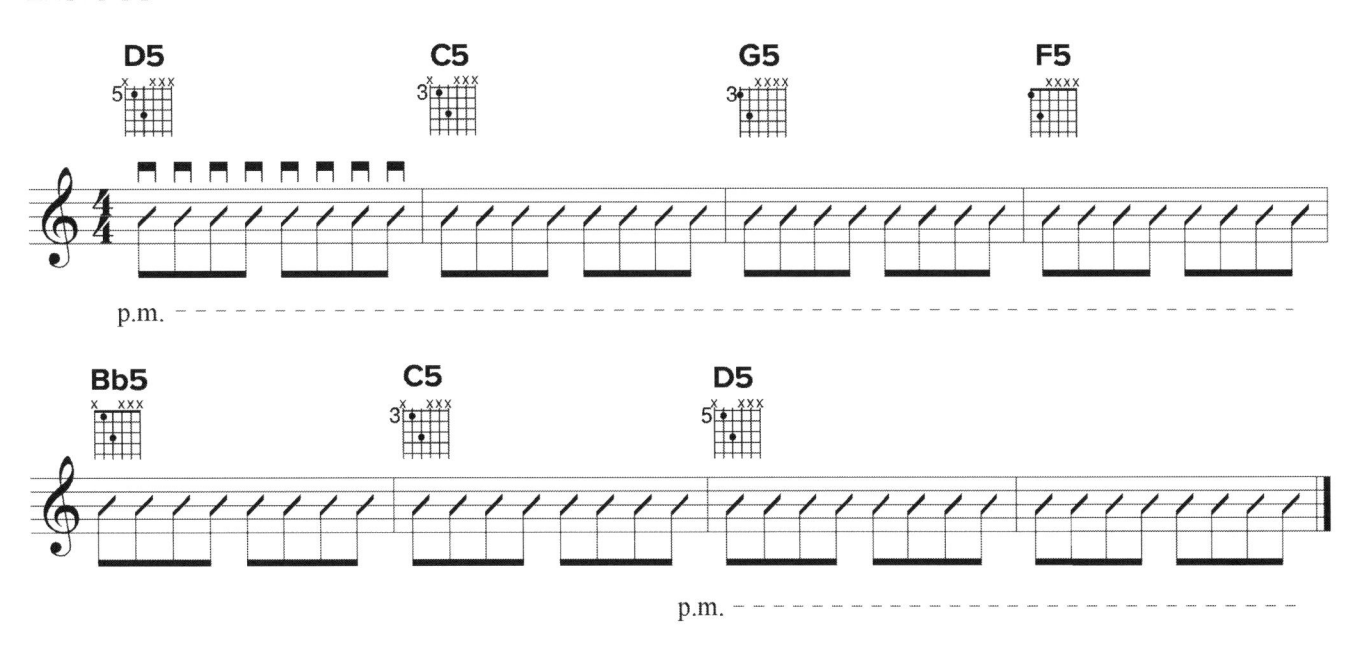

D5	C5	G5	F5

p.m.

Bb5	C5	D5	

p.m.

Exercise 5

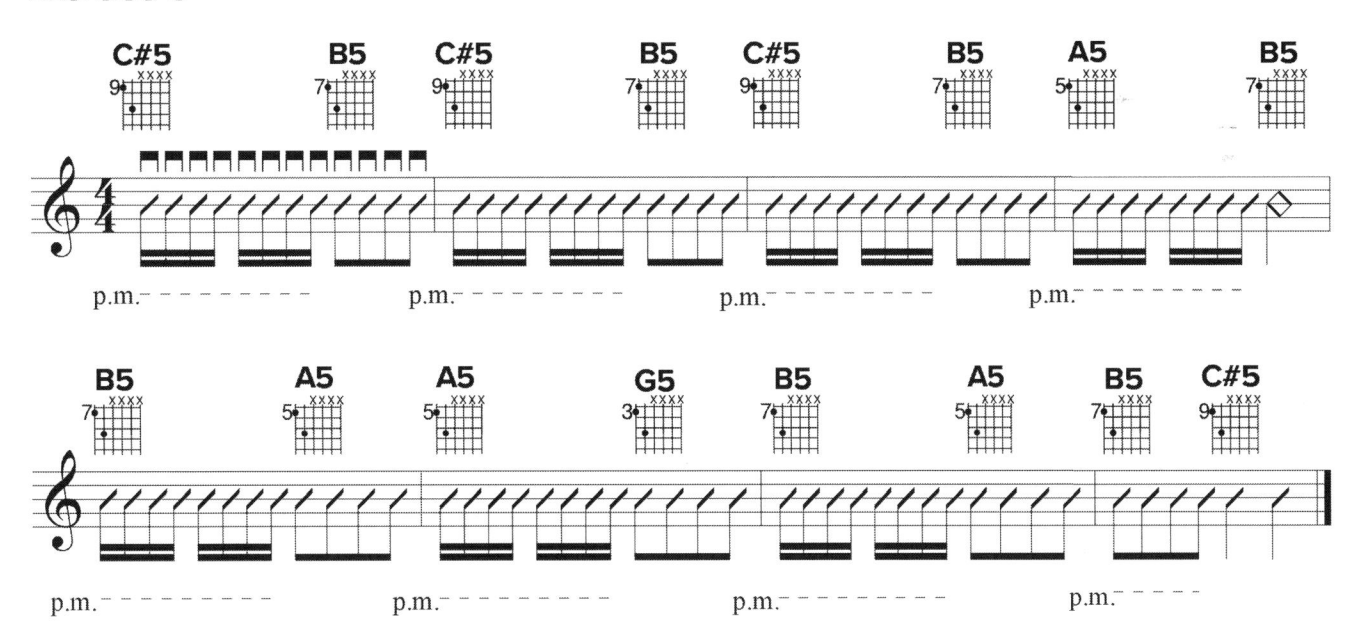

C#5	B5	C#5	B5	C#5	B5	A5	B5

p.m.   p.m.   p.m.   p.m.

B5	A5	A5	G5	B5	A5	B5	C#5

p.m.   p.m.   p.m.   p.m.

Accent Marks

In the following exercises, accent marks are used to give the palm muting a different feel. Accent marks are the sideways "v" shaped marks seen above the measure. This means that you give those beats a little more punch or hit them slightly harder to get a sound that highlights the indicated beat. Even though you'll want to usually count eighth notes as one-and-two-and-three-and-four-and, in the case of accent marks, it can be useful to count each accent as one, so that every time you say "one" you are hitting the accent. In exercise 6, for example, you could count it as one-two-three, one-two-three, one-two. Practice this slowly until you get the feel.

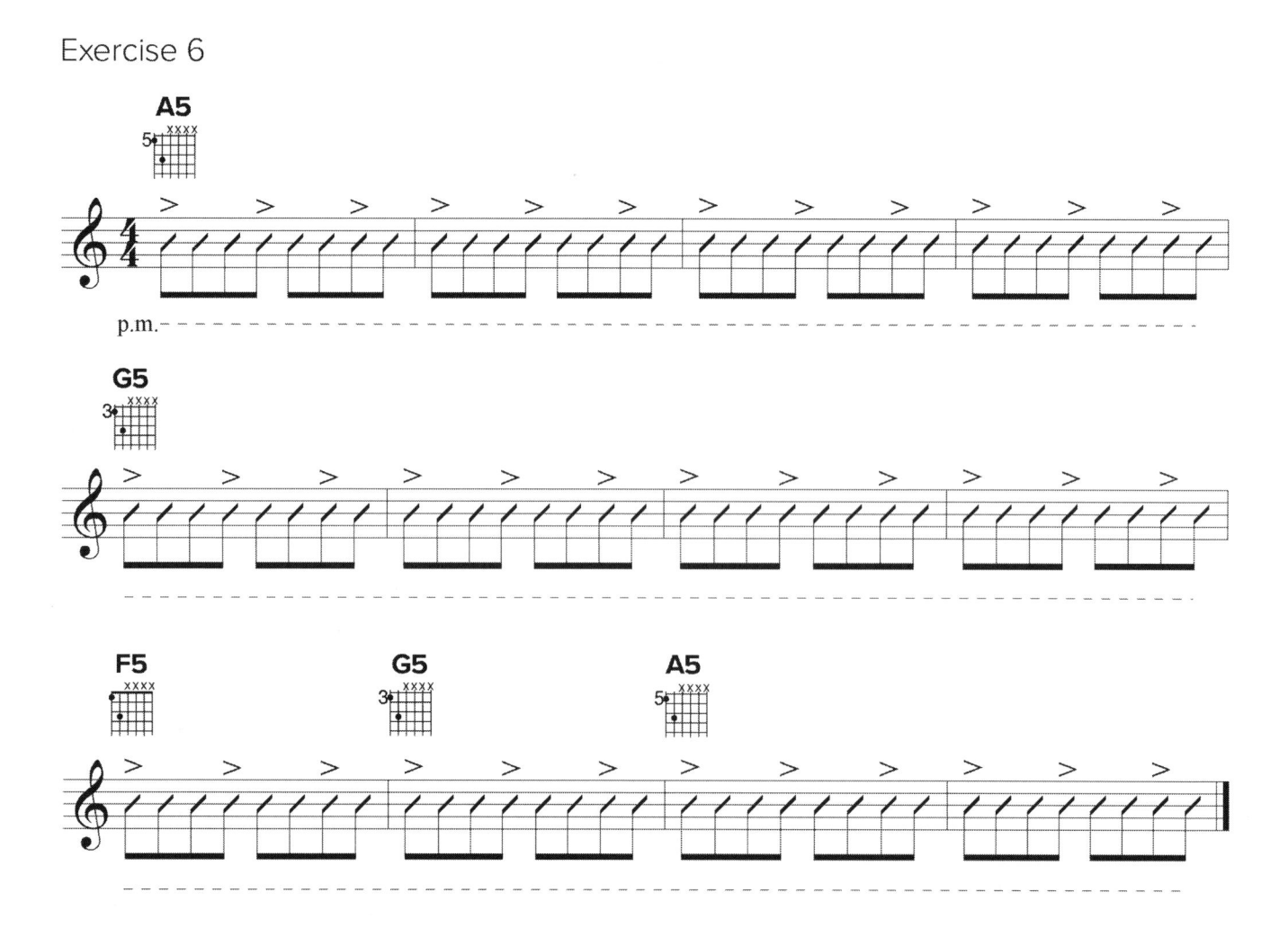

Exercise 6

Exercise 7

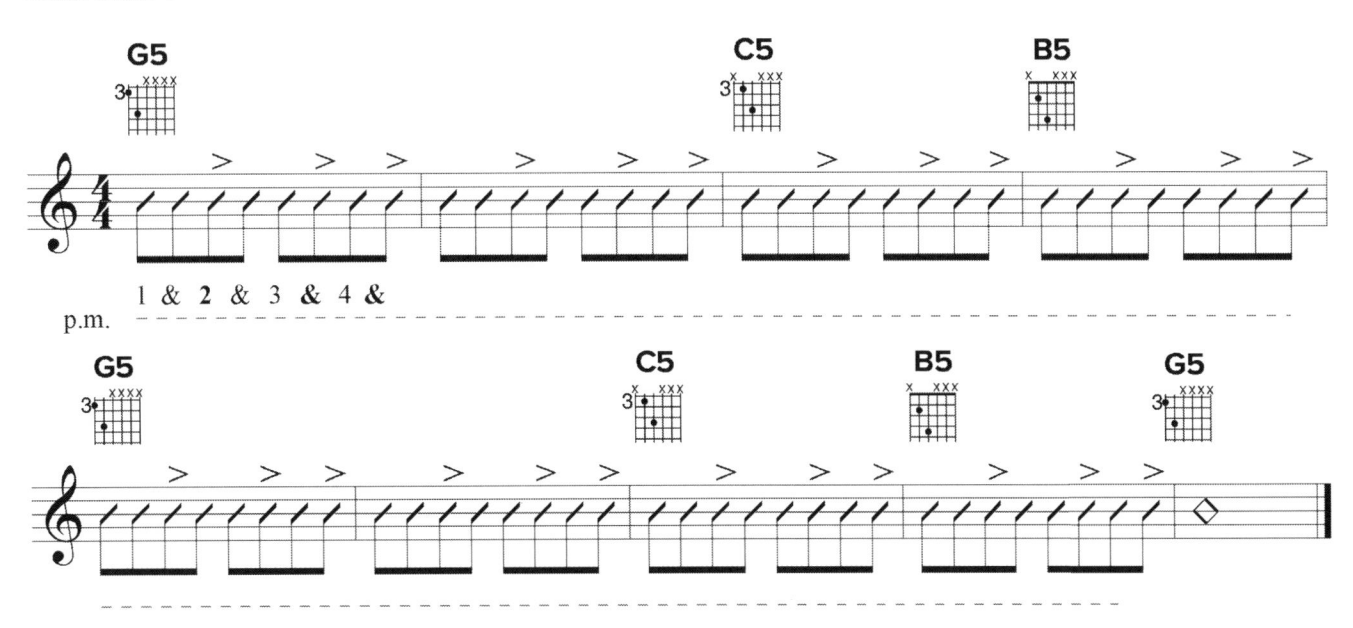

Exercise 8

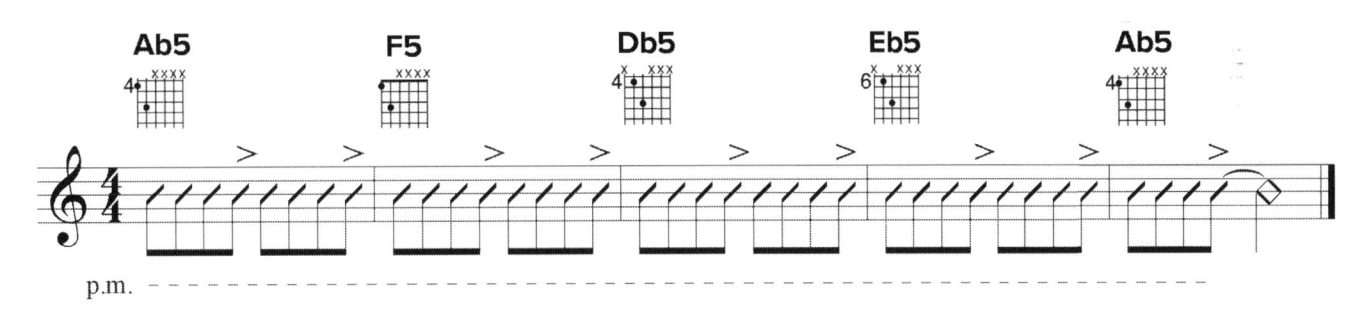

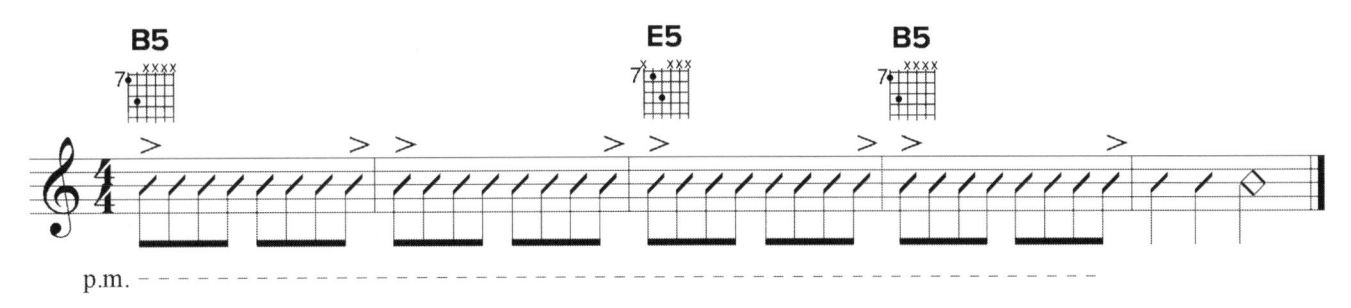

Exercise 9

The Impossible Room

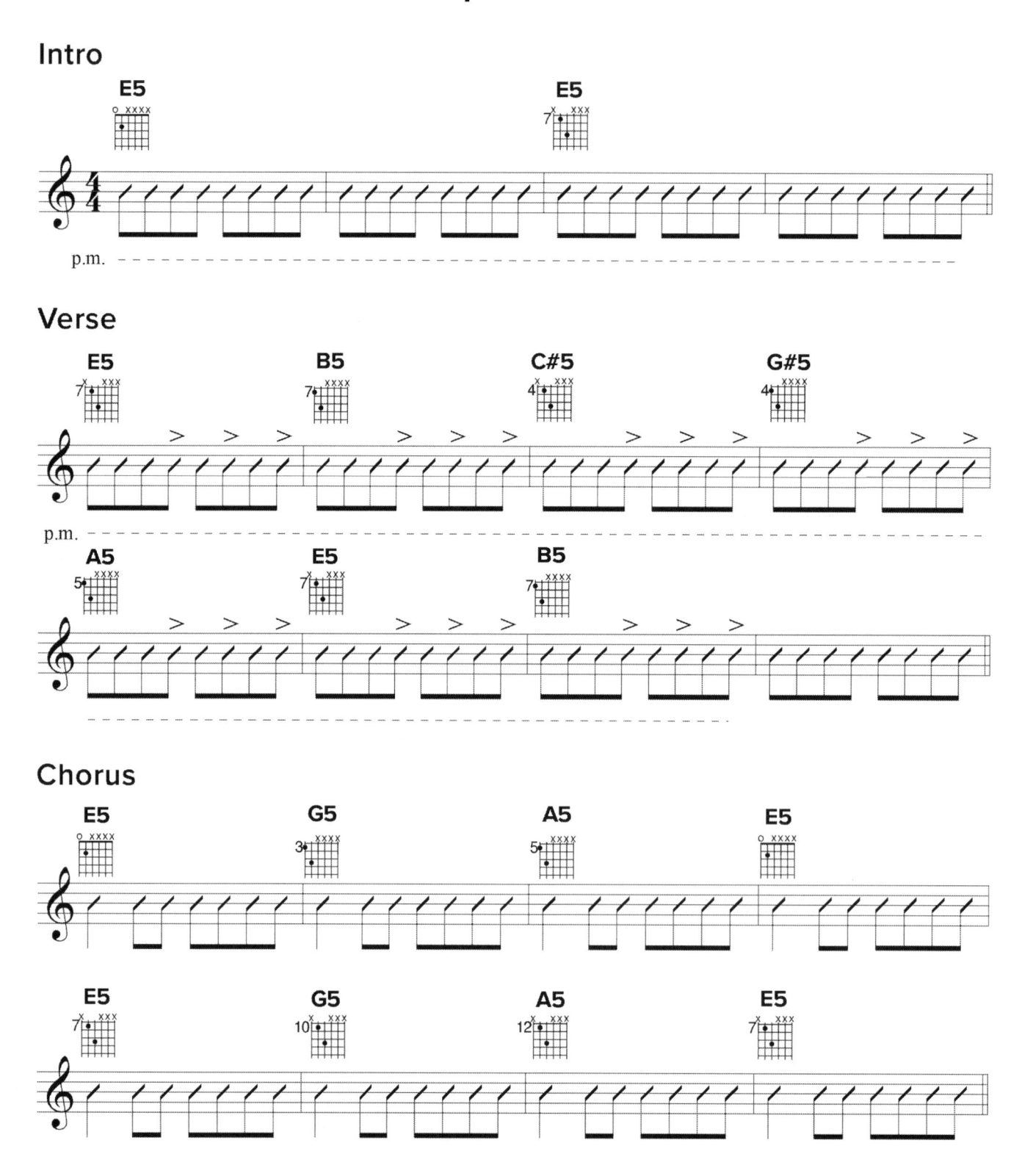

Intro

E5   E5

p.m.

Verse

E5   B5   C#5   G#5

p.m.

A5   E5   B5

Chorus

E5   G5   A5   E5

E5   G5   A5   E5

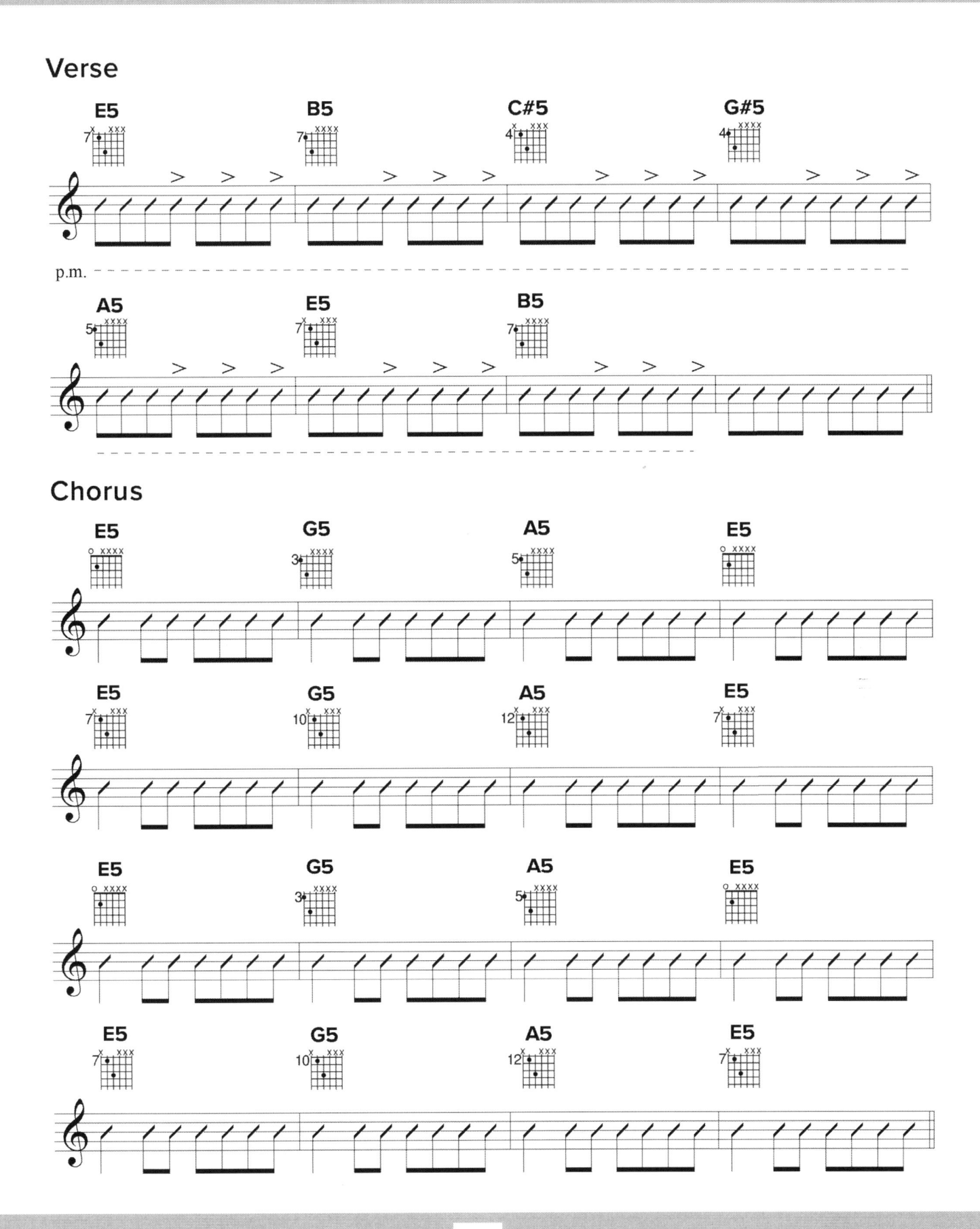

Verse

Chorus

Bridge

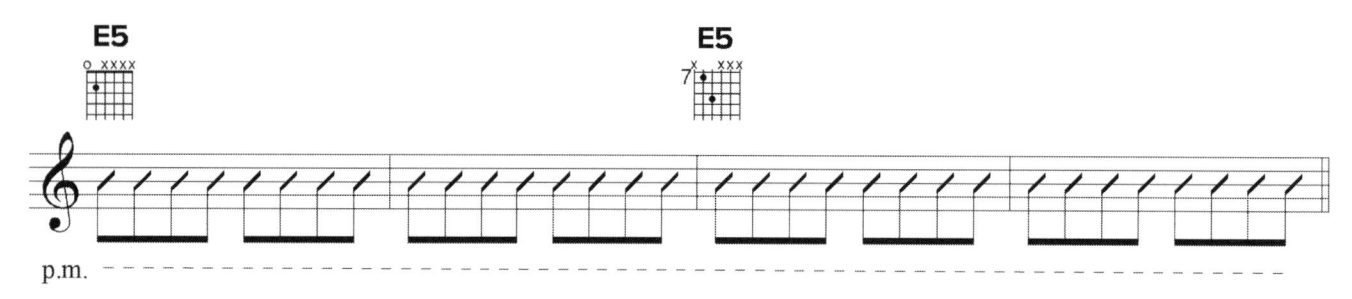

E5   **E5**

p.m.

Chorus

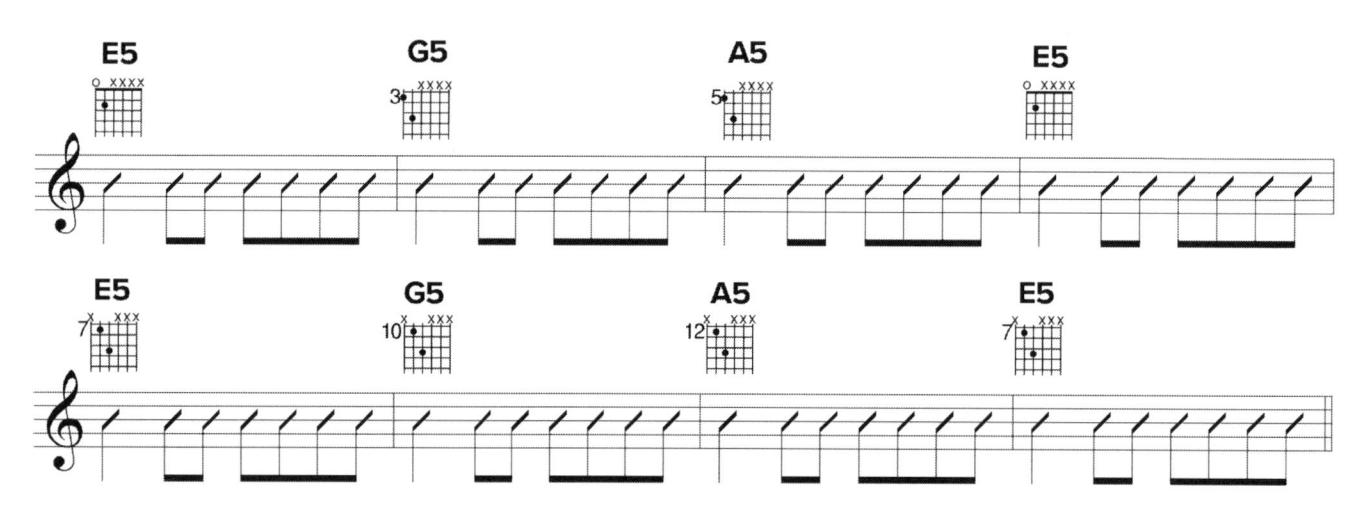

E5   **G5**   **A5**   **E5**

E5   **G5**   **A5**   **E5**

Outro

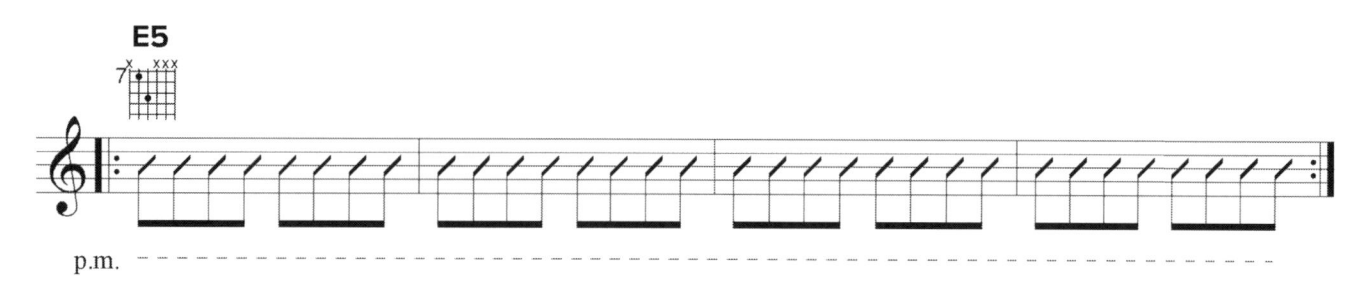

E5

p.m.

Lesson 6:
Three Note Power Chords

Now that you've learned all the basic power chords, we can start expanding them. The first step is to simply add the octave of the root to each chord. The result: fuller sounding power chords. Many songs utilize both two-note and three-note power chords. This is done to add variety and contrast, to make songs more interesting to the listener. It is also done for arrangement purposes. In other words, sometime two-note power chords sound better, sometimes three. It just depends on the song.

To play these three note power chords, simply add the fourth finger to the string below the third finger. This can be seen in the chord diagrams below.

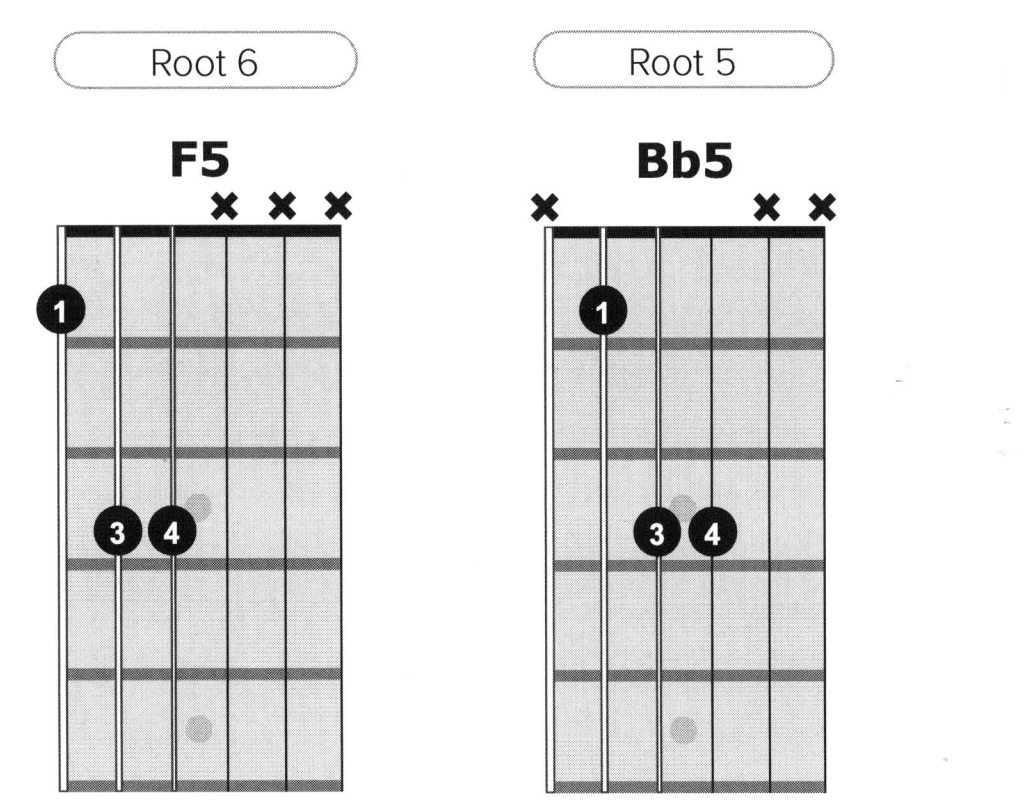

Root 6

F5

Root 5

Bb5

Try it: Practice the F5 and Bb5 chords below.

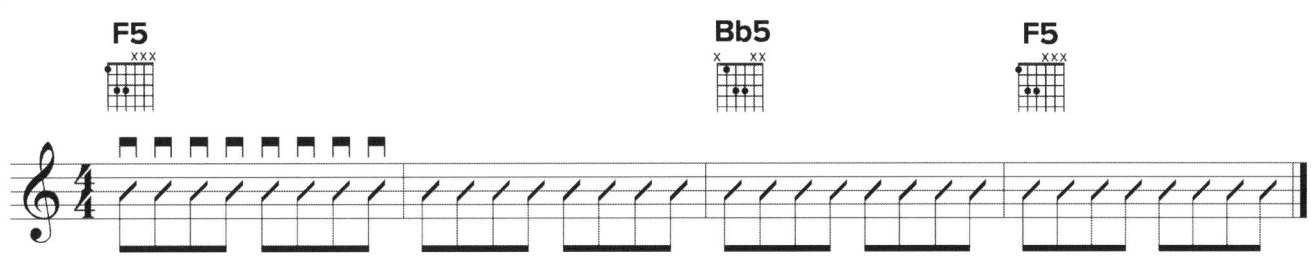

Exercise 1

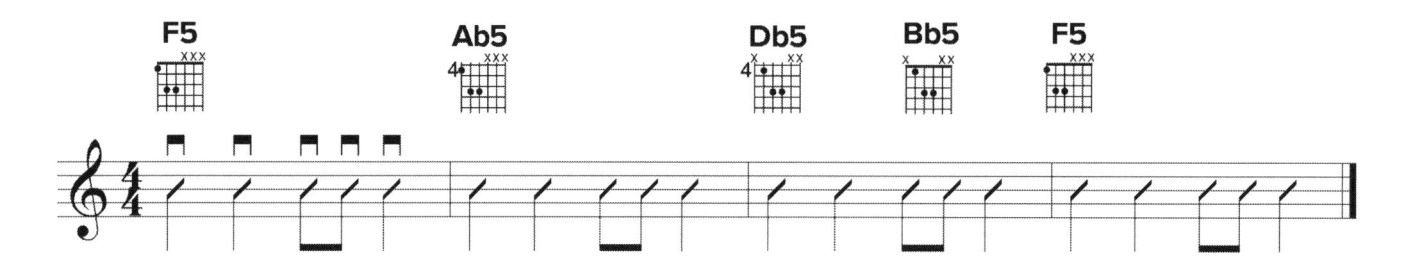

| F5 | Ab5 | Db5 | Bb5 | F5 |

Exercise 2

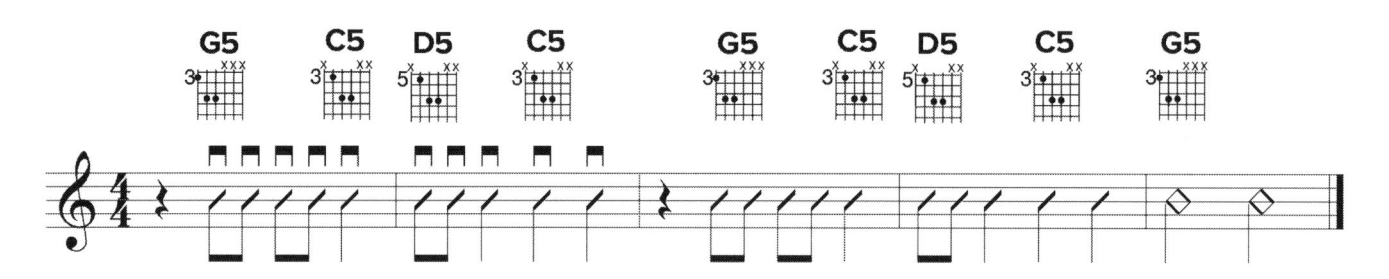

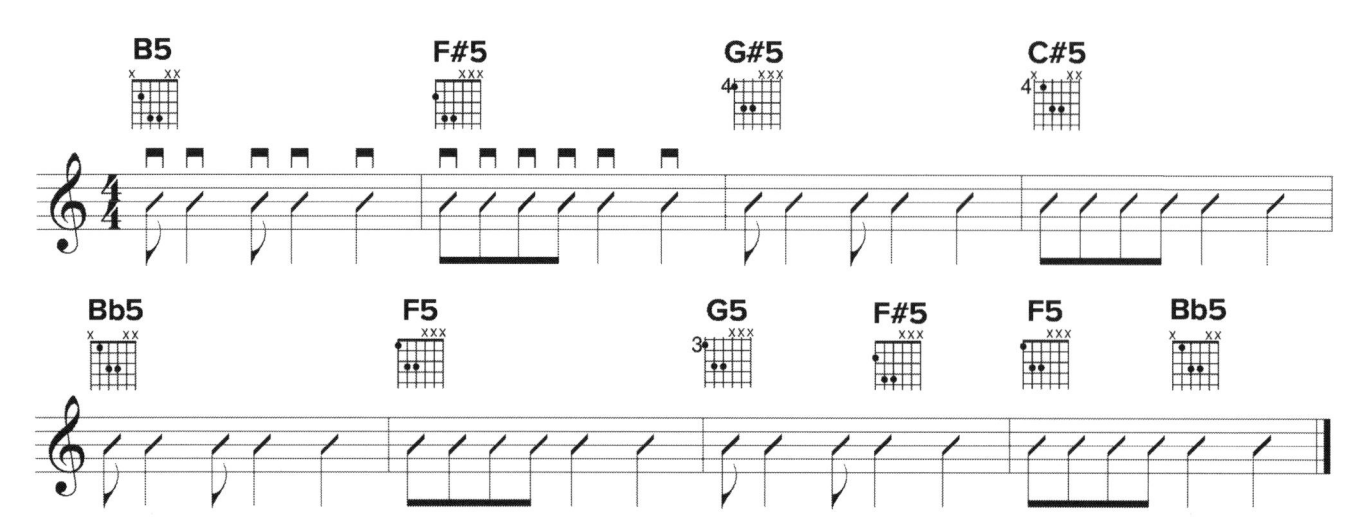

| G5 | C5 | D5 | C5 | G5 | C5 | D5 | C5 | G5 |

Exercise 3

| B5 | F#5 | G#5 | C#5 |

| Bb5 | F5 | G5 | F#5 | F5 | Bb5 |

Exercise 4

Exercise 5

Exercise 6

Exercise 7

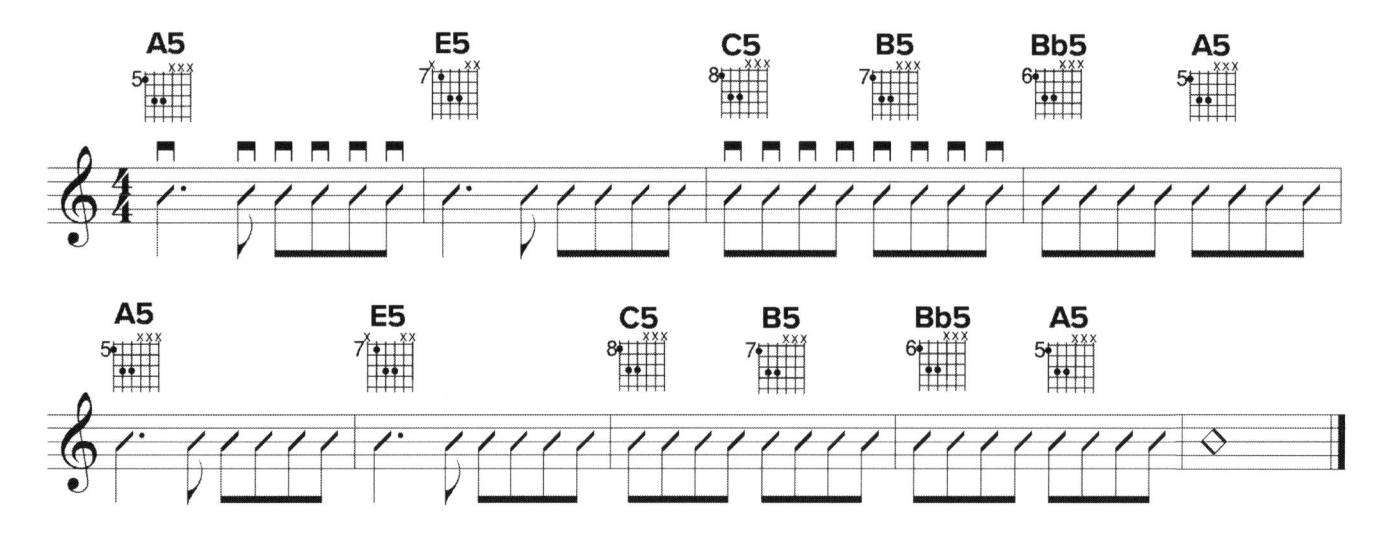

Exercise 8: Note that this exercise combines both two and three note power chords.

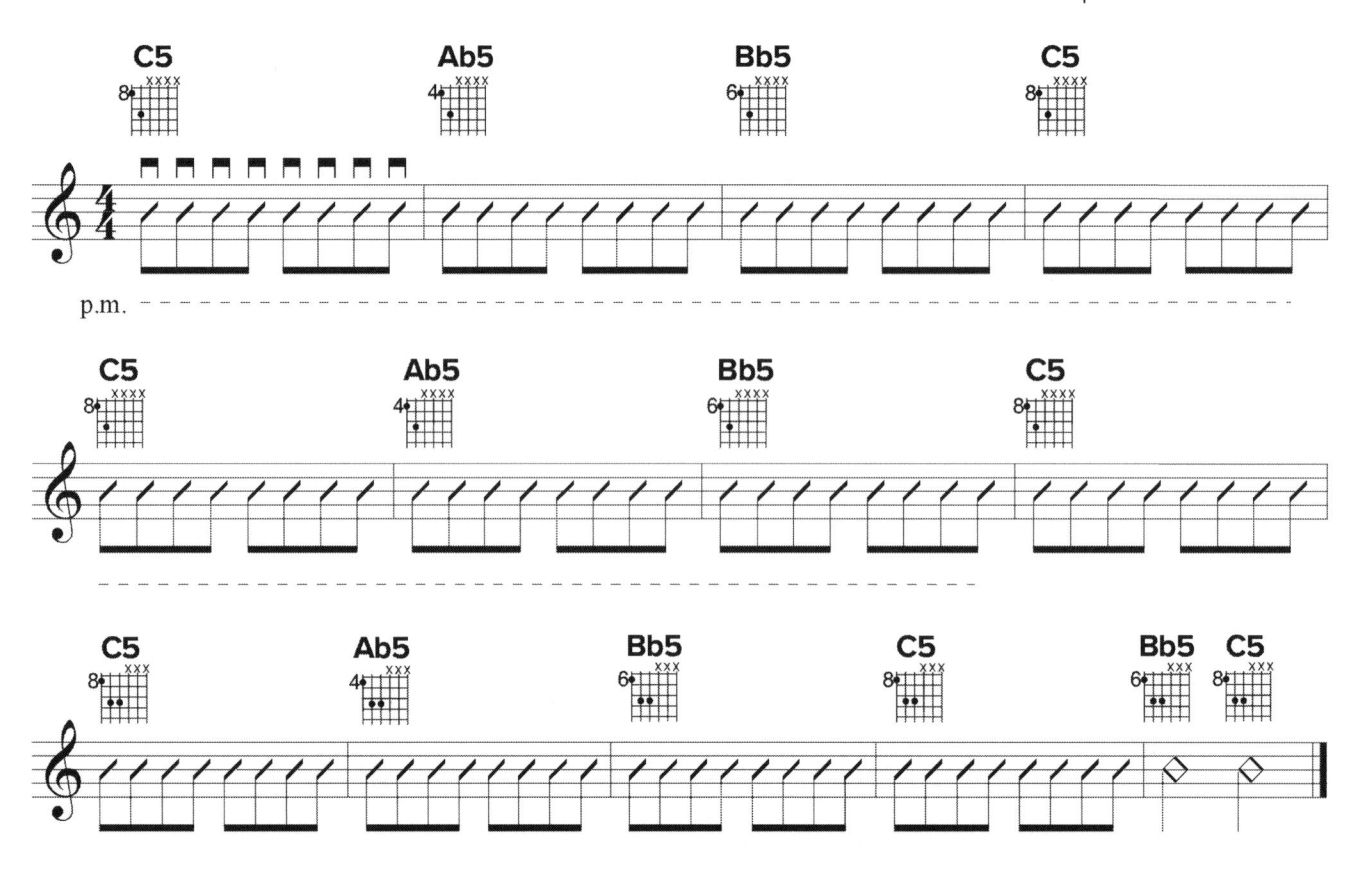

p.m.

Exercise 9

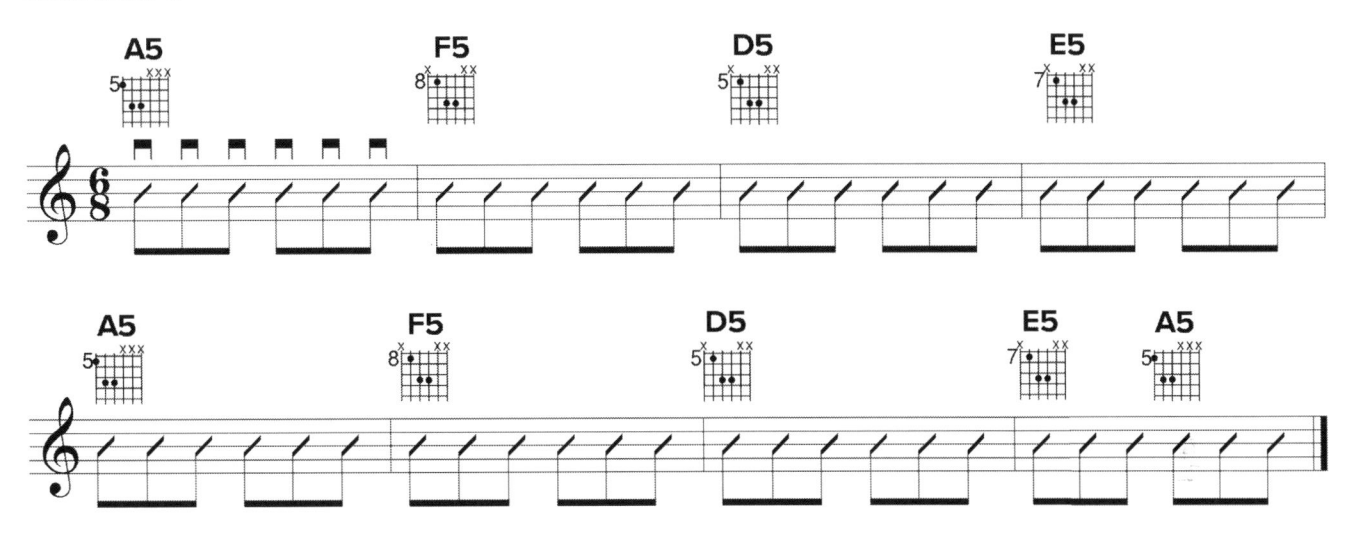

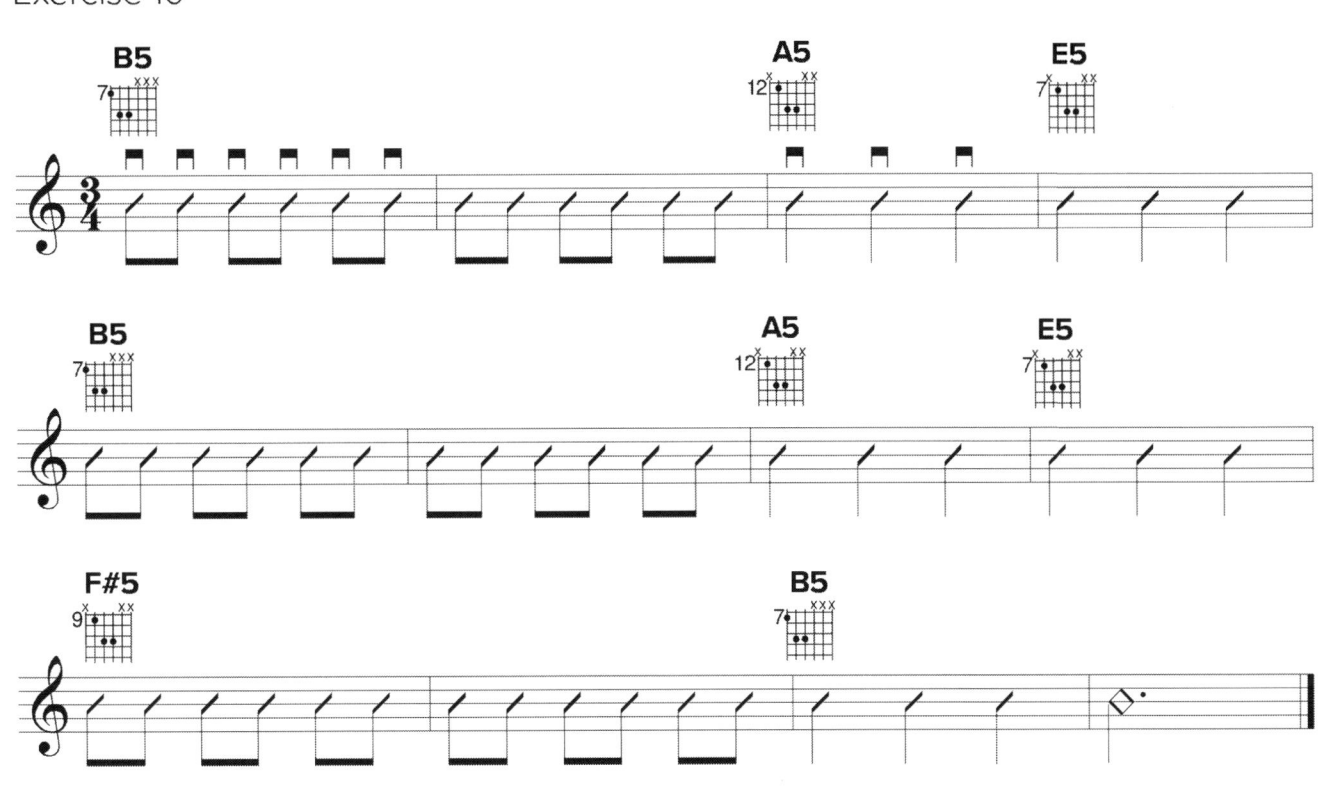

Exercise 10

Center Cut Blues

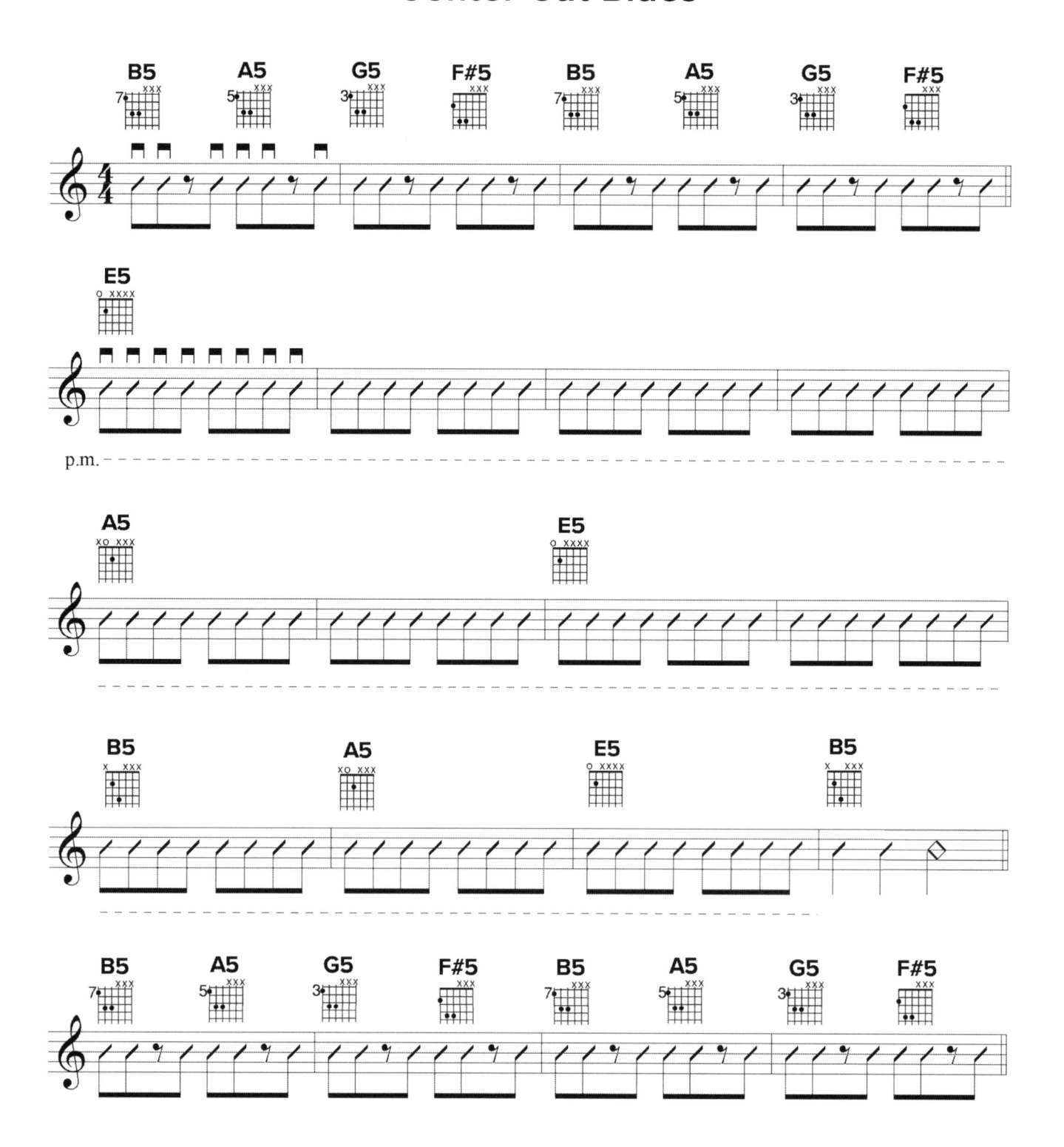

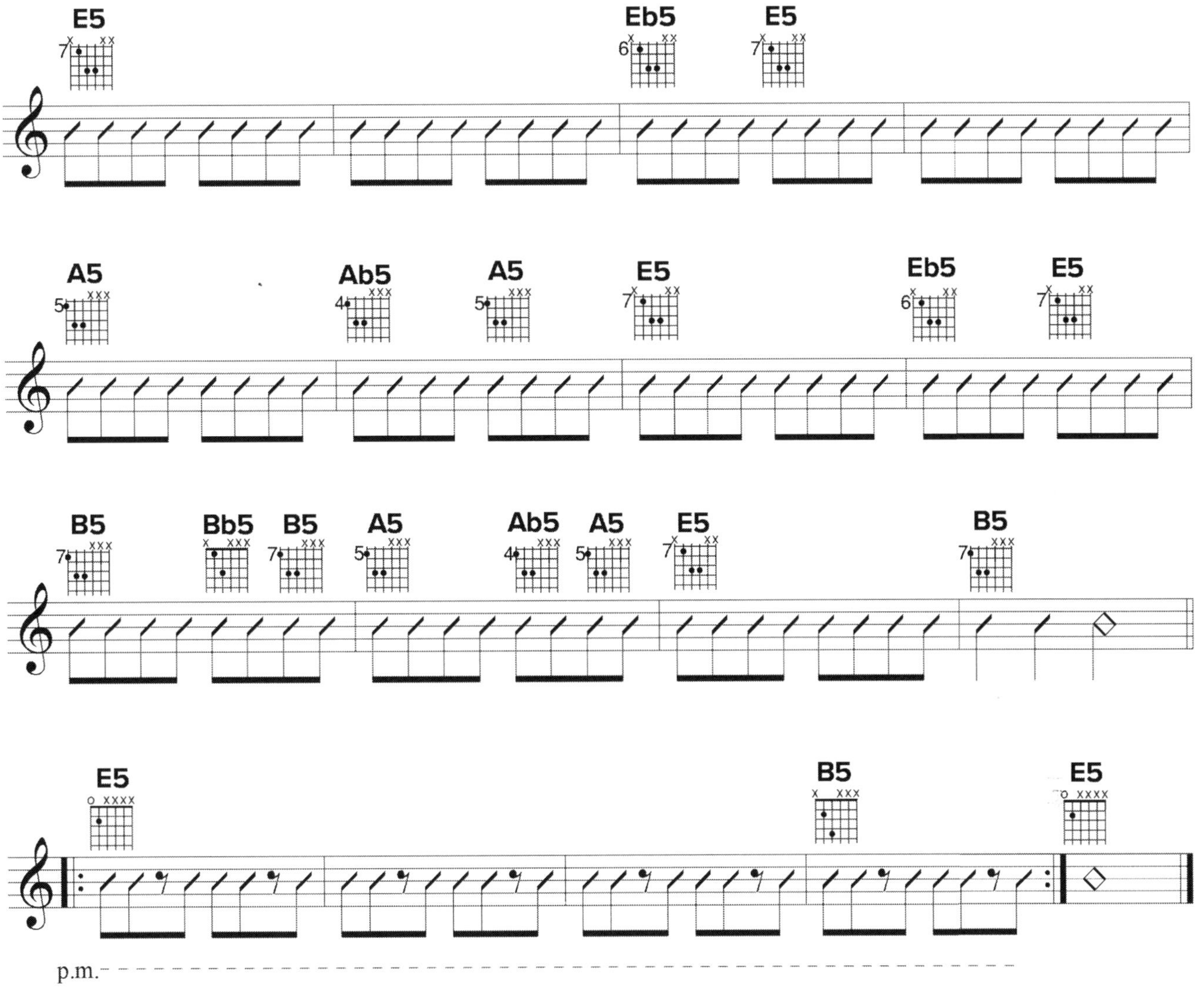
E5
Eb5
E5
A5
Ab5
A5
E5
Eb5
E5
B5
Bb5
B5
A5
Ab5
A5
E5
B5
E5
B5
E5
p.m.

Empowered

Intro

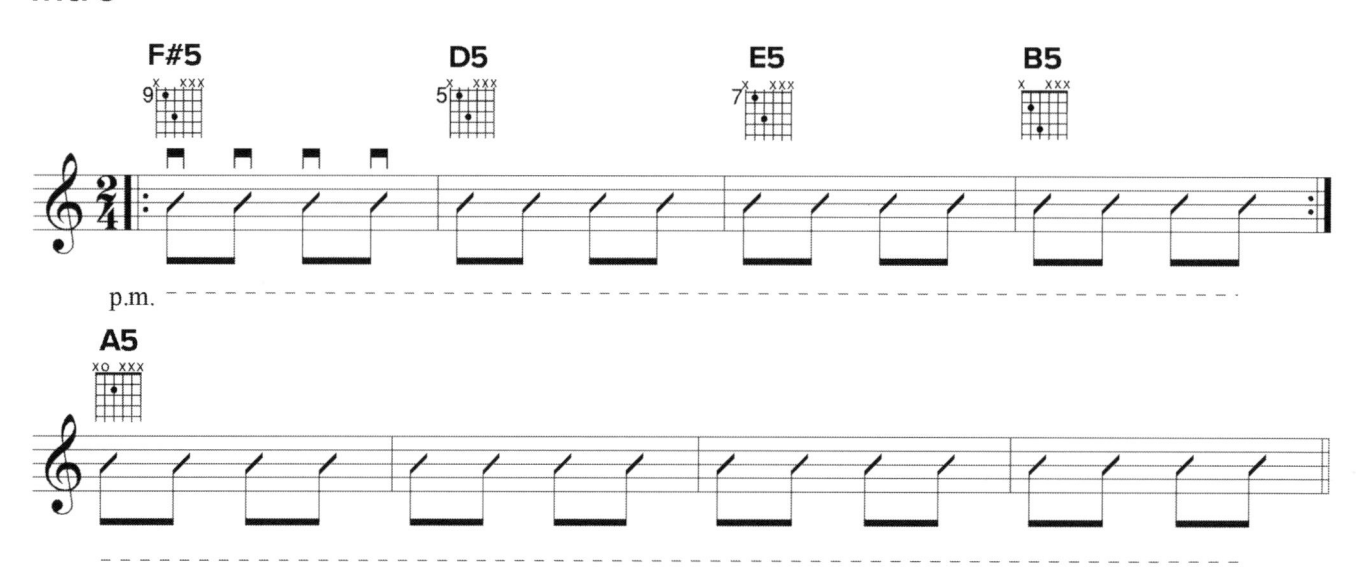

F#5 D5 E5 B5

p.m.

A5

Verse

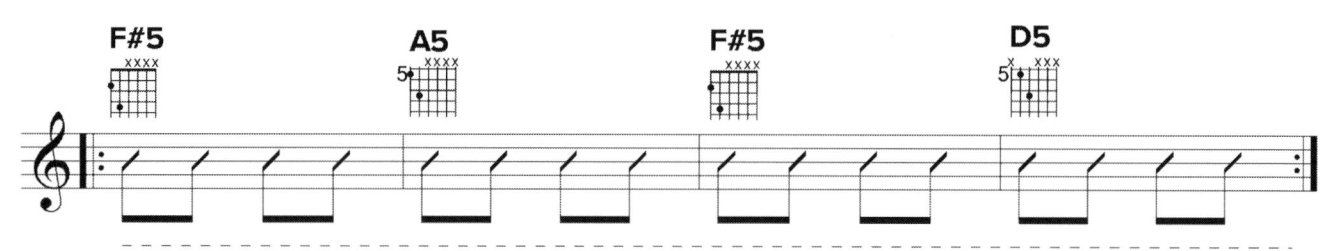

F#5 A5 F#5 D5

Pre-Chorus

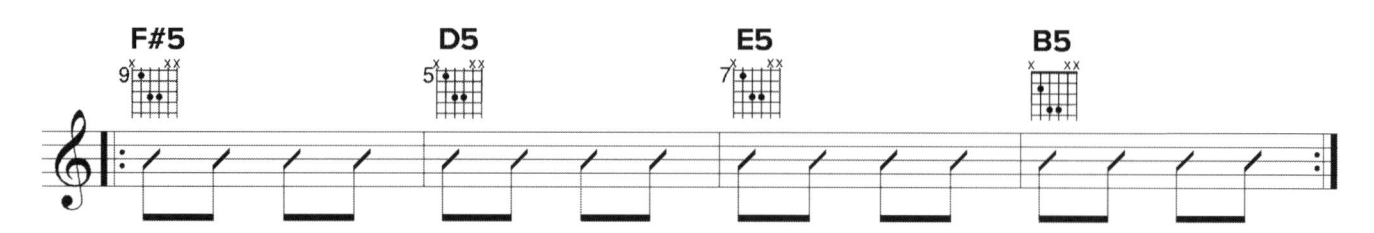

F#5 D5 E5 B5

Chorus

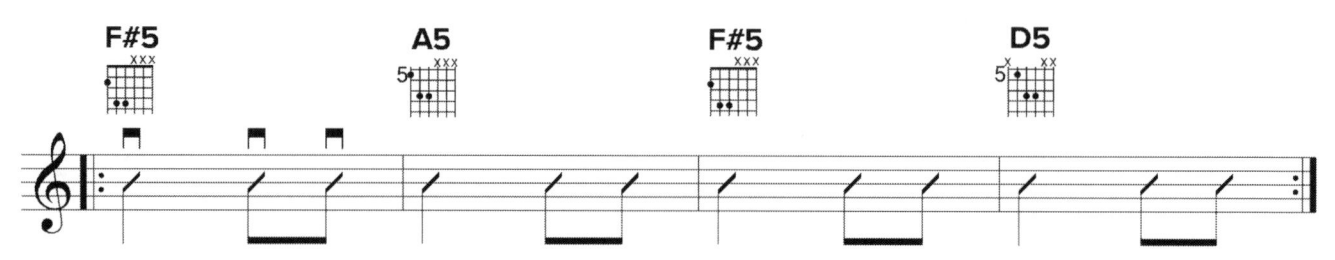

F#5 A5 F#5 D5

Verse

Pre-Chorus

Chorus

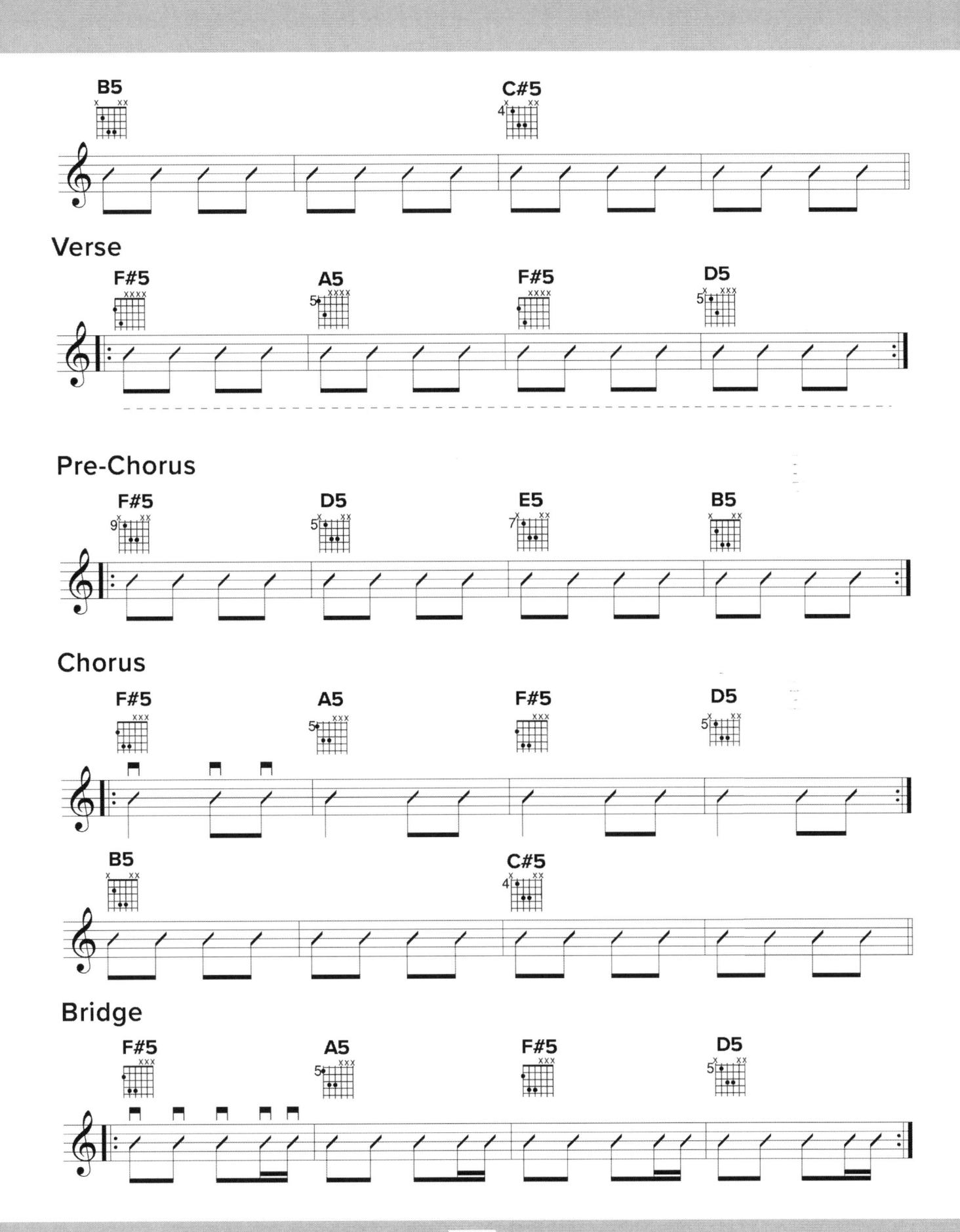

Bridge

Verse

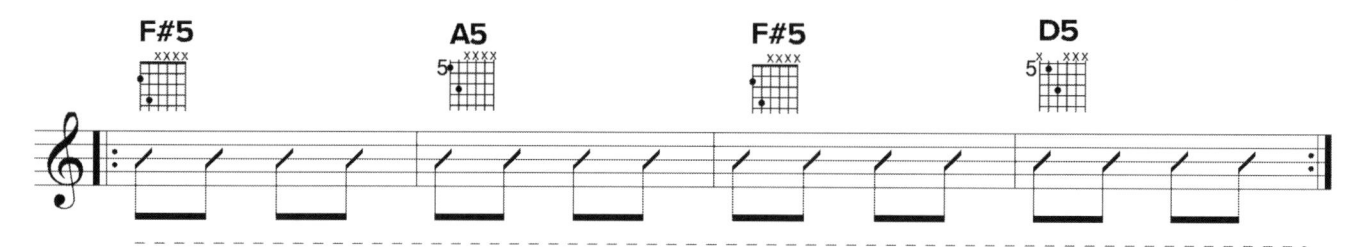

| F#5 | A5 | F#5 | D5 |

Pre-Chorus

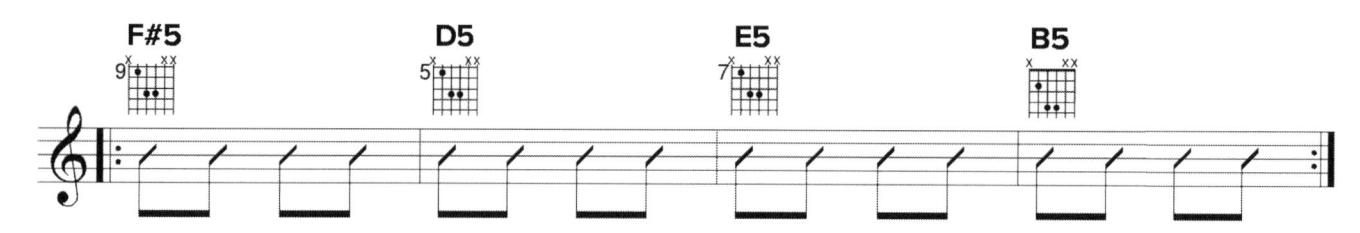

| F#5 | D5 | E5 | B5 |

Chorus

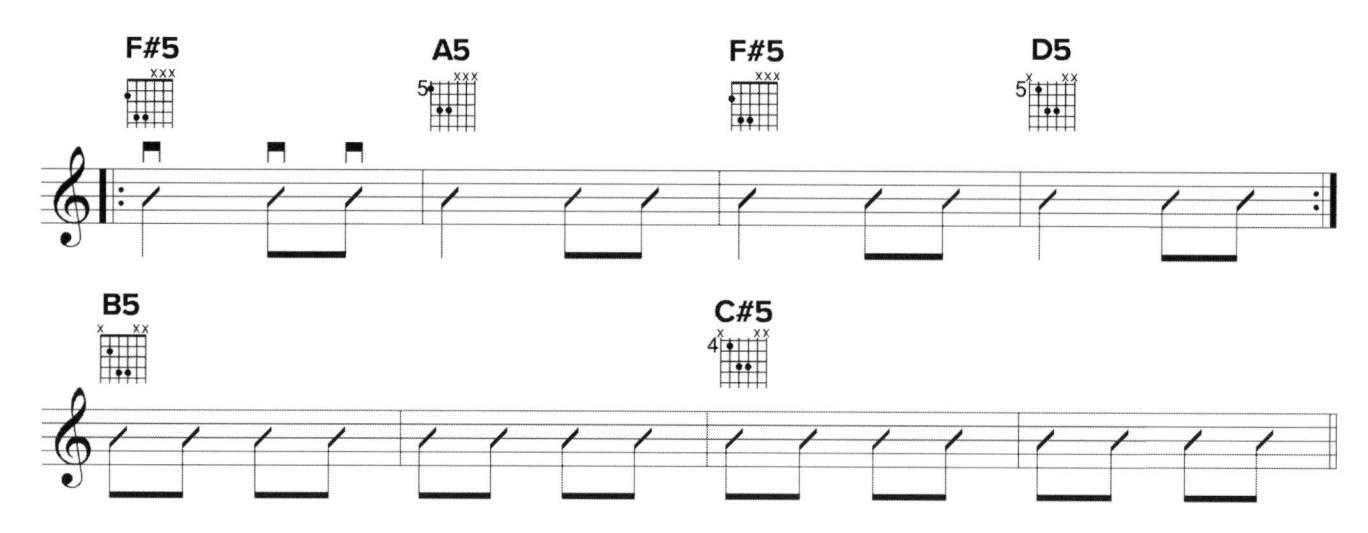

| F#5 | A5 | F#5 | D5 |
| B5 | | C#5 | |

Outro

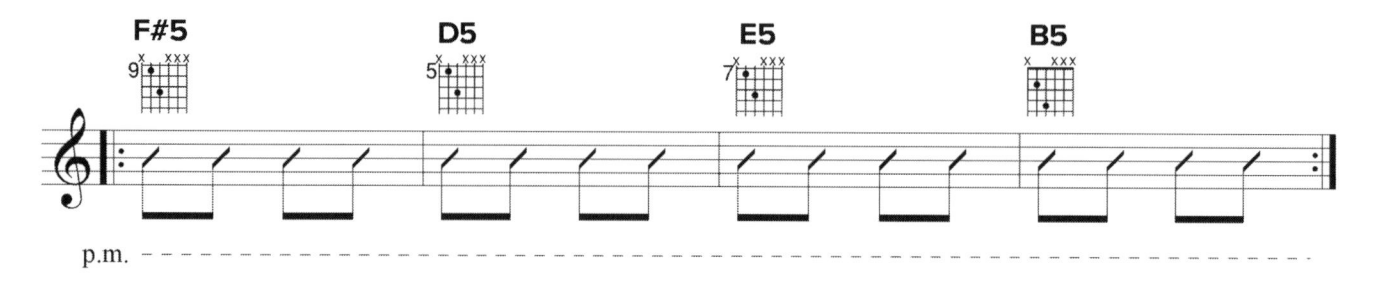

| F#5 | D5 | E5 | B5 |

p.m. -

The Seattle Battle

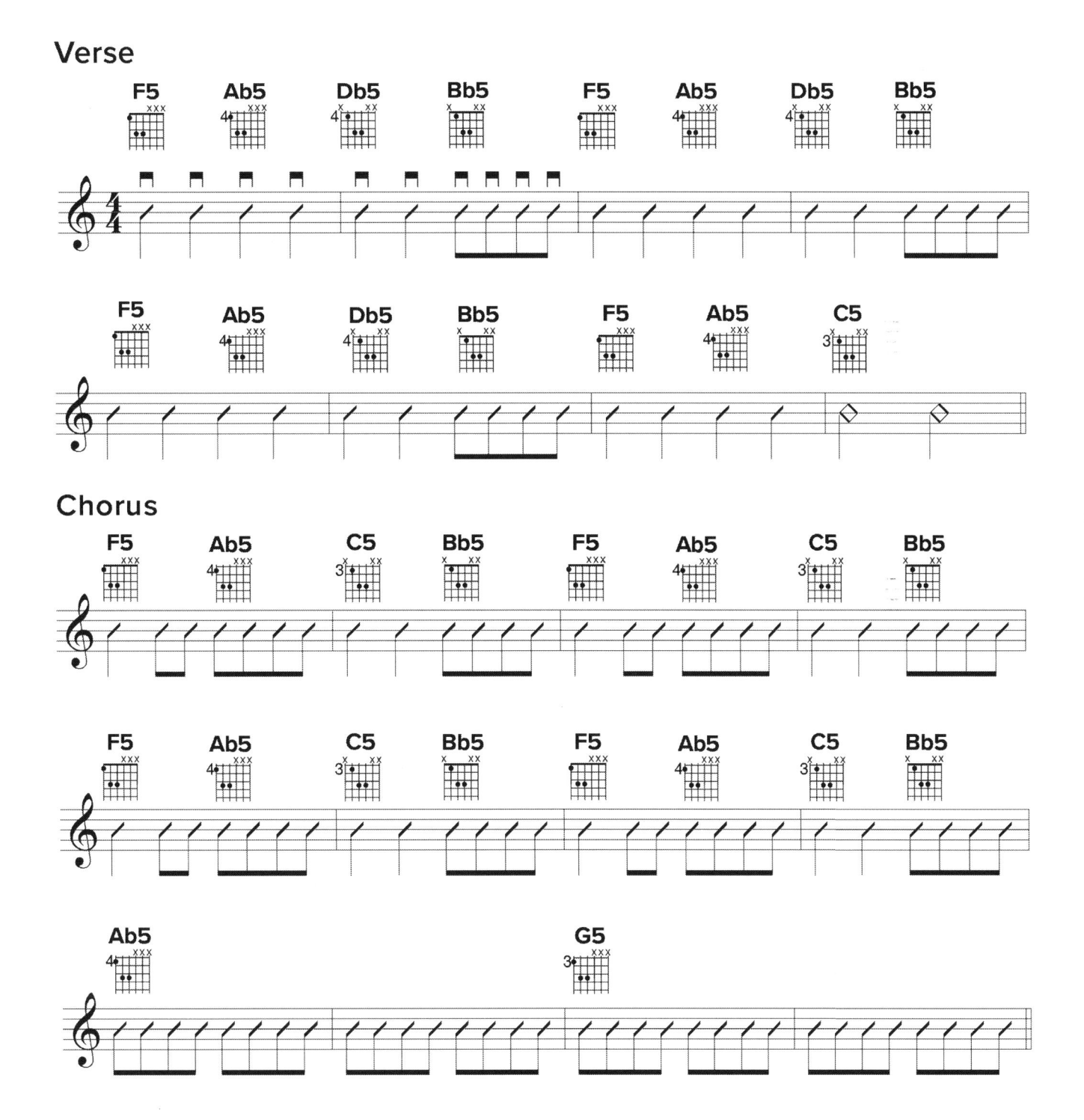

Verse

| F5 | Ab5 | Db5 | Bb5 | F5 | Ab5 | Db5 | Bb5 |

| F5 | Ab5 | Db5 | Bb5 | F5 | Ab5 | C5 |

Chorus

| F5 | Ab5 | C5 | Bb5 | F5 | Ab5 | C5 | Bb5 |

| F5 | Ab5 | C5 | Bb5 | F5 | Ab5 | C5 | Bb5 |

| Ab5 | G5 |

Verse

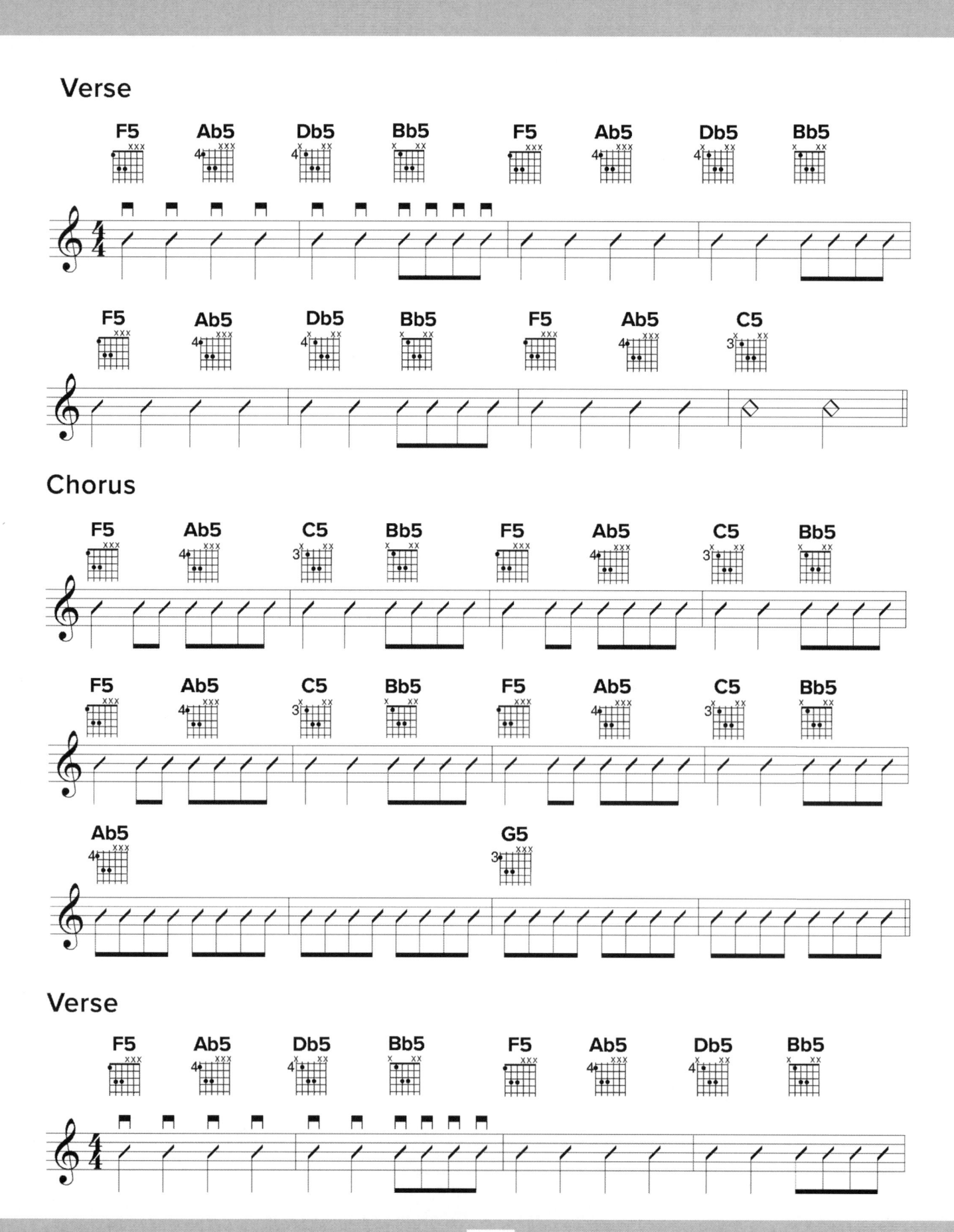

| F5 | Ab5 | Db5 | Bb5 | F5 | Ab5 | Db5 | Bb5 |

| F5 | Ab5 | Db5 | Bb5 | F5 | Ab5 | C5 |

Chorus

| F5 | Ab5 | C5 | Bb5 | F5 | Ab5 | C5 | Bb5 |

| F5 | Ab5 | C5 | Bb5 | F5 | Ab5 | C5 | Bb5 |

| Ab5 | | G5 | |

Verse

| F5 | Ab5 | Db5 | Bb5 | F5 | Ab5 | Db5 | Bb5 |

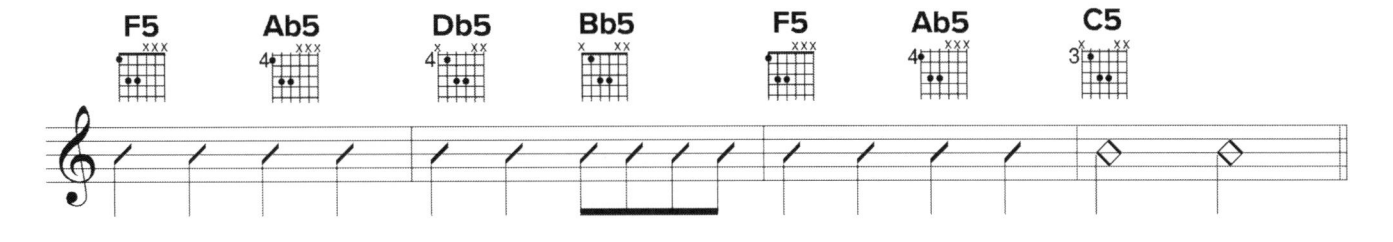

Chorus

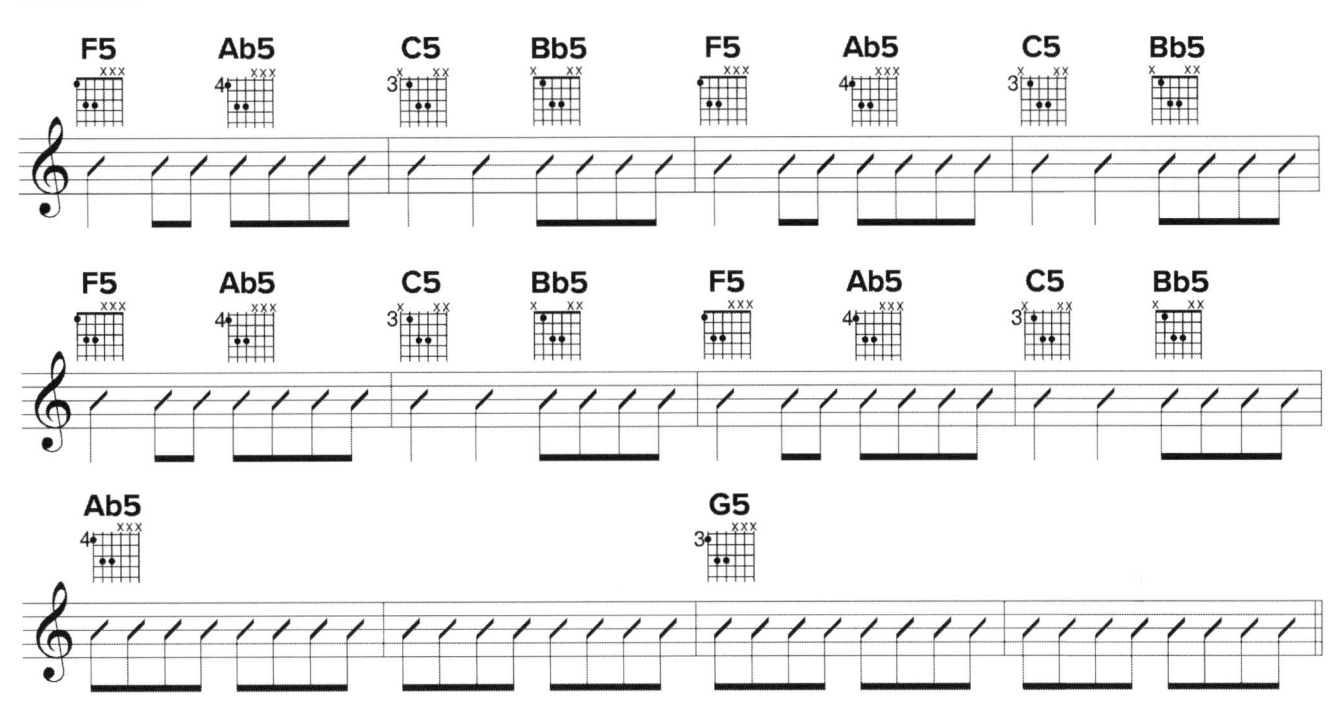

Bridge

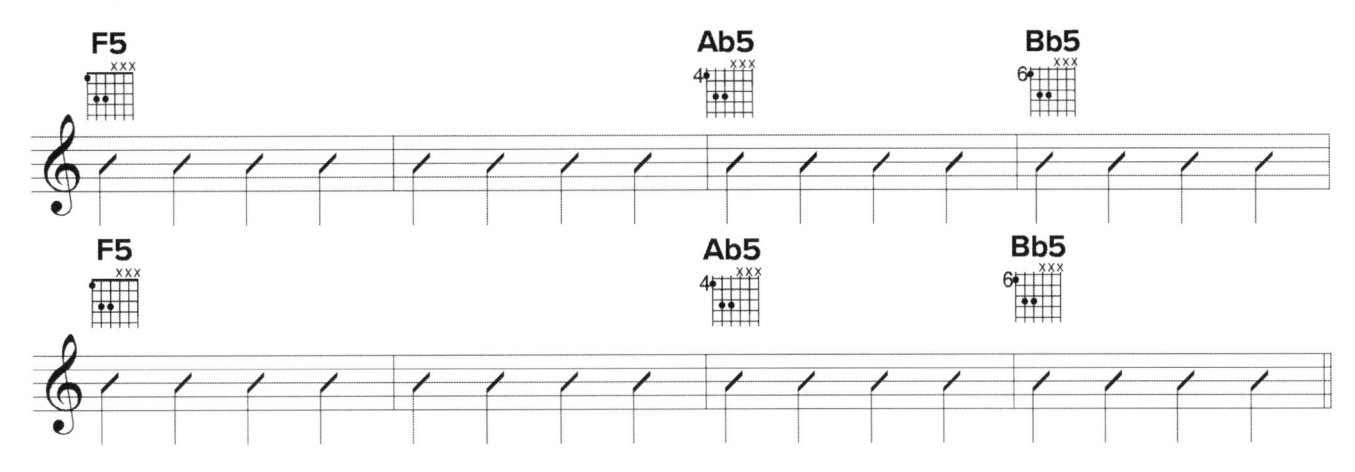

(continued on next page)

Chorus

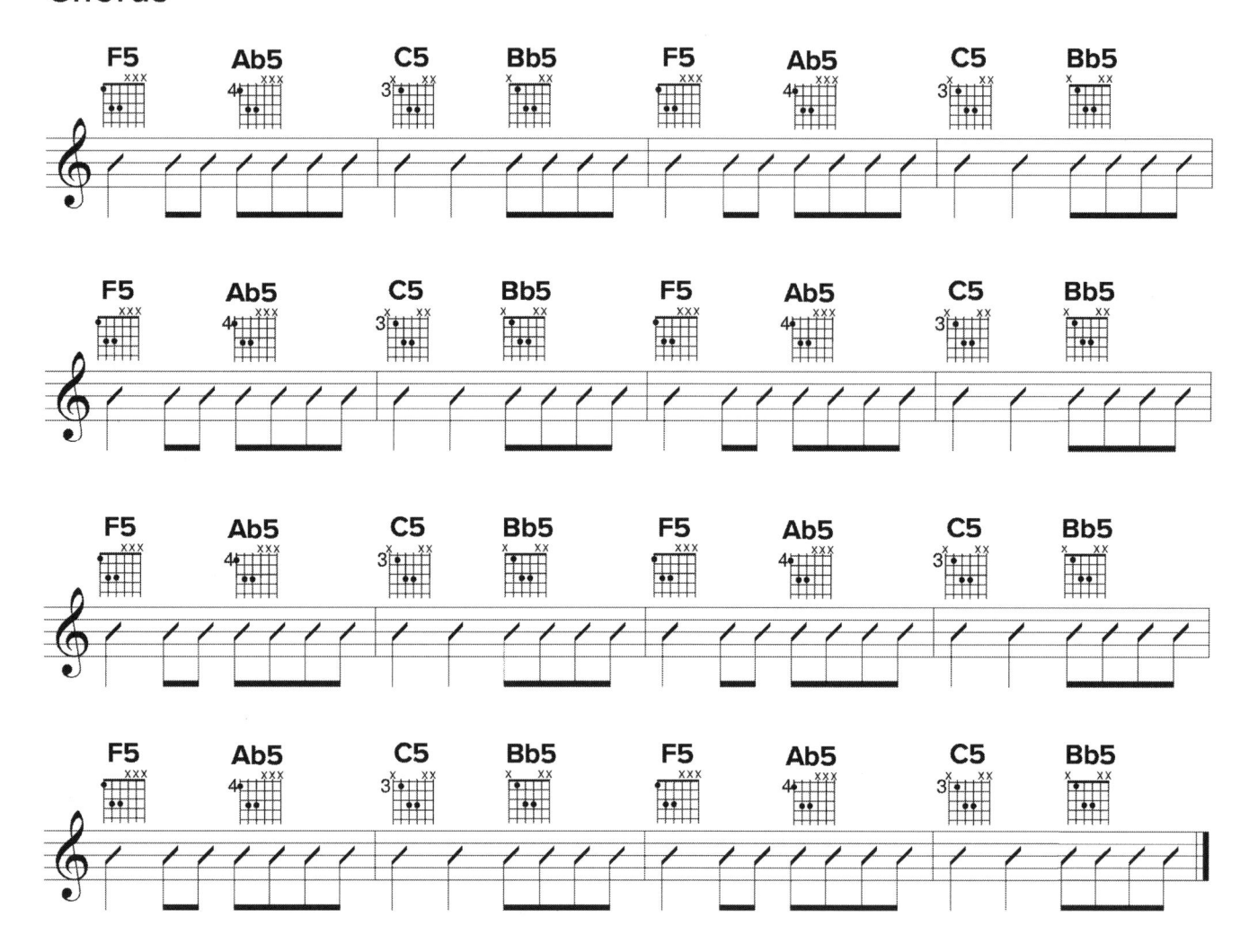

Slow and Low

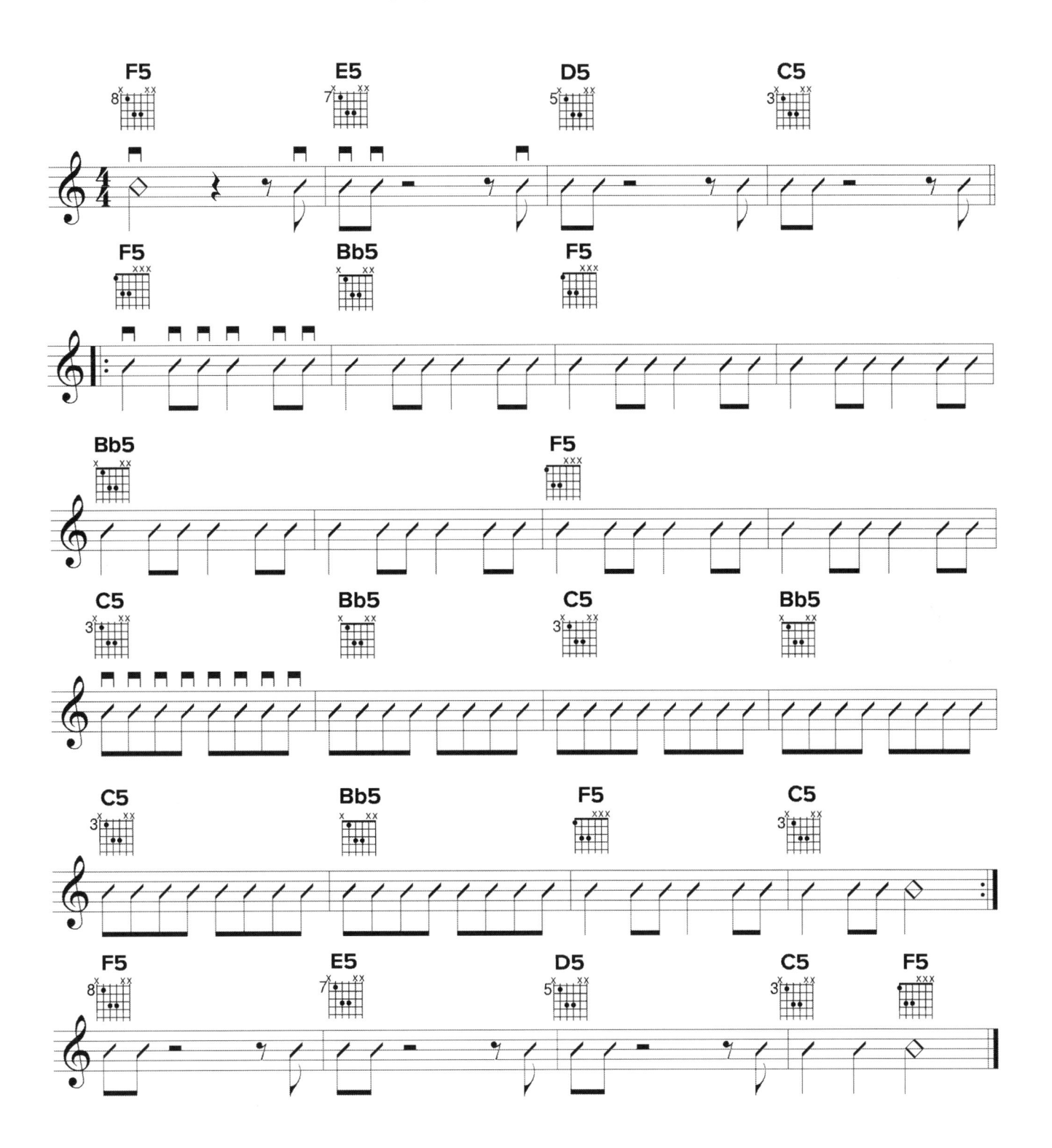

Lesson 7:
Root 4 Power Chords

Power chords whose roots fall on the fourth string are not as common as root 5 and root 6 power chords, but they are still worth learning. They work in the same manner as the other two types, where the root of the chord is on string four, and the fifth of the chord is on the next string (the third string in this case), two frets higher. However, when adding a third note to a root 4 power chord, the pinky moves up one additional fret. (See chart).

In this lesson, you will get a chance to learn both two-note and three-note root 4 power chords. Then you will be given opportunities to practice them along with the chords already covered in this book.

Natural Note Roots

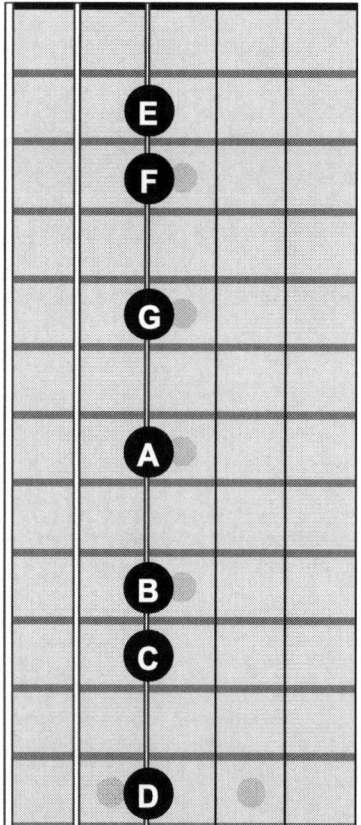

Sharp and Flat Roots

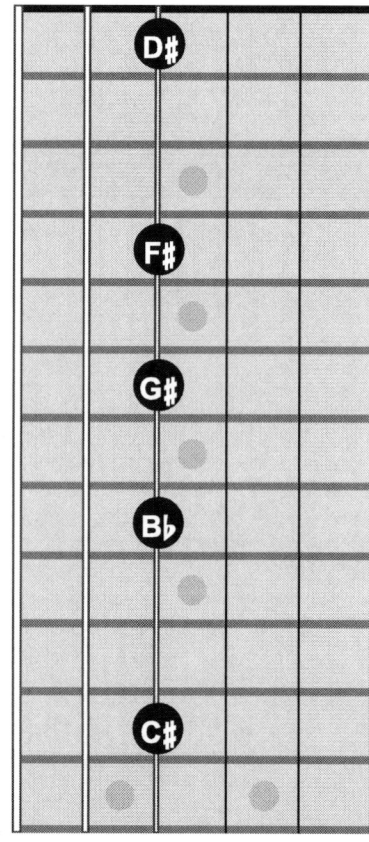

Two Note Example   Three Note Example

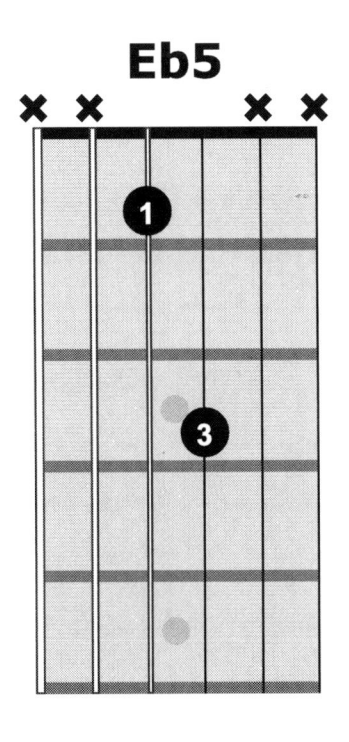

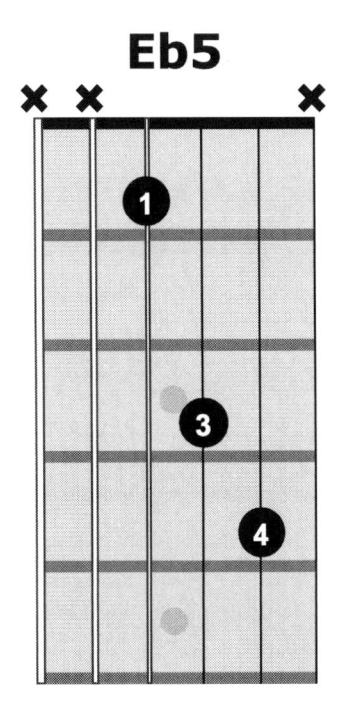

Eb5   **Eb5**

Practicing Root 4 Power Chords

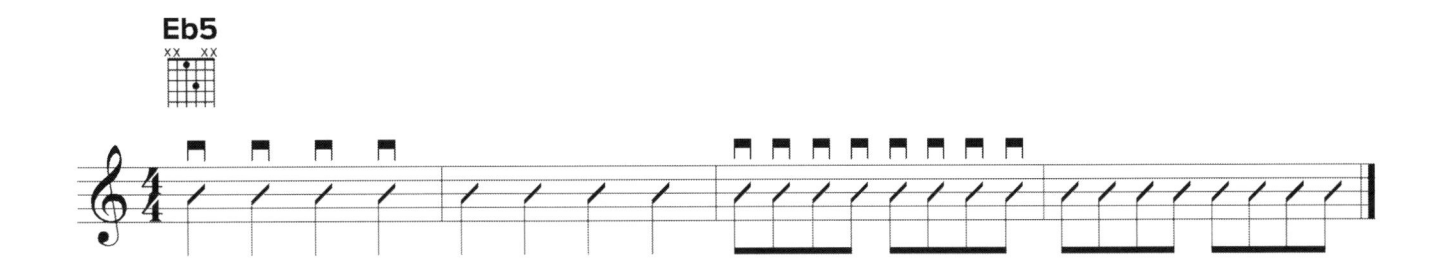

Exercise 1

Eb5

Exercise 2

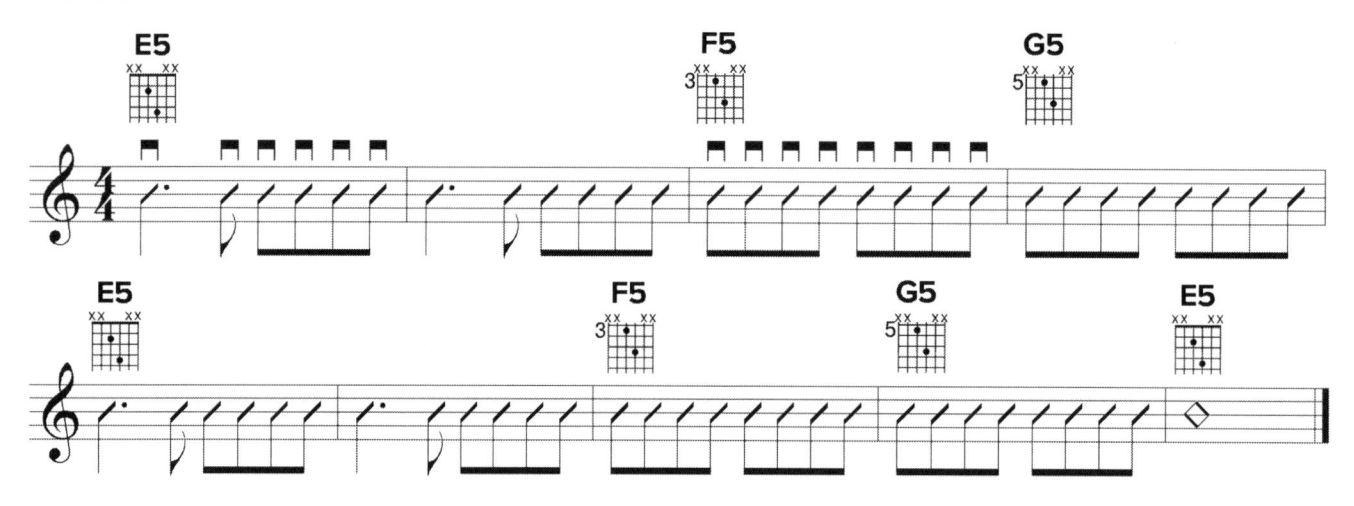

Exercise 3

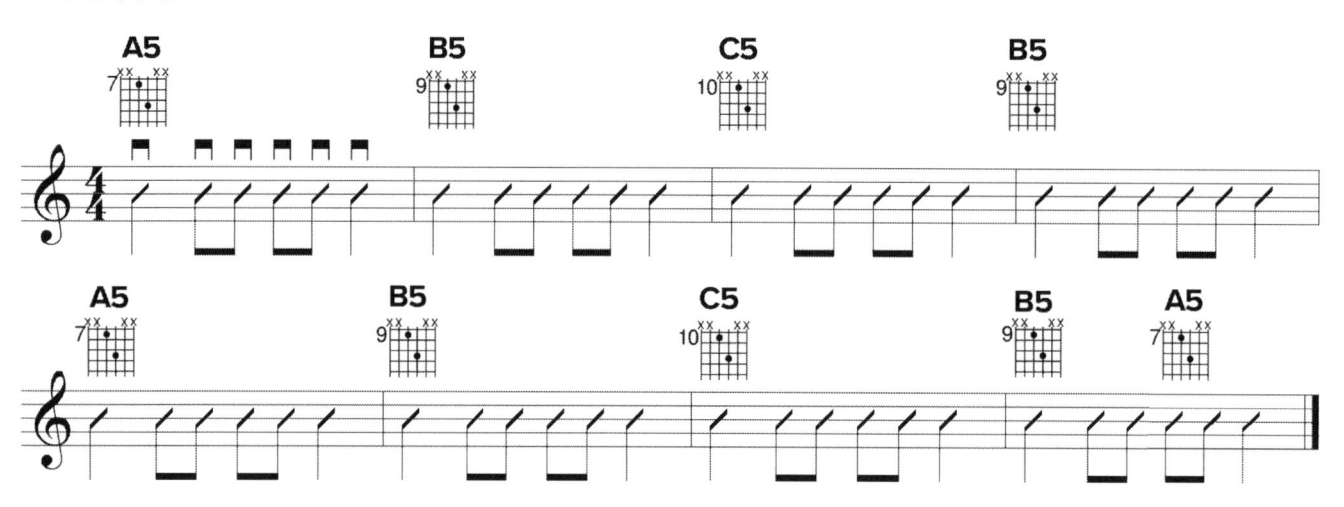

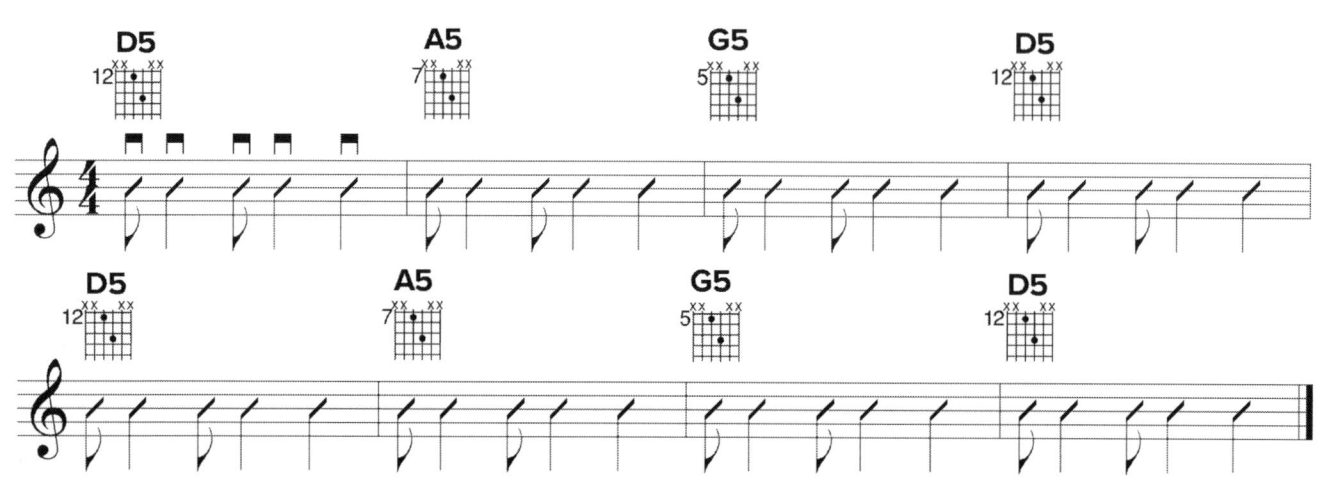

Exercise 4

Exercise 5

| Eb5 | Ab5 | Eb5 | Bb5 |
| Eb5 | Ab5 | Eb5 | Bb5 | Eb5 |

Exercise 6

| G5 | Gb5 G5 G5 | Gb5 G5 F5 | E5 F5 F5 | E5 F5 |
| G5 | Gb5 G5 G5 | Gb5 G5 A#5 | A5 A#5 G5 | Gb5 G5 |

Exercise 7

| C#5 A#5 | F#5 G#5 | C#5 A#5 | F#5 G#5 |
| A#5 | G#5 | A#5 G#5 | C#5 |

In the following exercises, no chord boxes are given. Therefore, you'll want to assume that the chords are all two-note, root 4 power chords. This is done to help you learn the names and positions of the chords better.

Exercise 8

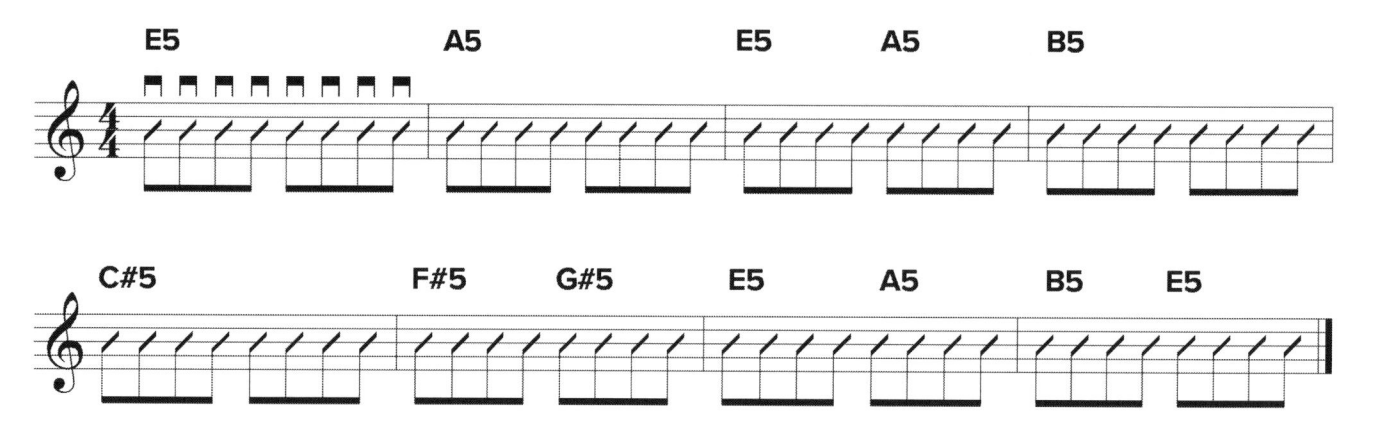

| E5 | A5 | E5 | A5 | B5 |

| C#5 | F#5 | G#5 | E5 | A5 | B5 | E5 |

Exercise 9

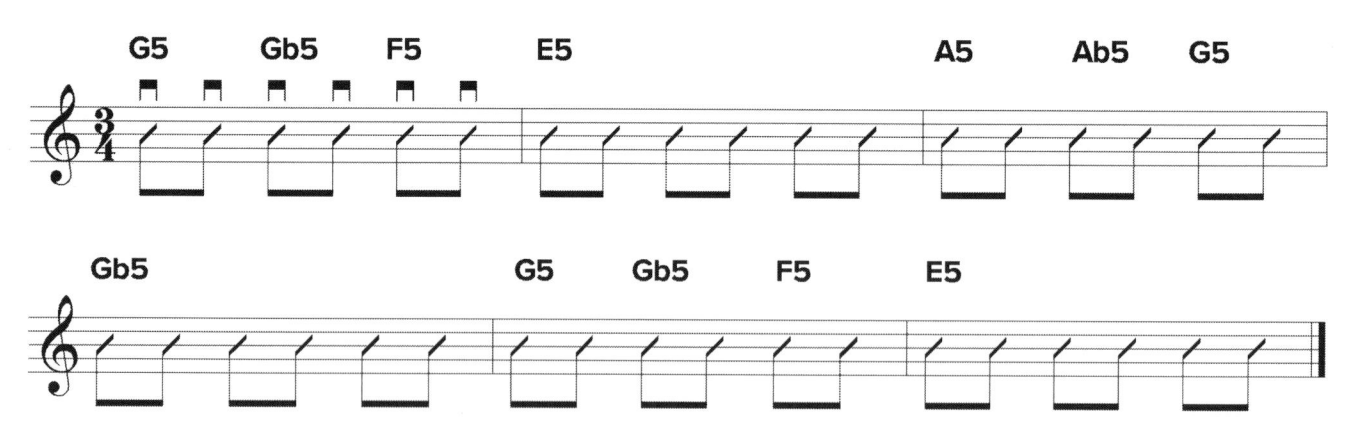

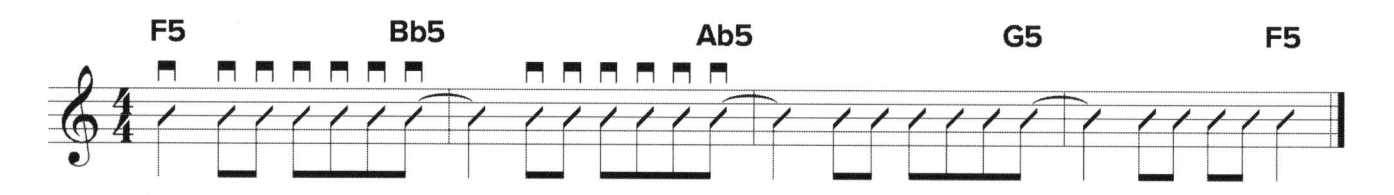

| G5 | Gb5 | F5 | E5 | A5 | Ab5 | G5 |

| Gb5 | G5 | Gb5 | F5 | E5 |

Exercise 10

| F5 | Bb5 | Ab5 | G5 | F5 |

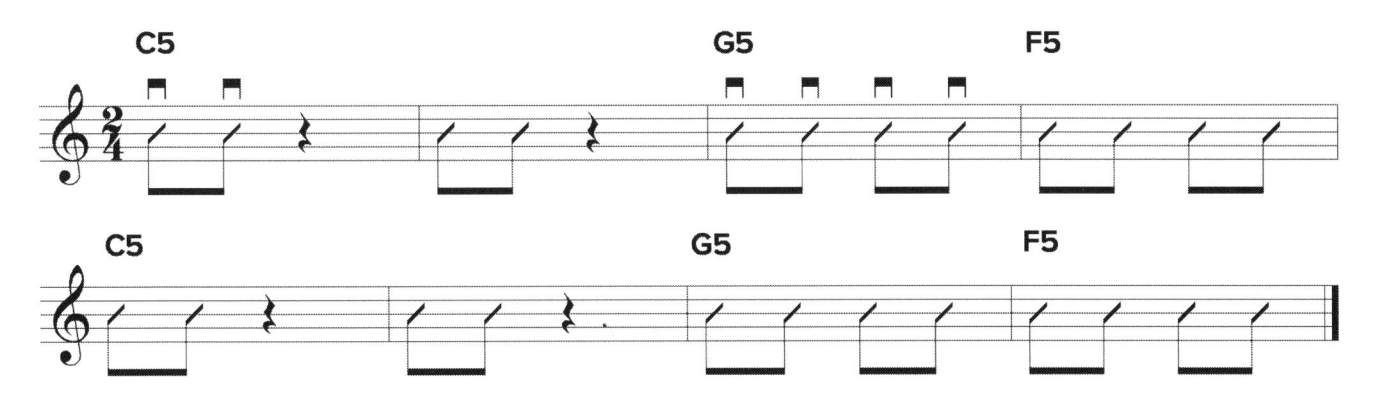

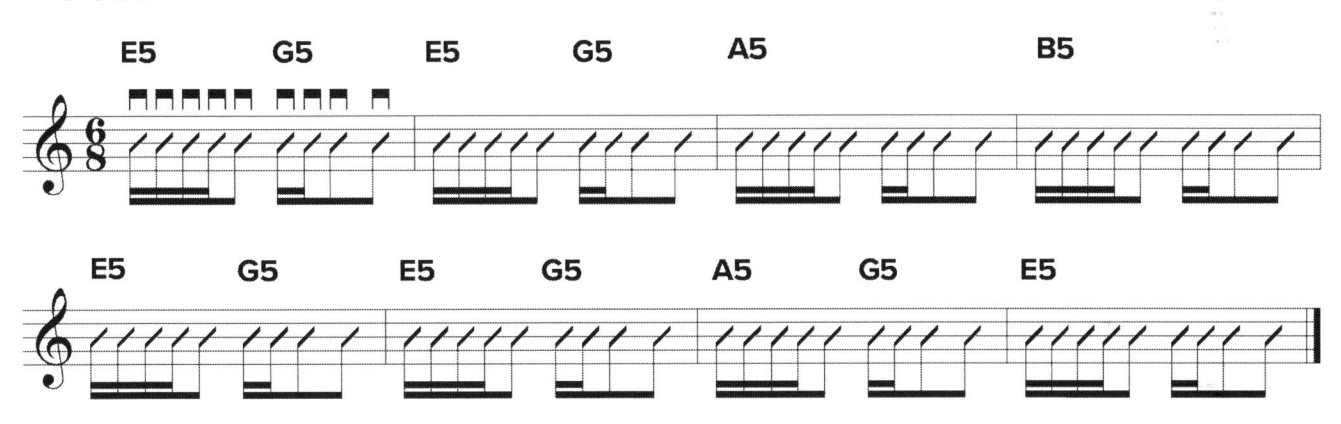

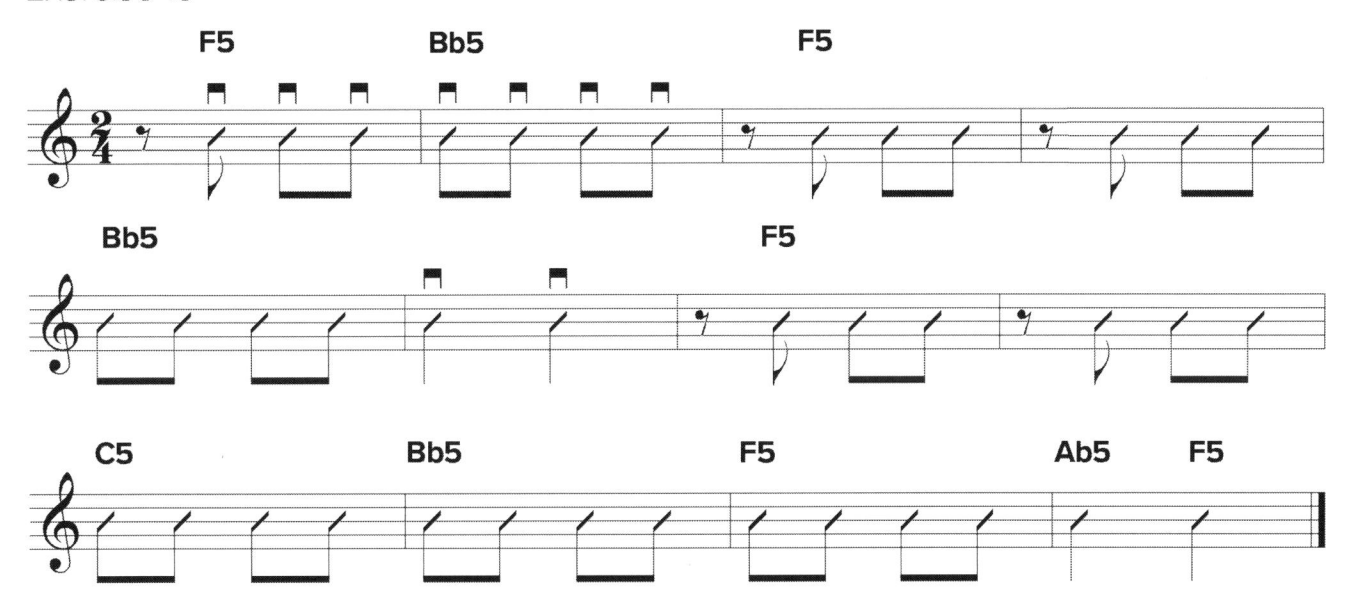

Exercise 11

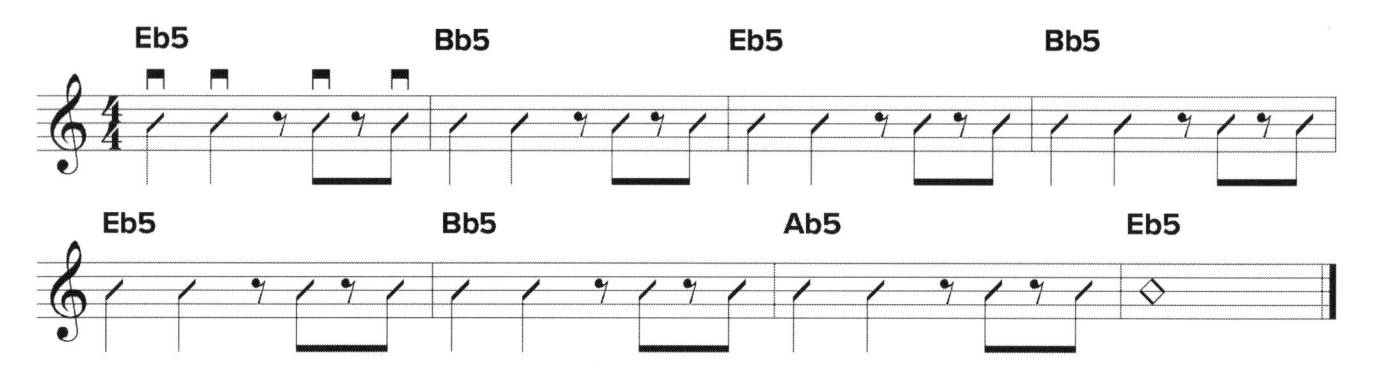

Exercise 14

Exercise 15: Since there are two places to play D5, I'd suggest using the open version for this exercise.

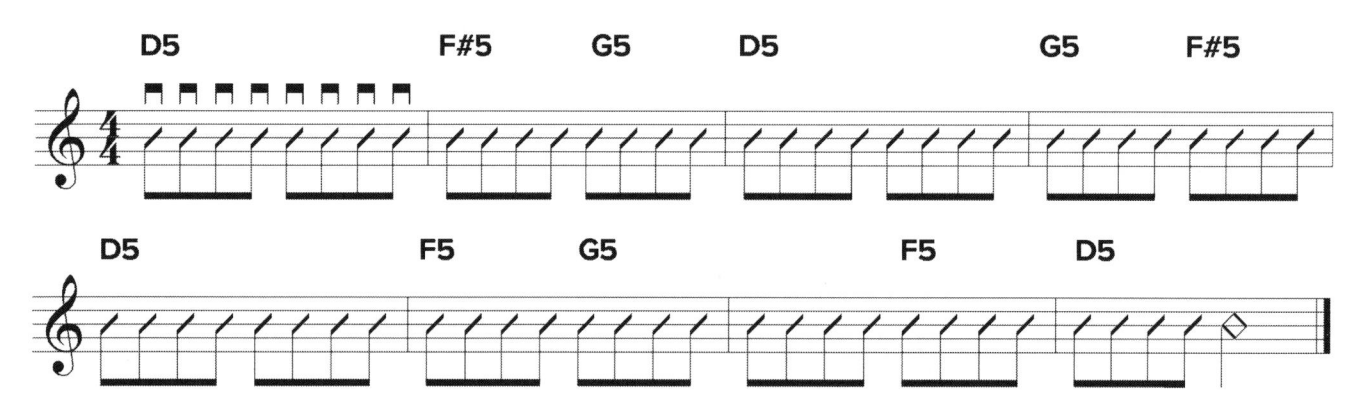

Exercise 16

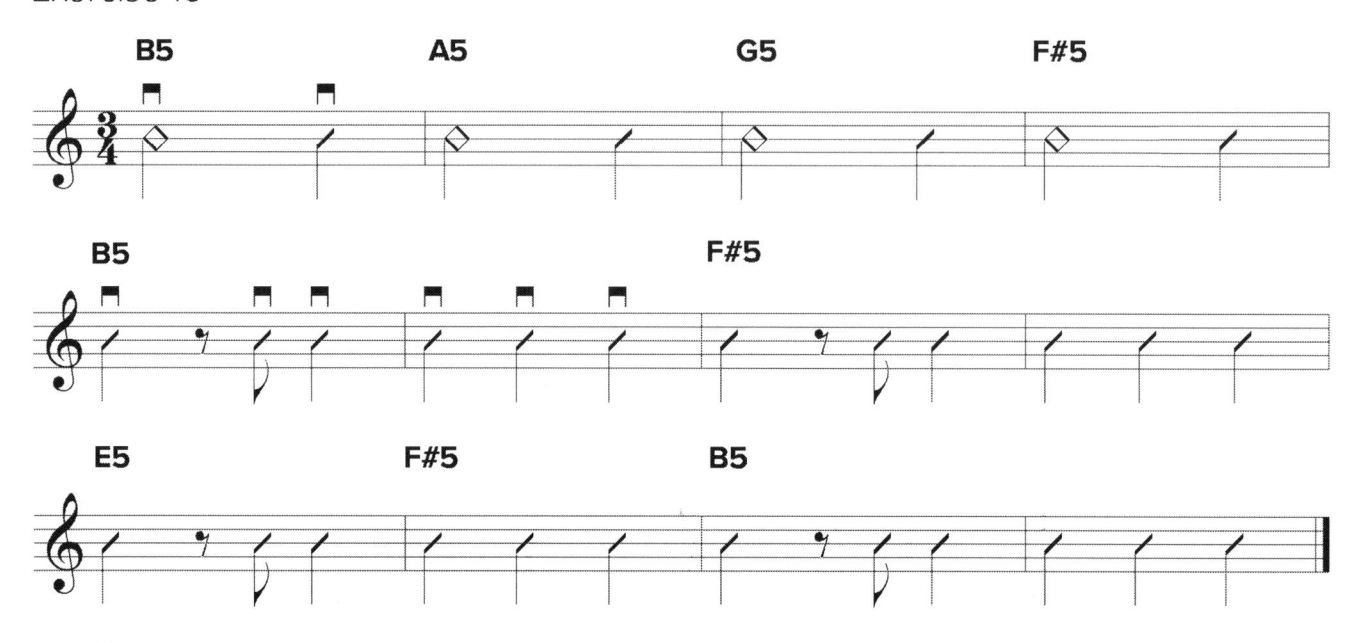

The following exercises include the three note versions of the root 4 power chords. (See page 83).

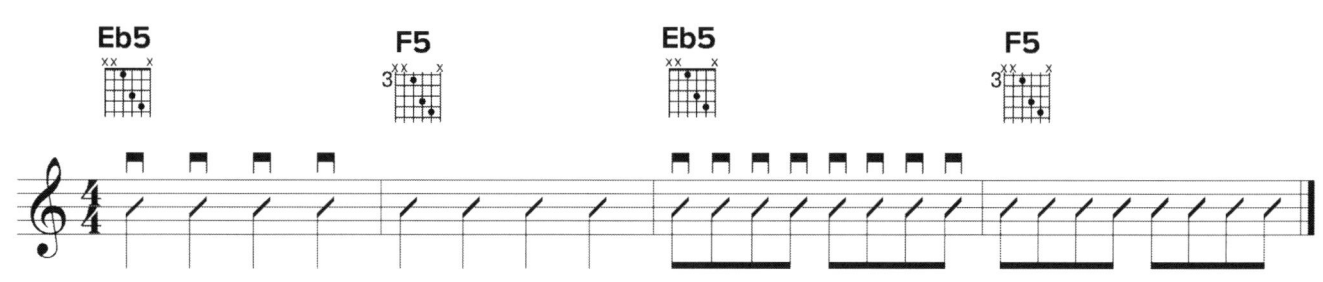

Exercise 17

Exercise 18

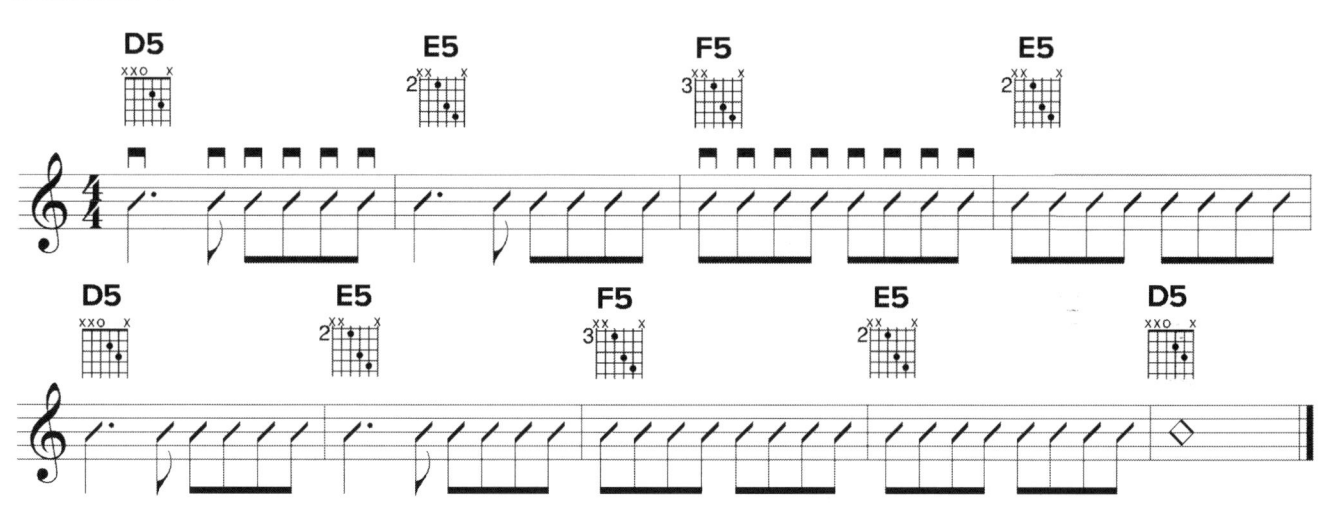

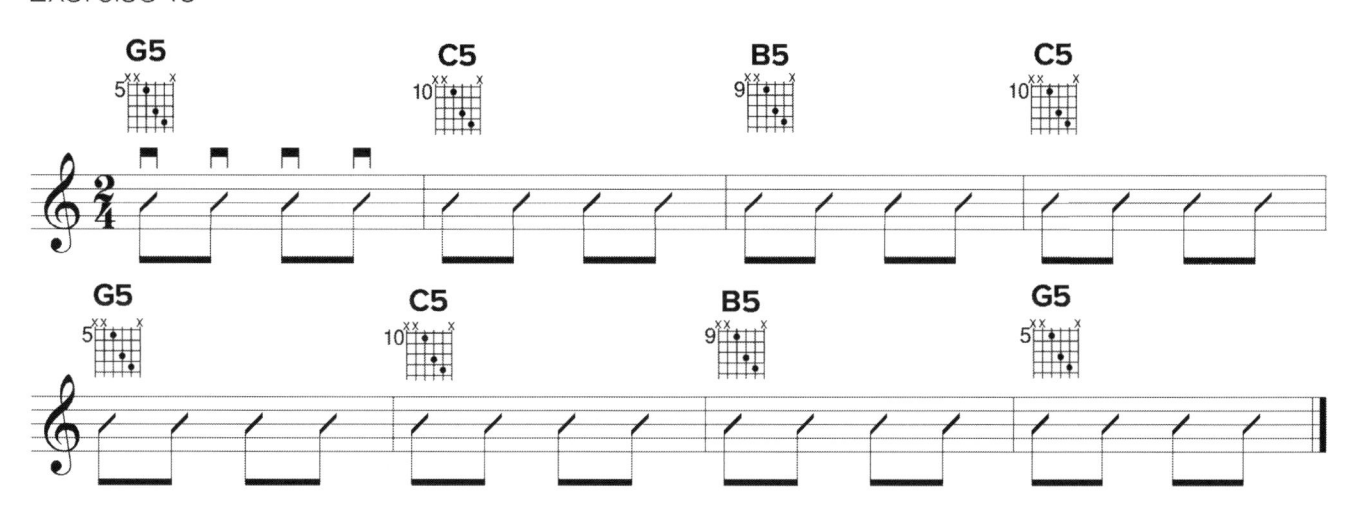

Exercise 19

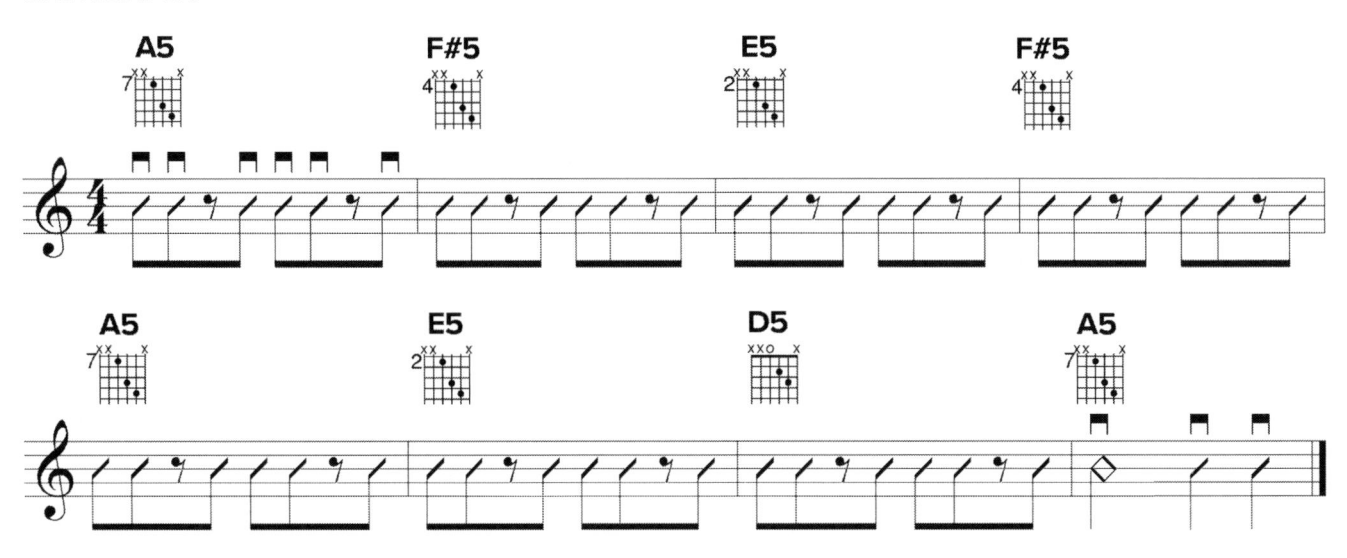

Exercise 20

Exercise 21: Be sure to note the repeat sign.

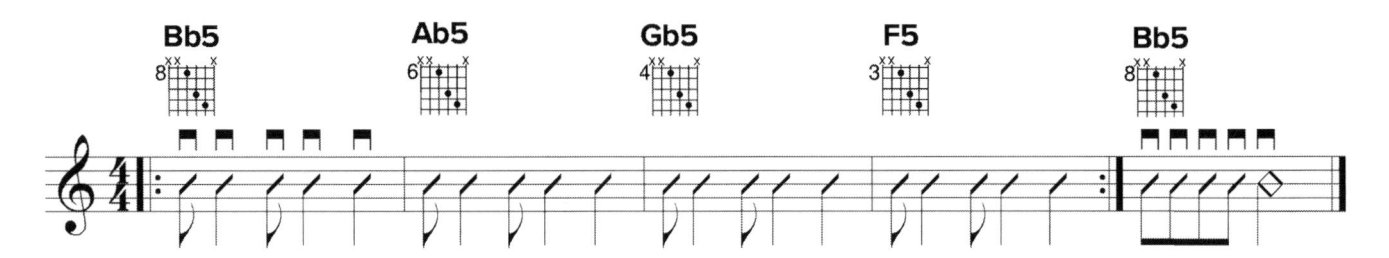

Exercise 22

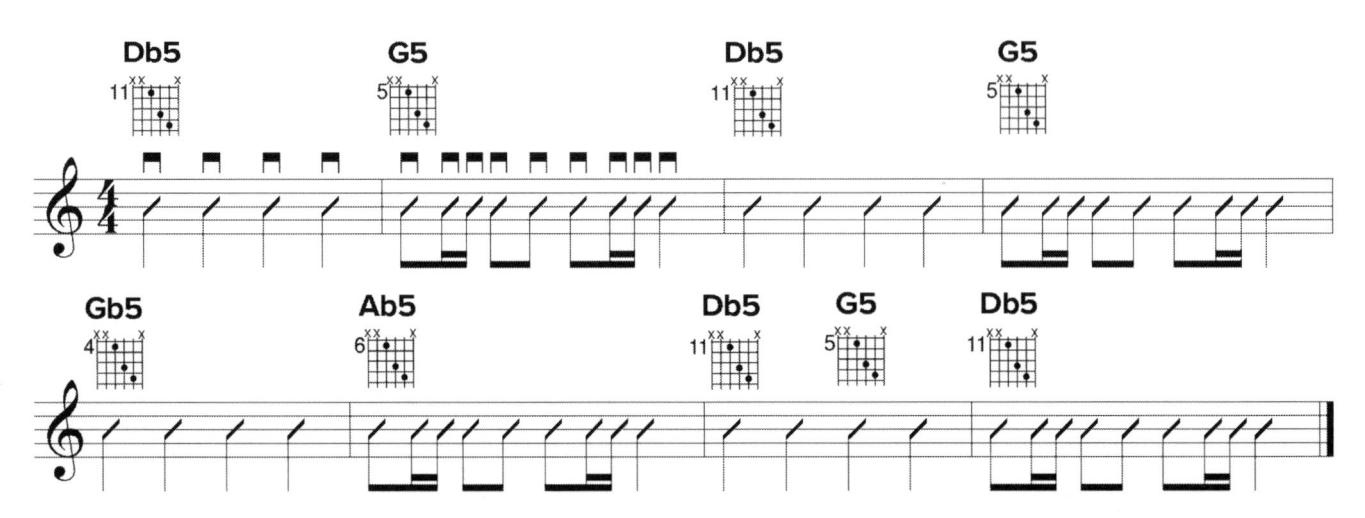

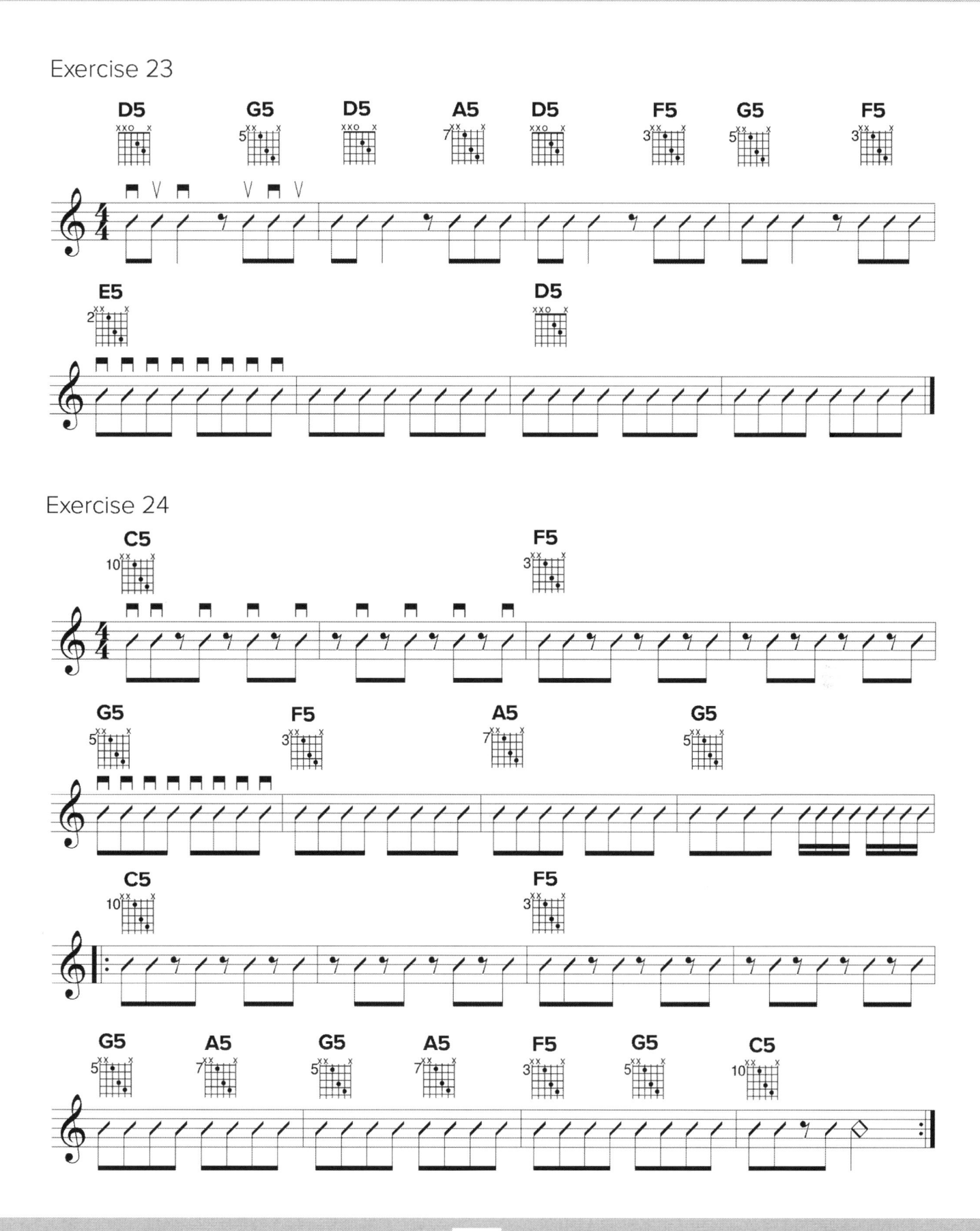

Exercise 23

Power Chord Review

The following review exercises combine the root 4 chords with root 5 and root 6, so be sure to read carefully.

Review 1

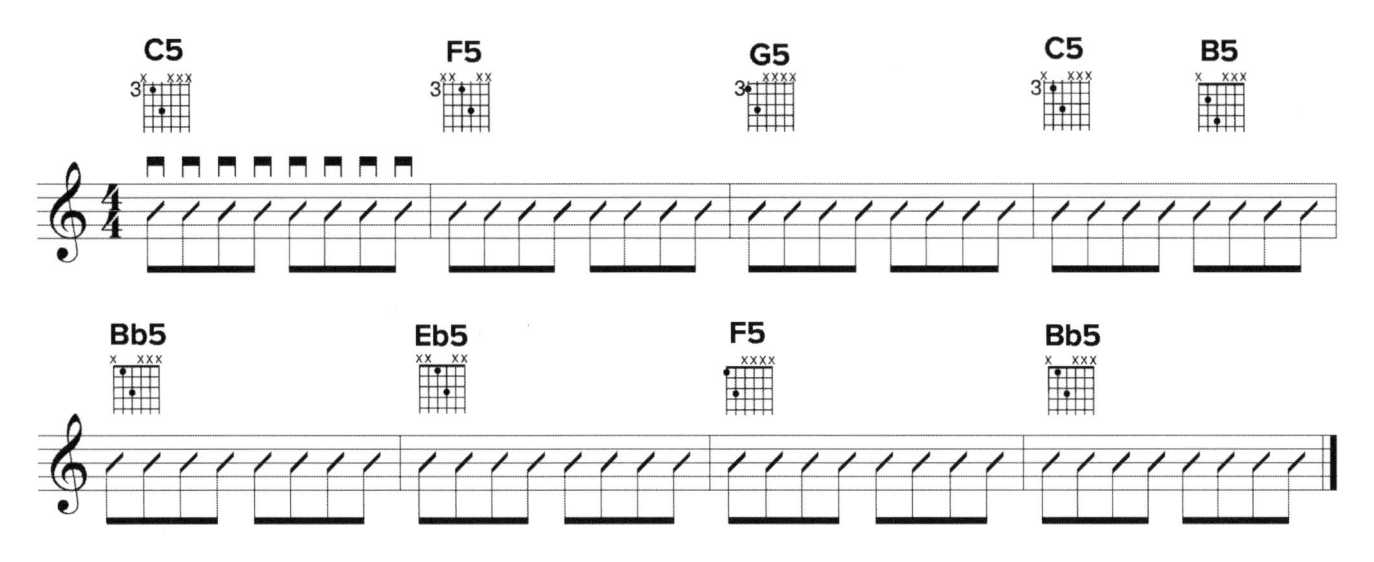

Review 2

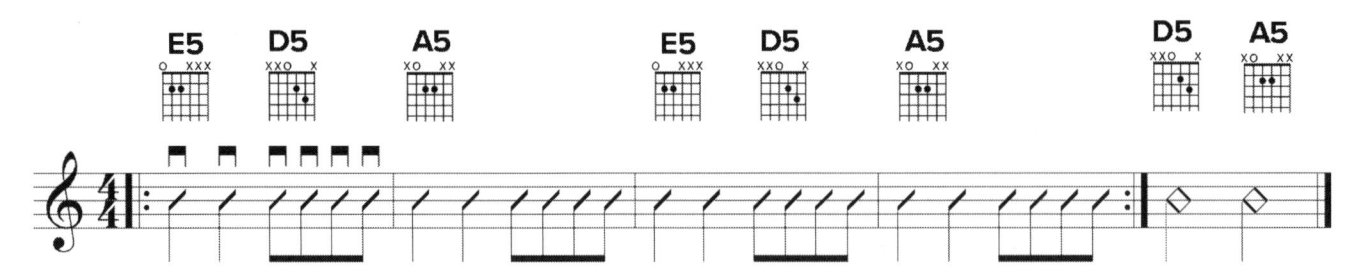

Review 3

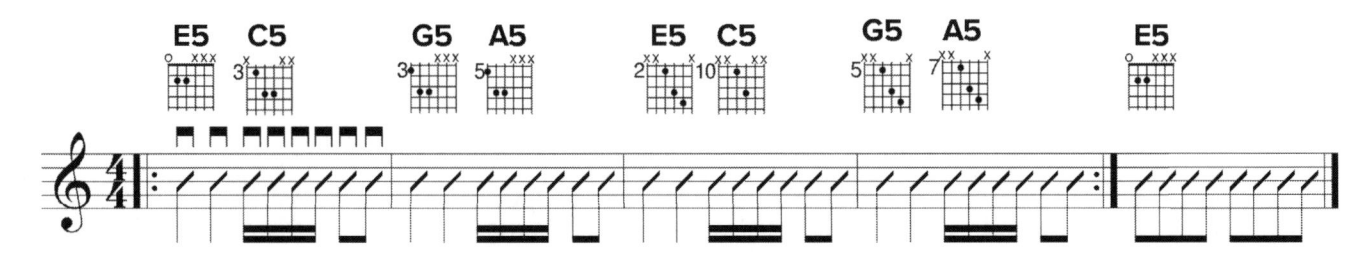

Review 4

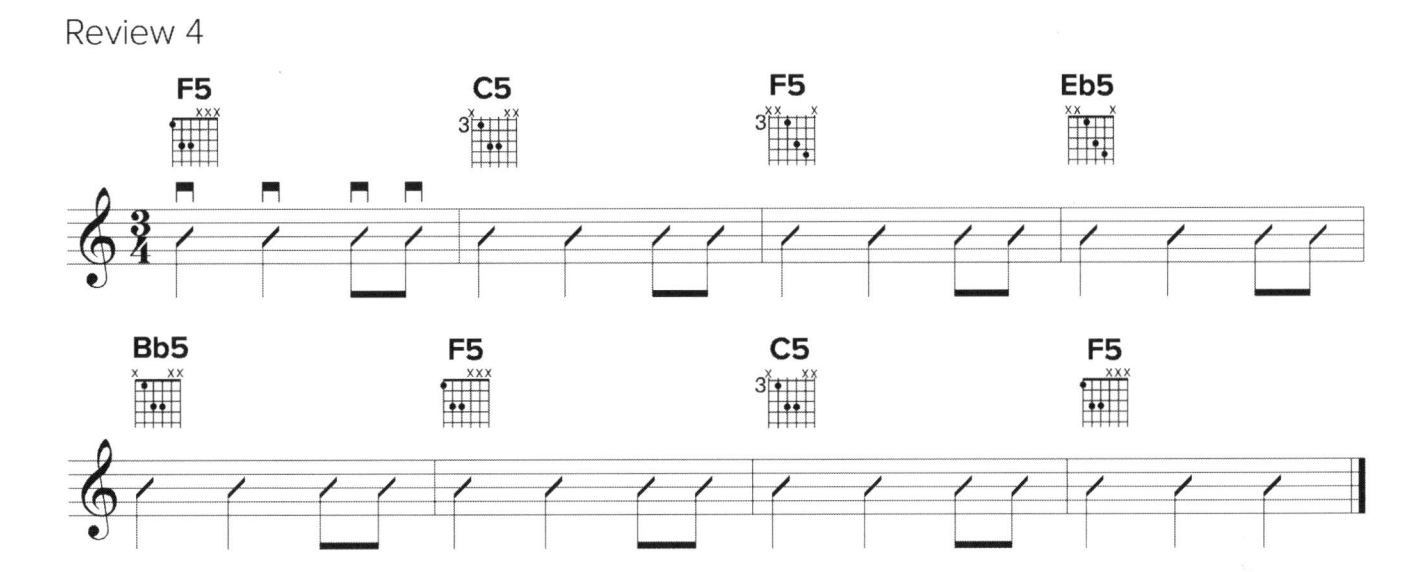

Review 5: Note the palm mute in line 1 and the switch to three note power chords in line 2.

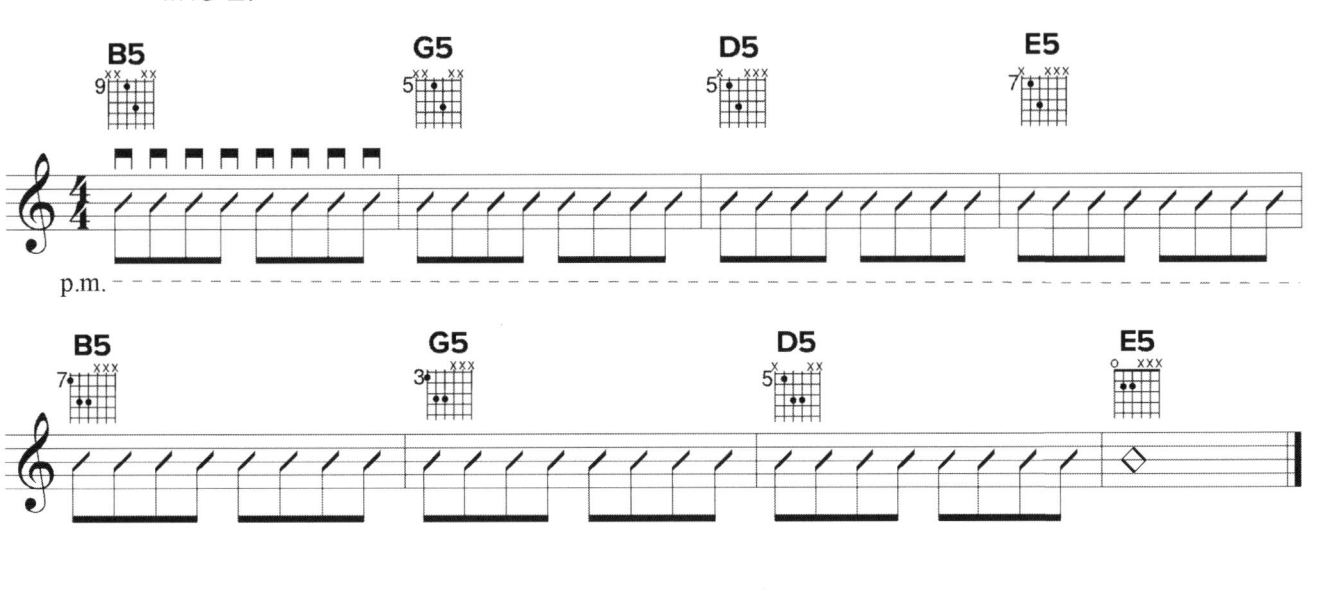

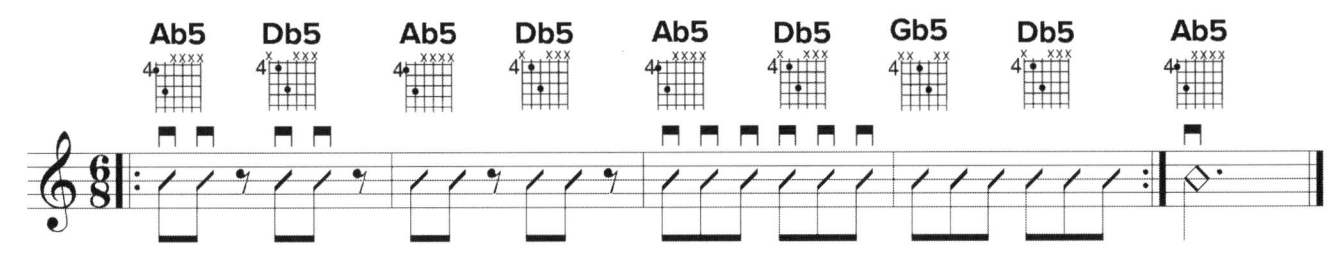

Review 6

The Arrival

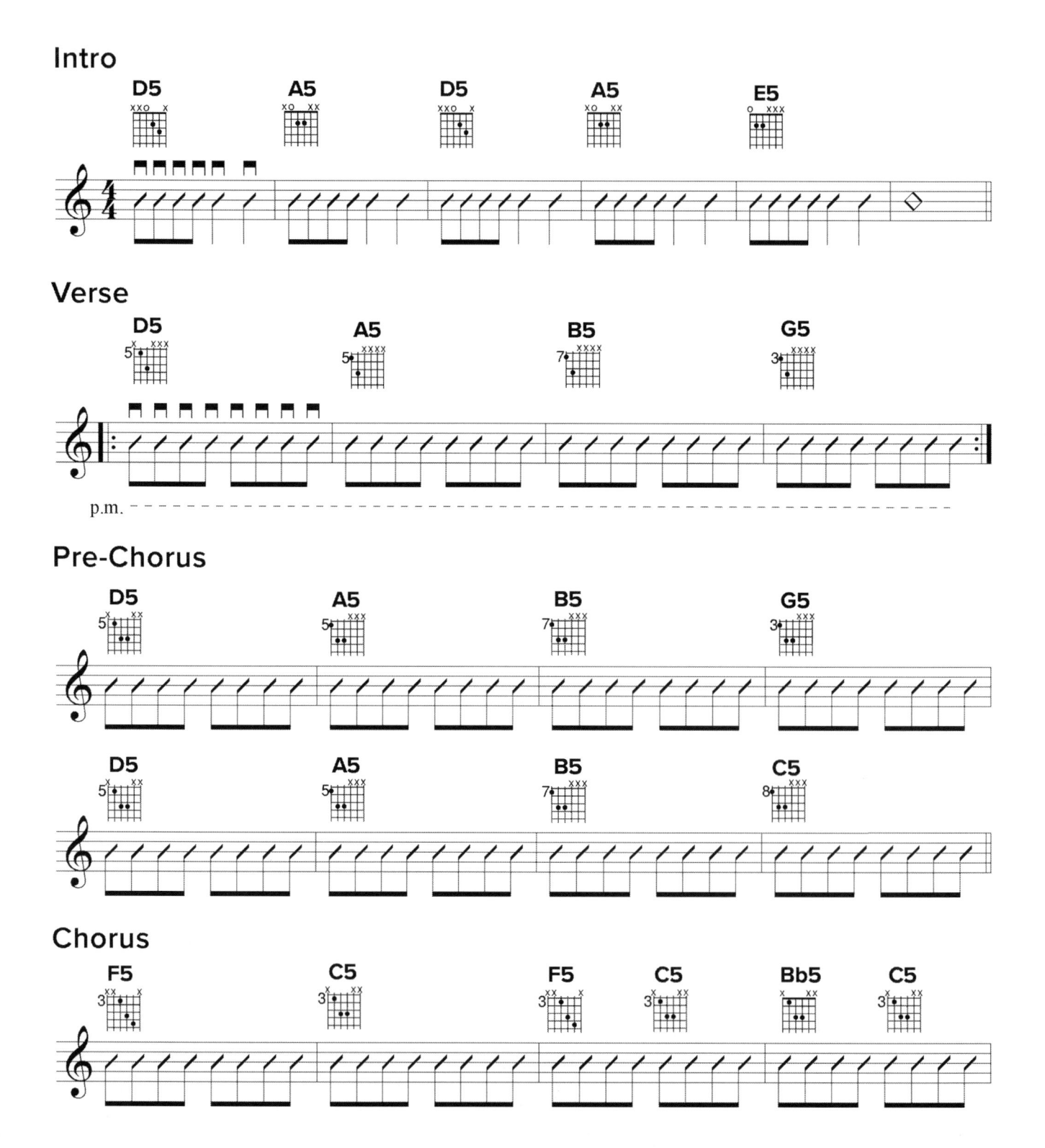

Intro

| D5 | A5 | D5 | A5 | E5 | |

Verse

| D5 | A5 | B5 | G5 |

p.m.

Pre-Chorus

| D5 | A5 | B5 | G5 |
| D5 | A5 | B5 | C5 |

Chorus

| F5 | C5 | F5 | C5 | Bb5 | C5 |

| F5 | C5 | F5 | C5 | Bb5 | A5 |

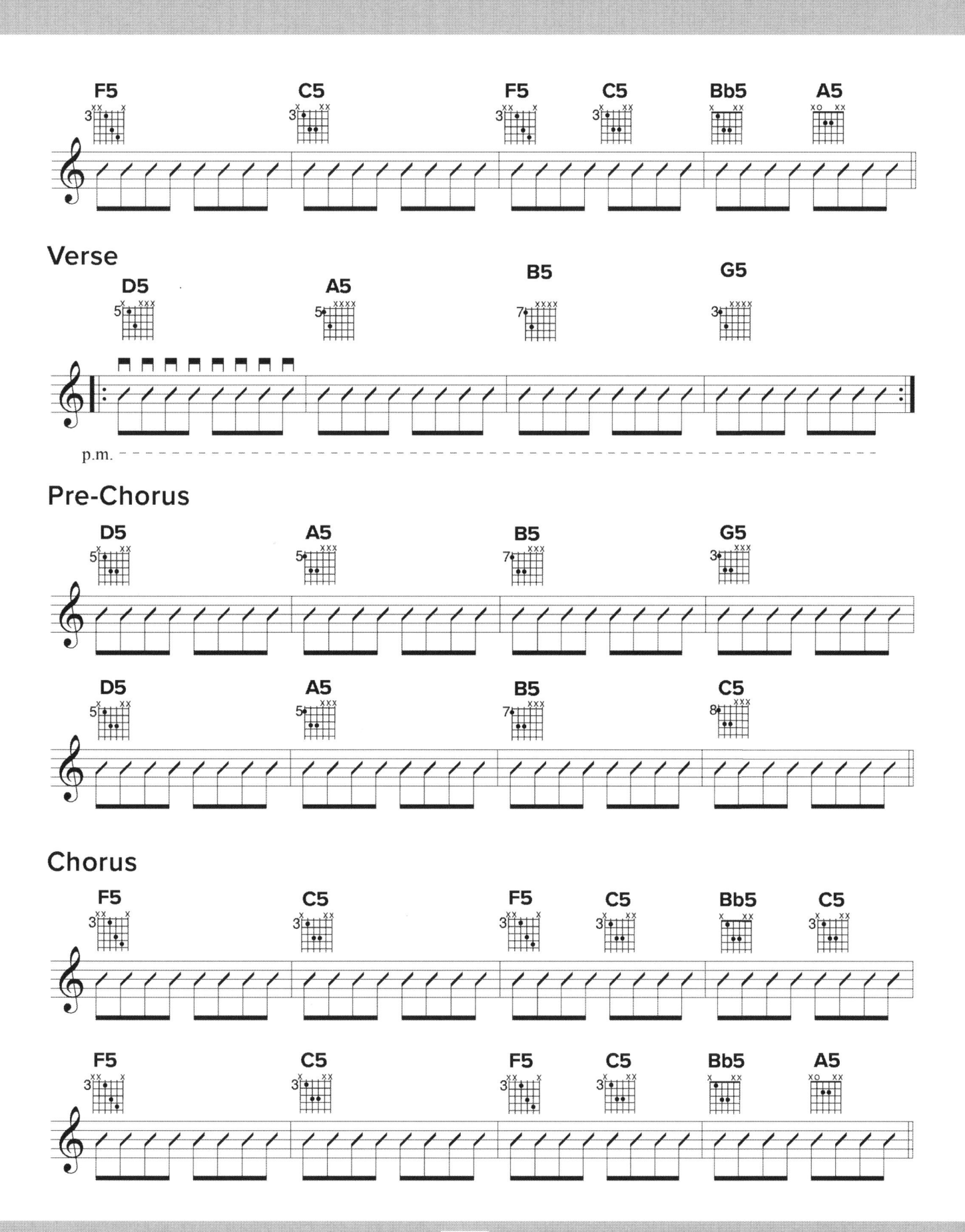

Verse

| D5 | A5 | B5 | G5 |

p.m.

Pre-Chorus

| D5 | A5 | B5 | G5 |

| D5 | A5 | B5 | C5 |

Chorus

| F5 | C5 | F5 | C5 | Bb5 | C5 |

| F5 | C5 | F5 | C5 | Bb5 | A5 |

Bridge

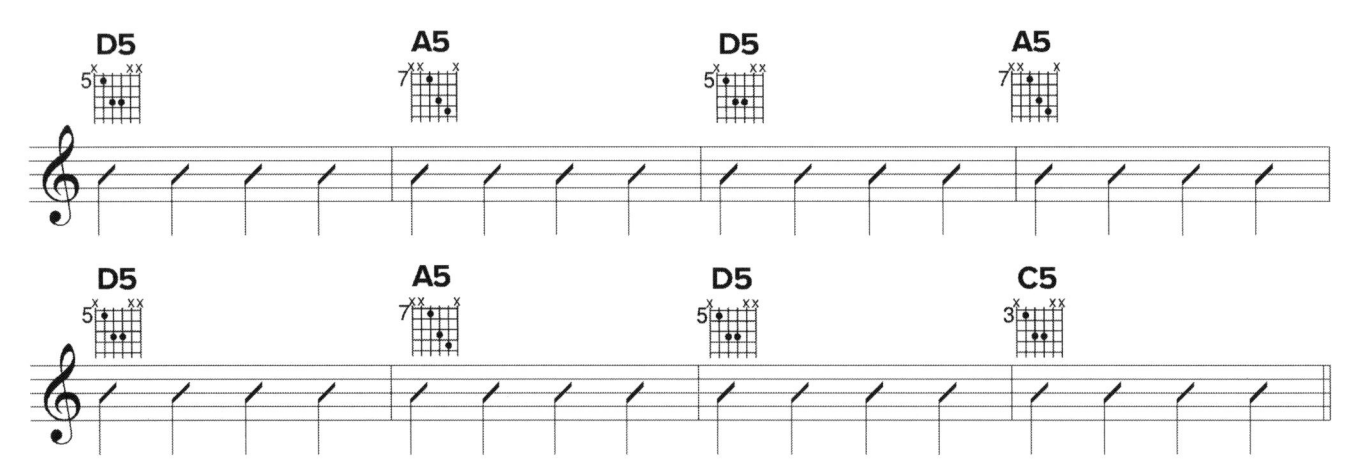

D5	A5	D5	A5
D5	A5	D5	C5

Chorus

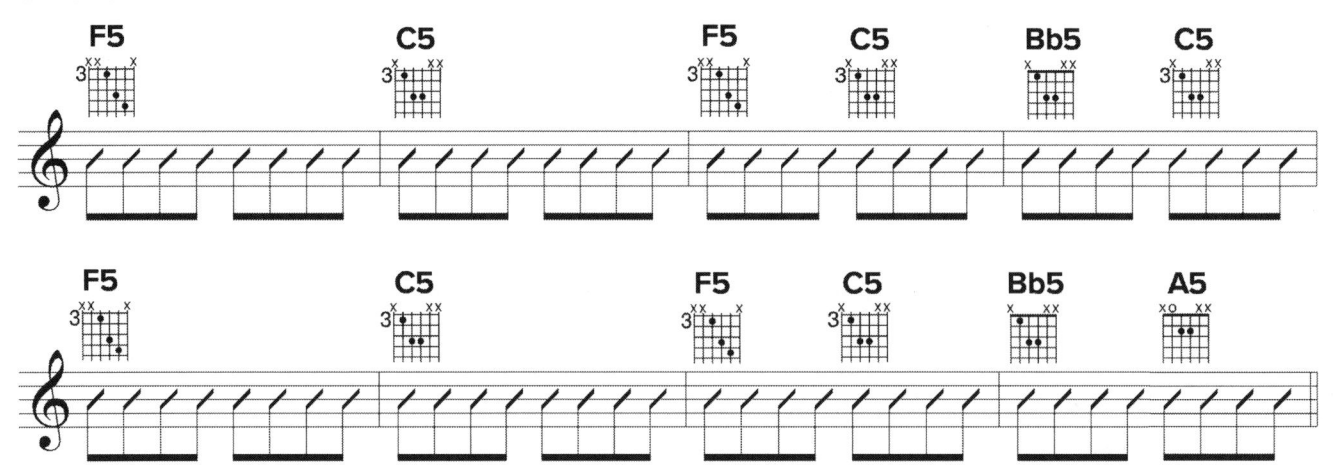

F5	C5	F5	C5	Bb5	C5
F5	C5	F5	C5	Bb5	A5

Outro

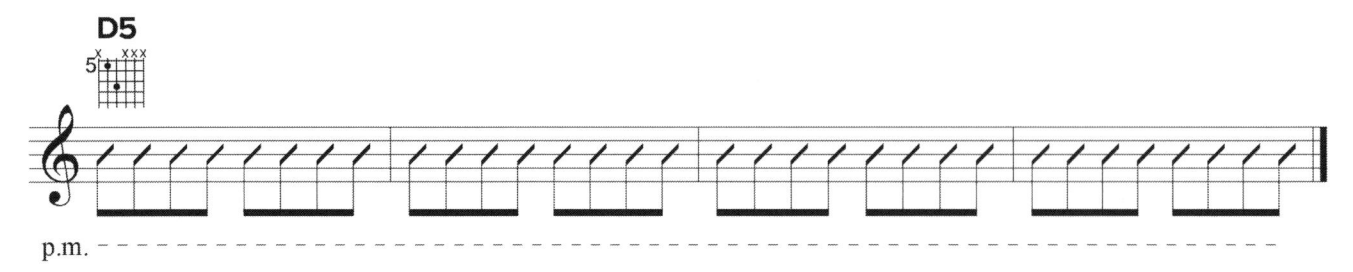

D5

p.m. -

School is Over

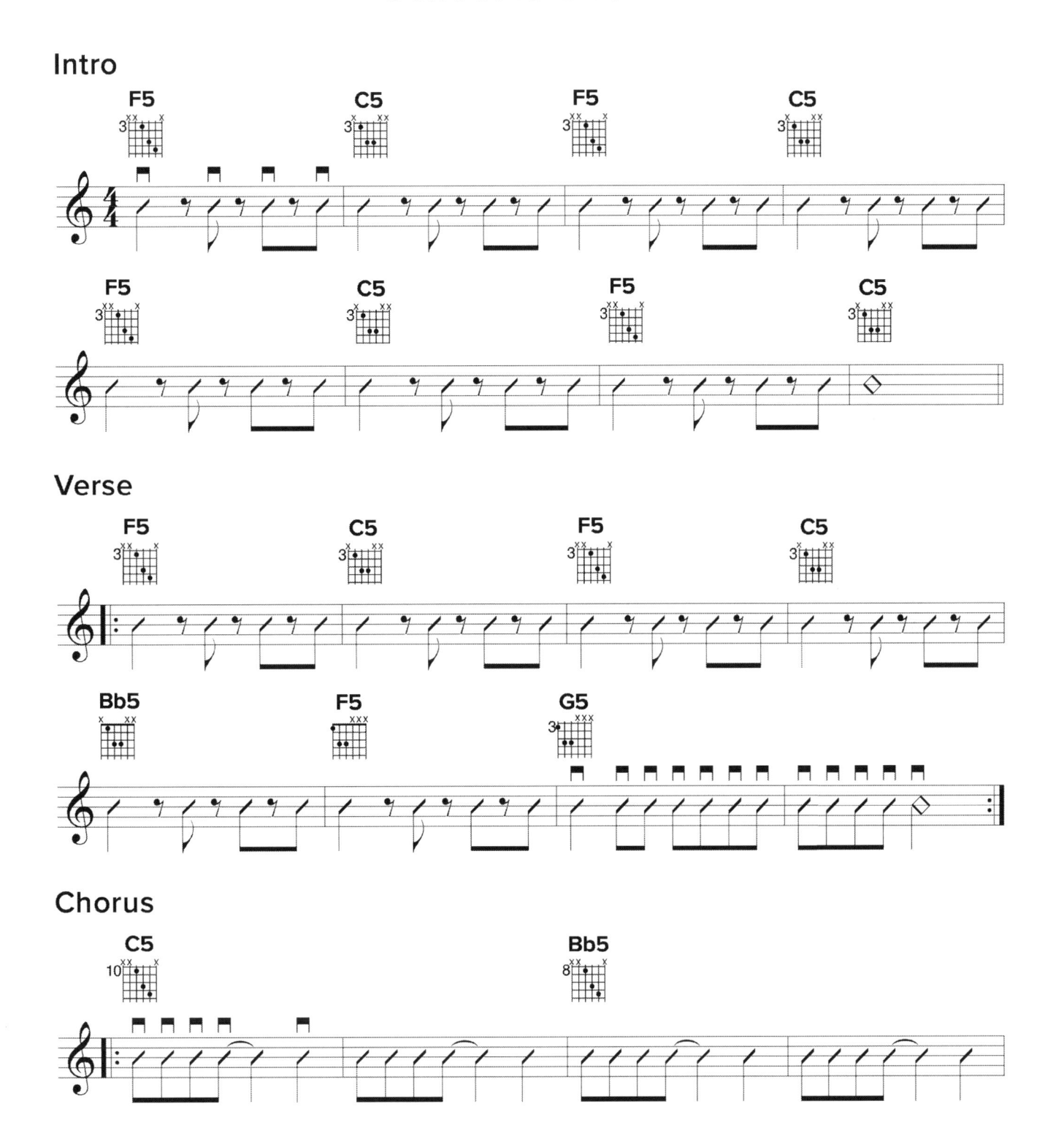

Intro

Verse

Chorus

Verse

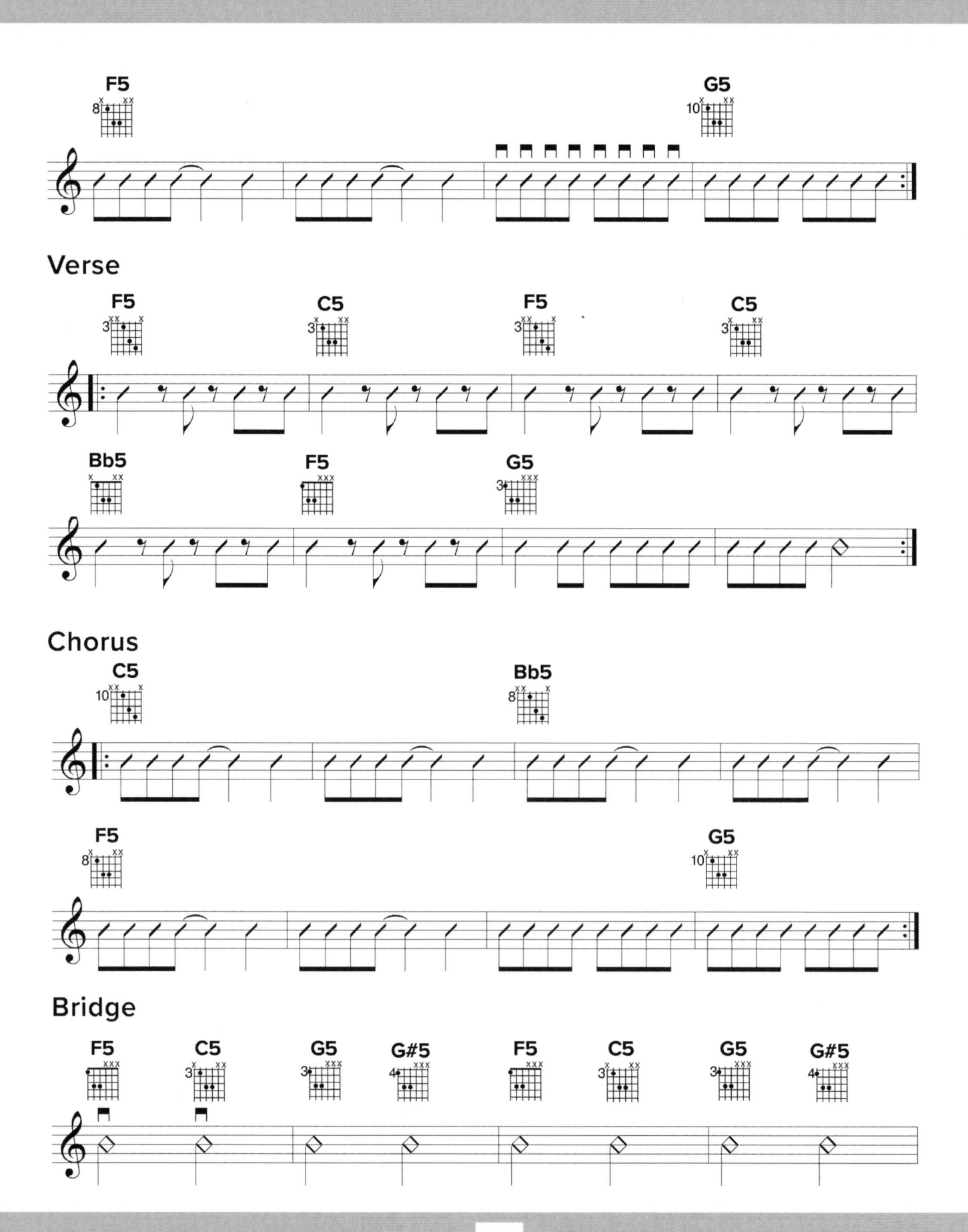

Chorus

Bridge

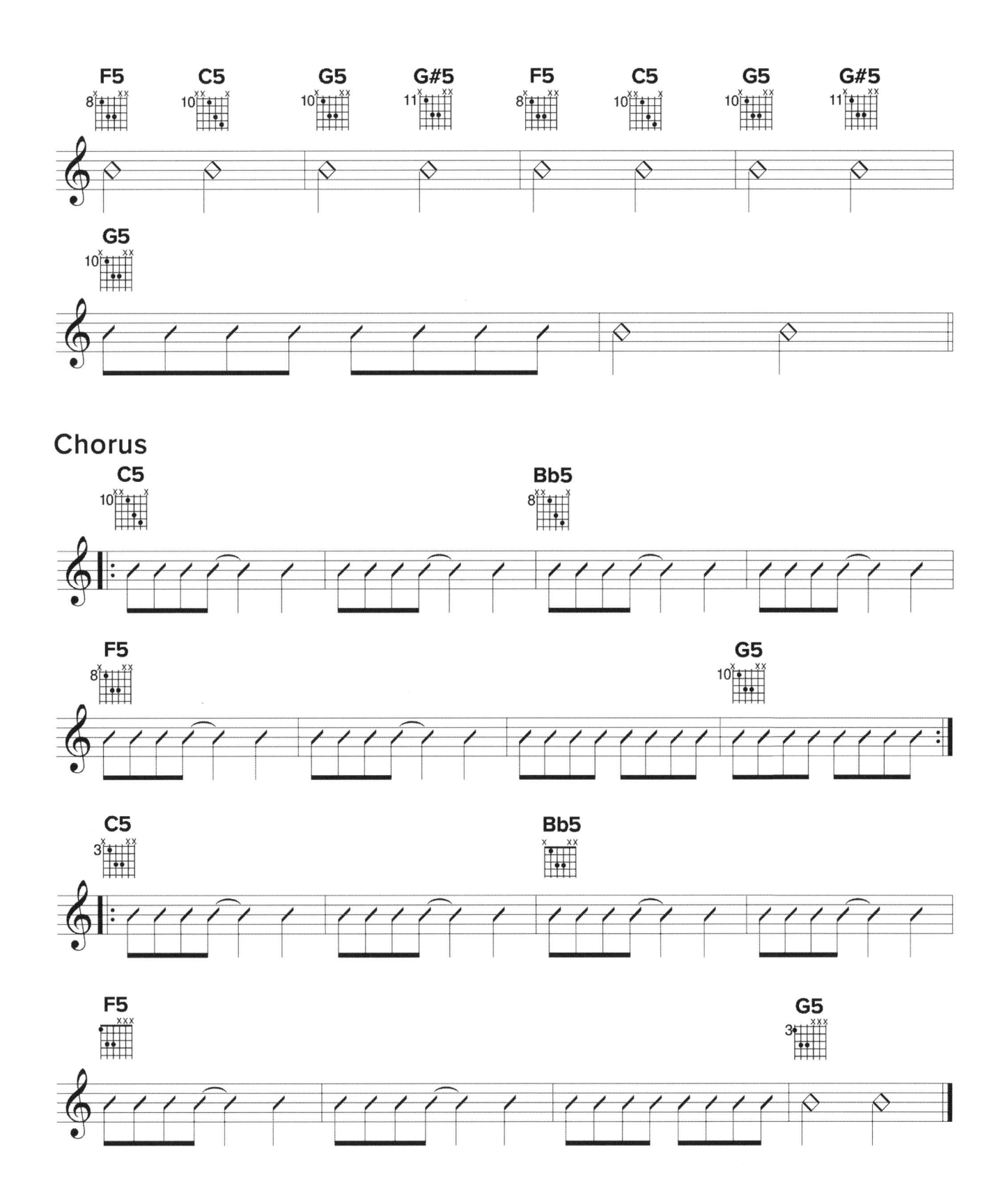

Chorus

Rule the Rulers

Verse

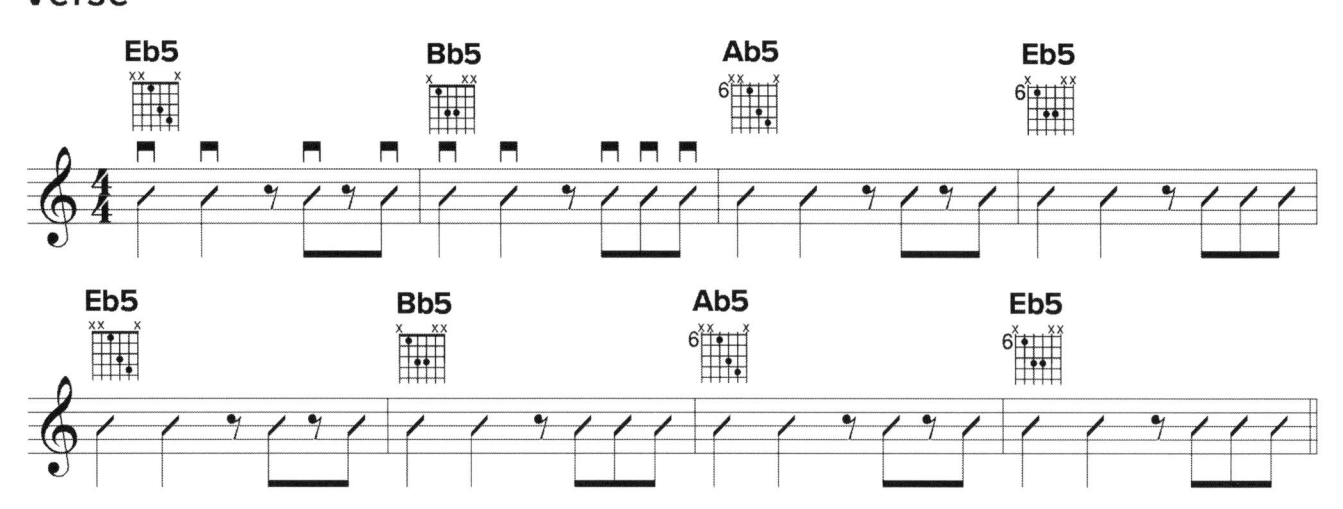

Chorus

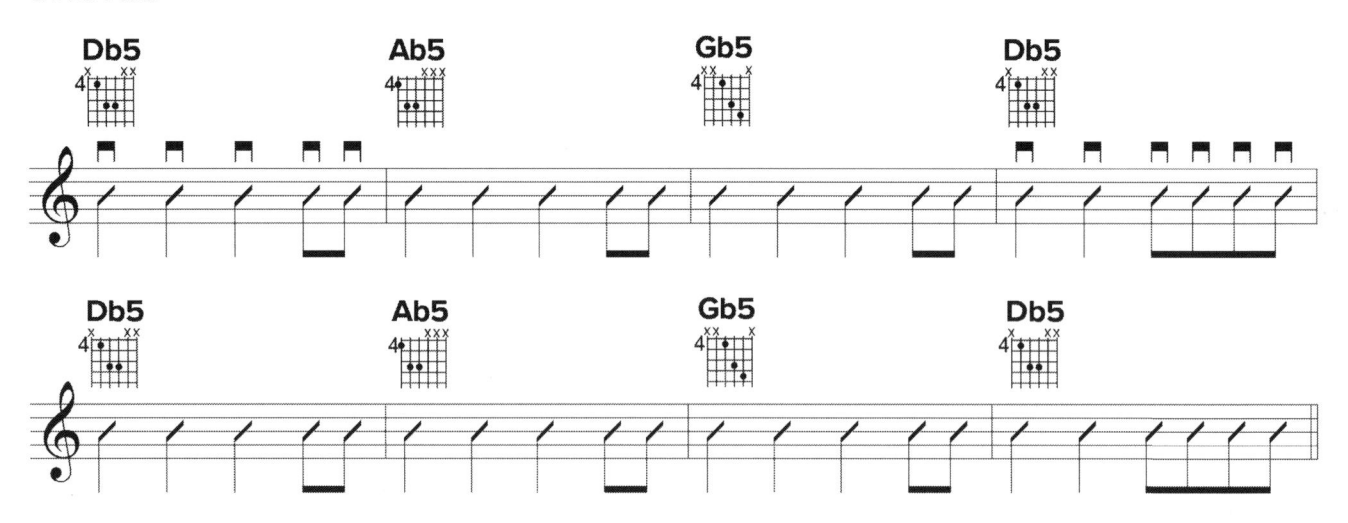

Verse

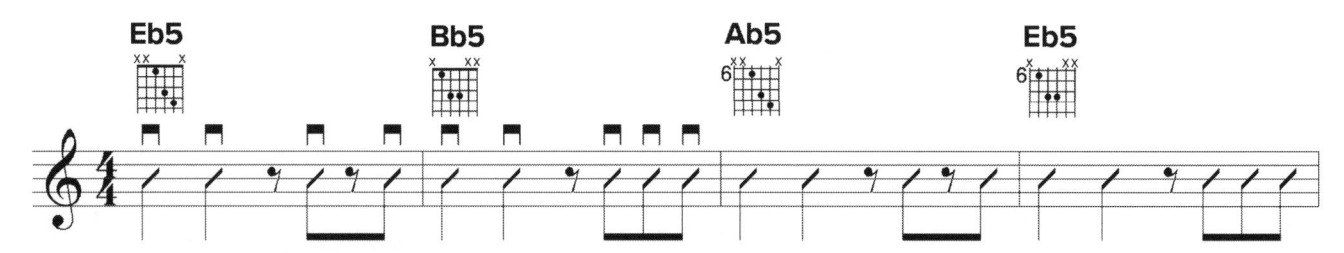

Chorus

Bridge

Verse

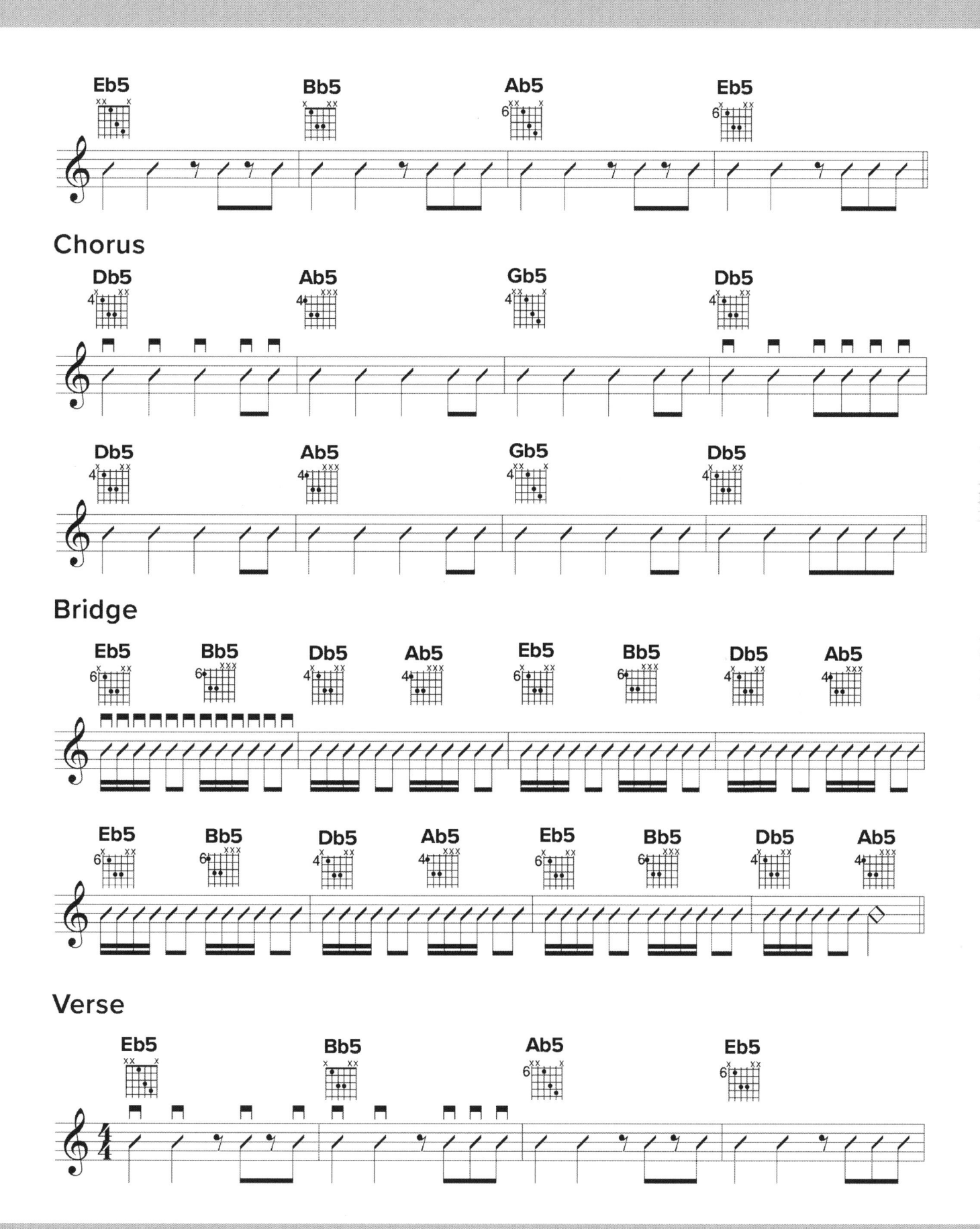

Chorus

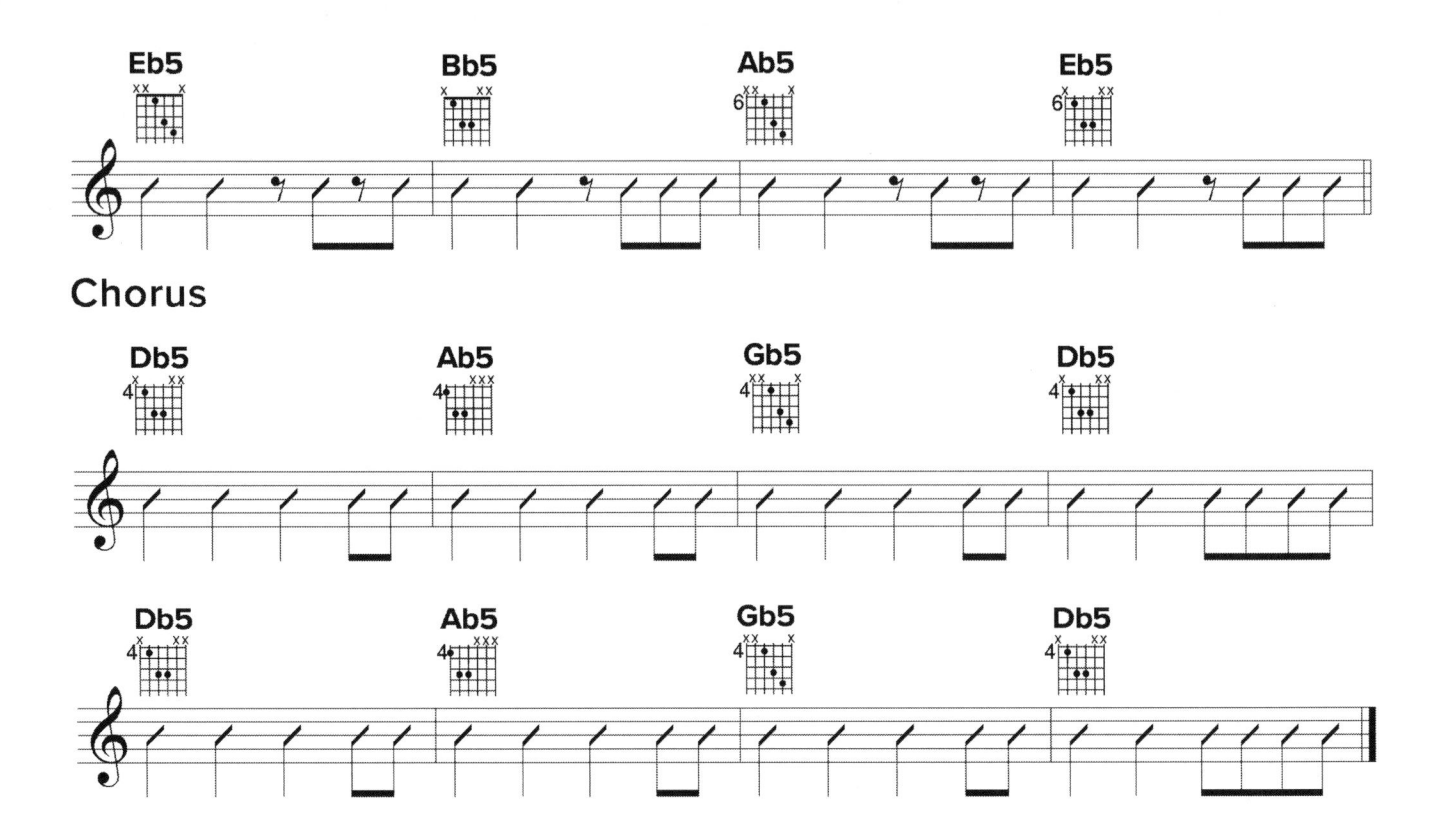

Lesson 8:
Inverted Power Chords

Now that we've learned the most commonly used versions of the power chords, we are going to take a look at a less common version called the inverted power chord. The inverted power chord contains the same notes as the regular power chords, but they are played with the 5th as the lowest note rather than the root. As such, these power chords are sometimes noted as slash chords.

A slash chord is a chord whose lowest note is no longer the root of the chord, such as C/G. In this example, you would play a regular C major chord, but the lowest note would now be the note G, found on the sixth string, third fret.

This idea can be applied to power chords as well. So if you have a power chord labeled C5/G, this means that the chord is C5, but the lowest note is now G.

Since the chords are now inverted, the roots for these chords will fall on strings 5, 4, and 3, instead of 6, 5, and 4.

See the charts below.

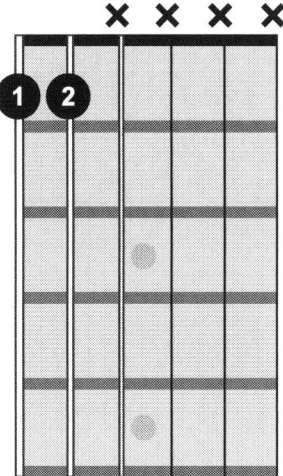

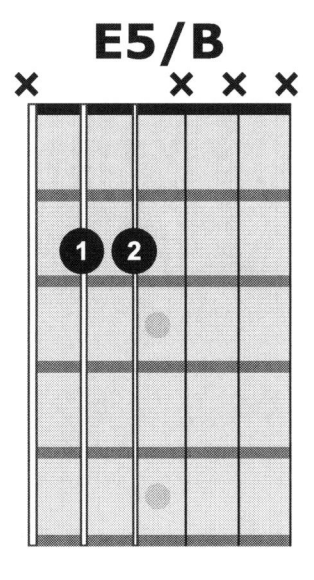

Root 5	Root 4	Root 3
Bb5/F	**E5/B**	**A5/E**

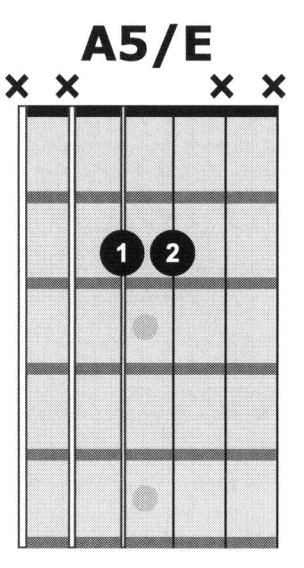

Practicing Root 5 Inverted Power Chords

In the following exercises, practice the inverted power chords with their roots on the 5th string.

Exercise 1

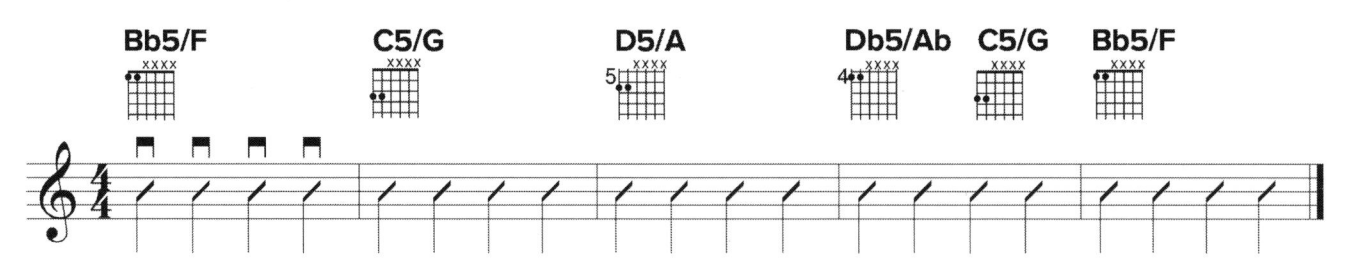

Bb5/F   **C5/G**   **D5/A**   **Db5/Ab**   **C5/G**   **Bb5/F**

Exercise 2

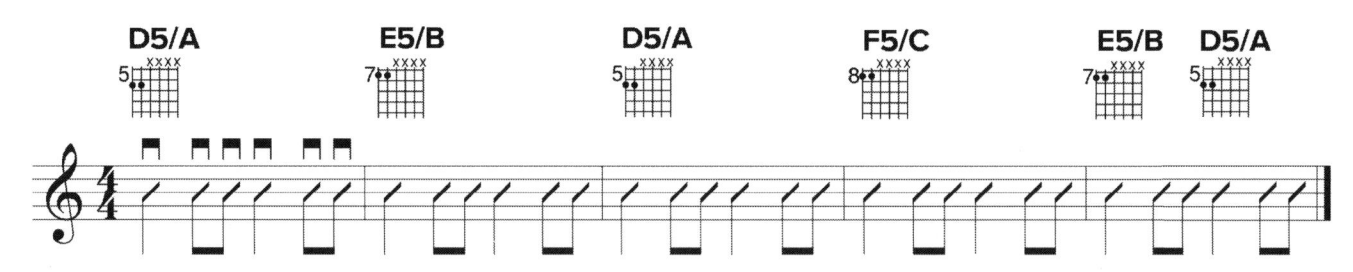

D5/A   **E5/B**   **D5/A**   **F5/C**   **E5/B**   **D5/A**

Exercise 3

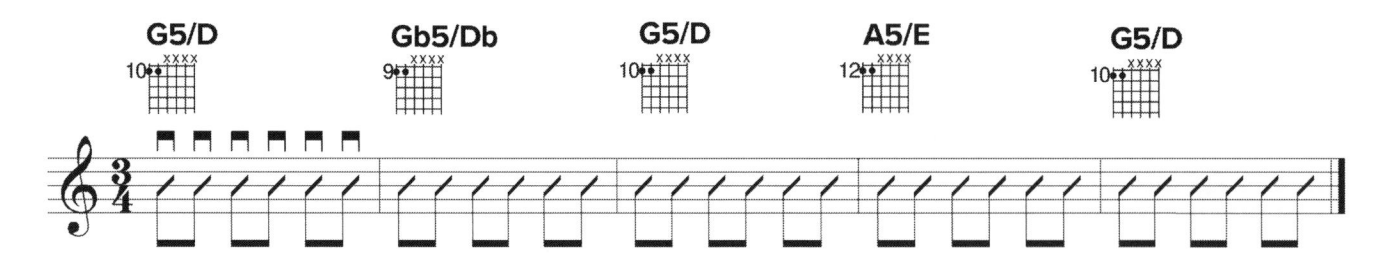

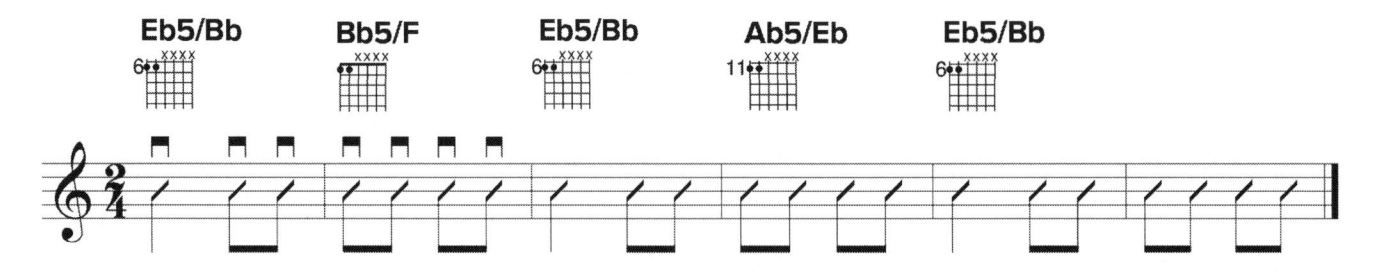

G5/D   **Gb5/Db**   **G5/D**   **A5/E**   **G5/D**

Exercise 4

Eb5/Bb   **Bb5/F**   **Eb5/Bb**   **Ab5/Eb**   **Eb5/Bb**

Exercise 5

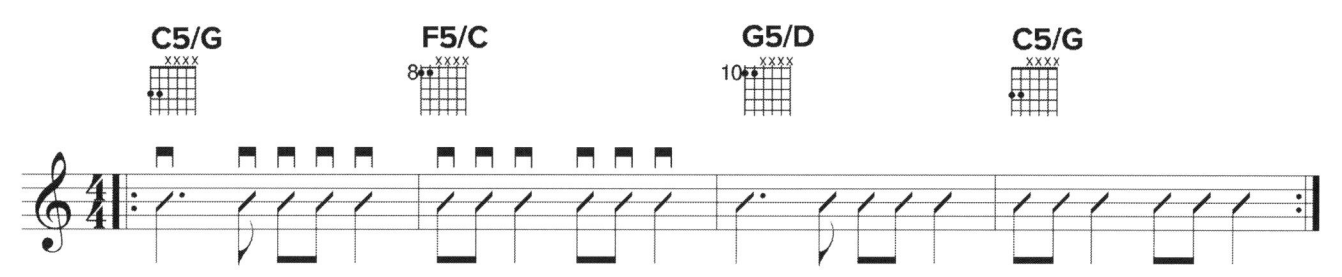

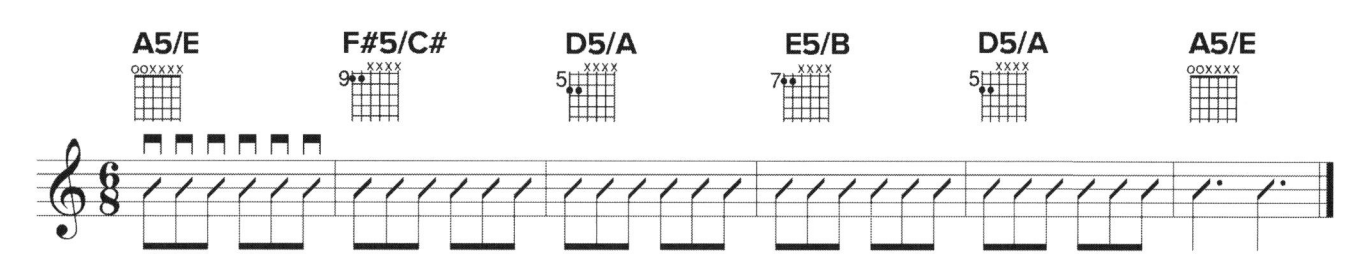

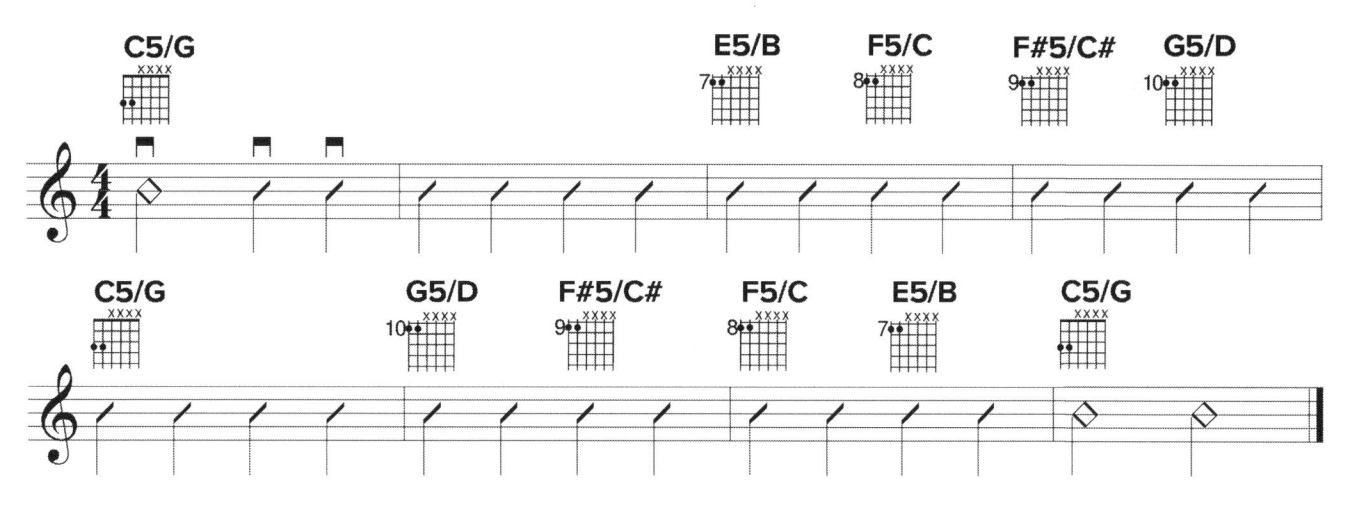

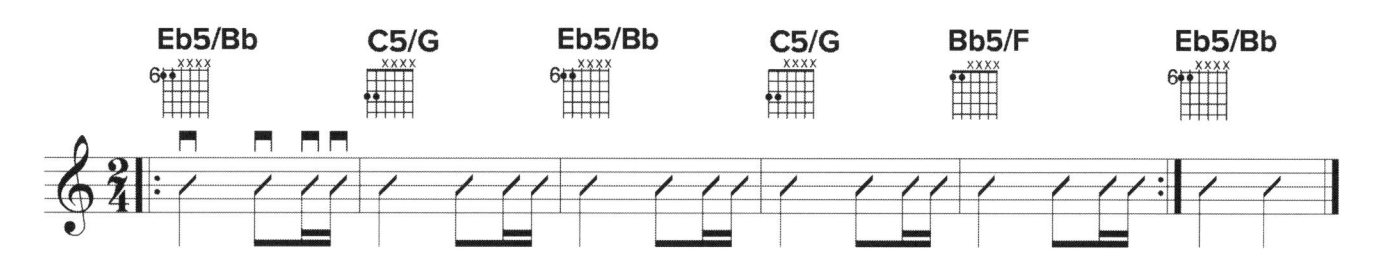

Exercise 9

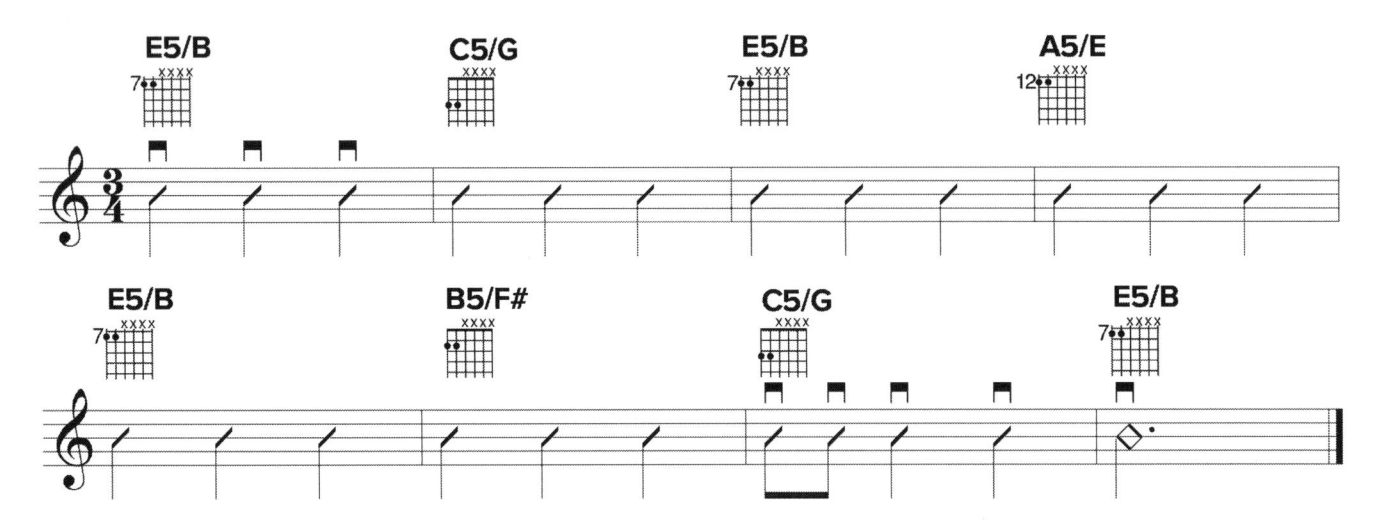

Exercise 10

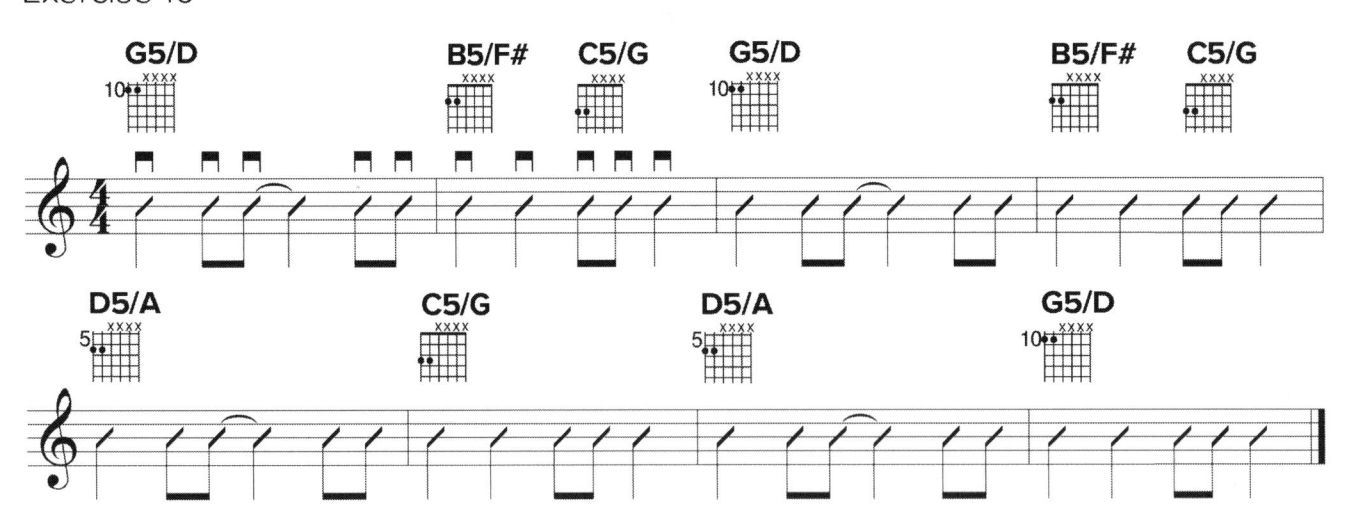

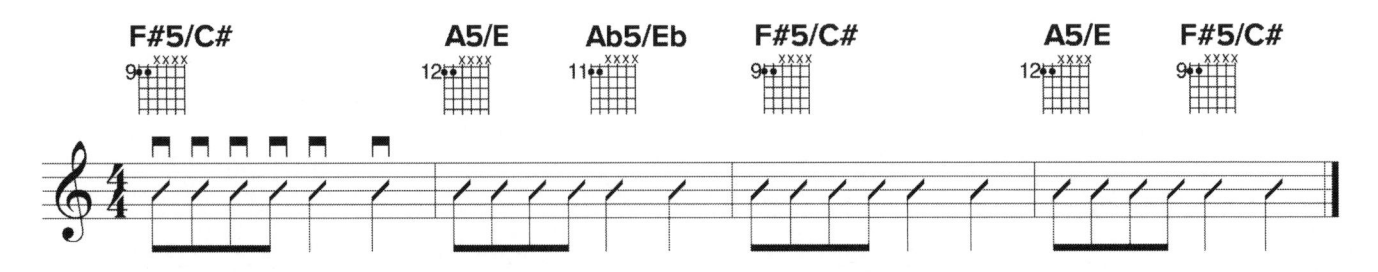

Exercise 11

The chord boxes have been omitted in the following exercises to test your memory.

Exercise 12

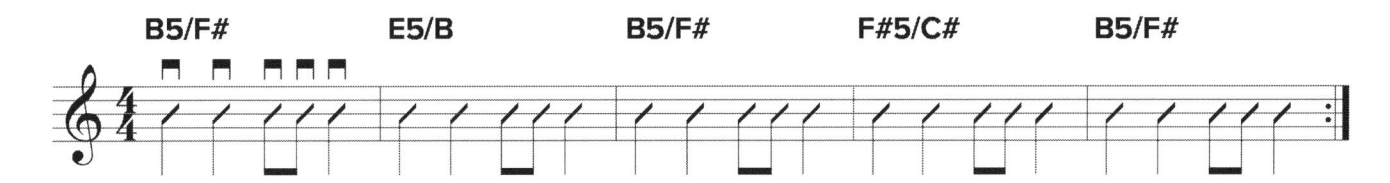

| B5/F# | E5/B | B5/F# | F#5/C# | B5/F# |

Exercise 13

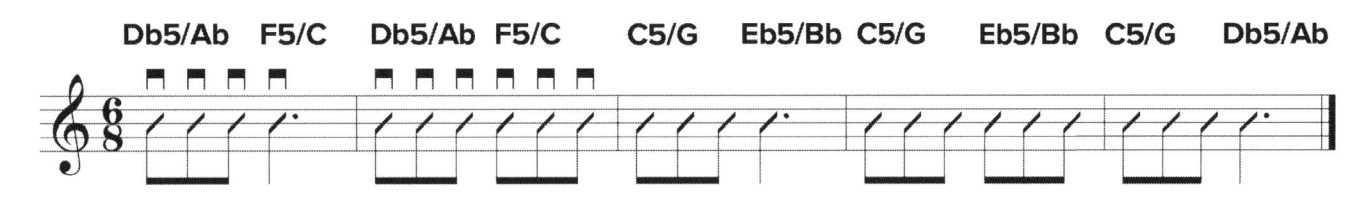

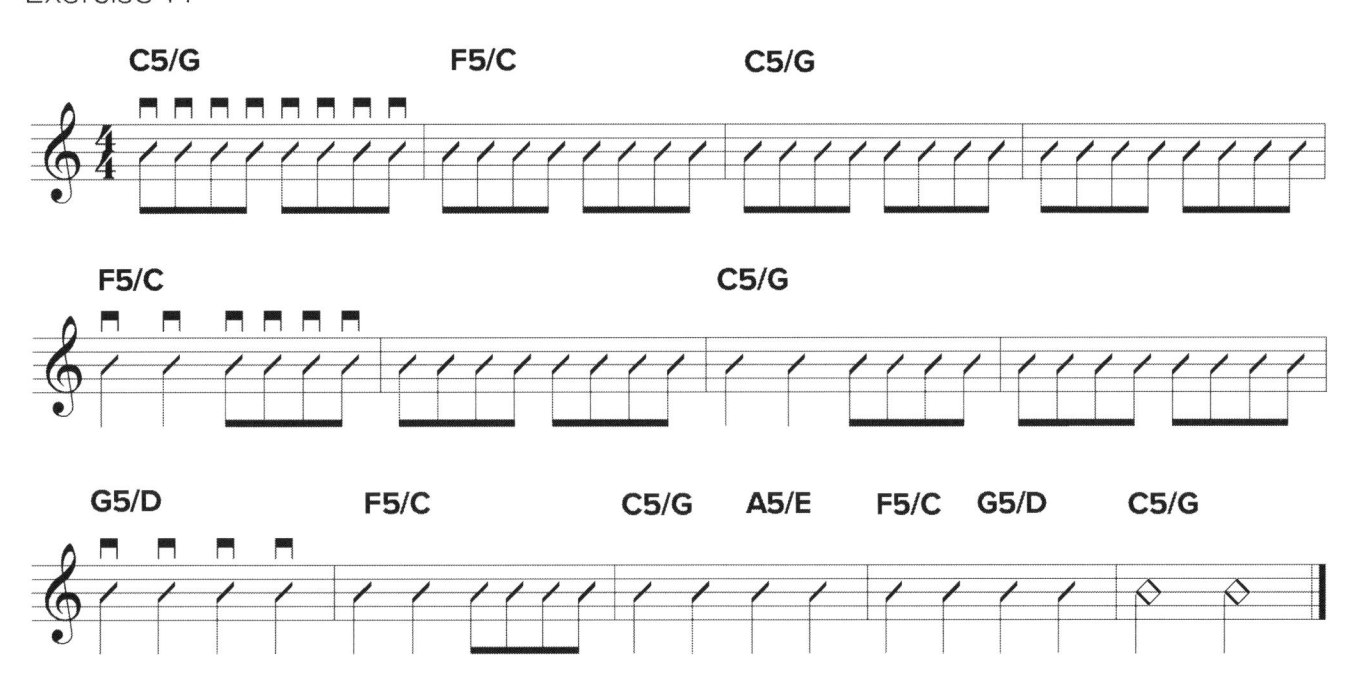

| Db5/Ab F5/C | Db5/Ab F5/C | C5/G Eb5/Bb C5/G | Eb5/Bb C5/G | Db5/Ab |

Exercise 14

| C5/G | F5/C | C5/G | |

| F5/C | | C5/G | |

| G5/D | F5/C | C5/G A5/E | F5/C G5/D | C5/G |

Practicing Root 4 Inverted Power Chords

In the following exercises, practice the inverted power chords with their roots on the 4th string.

Exercise 1

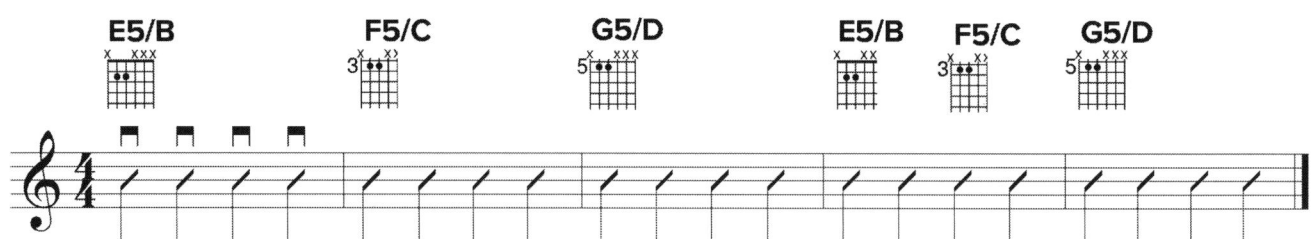

E5/B F5/C G5/D E5/B F5/C G5/D

Exercise 2

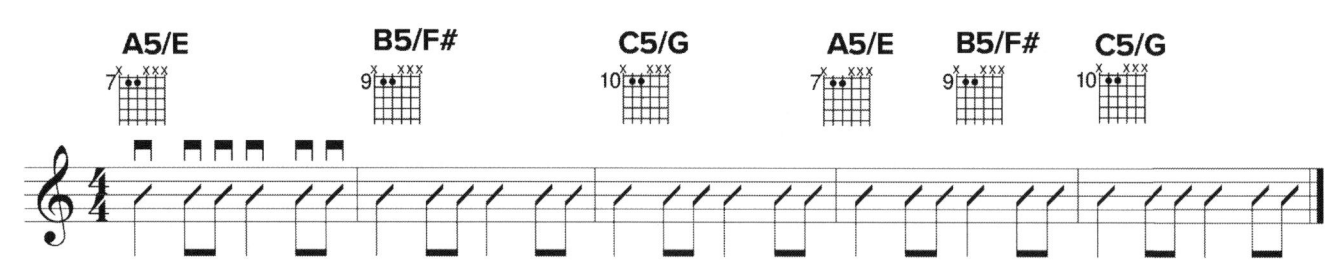

A5/E B5/F# C5/G A5/E B5/F# C5/G

Exercise 3

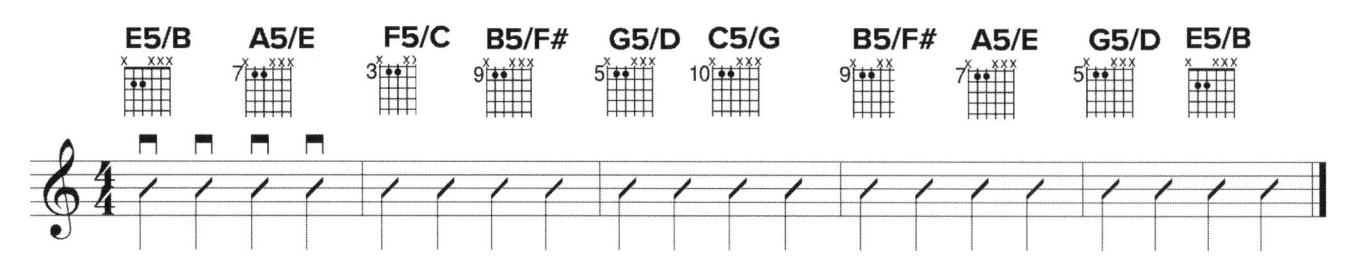

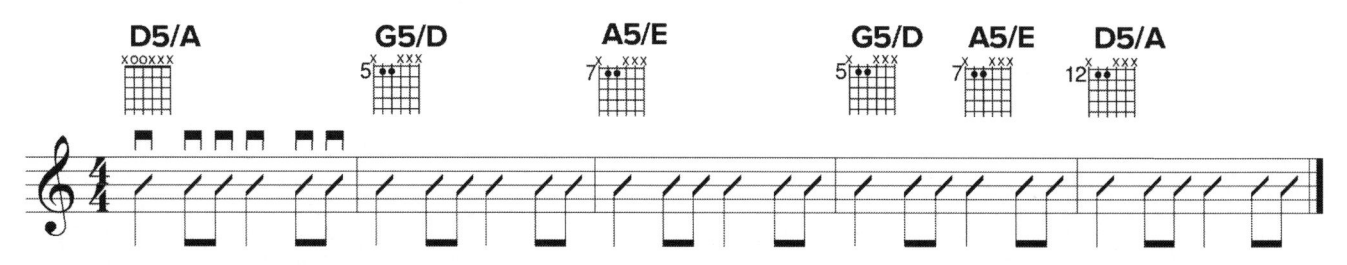

E5/B A5/E F5/C B5/F# G5/D C5/G B5/F# A5/E G5/D E5/B

Exercise 4

D5/A G5/D A5/E G5/D A5/E D5/A

Exercise 5

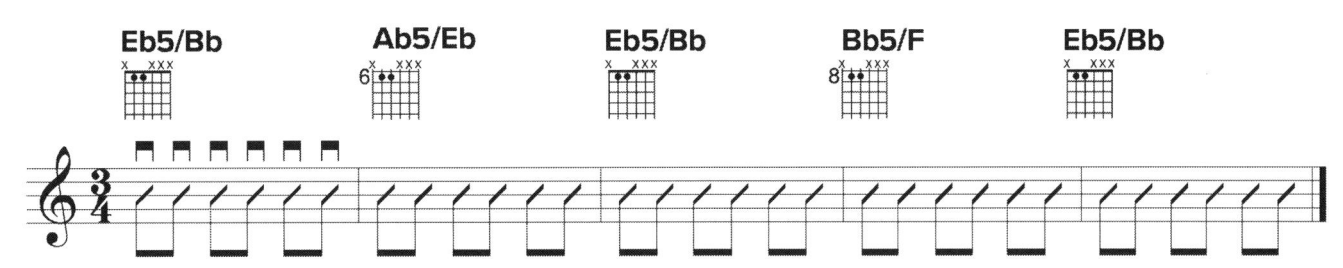

Eb5/Bb Ab5/Eb Eb5/Bb Bb5/F Eb5/Bb

Exercise 6

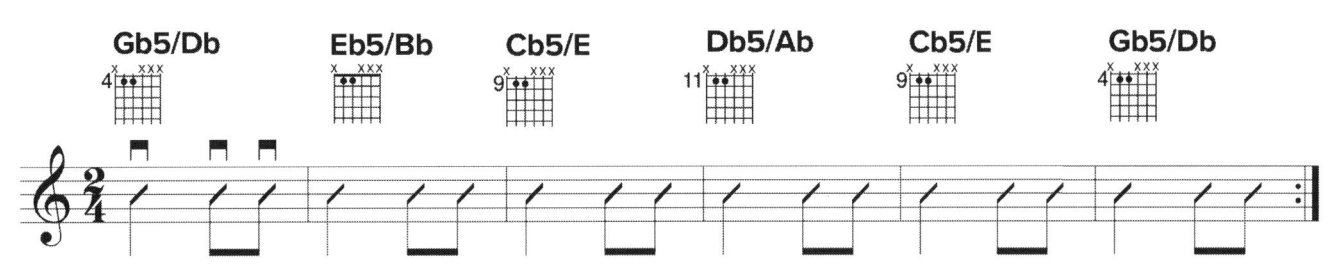

Gb5/Db Eb5/Bb Cb5/E Db5/Ab Cb5/E Gb5/Db

Exercise 7

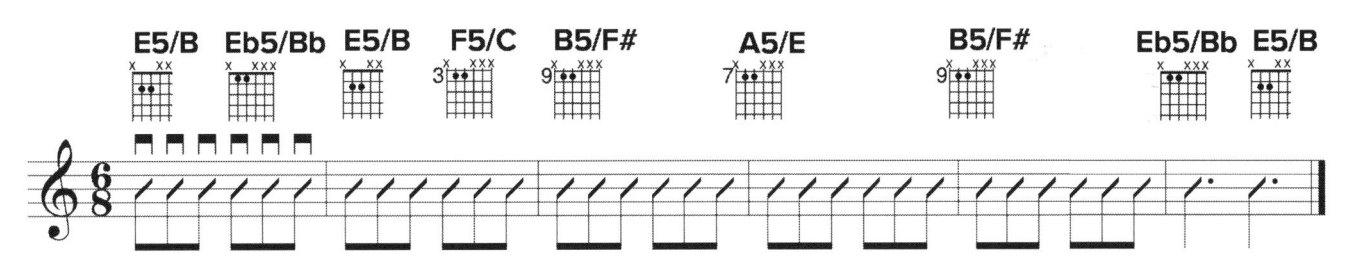

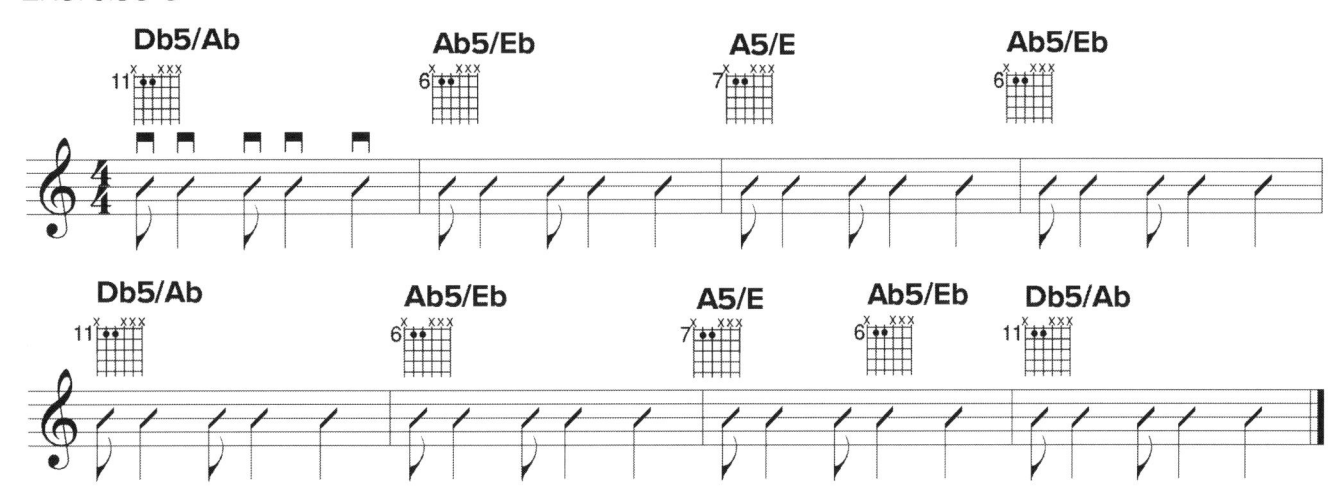

E5/B Eb5/Bb E5/B F5/C B5/F# A5/E B5/F# Eb5/Bb E5/B

Exercise 8

Db5/Ab Ab5/Eb A5/E Ab5/Eb

Db5/Ab Ab5/Eb A5/E Ab5/Eb Db5/Ab

The chord boxes have been omitted in the following exercises to test your memory.

Exercise 8

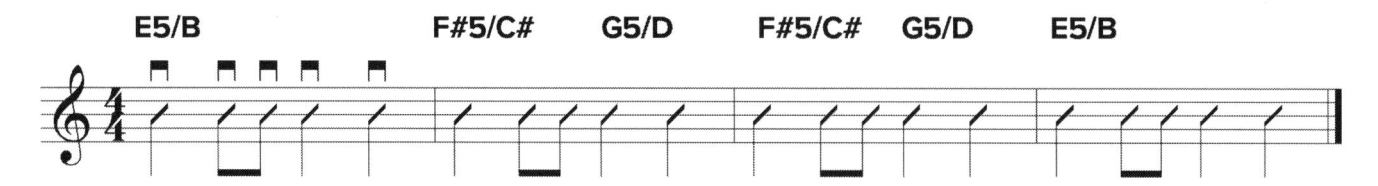

| E5/B | | F#5/C# | G5/D | F#5/C# | G5/D | E5/B |

Exercise 9: It is recommended that you use the open D5/A in the following exercise.

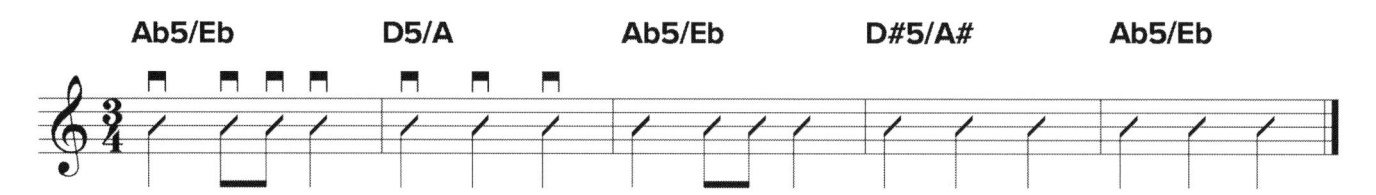

| Ab5/Eb | D5/A | Ab5/Eb | D#5/A# | Ab5/Eb |

Exercise 10

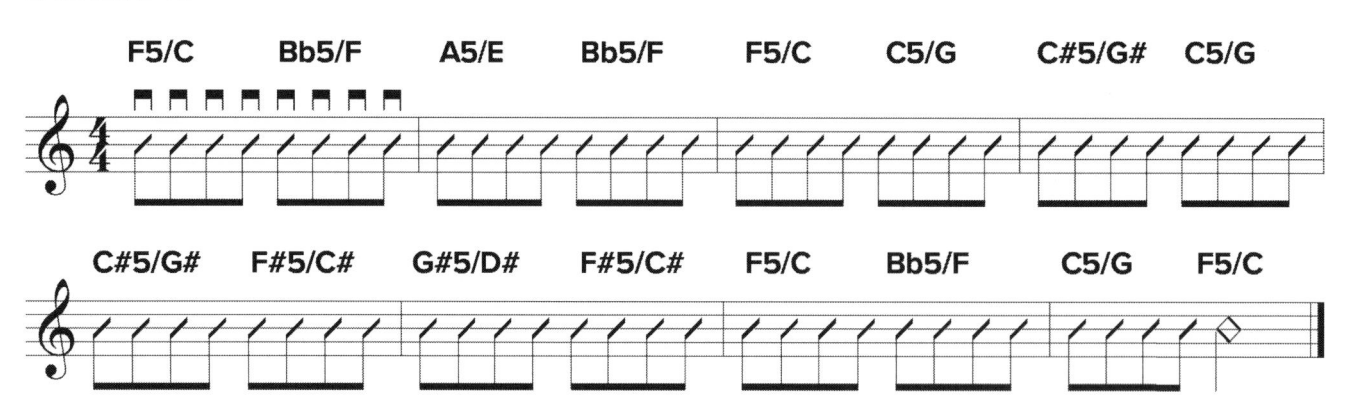

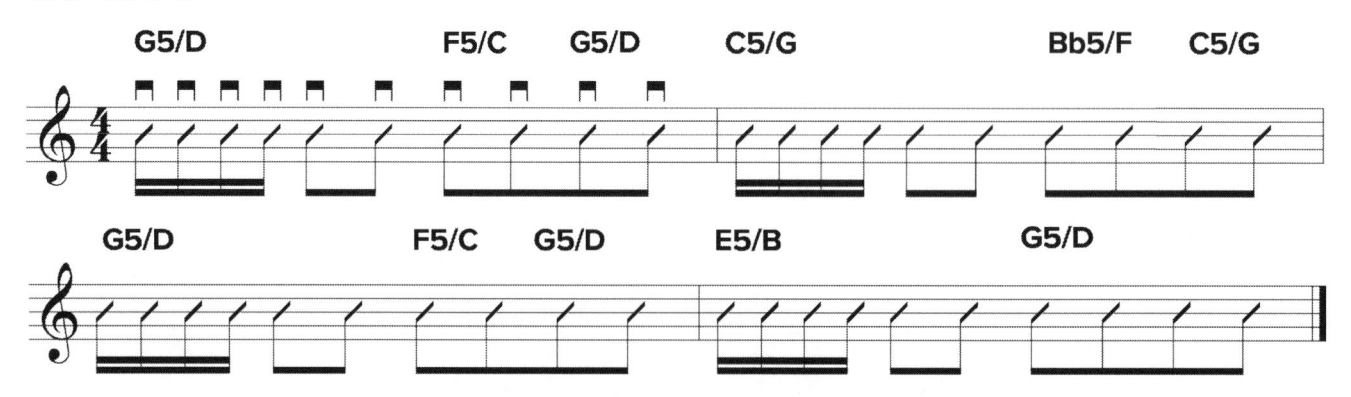

| F5/C | Bb5/F | A5/E | Bb5/F | F5/C | C5/G | C#5/G# | C5/G |

| C#5/G# | F#5/C# | G#5/D# | F#5/C# | F5/C | Bb5/F | C5/G | F5/C |

Exercise 11

| G5/D | | F5/C | G5/D | C5/G | | Bb5/F | C5/G |

| G5/D | | F5/C | G5/D | E5/B | | G5/D | |

The following exercises combine both the root 5 and root 4 inverted power chords.

Exercise 12

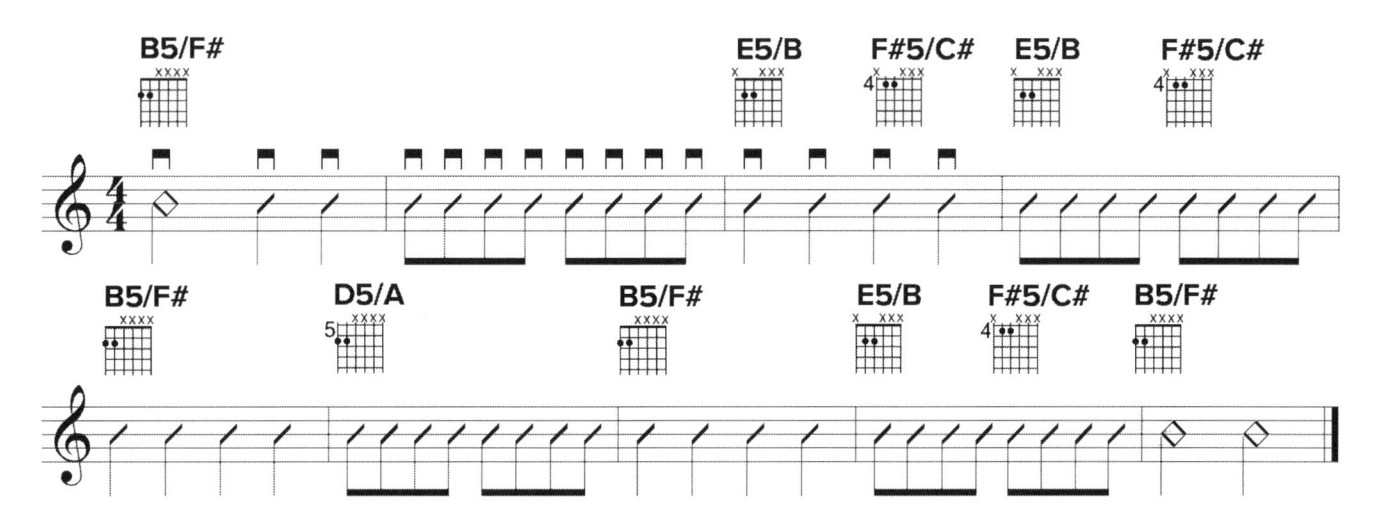

Exercise 13

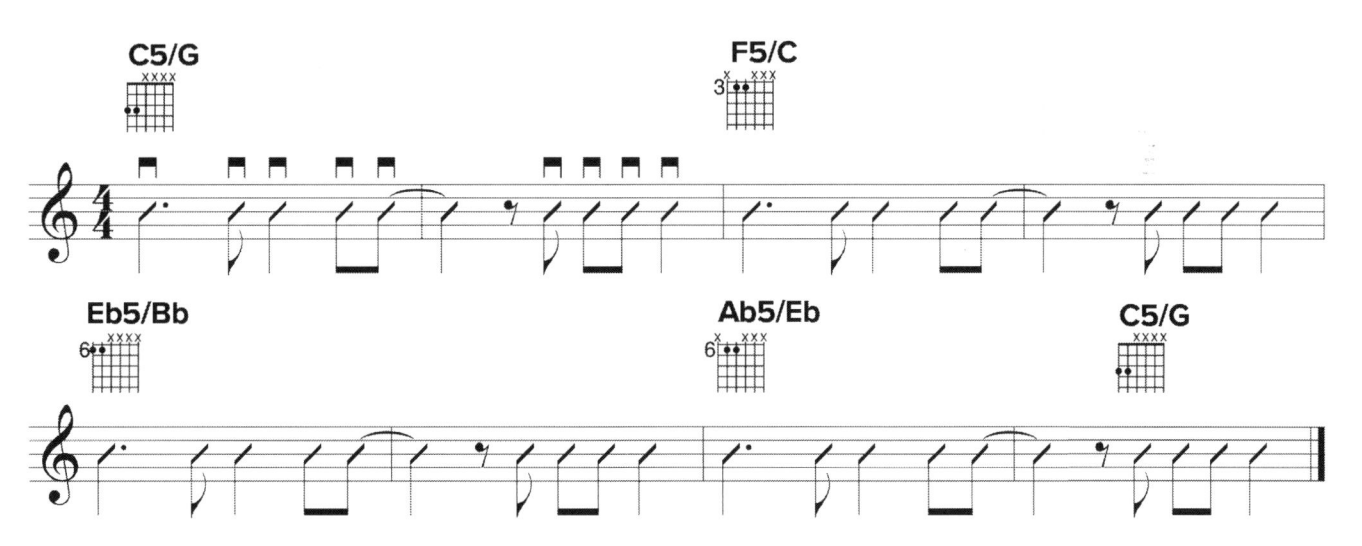

Exercise 14

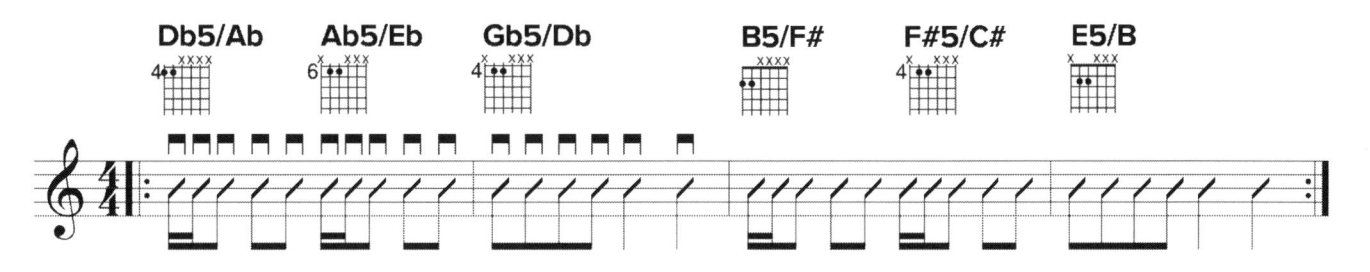

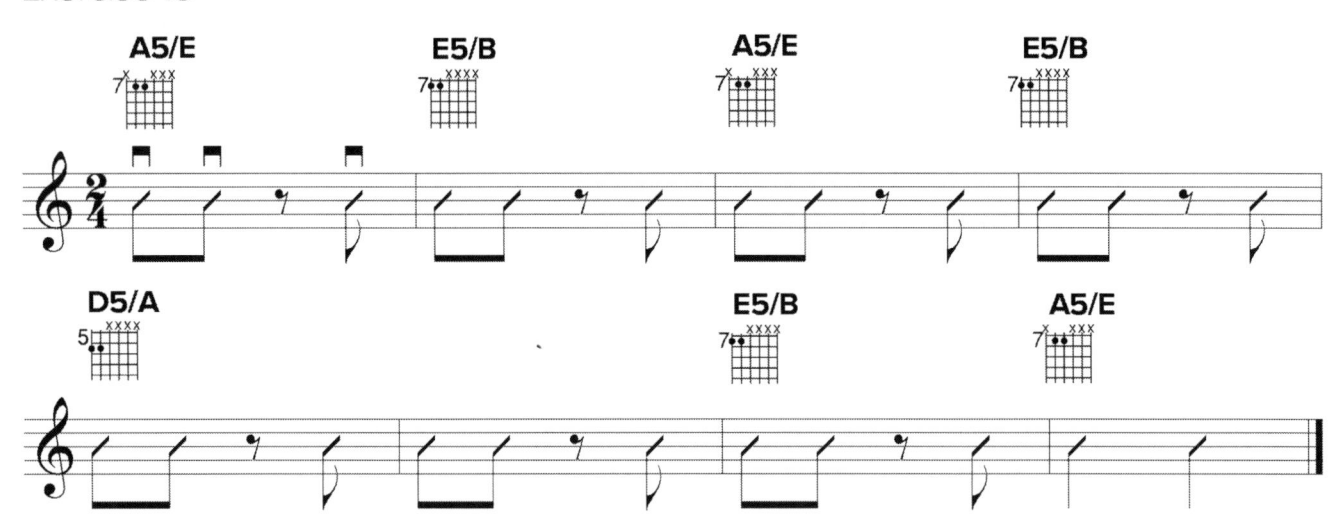

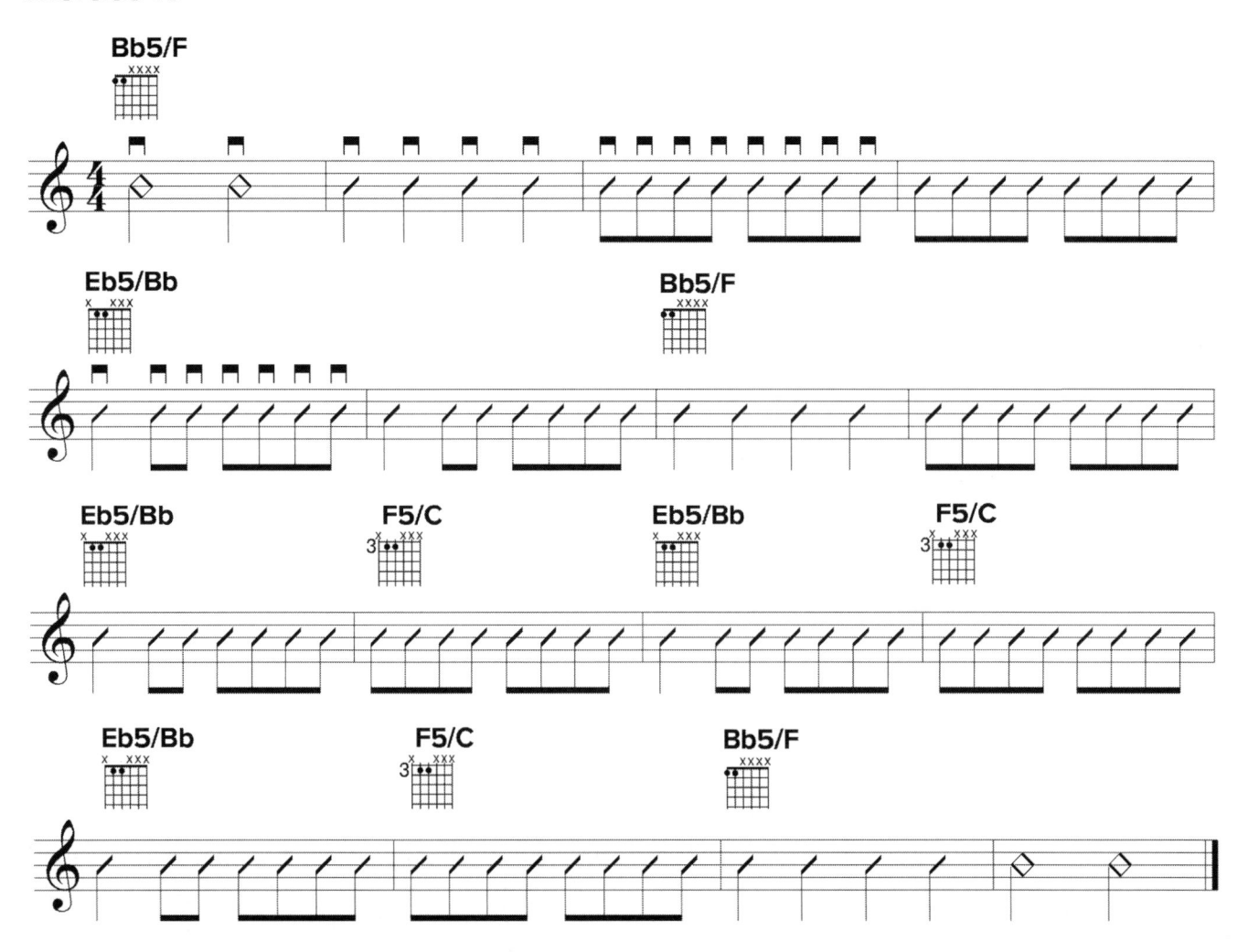

Exercise 15

Review: The following exercises combine the inverted power chords with the root position power chords learned earlier in the book.

Exercise 1

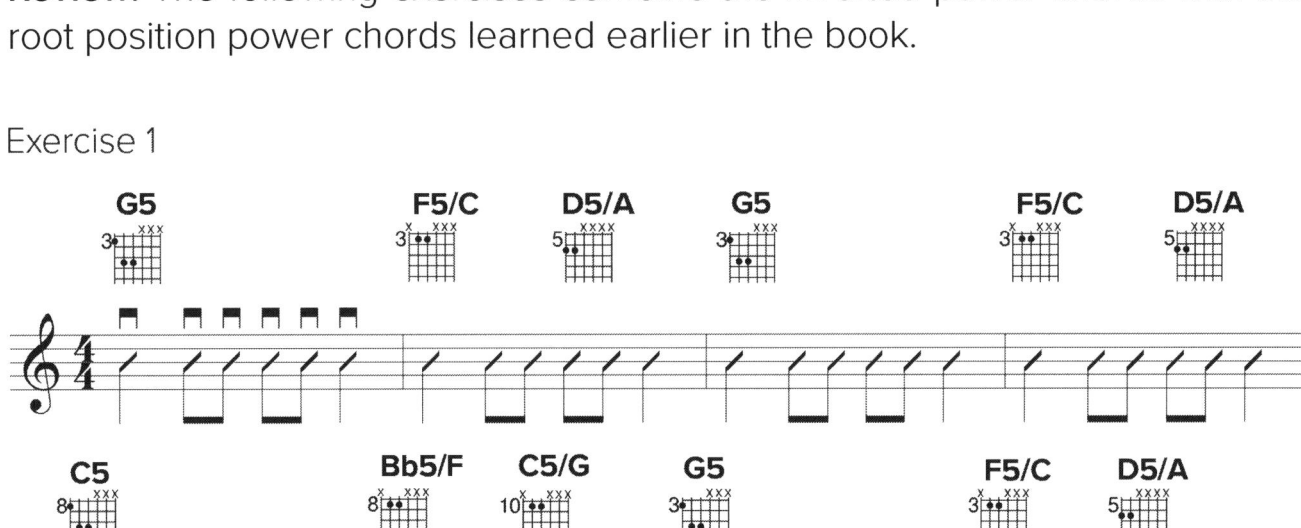

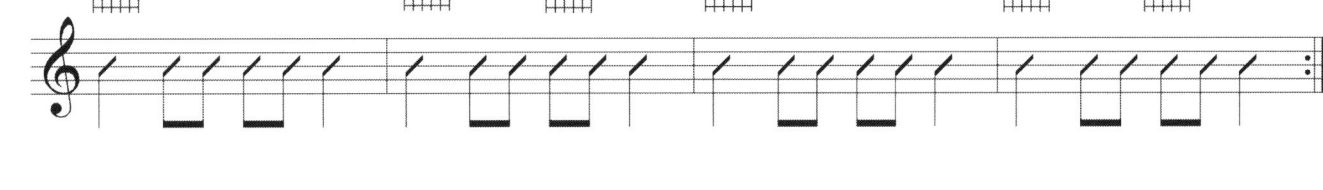

Exercise 2

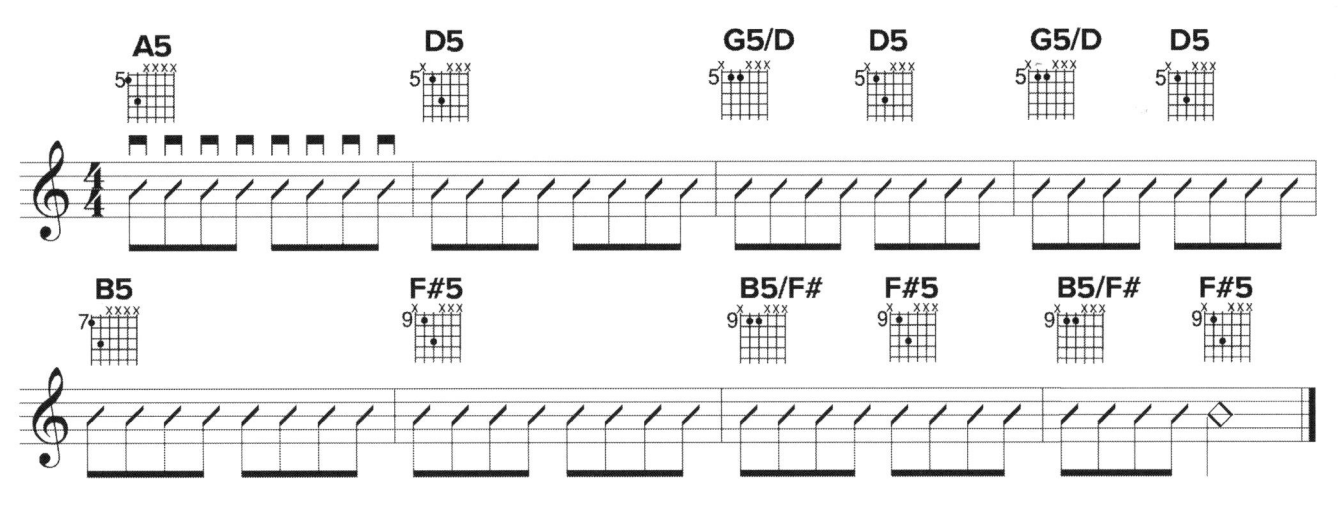

Exercise 3

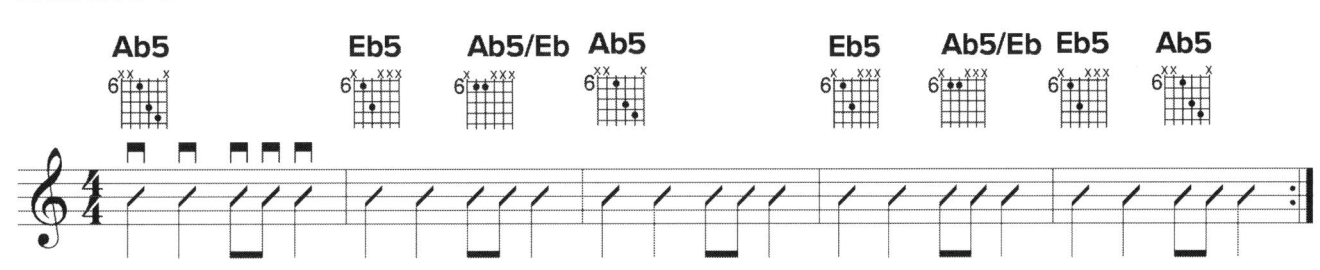

Exercise 4: Be sure to read this one carefully.

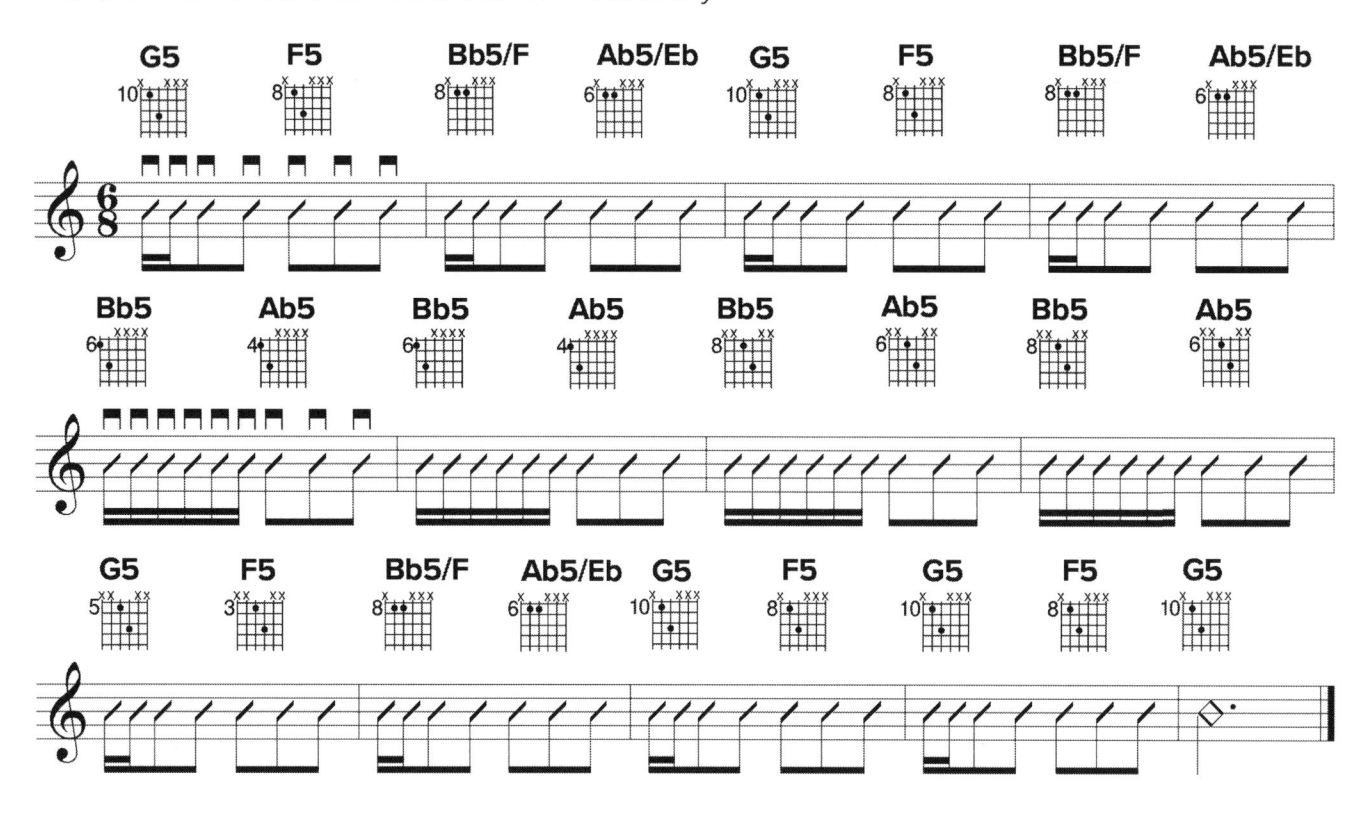

Exercise 5

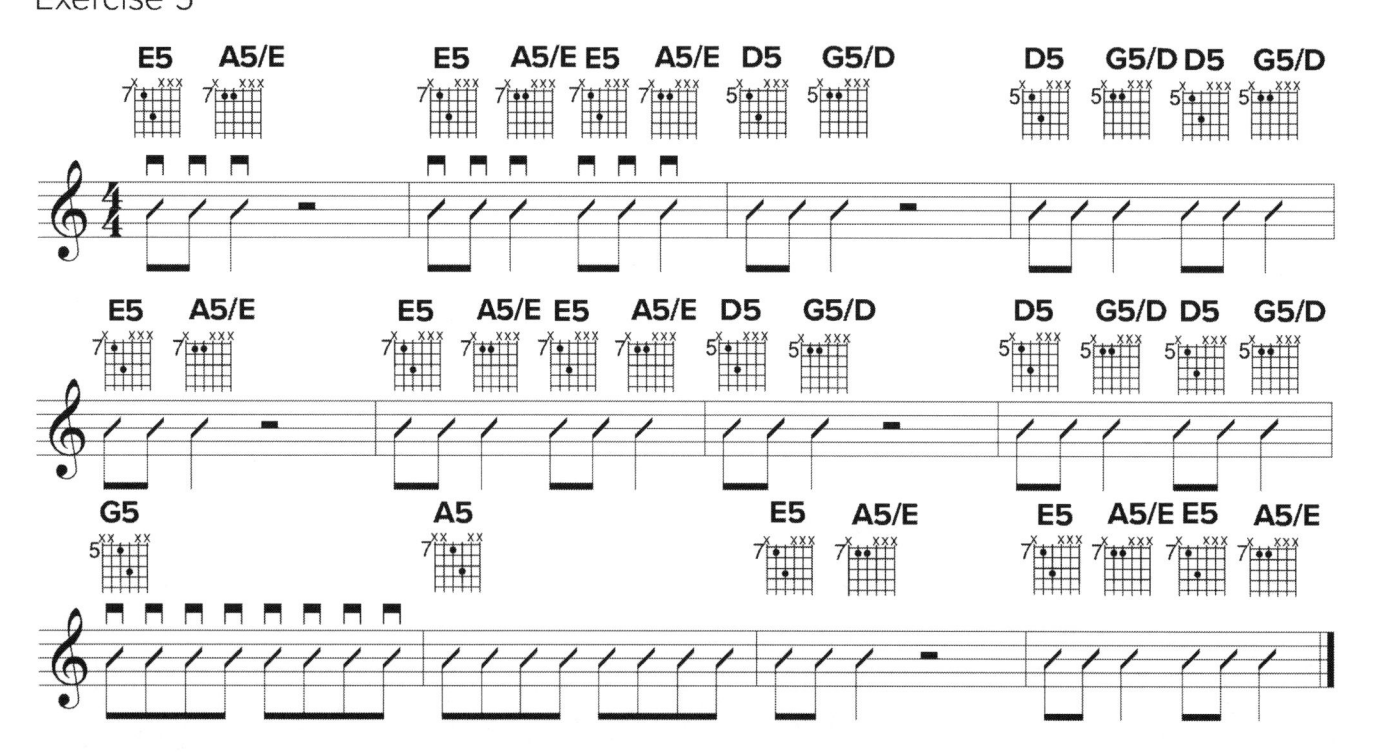

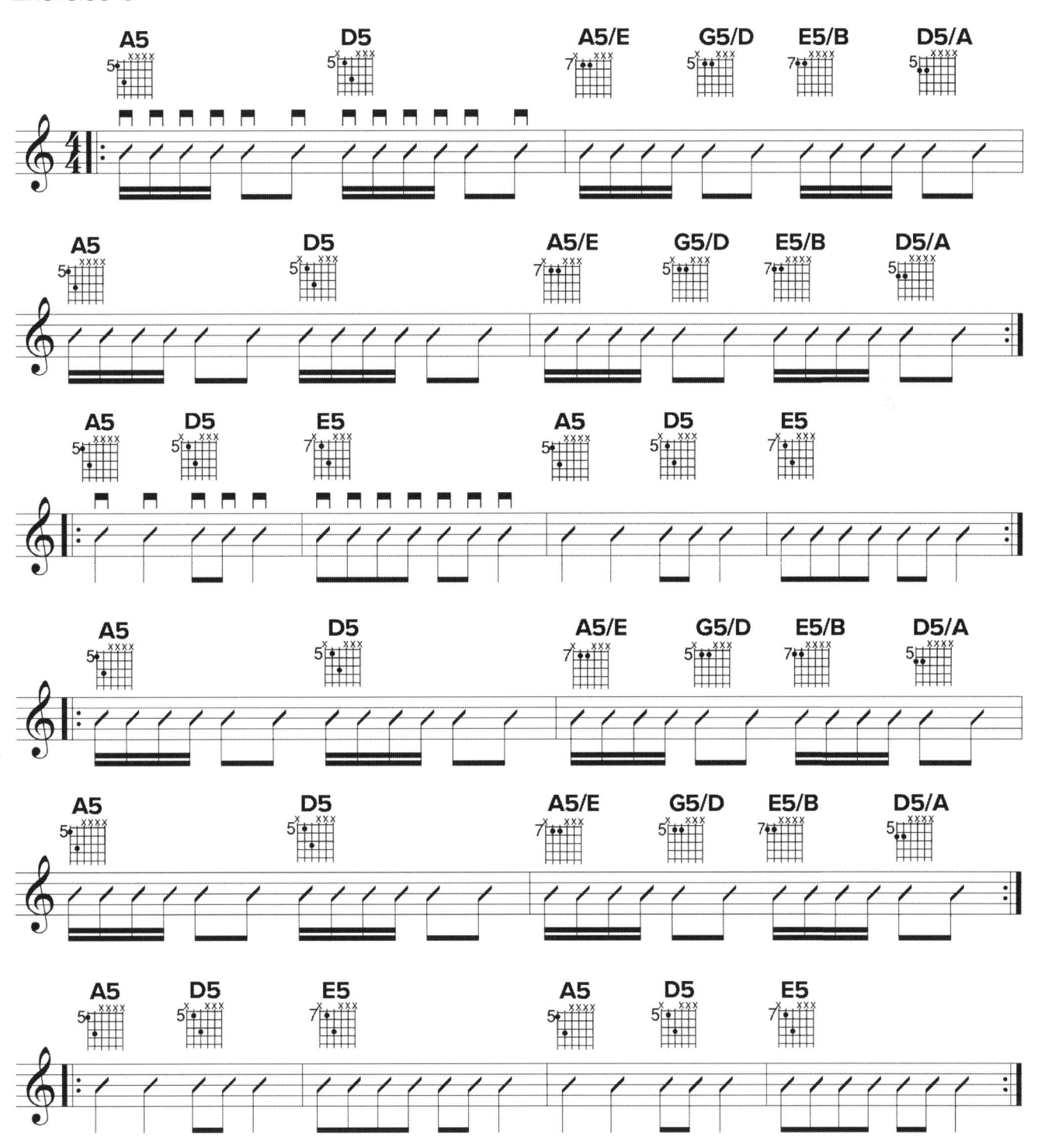

Exercise 6

Practicing Root 3 Inverted Power Chords

In this section, you will be practicing the inverted power chords with their roots on the third string.

Exercise 1

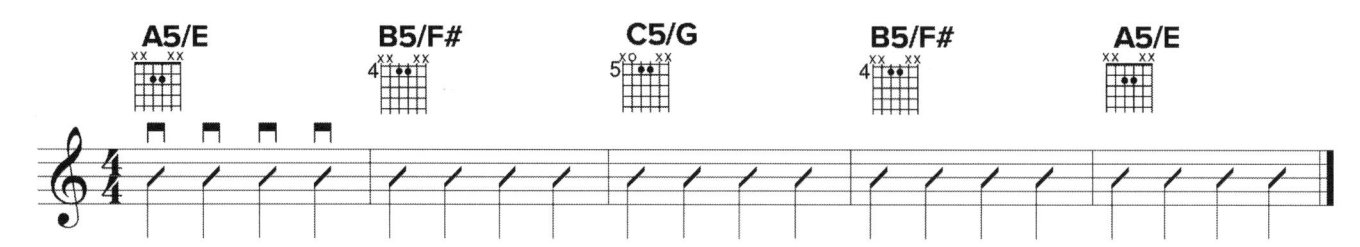

| A5/E | B5/F# | C5/G | B5/F# | A5/E |

Exercise 2

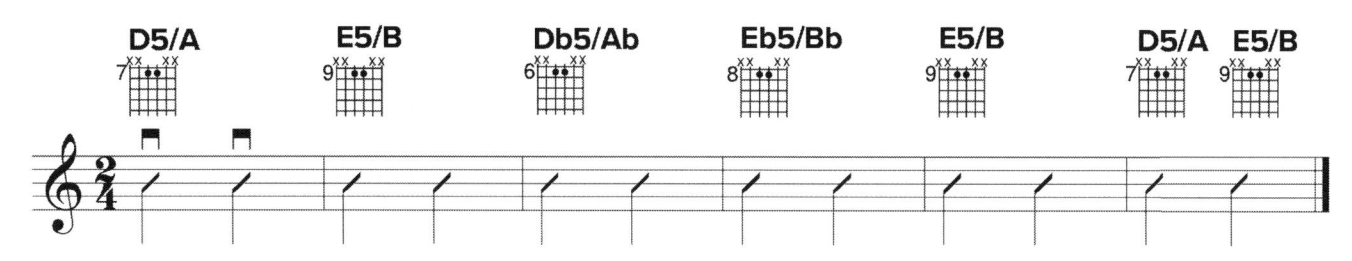

| D5/A | E5/B | Db5/Ab | Eb5/Bb | E5/B | D5/A | E5/B |

Exercise 3

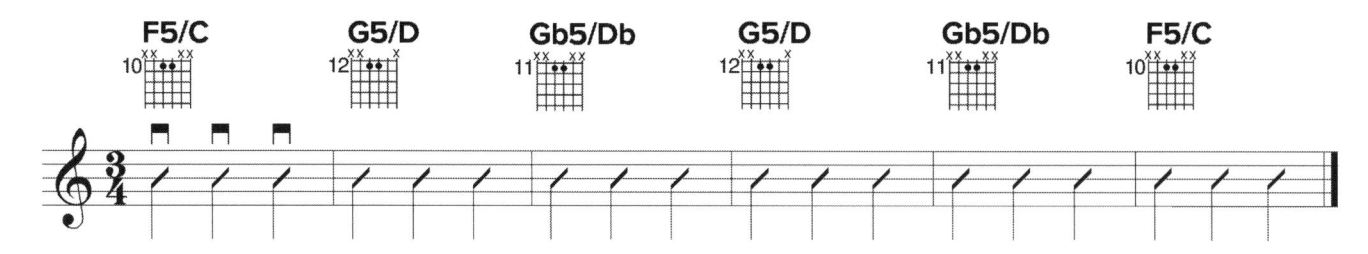

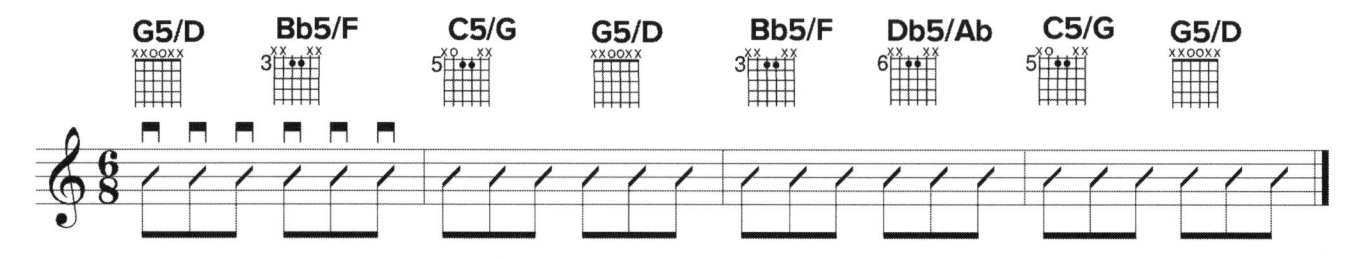

| F5/C | G5/D | Gb5/Db | G5/D | Gb5/Db | F5/C |

Exercise 4

| G5/D | Bb5/F | C5/G | G5/D | Bb5/F | Db5/Ab | C5/G | G5/D |

Exercise 5

| Bb5/F | Eb5/Bb | F5/C | Bb5/F |

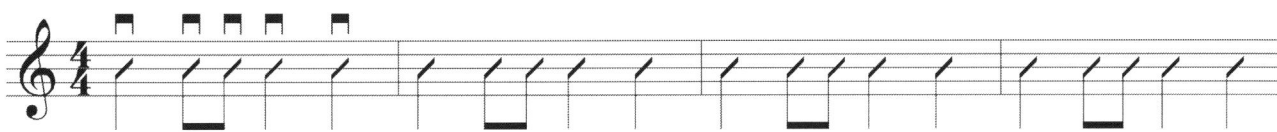

Exercise 6

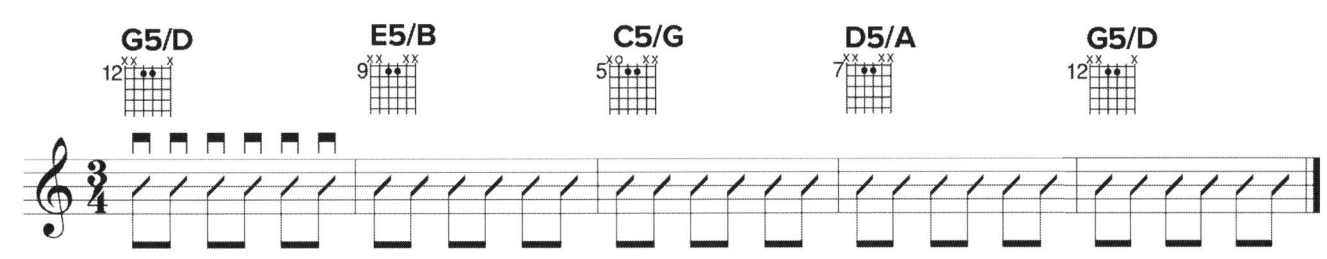

| G5/D | E5/B | C5/G | D5/A | G5/D |

Exercise 7

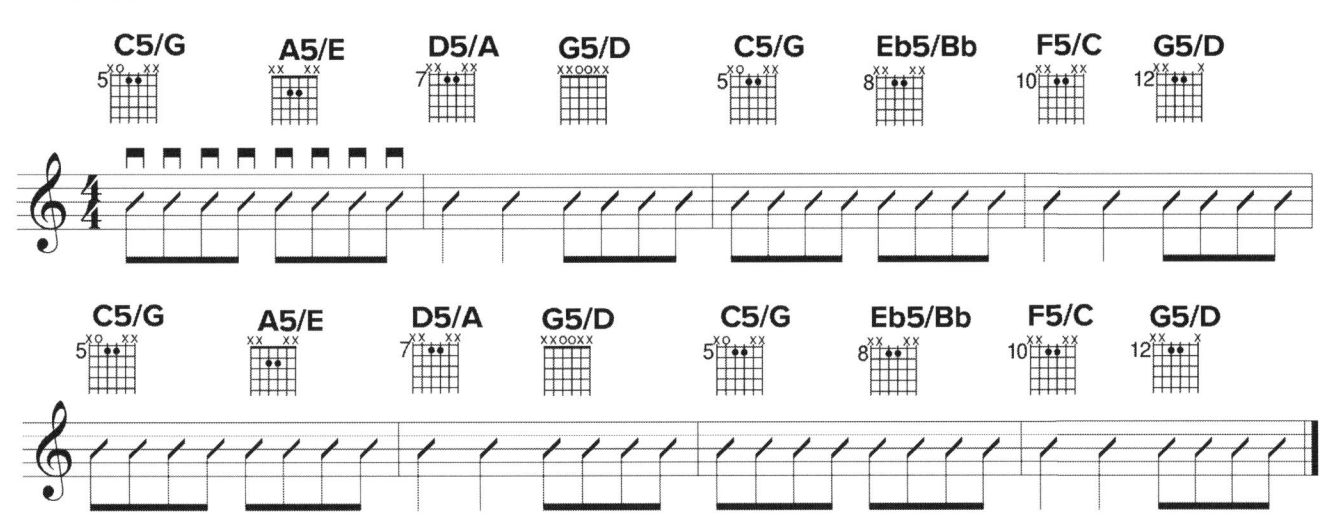

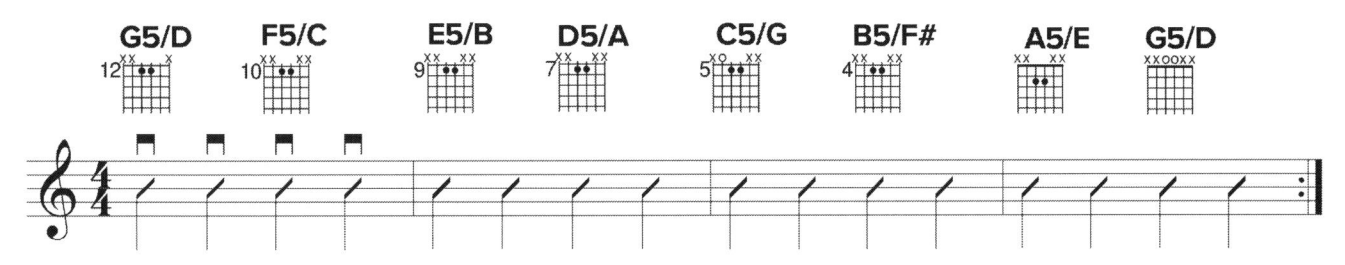

| C5/G | A5/E | D5/A | G5/D | C5/G | Eb5/Bb | F5/C | G5/D |

| C5/G | A5/E | D5/A | G5/D | C5/G | Eb5/Bb | F5/C | G5/D |

Exercise 8

| G5/D | F5/C | E5/B | D5/A | C5/G | B5/F# | A5/E | G5/D |

Exercise 9

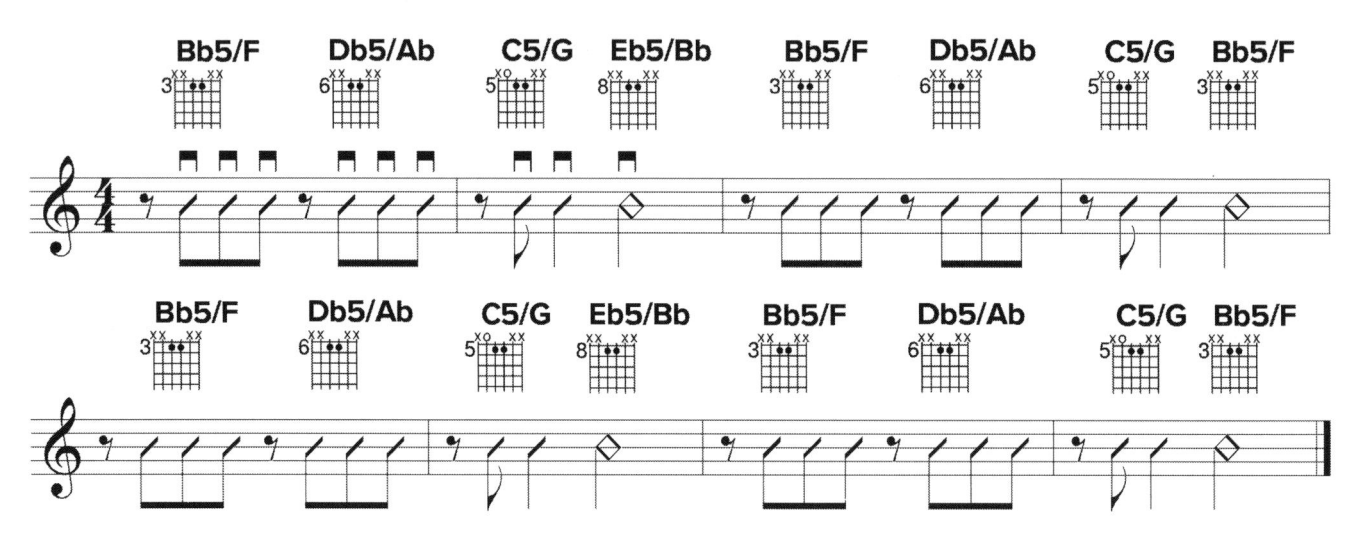

Exercise 10

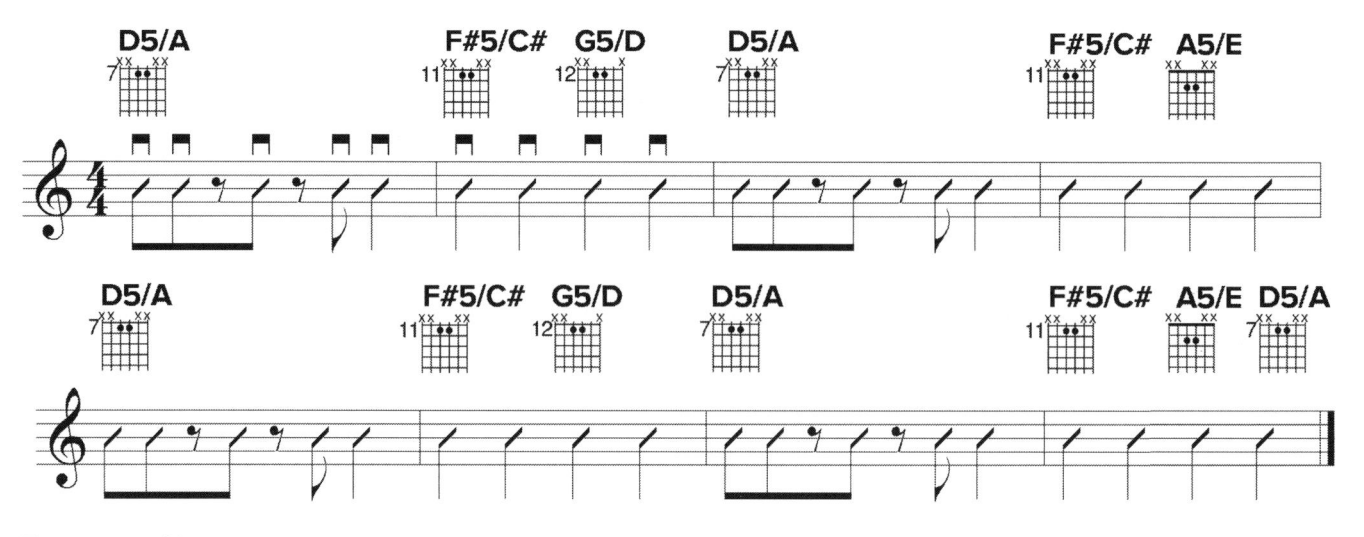

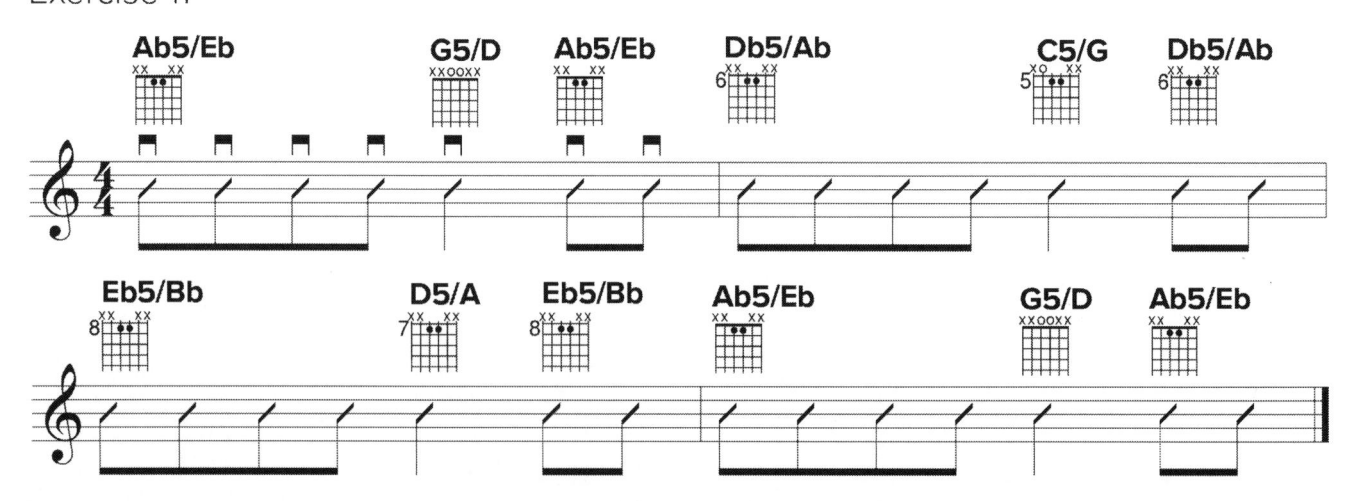

Exercise 11

The chord boxes have been omitted in the following exercises to test your memory.

Exercise 12

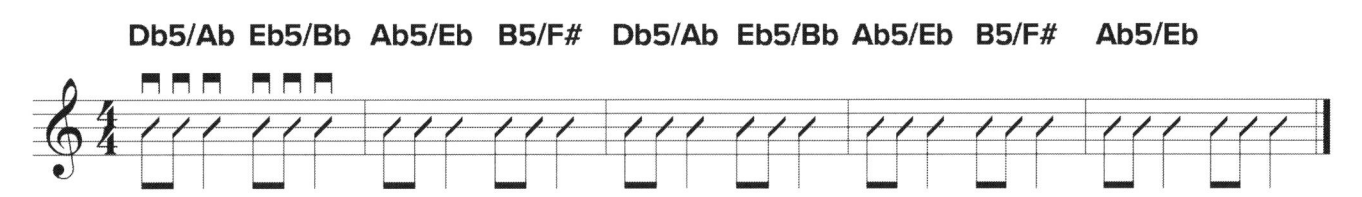

| Db5/Ab Eb5/Bb Ab5/Eb B5/F# | Db5/Ab Eb5/Bb Ab5/Eb B5/F# | Ab5/Eb |

Exercise 13: Use the open version of G5/D in the following exercise.

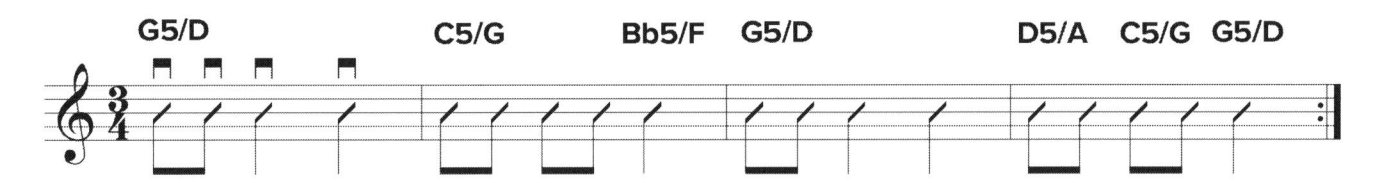

| G5/D | C5/G | Bb5/F G5/D | D5/A C5/G G5/D |

Exercise 14: Use the open version of the G5/D in this exercise too.

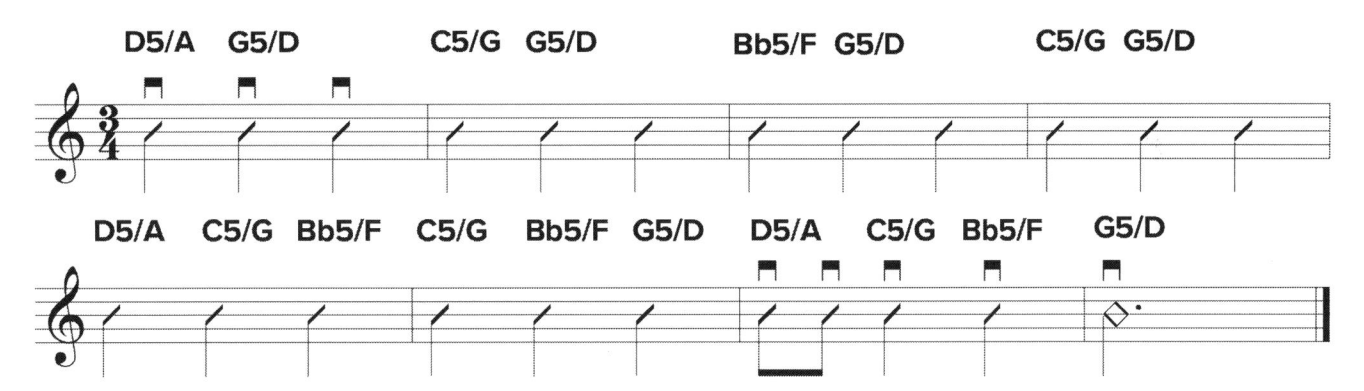

| D5/A G5/D | C5/G G5/D | Bb5/F G5/D | C5/G G5/D |
| D5/A C5/G Bb5/F | C5/G Bb5/F G5/D | D5/A C5/G Bb5/F | G5/D |

Exercise 15: And again, use the open version of the G5/D chord in this exercise.

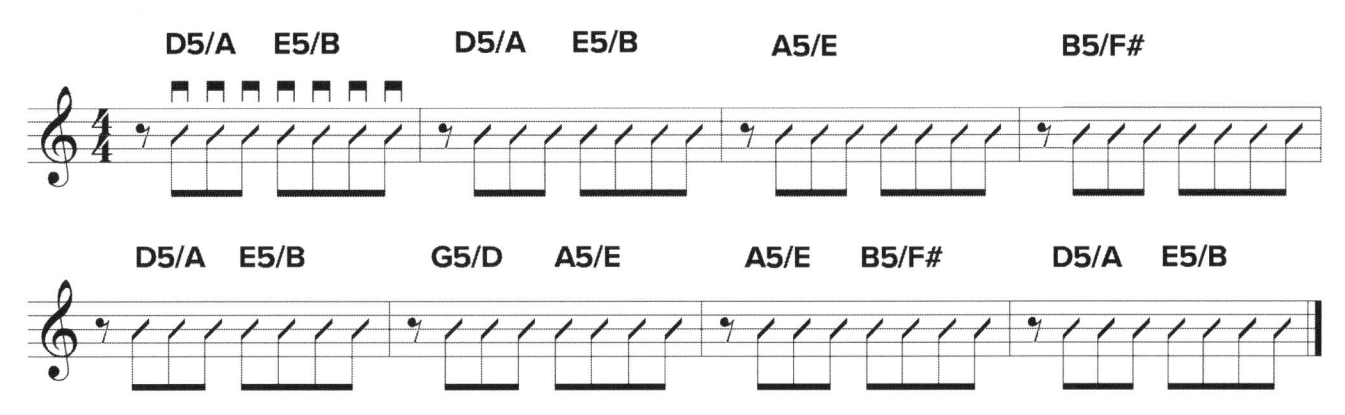

| D5/A E5/B | D5/A E5/B | A5/E | B5/F# |
| D5/A E5/B | G5/D A5/E | A5/E B5/F# | D5/A E5/B |

The following review exercises make use of root 5, root 4, and root 3 inverted power chords, so be sure to read them carefully.

Review Exercise 1

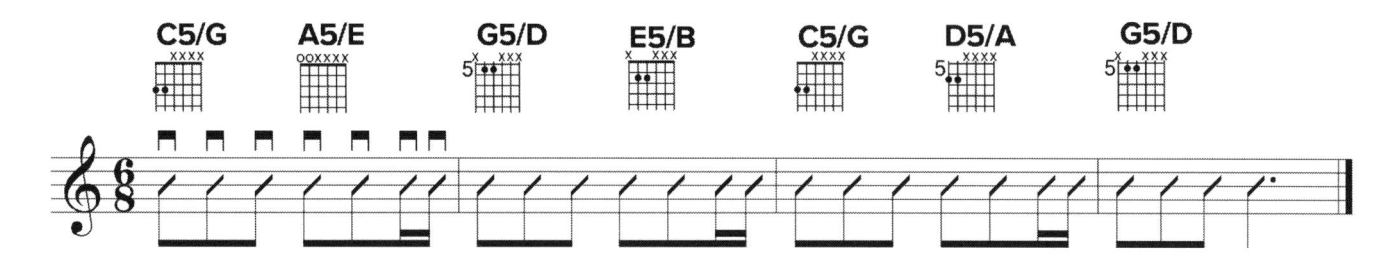

Review Exercise 2

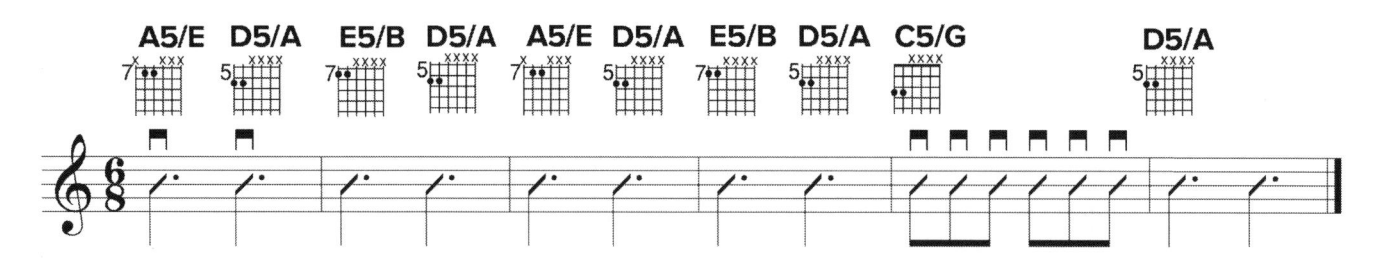

Review Exercise 3

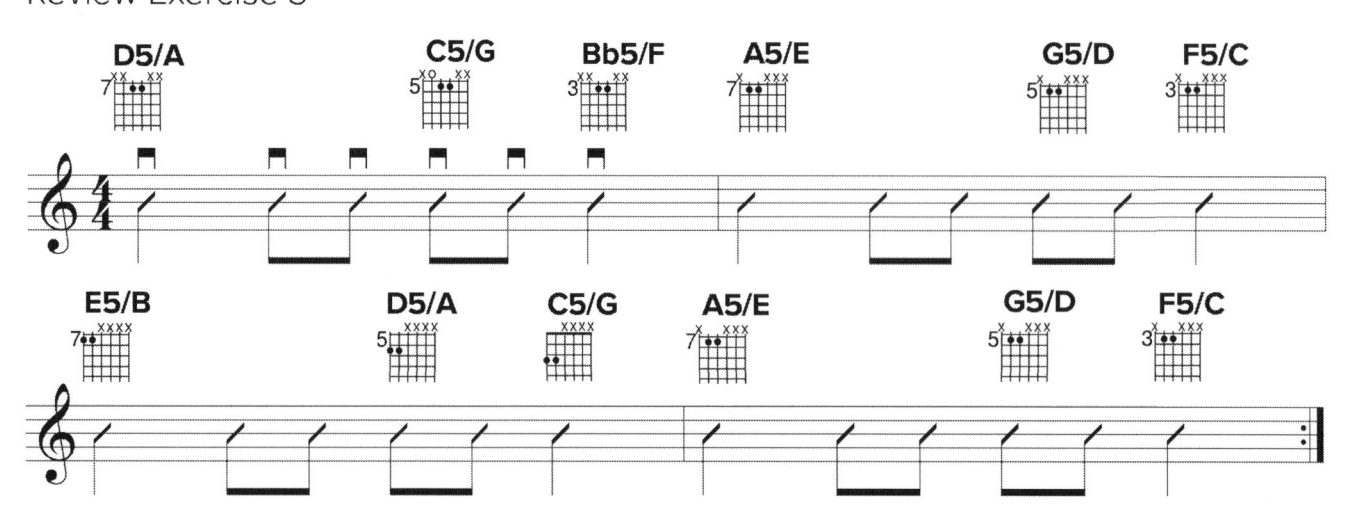

Review Exercise 4

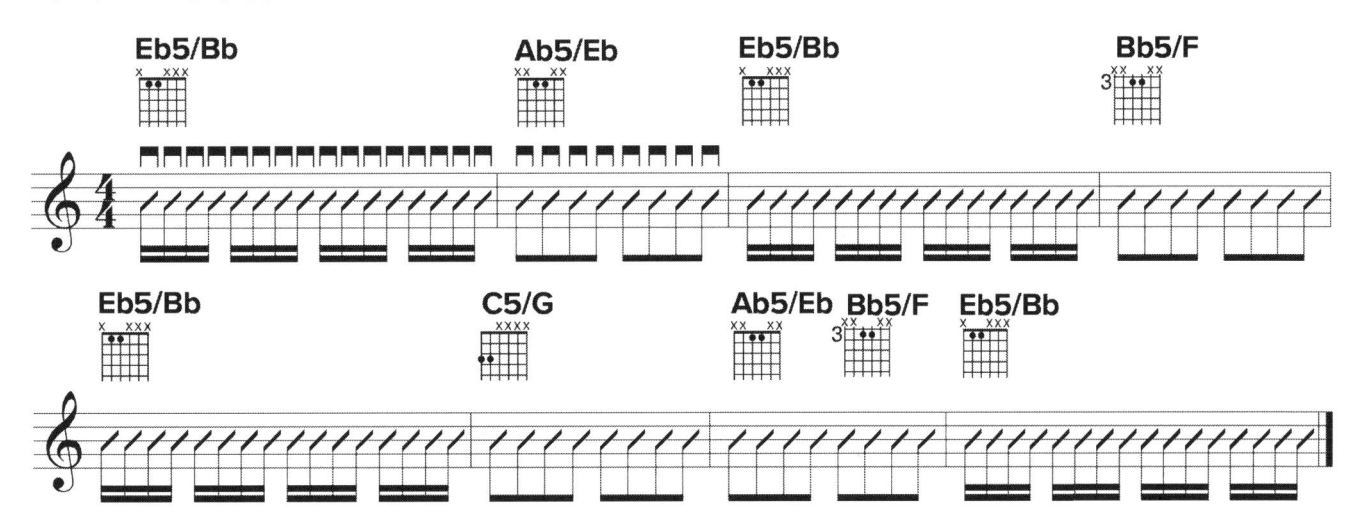

| Eb5/Bb | Ab5/Eb | Eb5/Bb | Bb5/F |

| Eb5/Bb | C5/G | Ab5/Eb | Bb5/F | Eb5/Bb |

Review Exercise 5

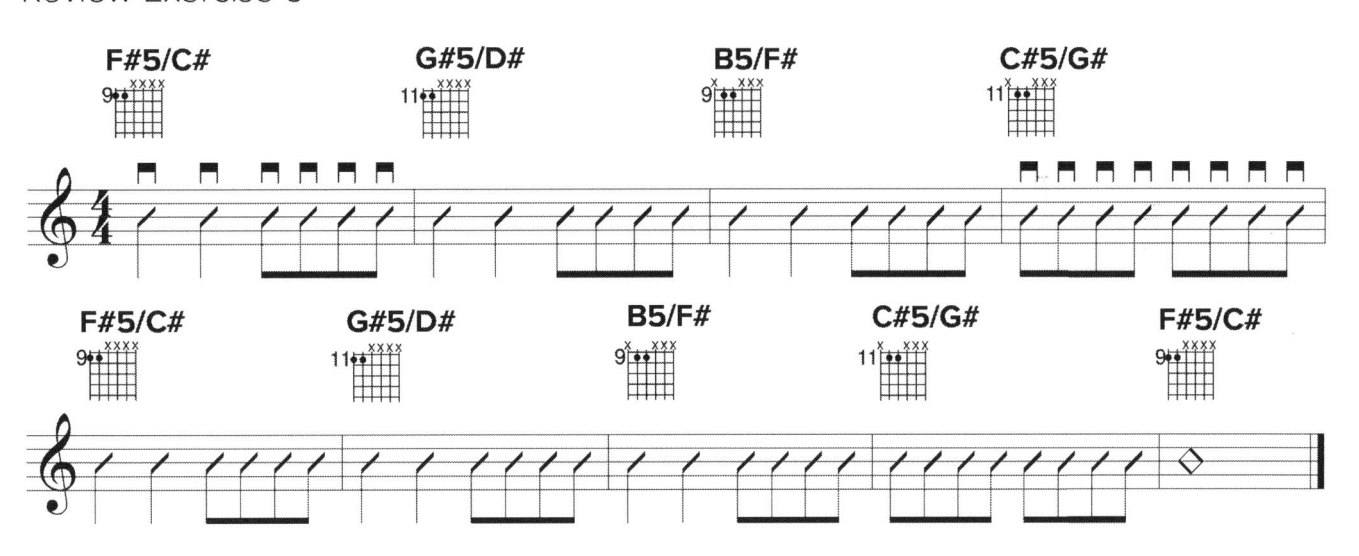

| F#5/C# | G#5/D# | B5/F# | C#5/G# |

| F#5/C# | G#5/D# | B5/F# | C#5/G# | F#5/C# |

Review Exercise 6

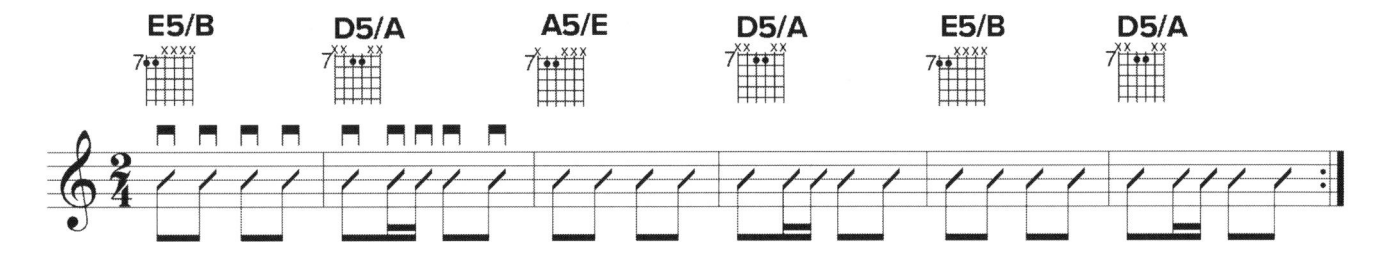

| E5/B | D5/A | A5/E | D5/A | E5/B | D5/A |

Review Exercise 7: Note the use of the palm mute in the first line.

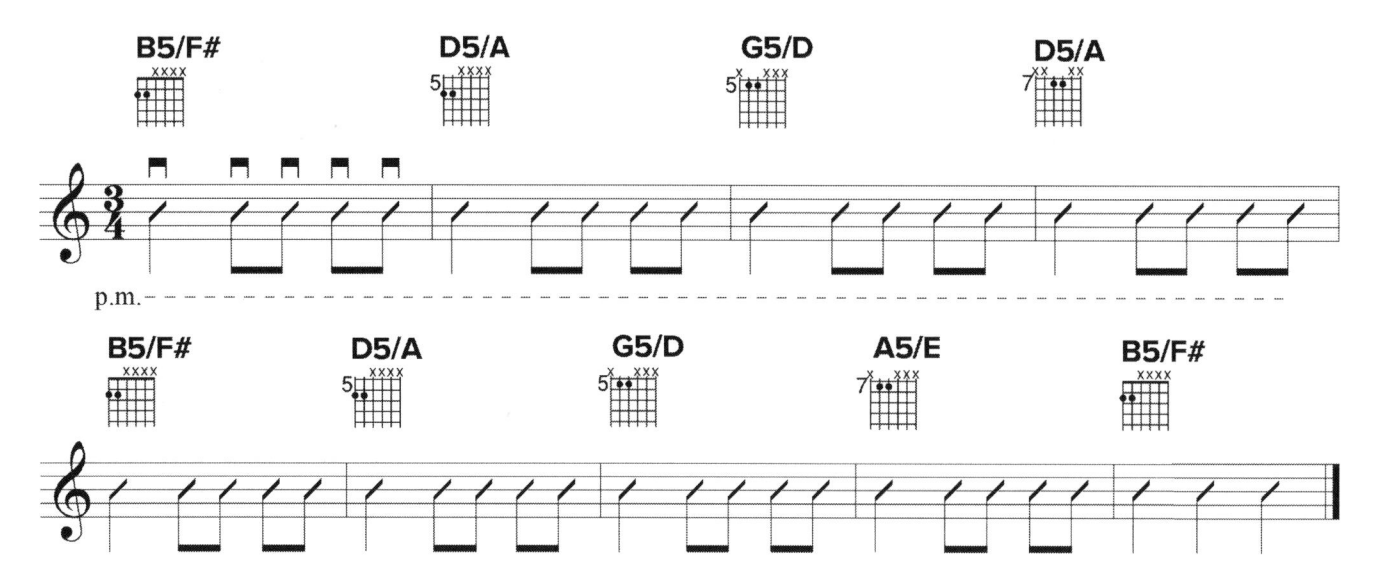

Review Exercise 8

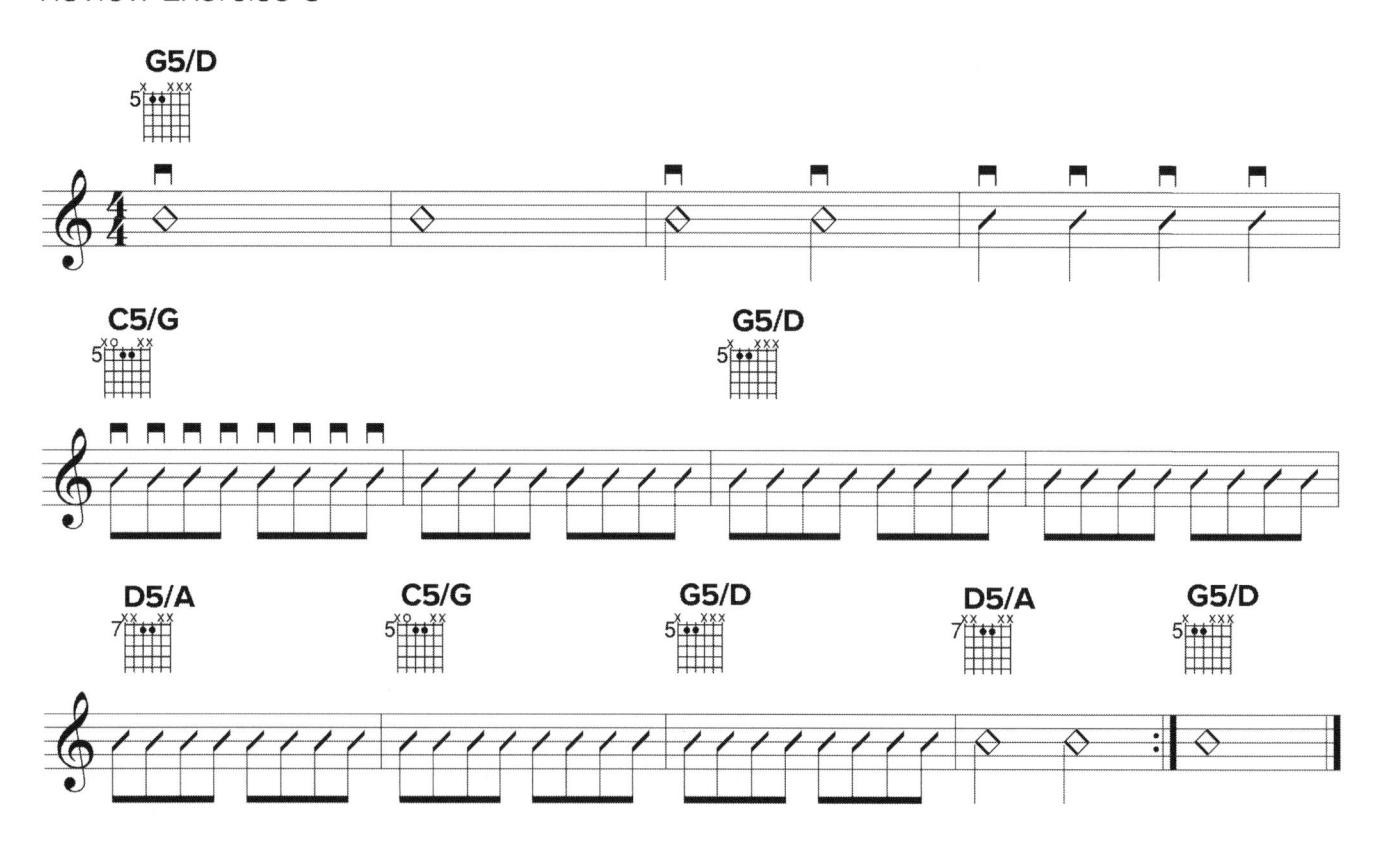

The following review songs contain all the different versions of the power chords we've studied so far. So again, read carefully. And have fun.

The Toy Box

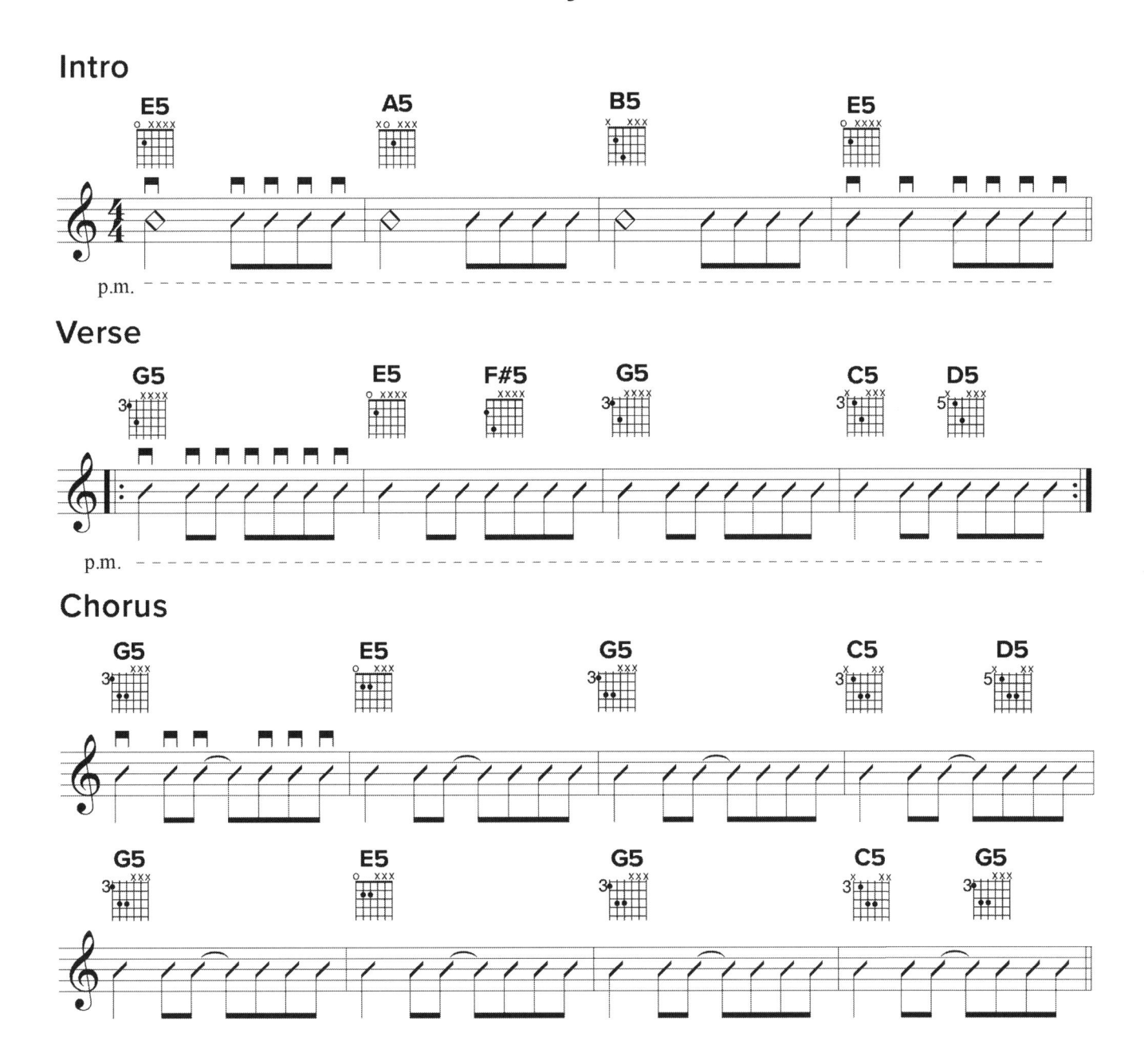

Intro

Verse

Chorus

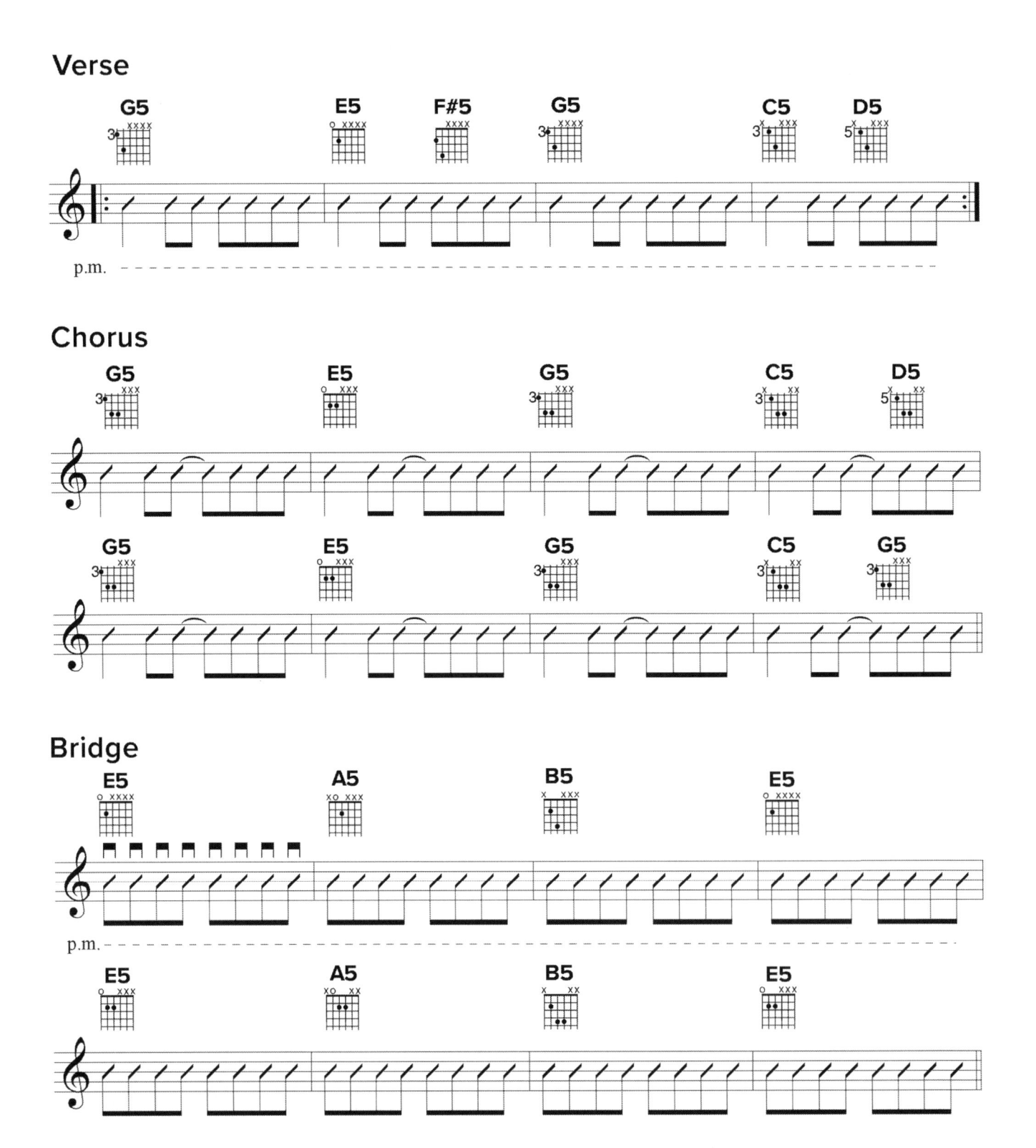

Verse

G5 E5 F#5 G5 C5 D5

p.m.

Chorus

G5 E5 G5 C5 D5

G5 E5 G5 C5 G5

Bridge

E5 A5 B5 E5

p.m.

E5 A5 B5 E5

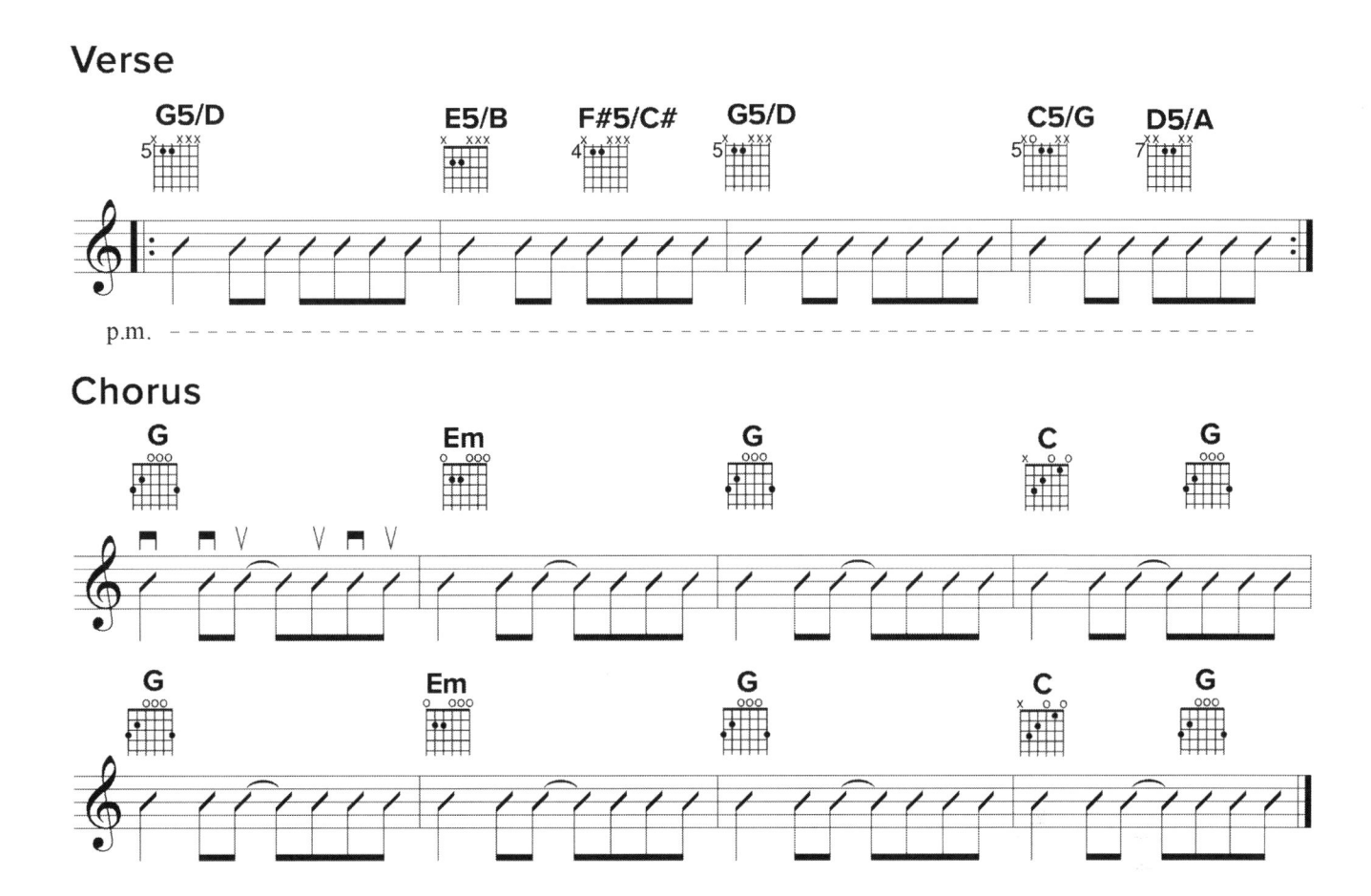

Verse

G5/D **E5/B** **F#5/C#** **G5/D** **C5/G** **D5/A**

p.m.

Chorus

G **Em** **G** **C** **G**

G **Em** **G** **C** **G**

Happy As Can Be
(Version 2)

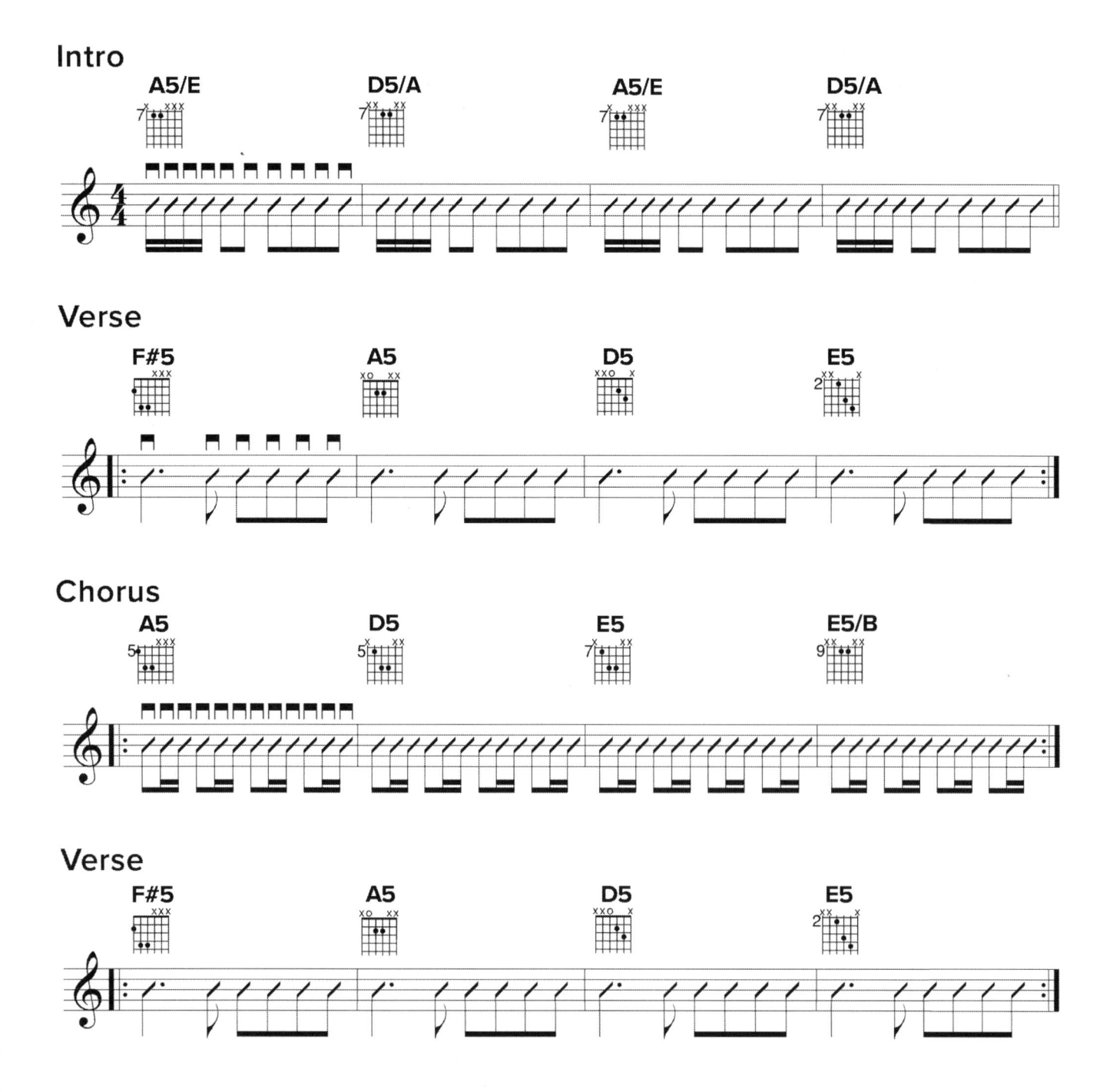

Intro

| A5/E | D5/A | A5/E | D5/A |

Verse

| F#5 | A5 | D5 | E5 |

Chorus

| A5 | D5 | E5 | E5/B |

Verse

| F#5 | A5 | D5 | E5 |

Chorus

| A5 | D5 | E5 | E5/B |

Bridge

| F#5/C# | A5/E | F#5/C# | A5/E | E5/B |

Chorus

| A5/E | D5/A | E5/B | E5 |

| A5 | D5 | E5 | A5 |

Lesson 9:
Three-Note Inverted Power Chords

The following power chords are essentially the same as the chords learned in the previous lesson. However, this time a third note (the fifth of the chord) has been added. This helps fill out the sound, giving you yet another option for power chord voicings.

Note that on the root 3 power chord, the fourth finger is used, which means that the reach for the additional note is one fret further than the root 5 and root 4 versions of the chord.

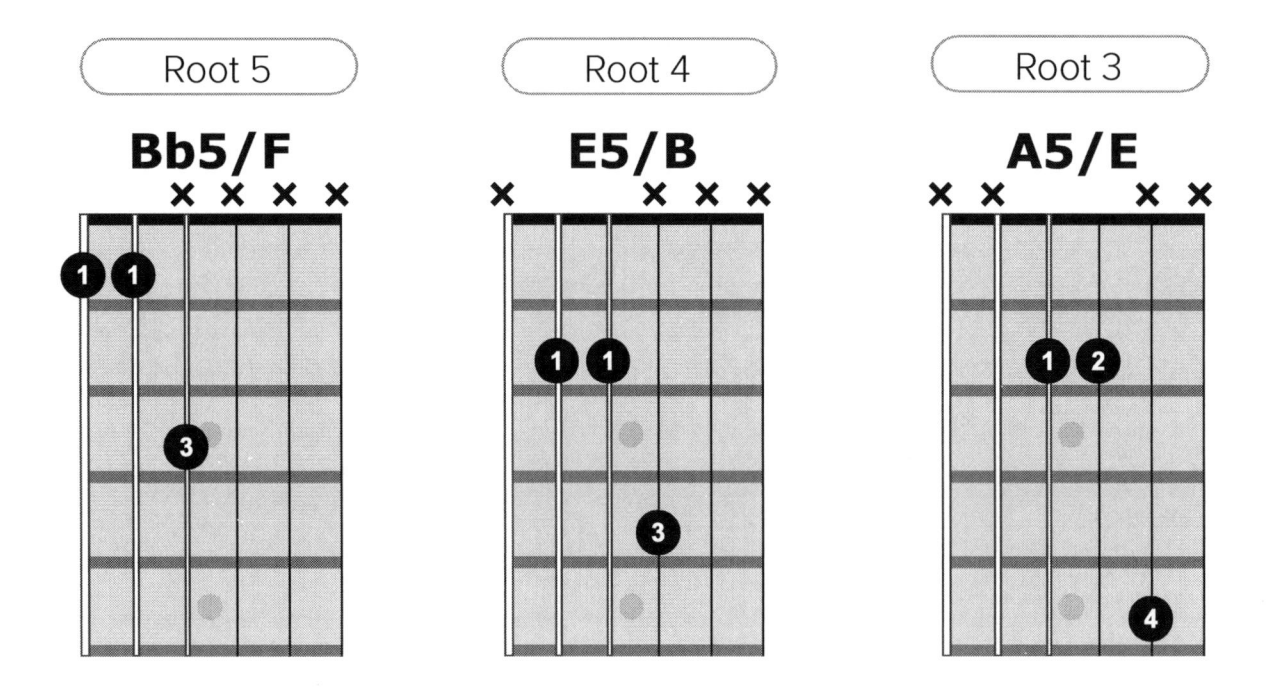

Root 5: Bb5/F

Root 4: E5/B

Root 3: A5/E

Practice the following Root 5 Exercises

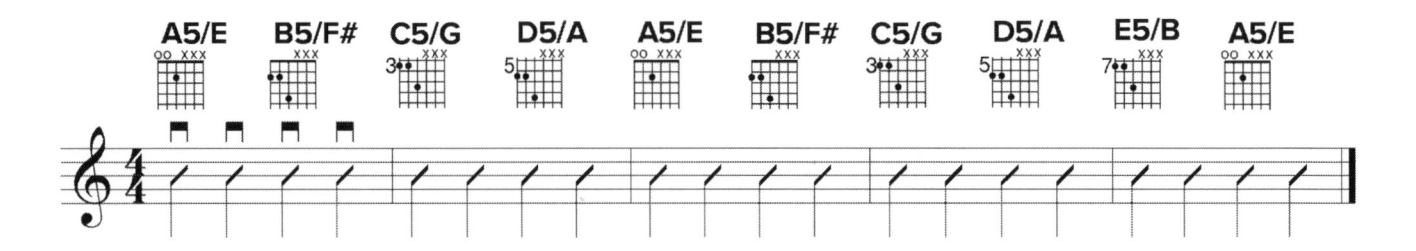

Exercise 1

A5/E — B5/F# — C5/G — D5/A — A5/E — B5/F# — C5/G — D5/A — E5/B — A5/E

Exercise 2

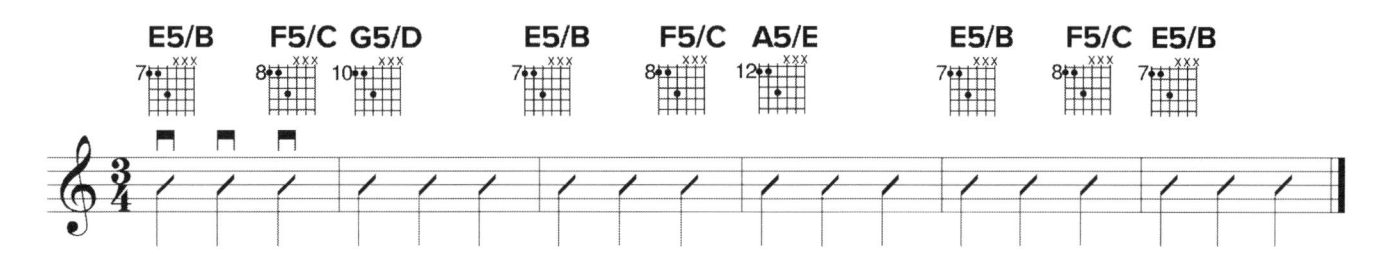

| E5/B | F5/C | G5/D | E5/B | F5/C | A5/E | E5/B | F5/C | E5/B |

3/4

Exercise 3

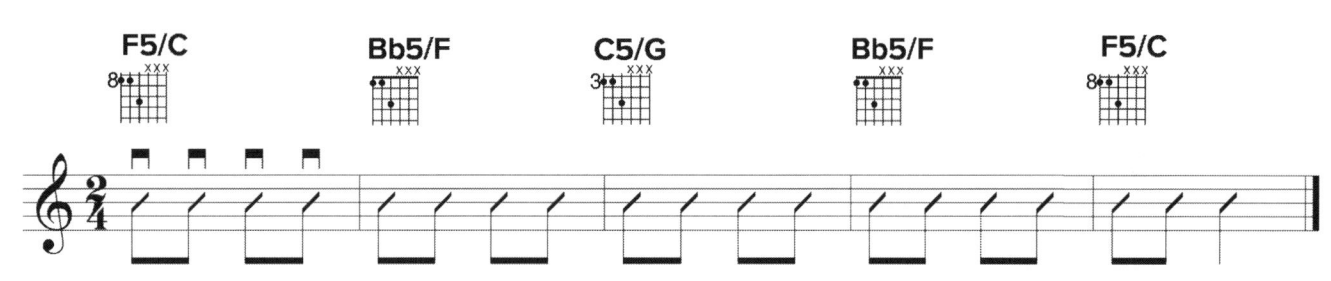

| F5/C | Bb5/F | C5/G | Bb5/F | F5/C |

2/4

Exercise 4

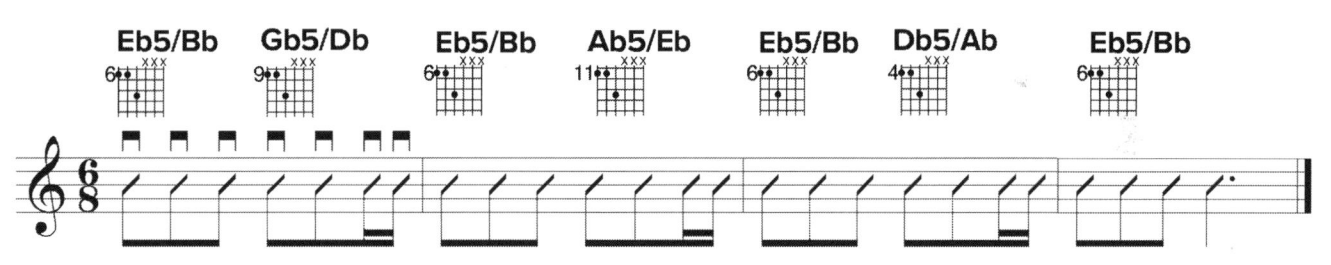

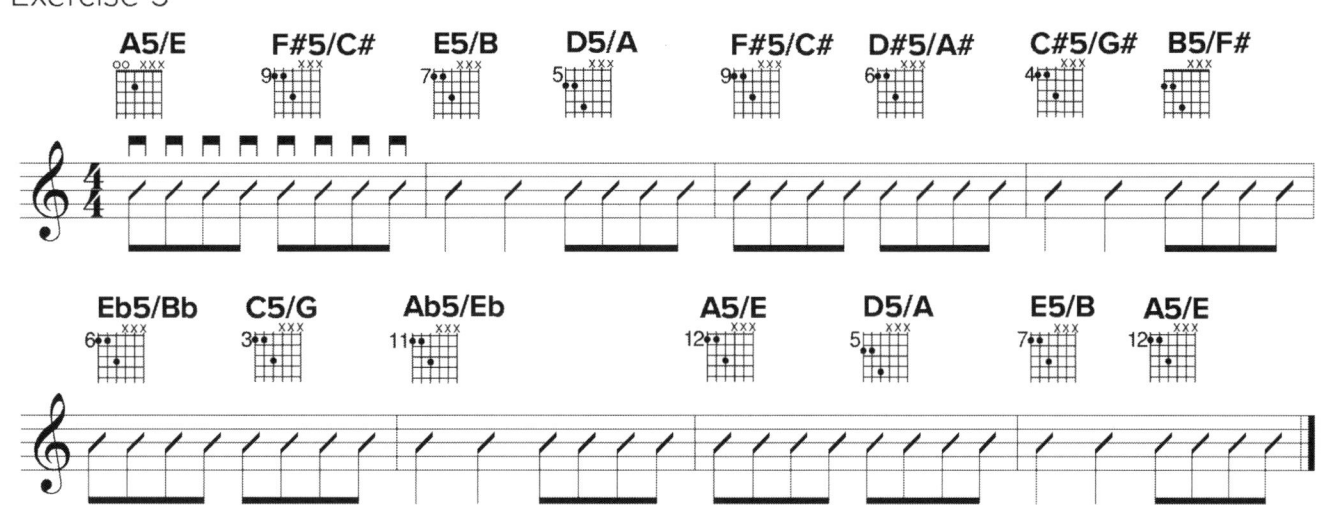

| Eb5/Bb | Gb5/Db | Eb5/Bb | Ab5/Eb | Eb5/Bb | Db5/Ab | Eb5/Bb |

6/8

Exercise 5

| A5/E | F#5/C# | E5/B | D5/A | F#5/C# | D#5/A# | C#5/G# | B5/F# |

4/4

| Eb5/Bb | C5/G | Ab5/Eb | A5/E | D5/A | E5/B | A5/E |

Practice the following Root 4 Exercises

Exercise 1

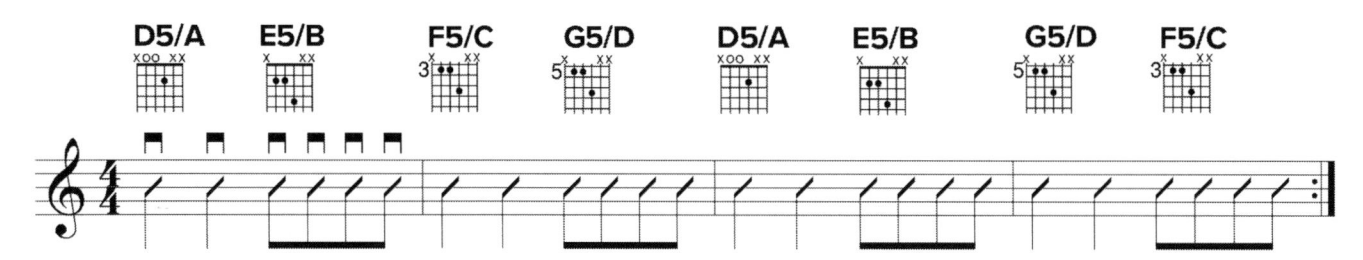

| D5/A | E5/B | F5/C | G5/D | D5/A | E5/B | G5/D | F5/C |

Exercise 2

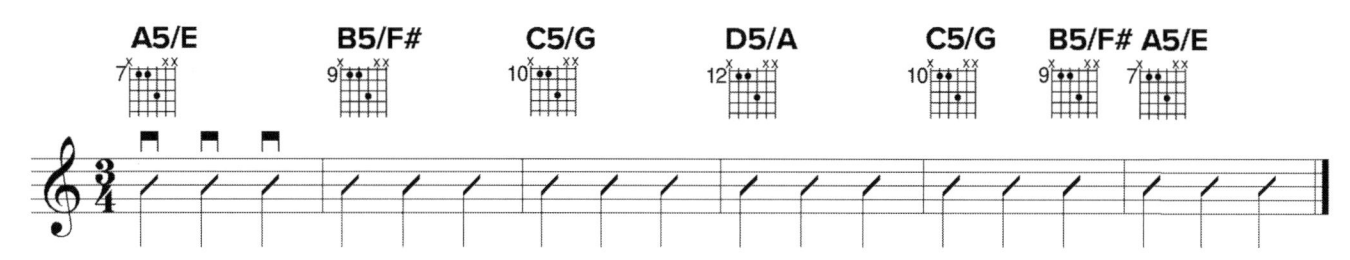

| A5/E | B5/F# | C5/G | D5/A | C5/G | B5/F# | A5/E |

Exercise 3

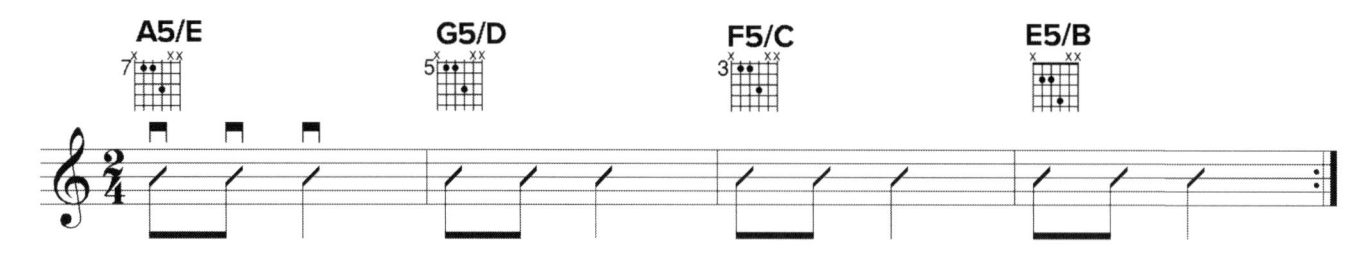

| A5/E | G5/D | F5/C | E5/B |

Exercise 4

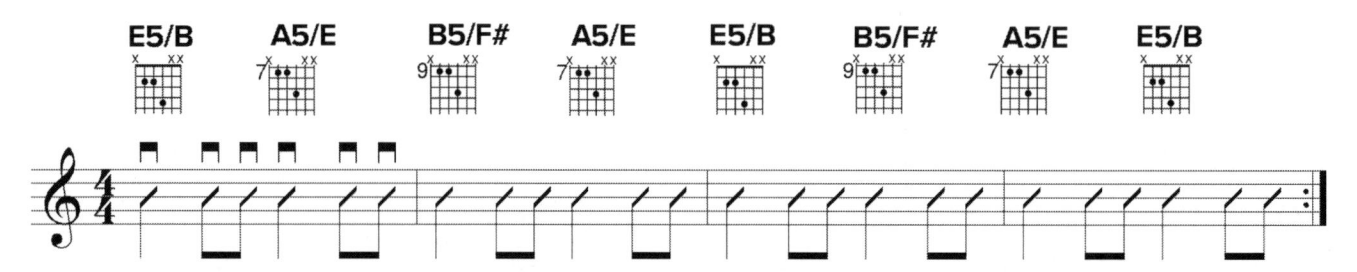

| E5/B | A5/E | B5/F# | A5/E | E5/B | B5/F# | A5/E | E5/B |

Exercise 5

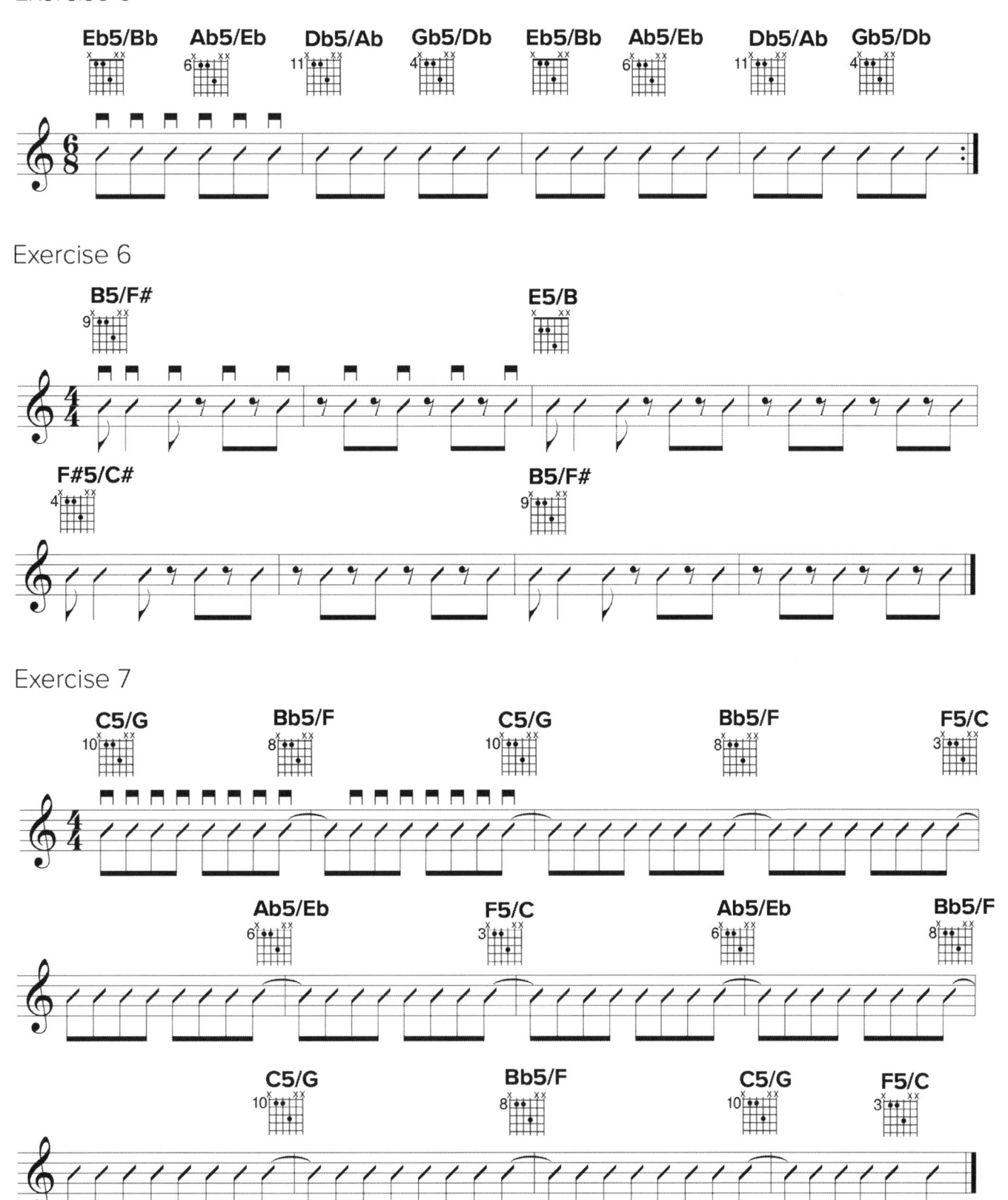

Eb5/Bb   Ab5/Eb   Db5/Ab   Gb5/Db   Eb5/Bb   Ab5/Eb   Db5/Ab   Gb5/Db

Exercise 6

B5/F#   E5/B

F#5/C#   B5/F#

Exercise 7

C5/G   Bb5/F   C5/G   Bb5/F   F5/C

Ab5/Eb   F5/C   Ab5/Eb   Bb5/F

C5/G   Bb5/F   C5/G   F5/C

Practice the following Root 3 Exercises

Exercise 1

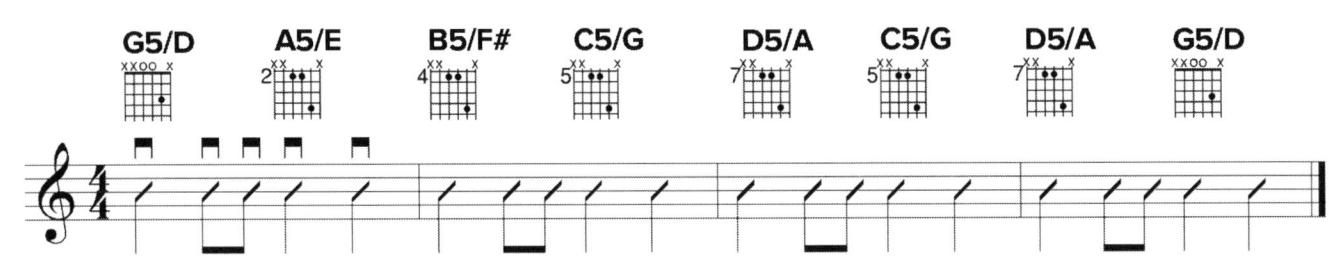

| G5/D | A5/E | B5/F# | C5/G | D5/A | C5/G | D5/A | G5/D |

Exercise 2

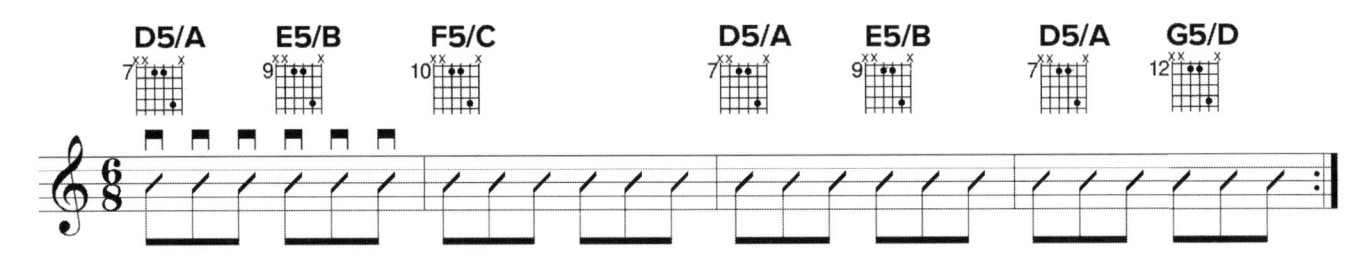

| D5/A | E5/B | F5/C | D5/A | E5/B | D5/A | G5/D |

Exercise 3

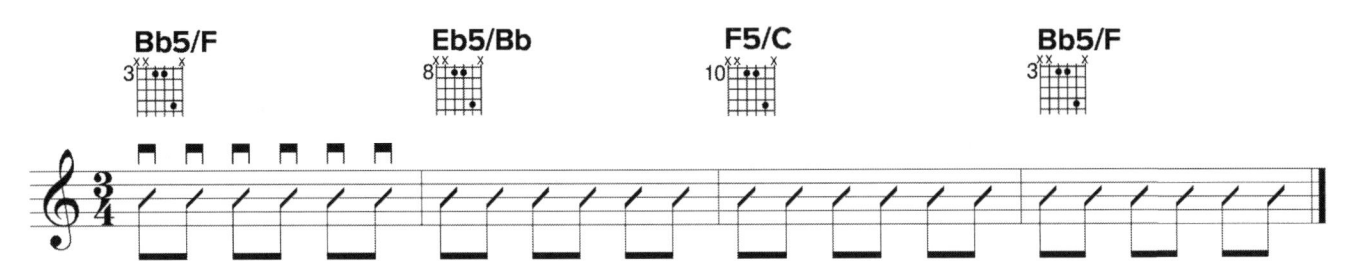

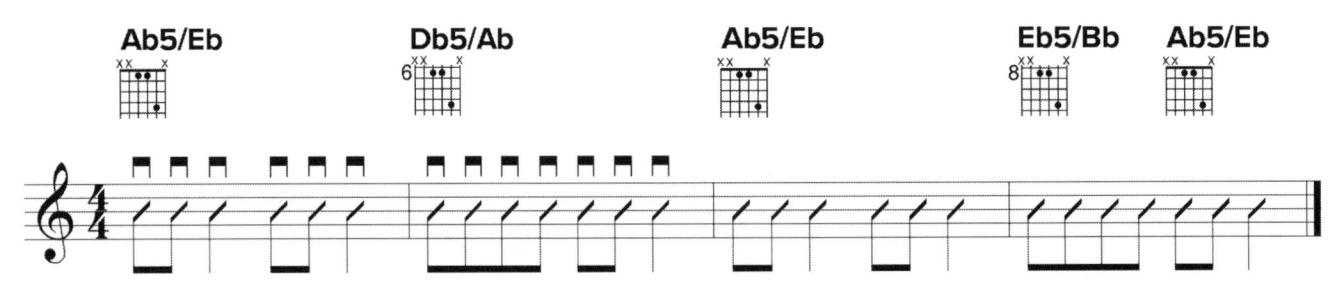

| Bb5/F | Eb5/Bb | F5/C | Bb5/F |

Exercise 4

| Ab5/Eb | Db5/Ab | Ab5/Eb | Eb5/Bb | Ab5/Eb |

Exercise 5

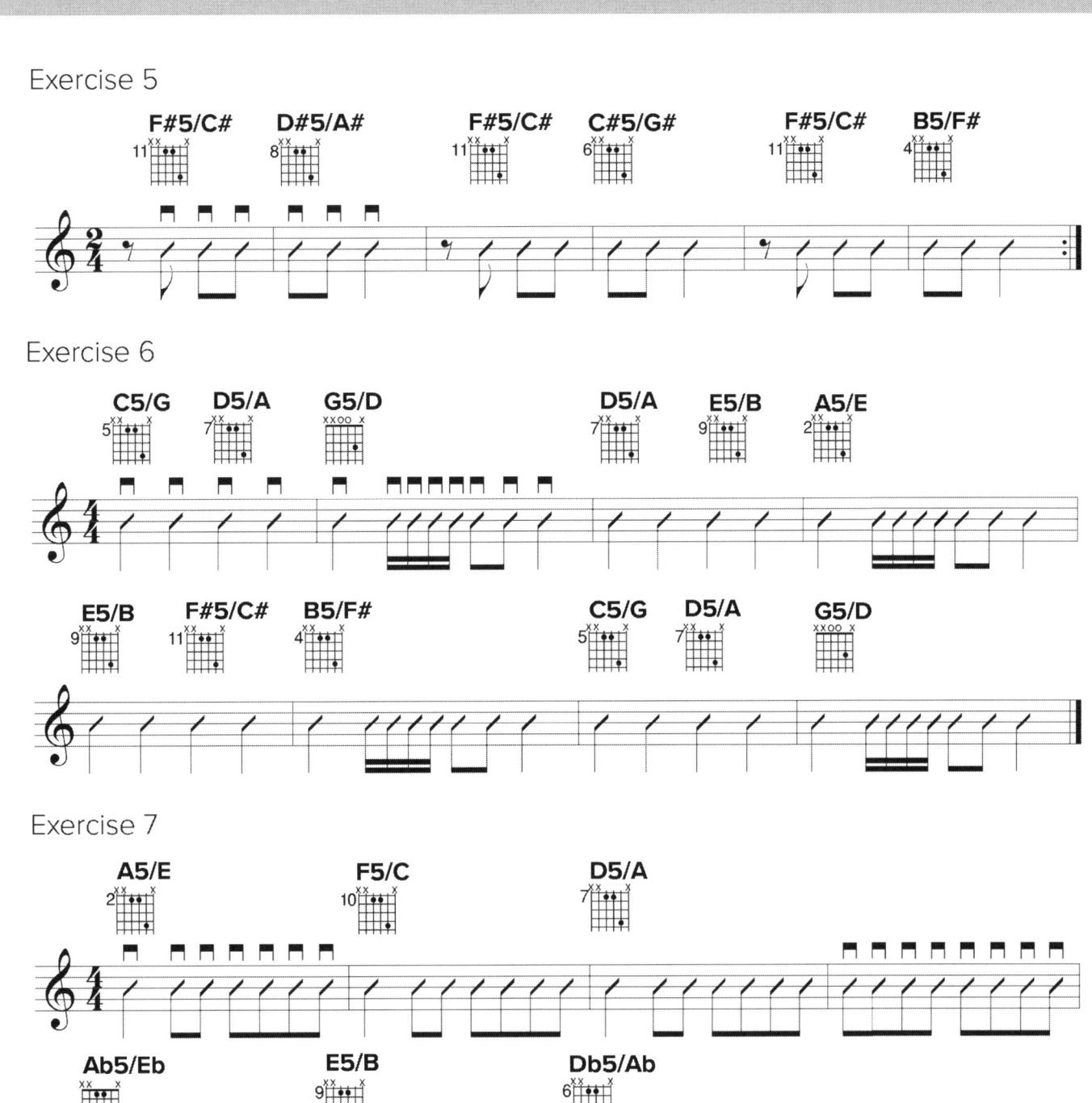

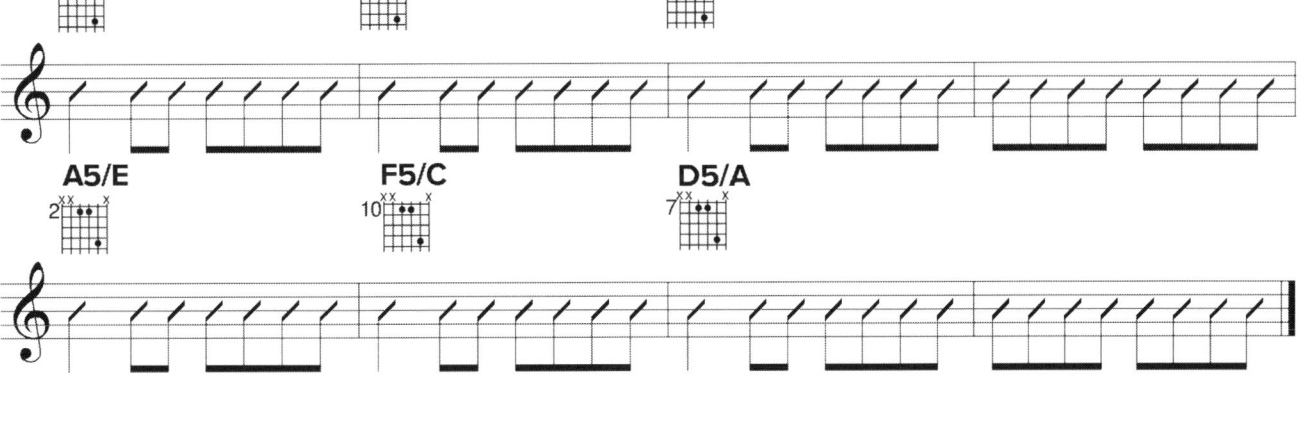

Exercise 6

Exercise 7

The next set of exercises contain all three inverted power chord types, so be sure to read them carefully.

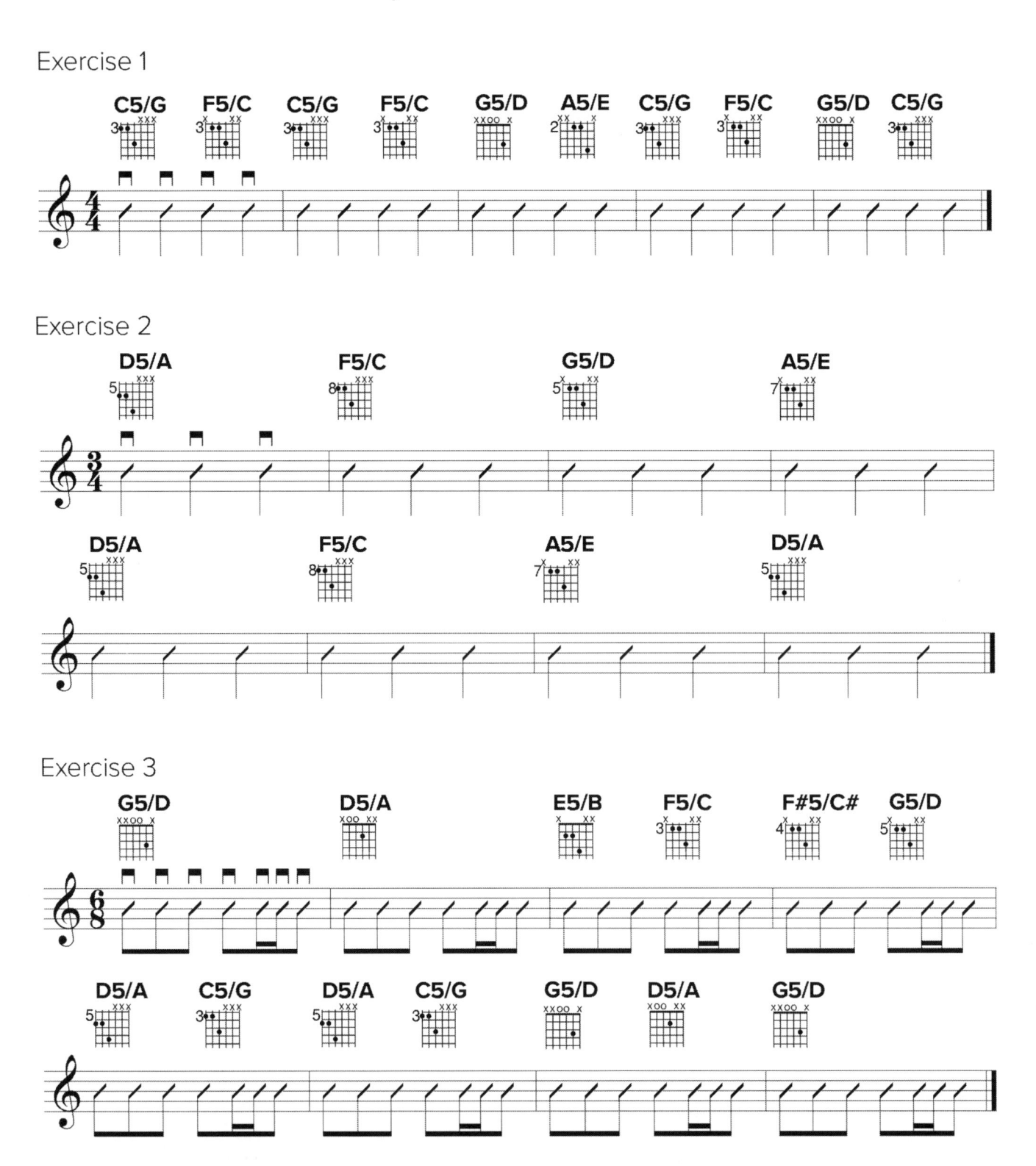

Exercise 1

C5/G F5/C C5/G F5/C G5/D A5/E C5/G F5/C G5/D C5/G

Exercise 2

D5/A F5/C G5/D A5/E

D5/A F5/C A5/E D5/A

Exercise 3

G5/D D5/A E5/B F5/C F#5/C# G5/D

D5/A C5/G D5/A C5/G G5/D D5/A G5/D

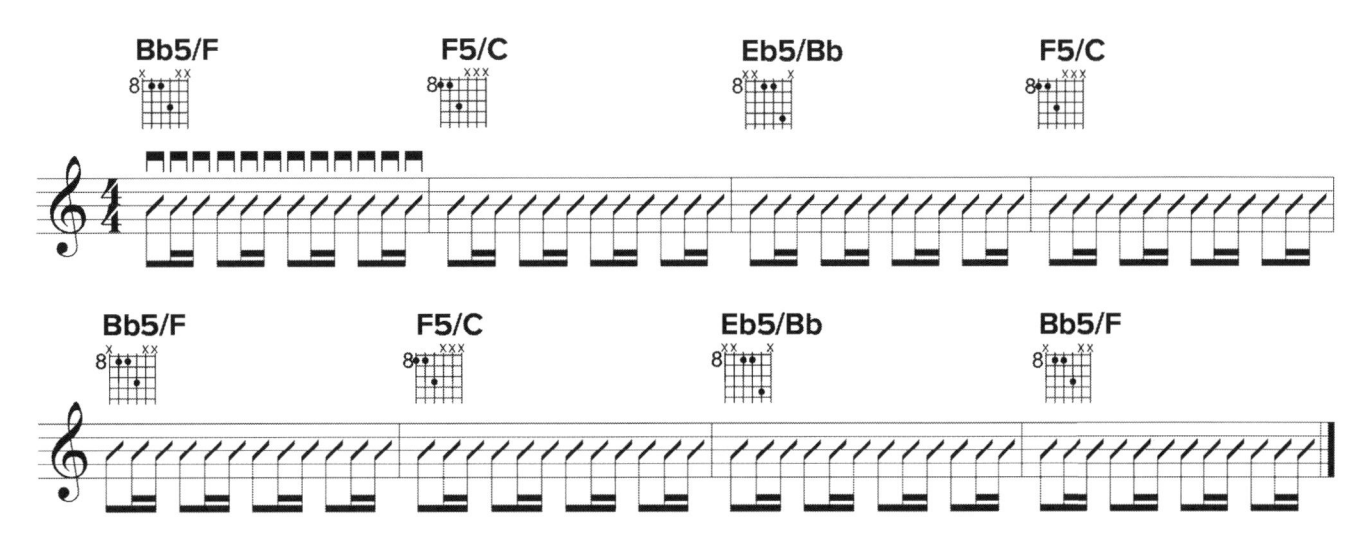

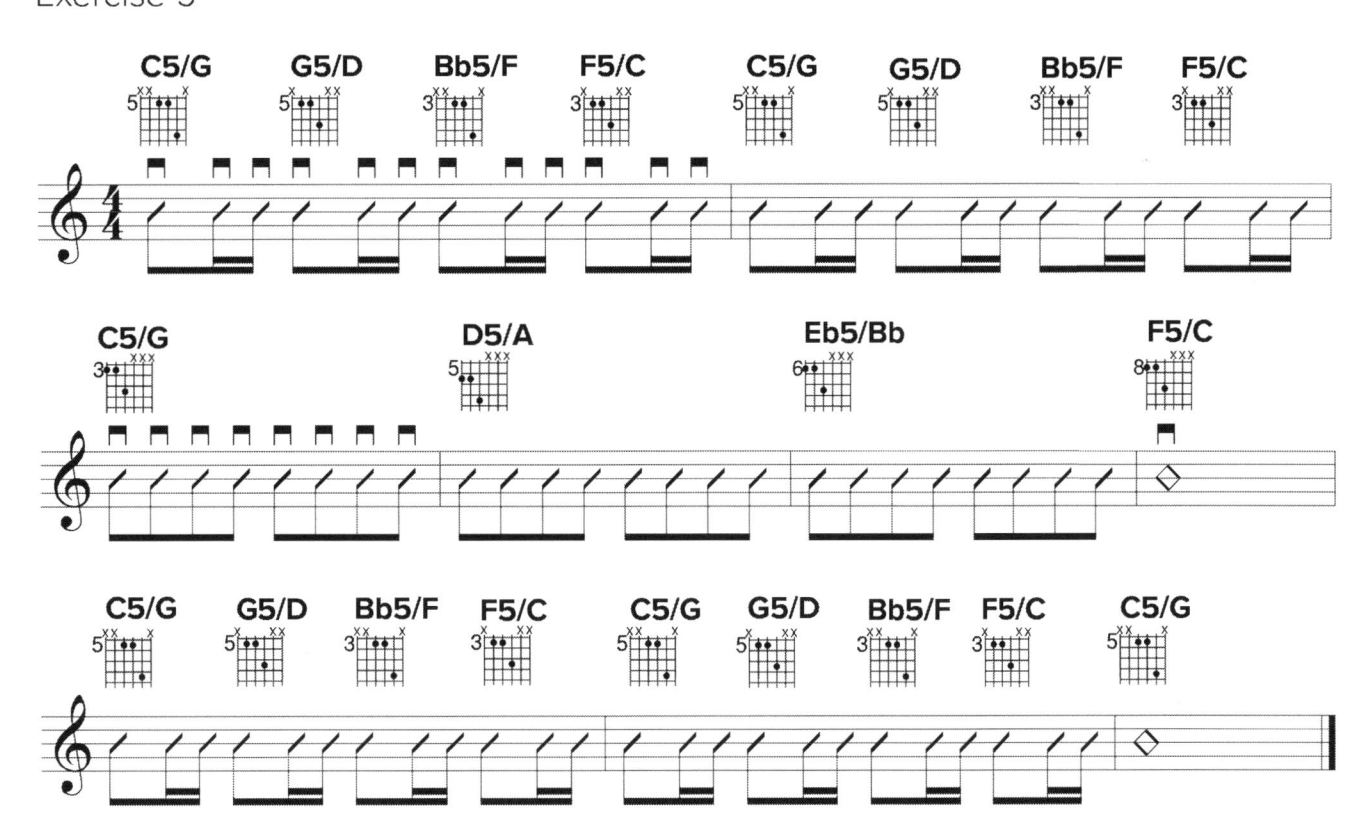

Exercise 4

Lesson 10: Review All Power Chords

This lesson is designed to help you see how you can use all the different power chords learned so far in this book together. So, again, be sure to read carefully. Also, you can use what's here to create your own versions of these exercises. For example, if you have an E5 power chord listed, and it says to play it as a three-note root 6 power chord, try playing different versions of that chord, such as a two-note, root 5 version.

Exercise 1

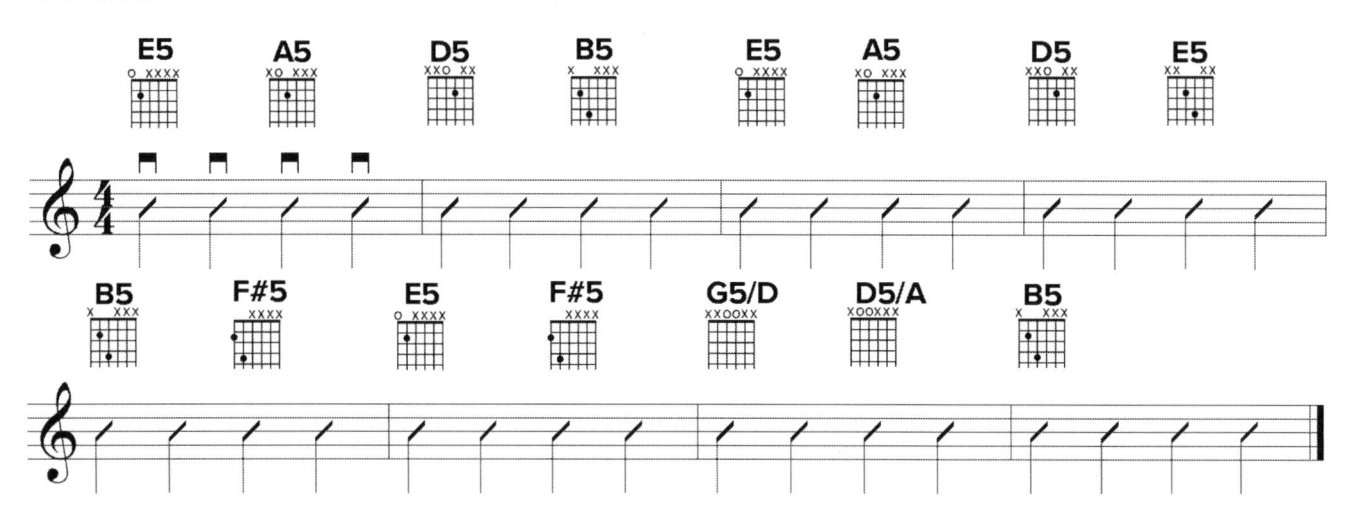

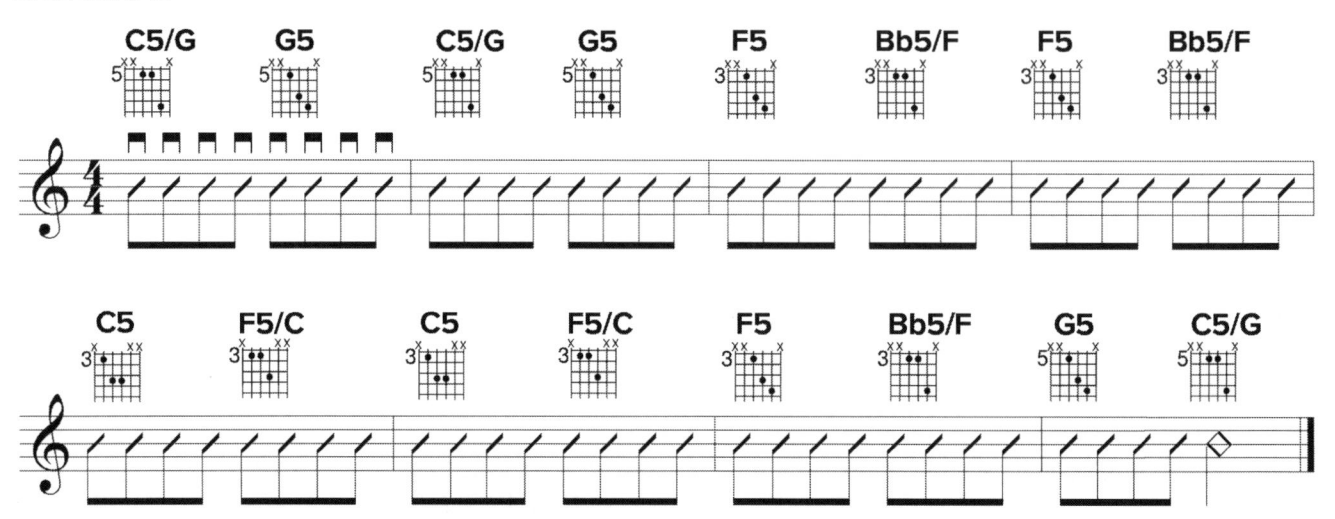

E5	A5	D5	B5	E5	A5	D5	E5

B5	F#5	E5	F#5	G5/D	D5/A	B5	

Exercise 2

C5/G	G5	C5/G	G5	F5	Bb5/F	F5	Bb5/F

C5	F5/C	C5	F5/C	F5	Bb5/F	G5	C5/G

137

Exercise 3

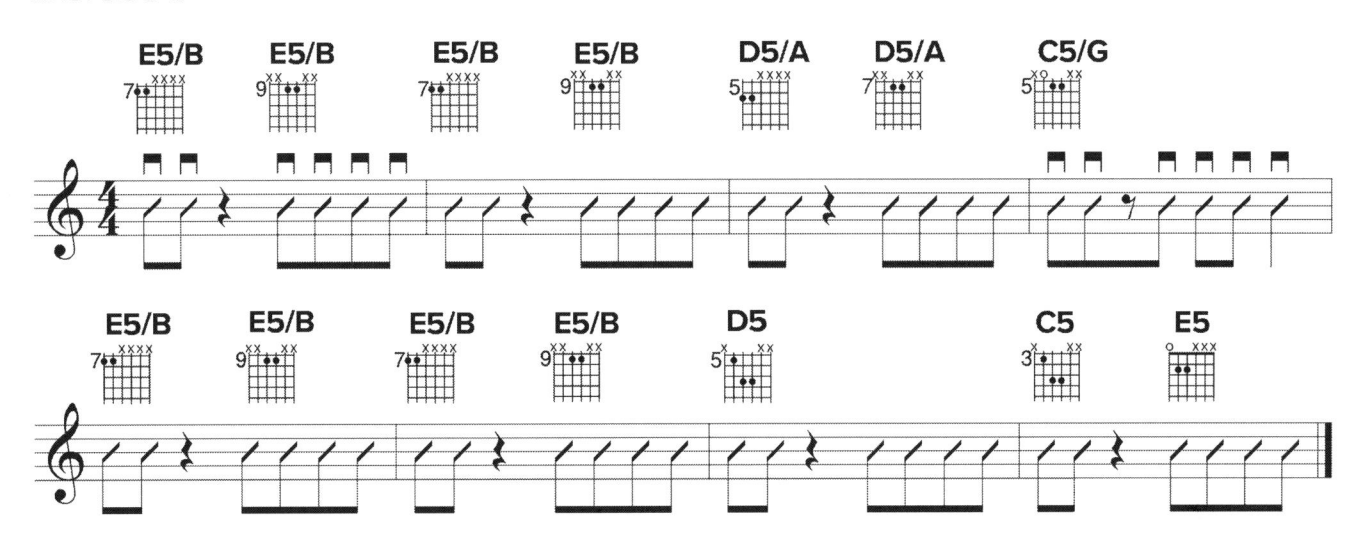

Exercise 4

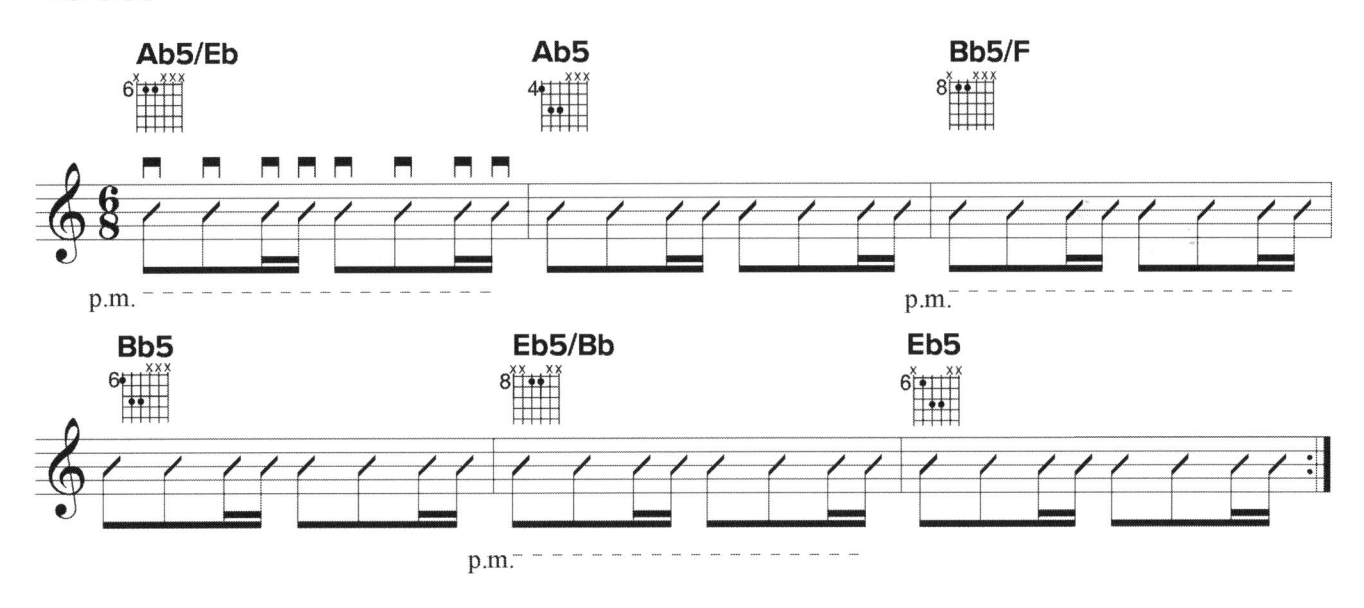

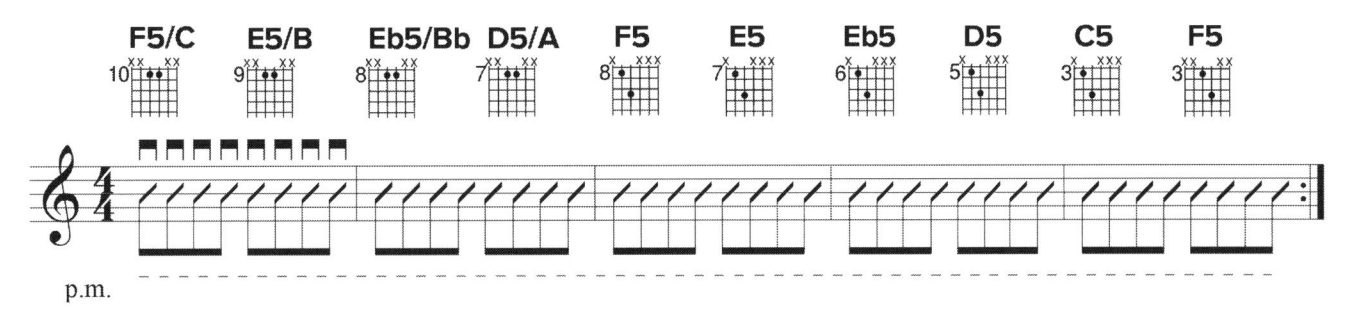

Exercise 5

The Nightmare Machine

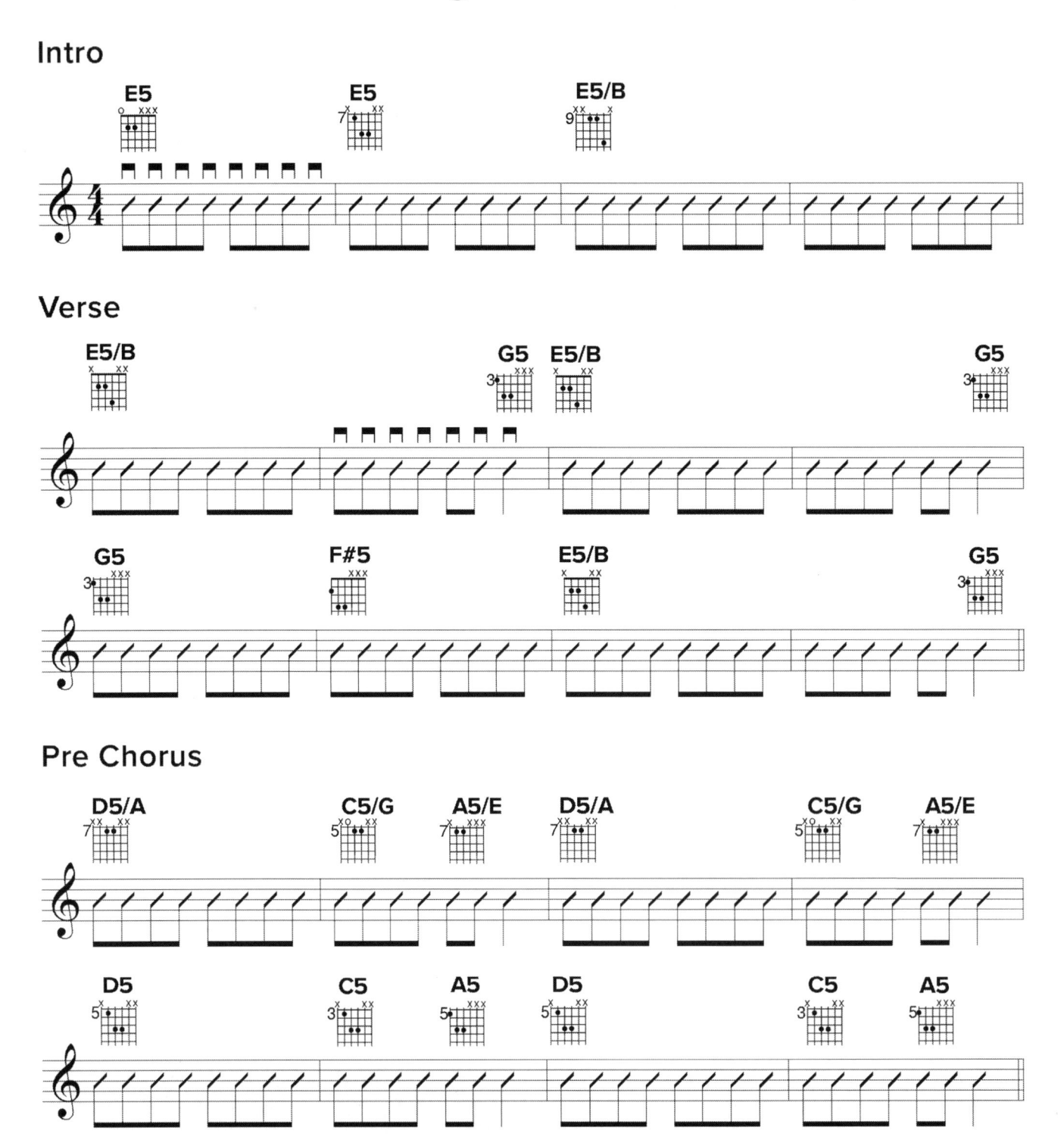

Intro

E5 E5 E5/B

Verse

E5/B G5 E5/B G5

G5 F#5 E5/B G5

Pre Chorus

D5/A C5/G A5/E D5/A C5/G A5/E

D5 C5 A5 D5 C5 A5

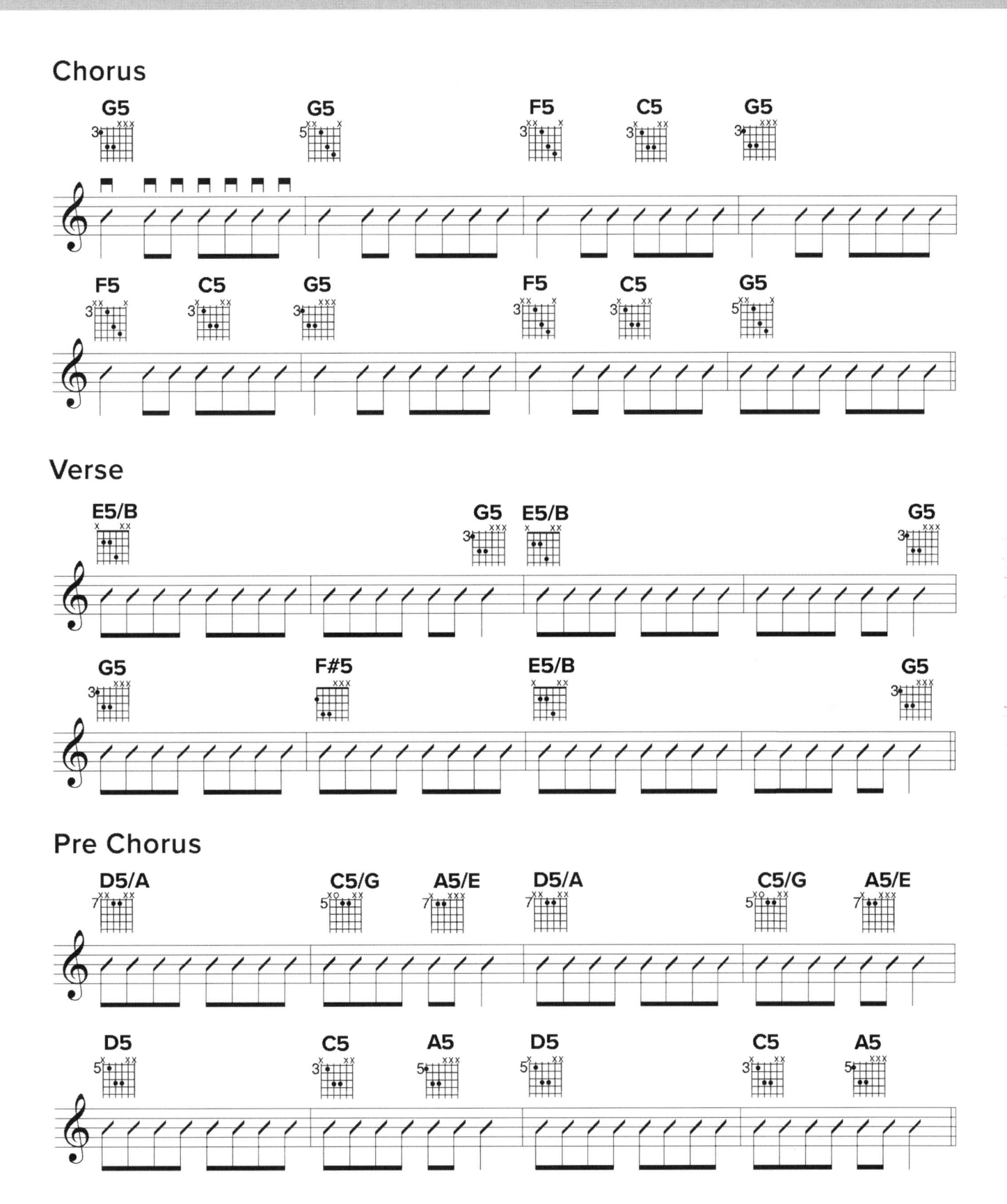

Chorus

G5	G5	F5	C5	G5

F5	C5	G5	F5	C5	G5

Verse

E5/B	G5	E5/B	G5

G5	F#5	E5/B	G5

Pre Chorus

D5/A	C5/G	A5/E	D5/A	C5/G	A5/E

D5	C5	A5	D5	C5	A5

Chorus

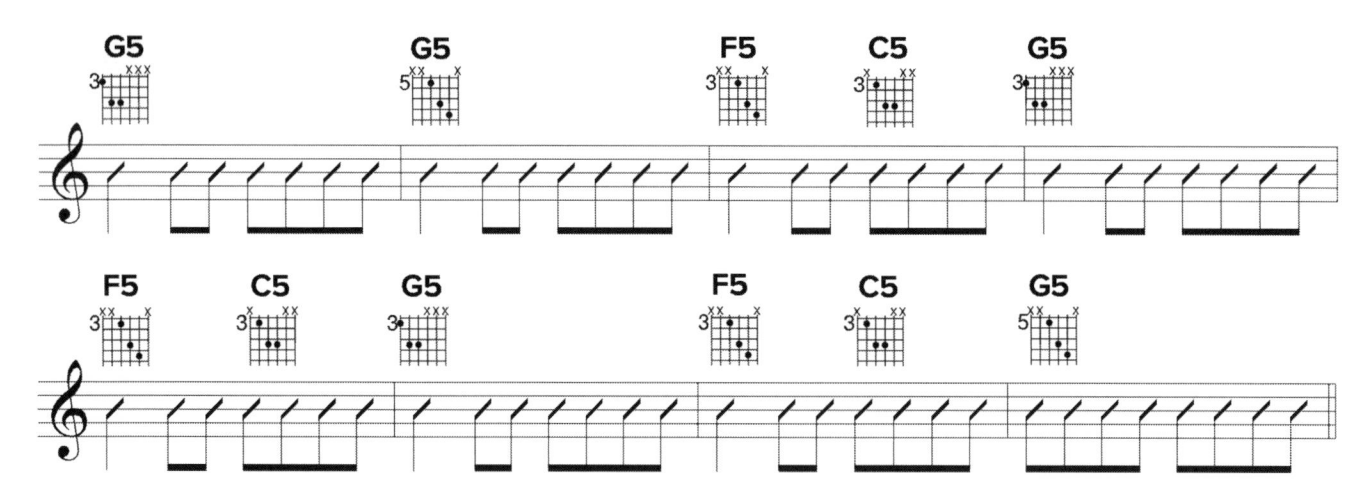

| G5 | G5 | F5 | C5 | G5 |

| F5 | C5 | G5 | F5 | C5 | G5 |

Bridge

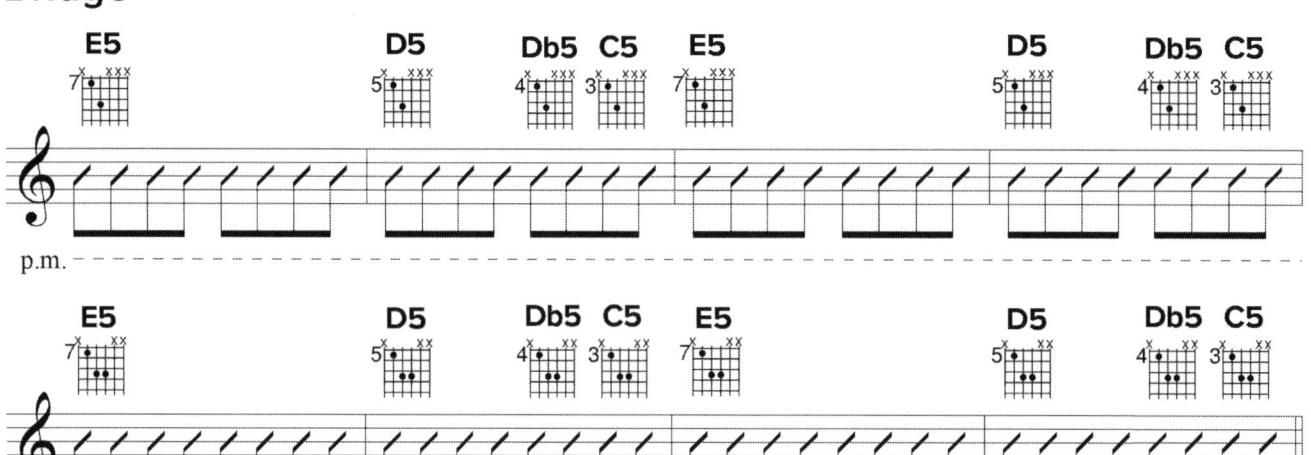

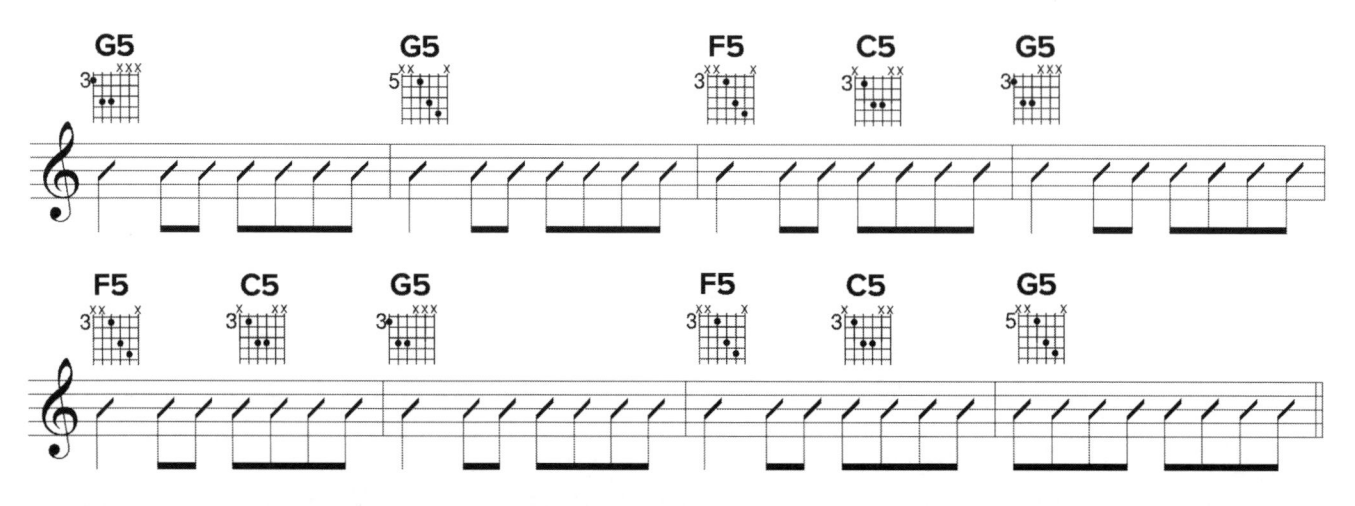

| E5 | D5 | Db5 | C5 | E5 | D5 | Db5 | C5 |

p.m.

| E5 | D5 | Db5 | C5 | E5 | D5 | Db5 | C5 |

Chorus

| G5 | G5 | F5 | C5 | G5 |

| F5 | C5 | G5 | F5 | C5 | G5 |

Chorus

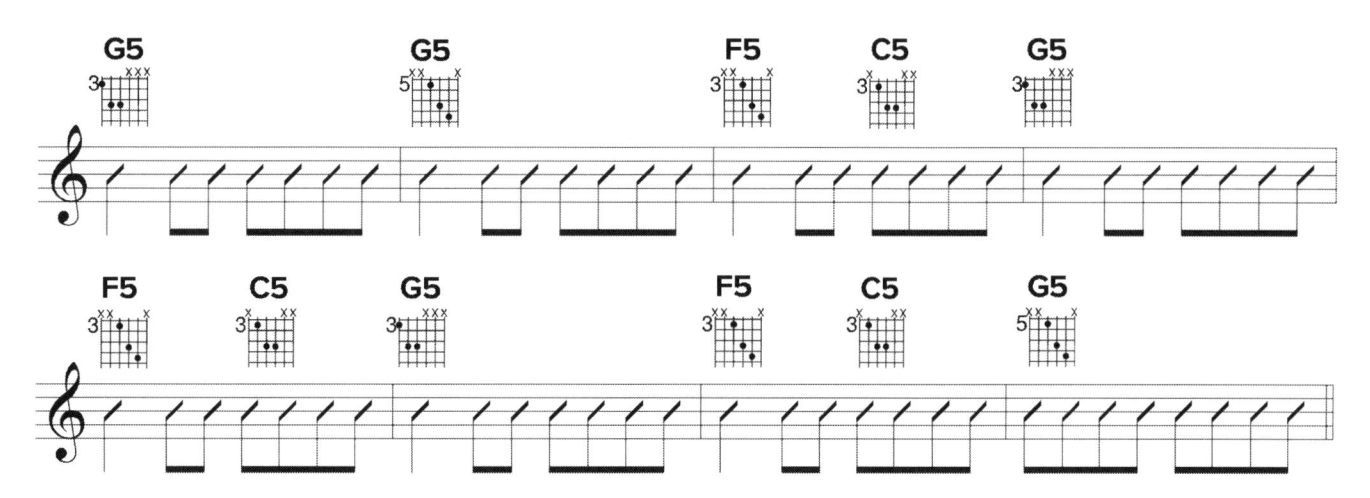

Outro

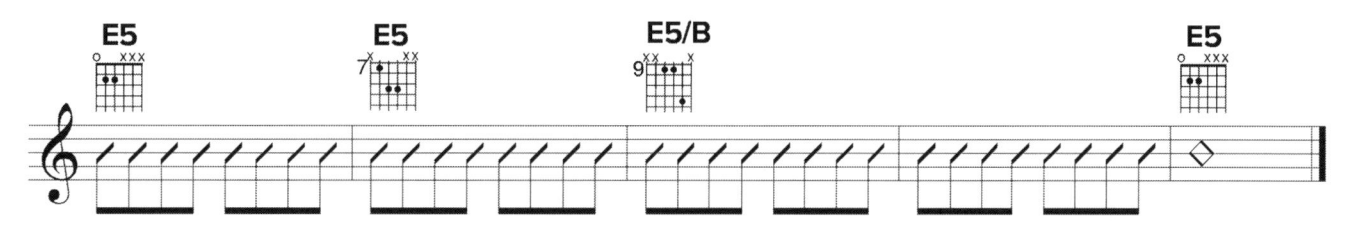

October Tornado

Intro

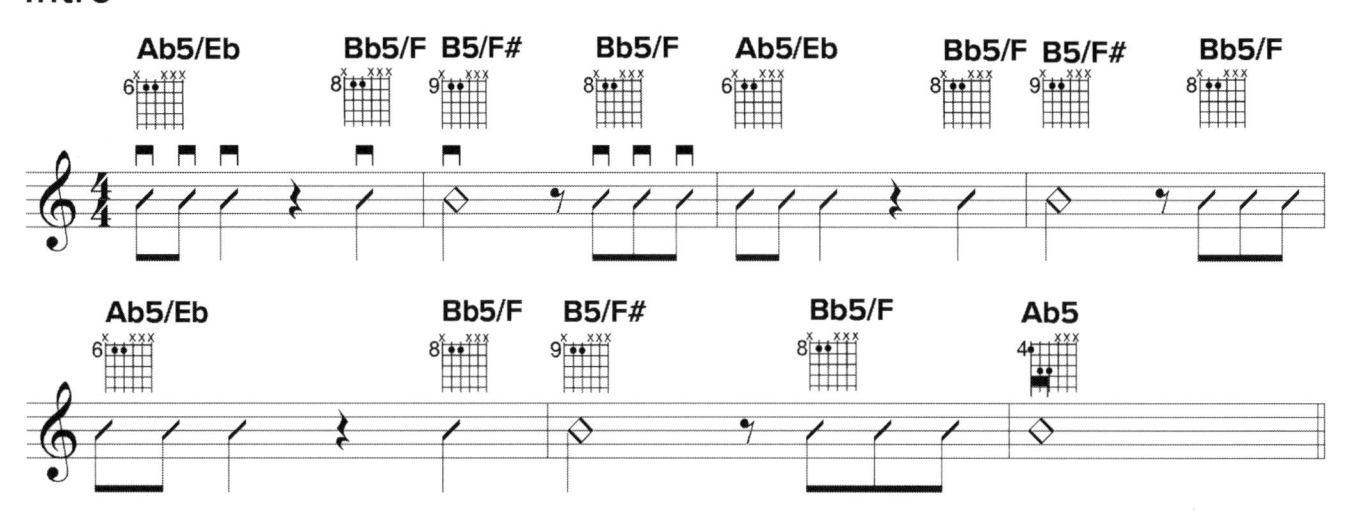

| Ab5/Eb | Bb5/F | B5/F# | Bb5/F | Ab5/Eb | Bb5/F | B5/F# | Bb5/F |

| Ab5/Eb | Bb5/F | B5/F# | Bb5/F | Ab5 |

Verse

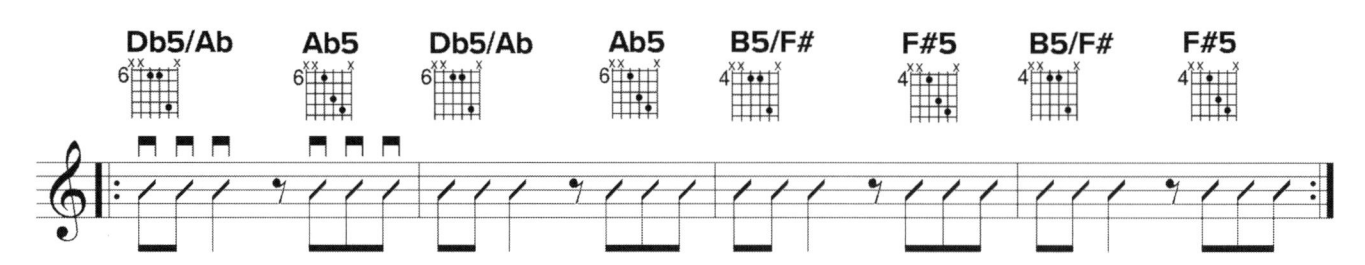

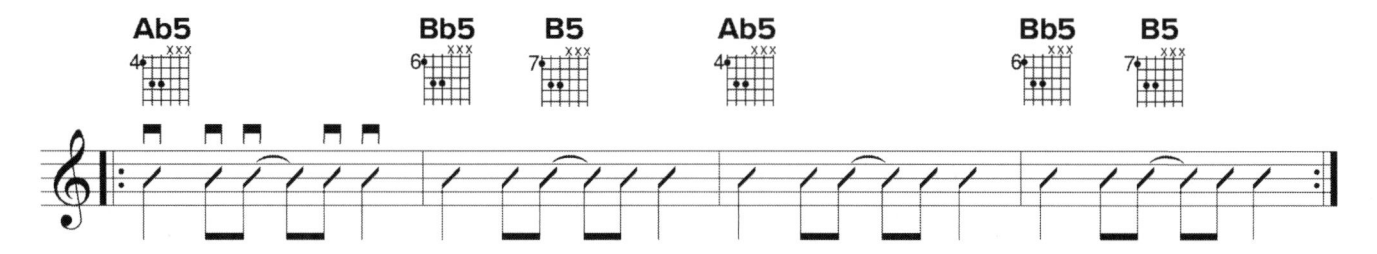

| Db5/Ab | Ab5 | Db5/Ab | Ab5 | B5/F# | F#5 | B5/F# | F#5 |

Chorus

| Ab5 | Bb5 | B5 | Ab5 | Bb5 | B5 |

Bridge

Verse

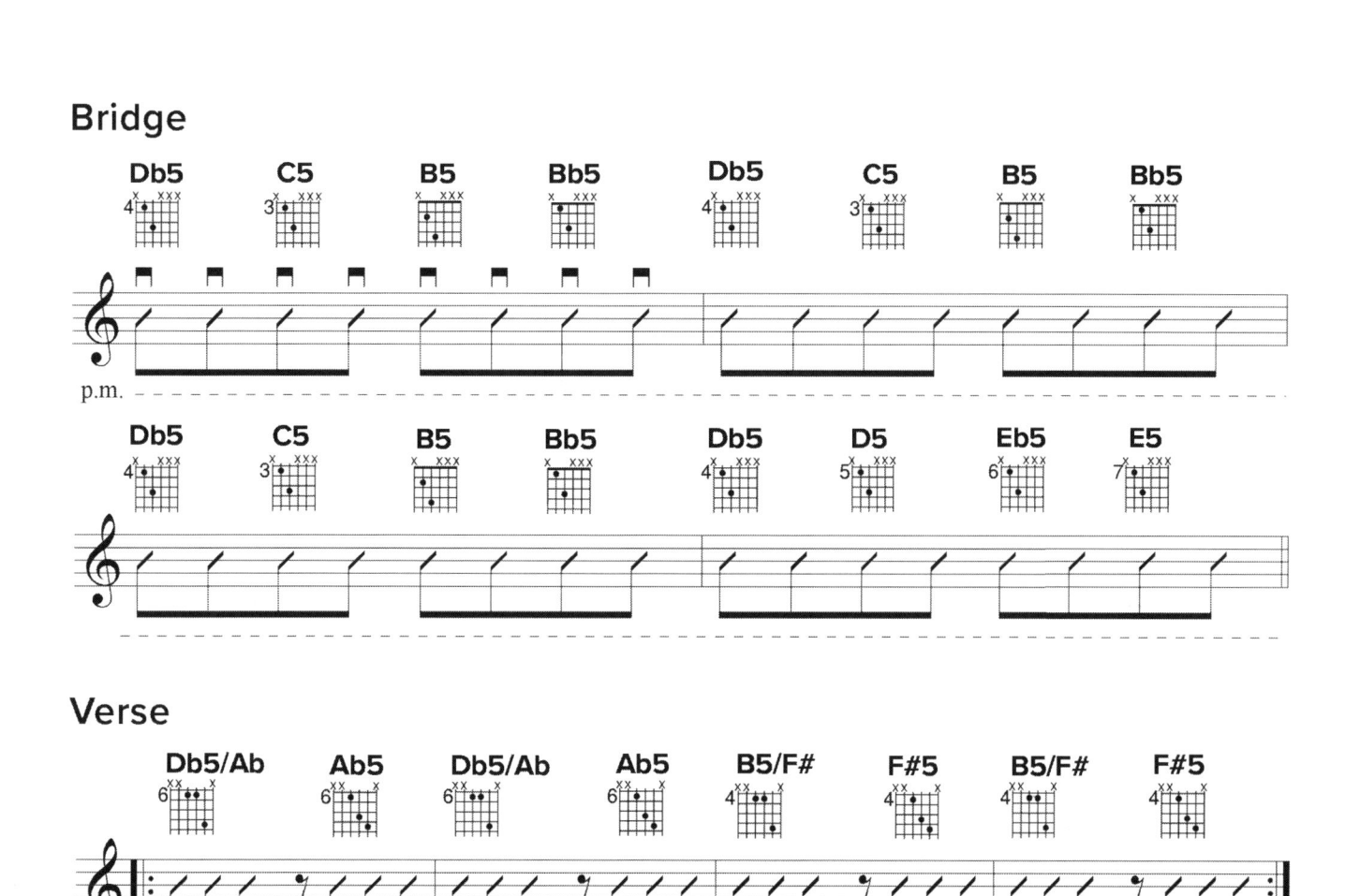

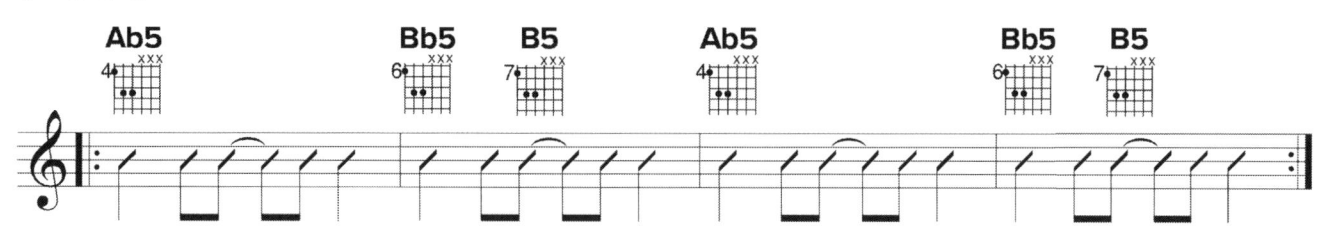

Chorus

Outro

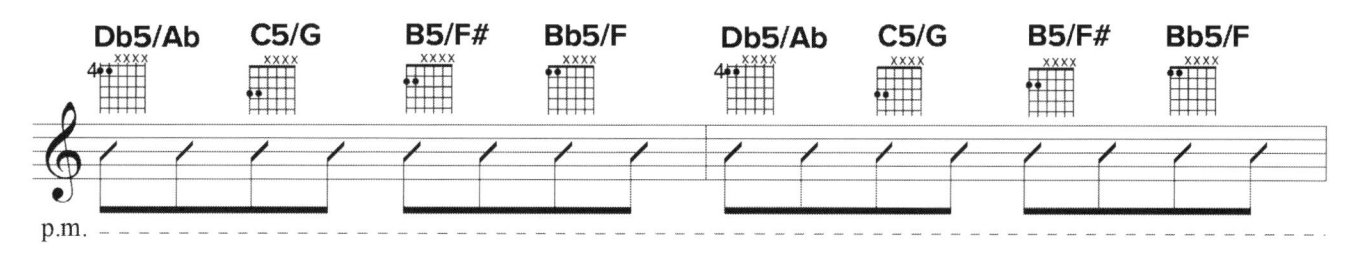

Outro (continued)

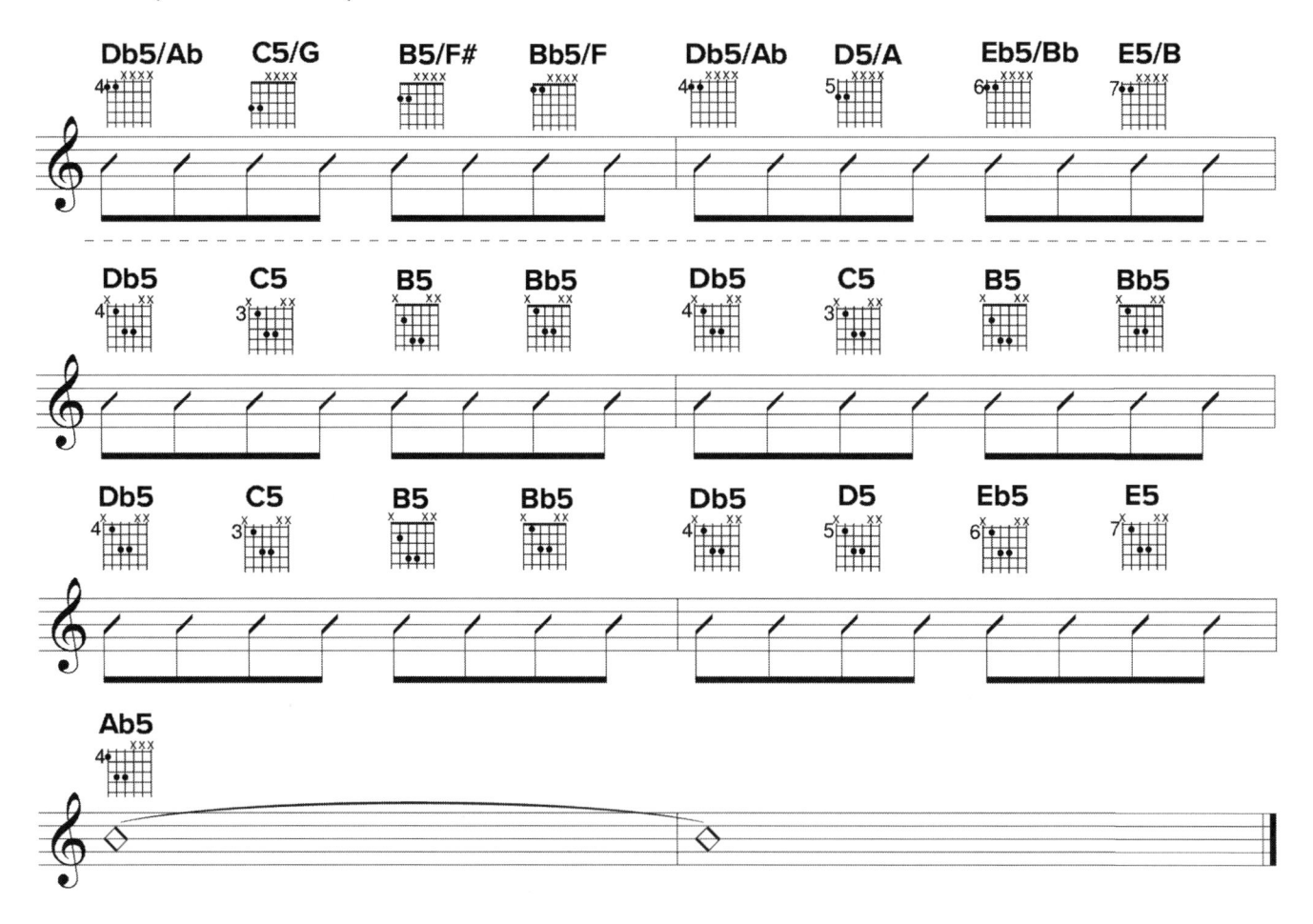

Fall for All

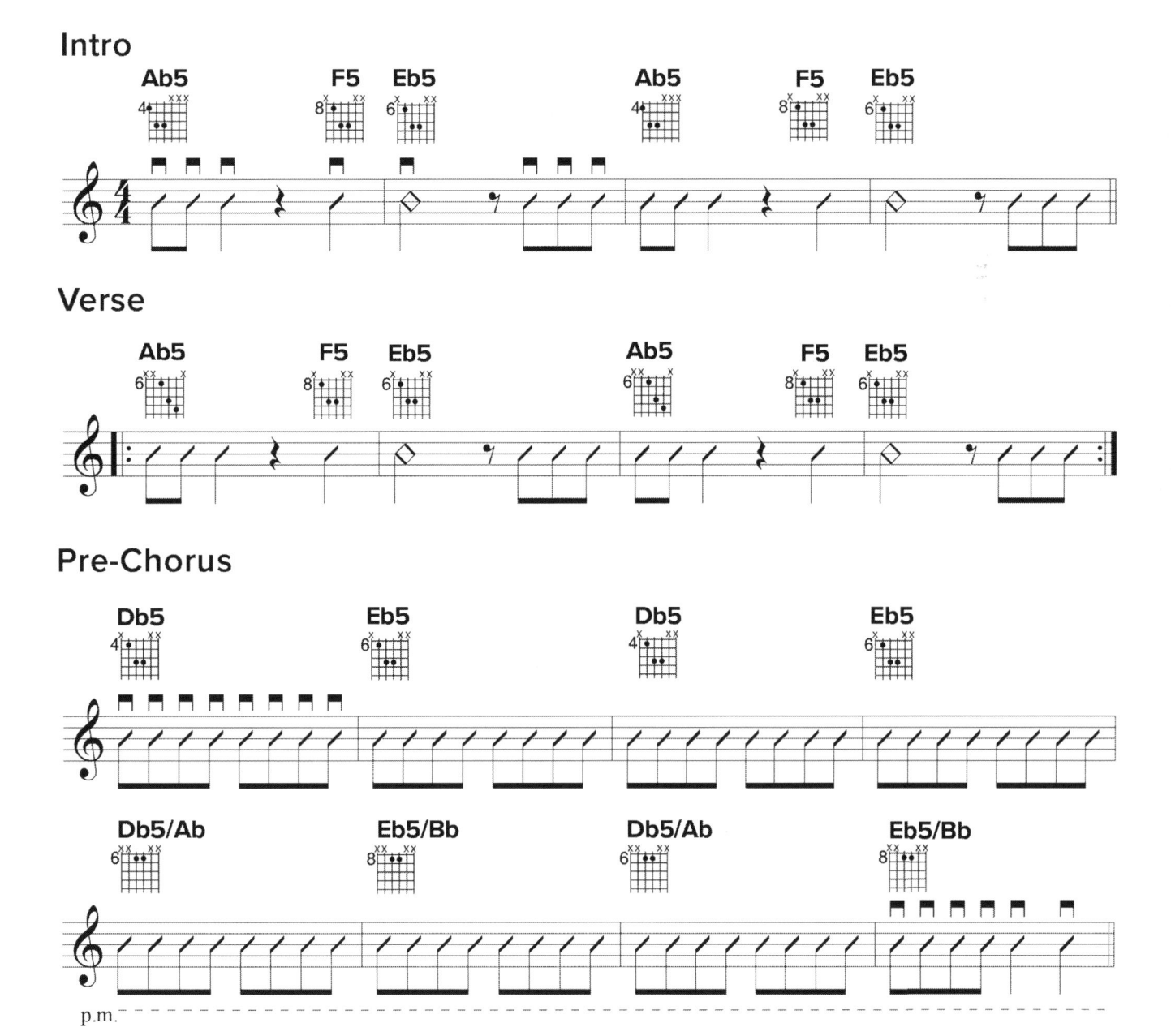

Intro

Ab5 F5 Eb5   Ab5 F5 Eb5

Verse

Ab5 F5 Eb5   Ab5 F5 Eb5

Pre-Chorus

Db5 Eb5 Db5 Eb5

Db5/Ab Eb5/Bb Db5/Ab Eb5/Bb

p.m.

Chorus

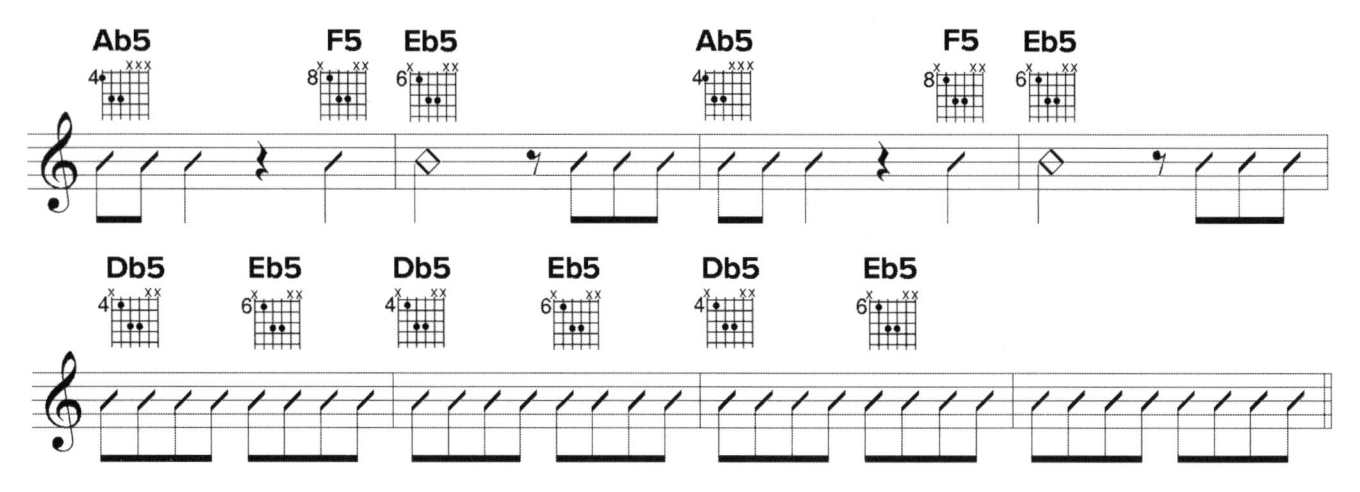

Verse

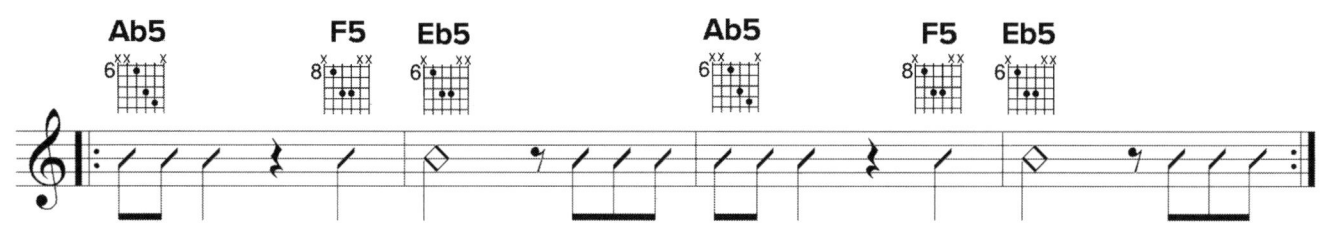

Pre-Chorus

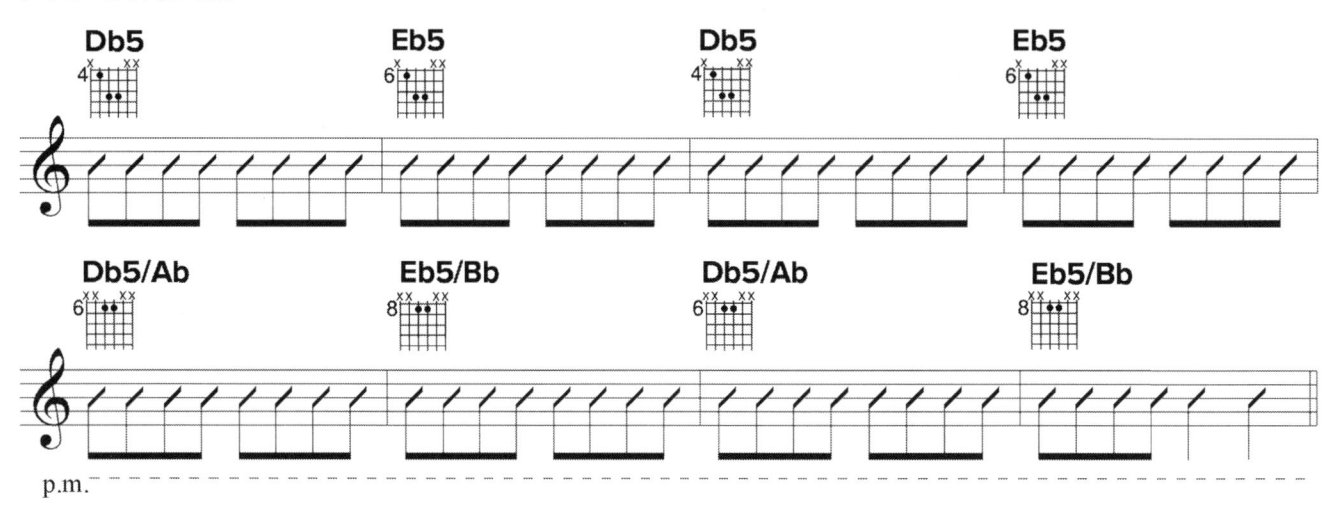

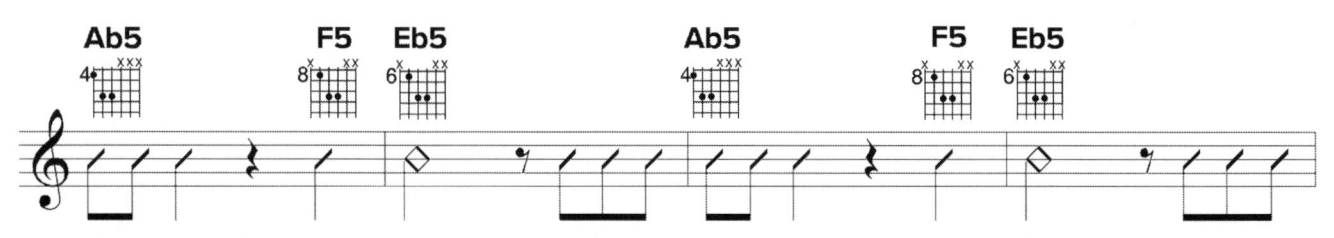

Chorus

Chorus (continued)

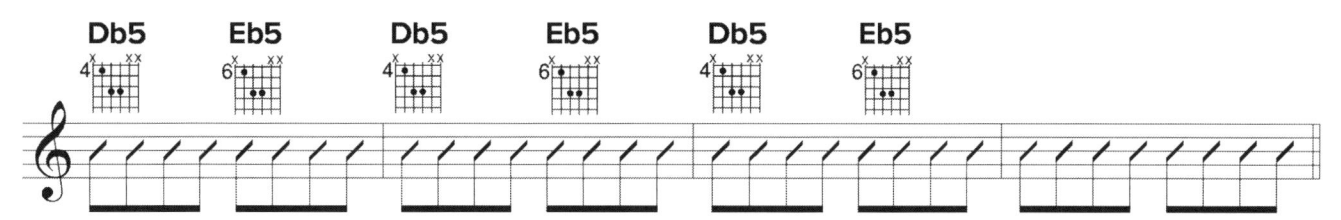

| Db5 | Eb5 | Db5 | Eb5 | Db5 | Eb5 |

Bridge

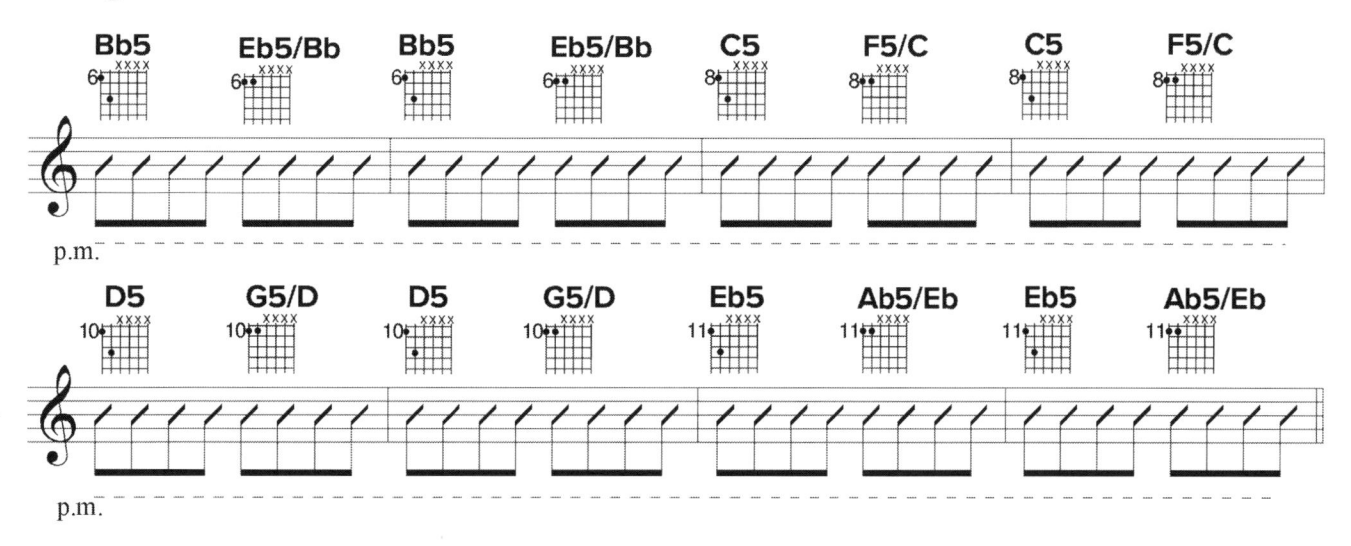

| Bb5 | Eb5/Bb | Bb5 | Eb5/Bb | C5 | F5/C | C5 | F5/C |

p.m.

| D5 | G5/D | D5 | G5/D | Eb5 | Ab5/Eb | Eb5 | Ab5/Eb |

p.m.

Verse

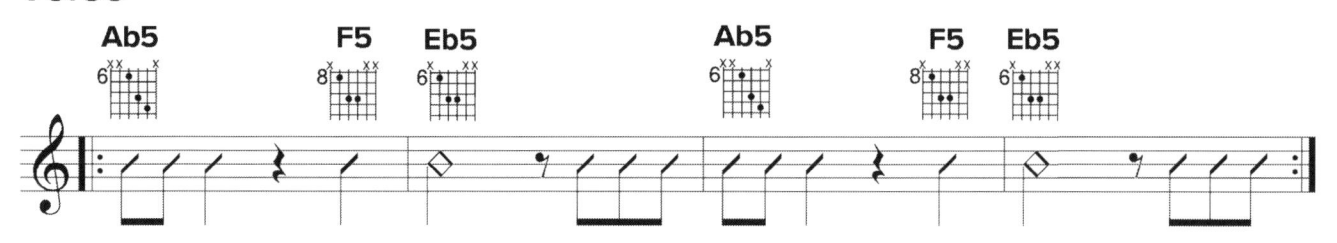

| Ab5 | F5 | Eb5 | Ab5 | F5 | Eb5 |

Pre-Chorus

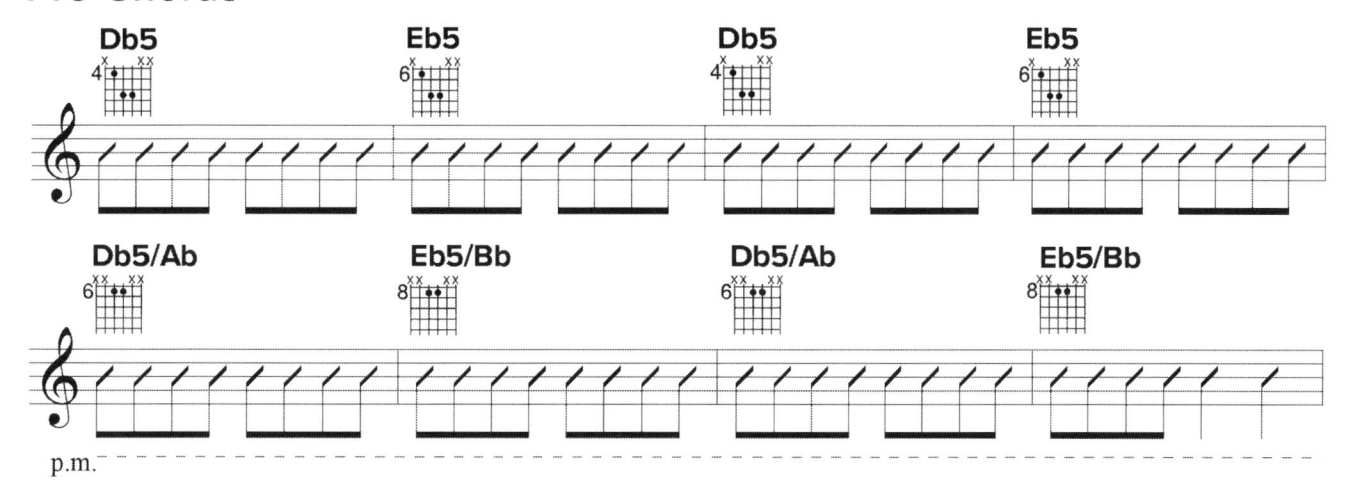

| Db5 | Eb5 | Db5 | Eb5 |

| Db5/Ab | Eb5/Bb | Db5/Ab | Eb5/Bb |

p.m.

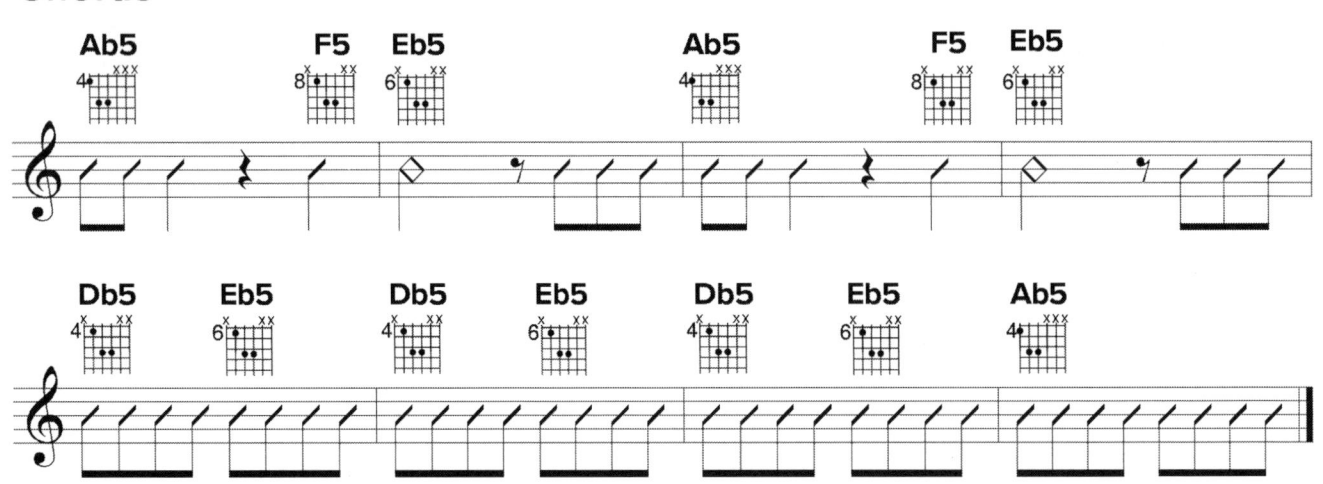

Chorus

Lesson 11:
Drop D Power Chords

Another way you can play power chords is to tune the last string (the thickest string) down to the pitch "D," hence the name "dropped-D power chords". As such, this tuning only effects chords whose roots are found on that string.

There are a couple of ways in which you can lower your low "E" string. The easiest way is to use a chromatic tuner. A chromatic tuner picks up any note, meaning it isn't guitar specific, and therefore is easier to use when changing the pitch of the string. To do this, simply tune your last string down one whole step, from standard tuning "E" down to the new pitch "D".

Another way you can drop your last string to D is to use a reference pitch. To do this, play the open D string (fourth string) and then listen to it. Then lower your last string until they sound alike, or in other words, a perfect octave apart.

Since the E string is now a D string, the rest of the notes on the string have moved as well. Therefore, the first fret is now D#/Eb, the next is E, etc. See the charts below.

Natural Notes

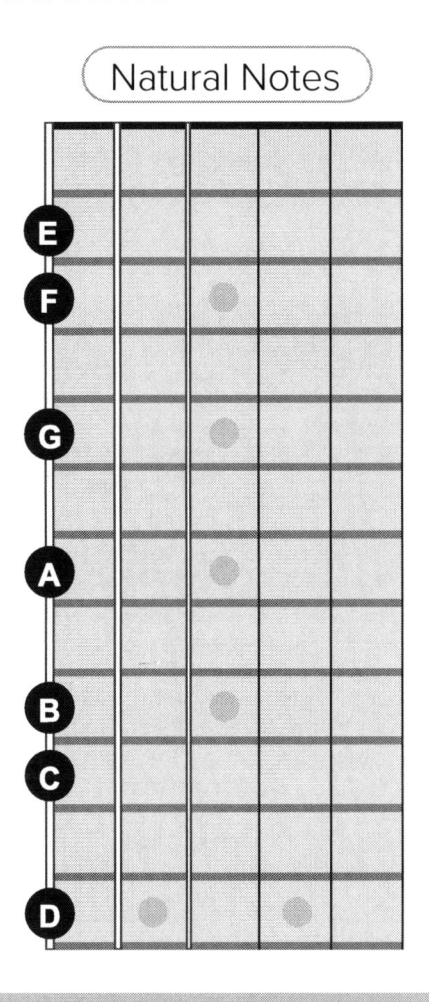

Sharps and Flats

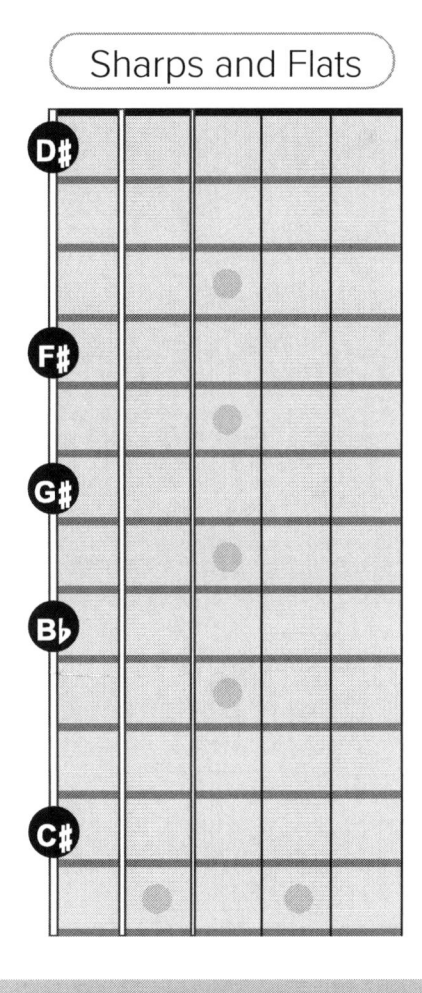

Drop D Power Chord Examples

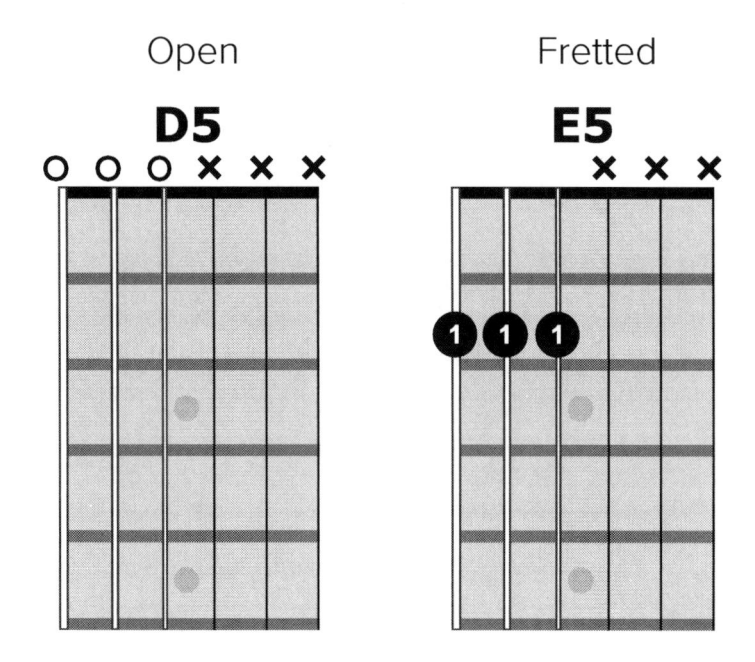

Open — **D5**

Fretted — **E5**

Practice the following Drop D Exercises

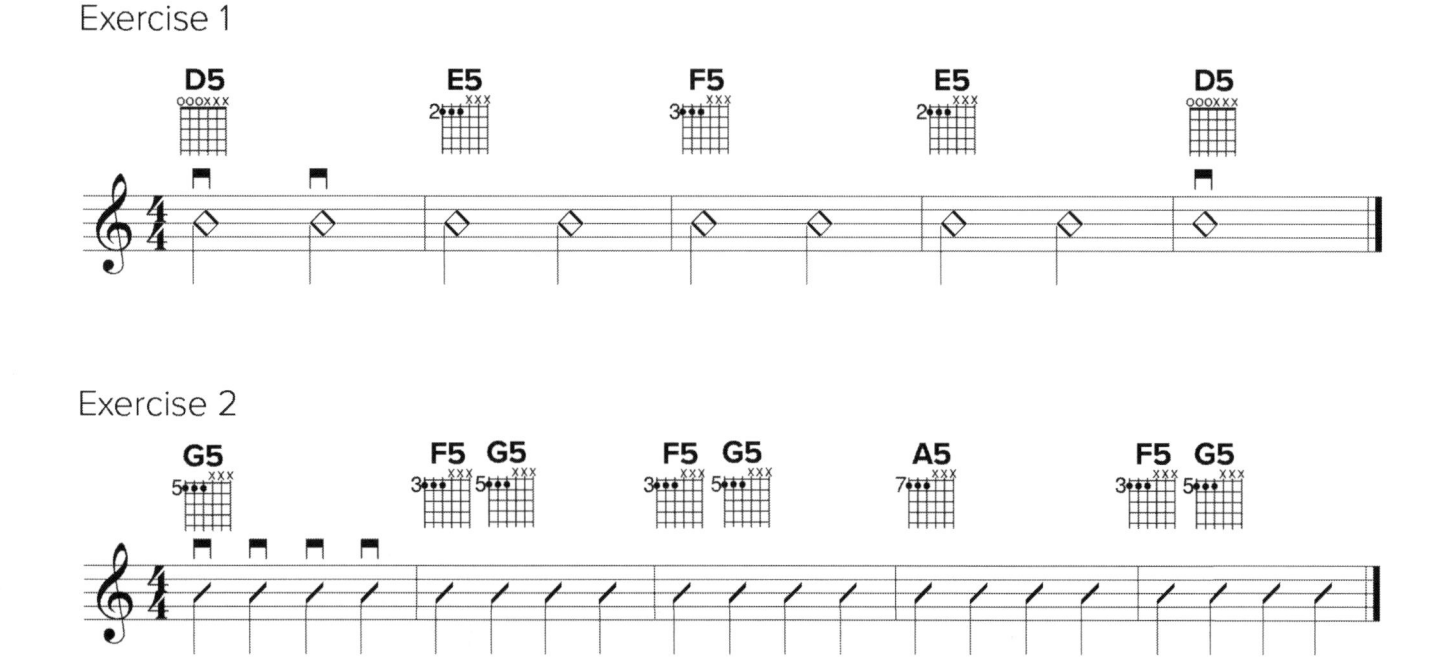

Exercise 1

D5   E5   F5   E5   D5

Exercise 2

G5   F5 G5   F5 G5   A5   F5 G5

Exercise 3

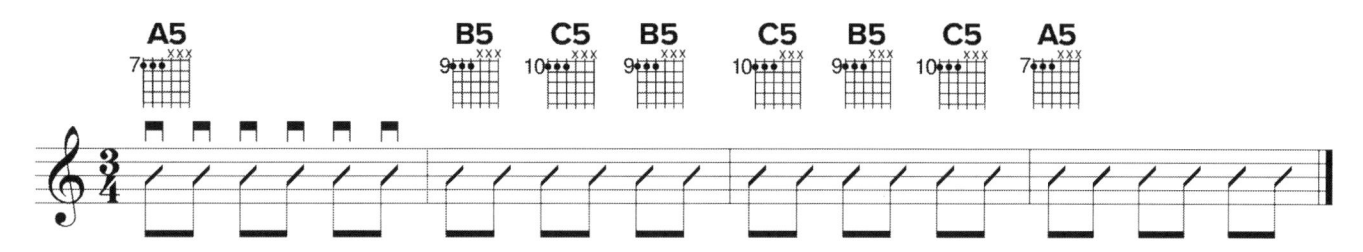

Exercise 4

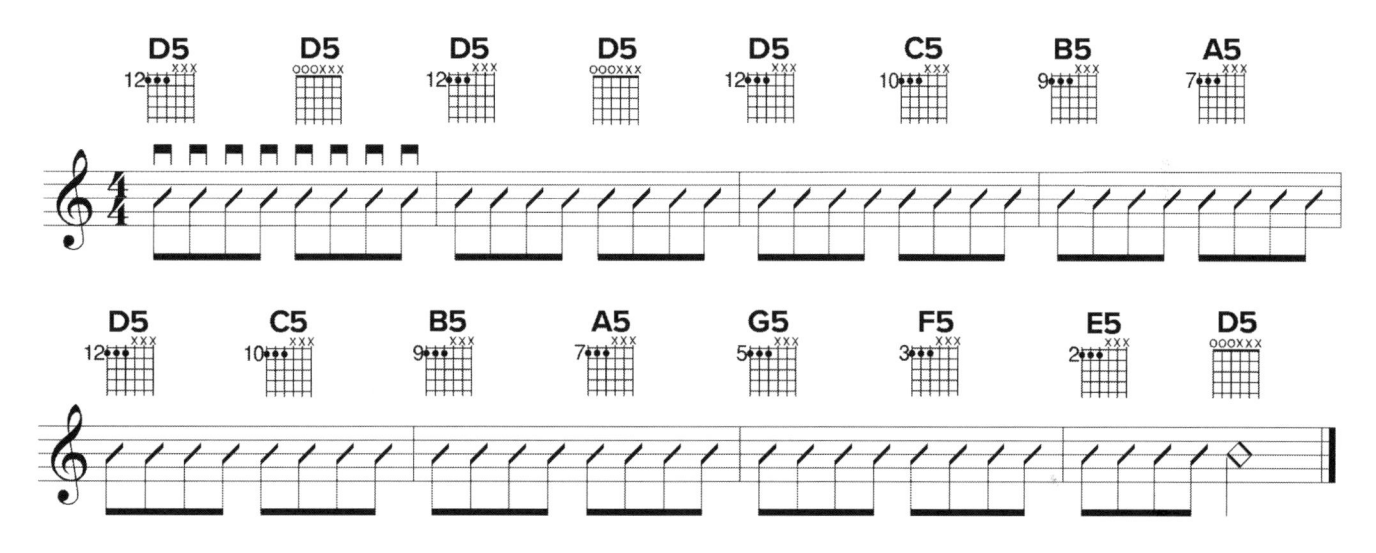

Exercise 5

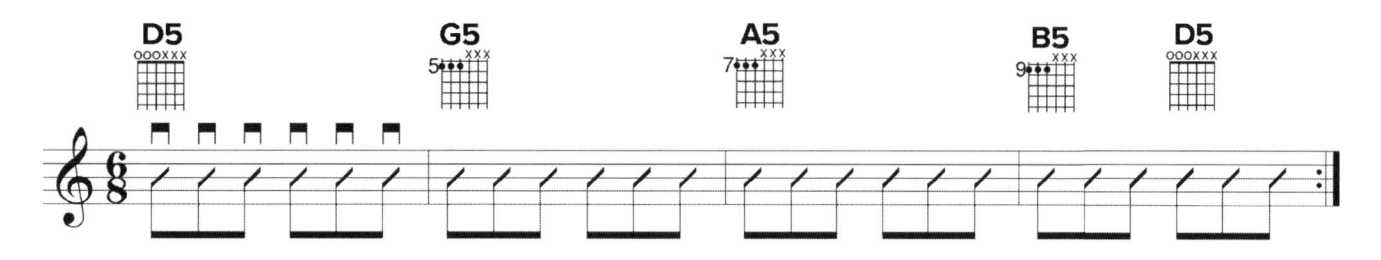

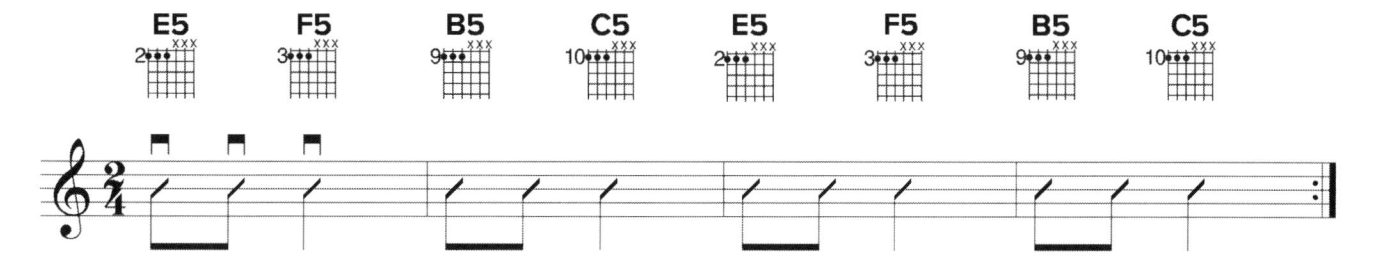

Exercise 6

Exercise 7

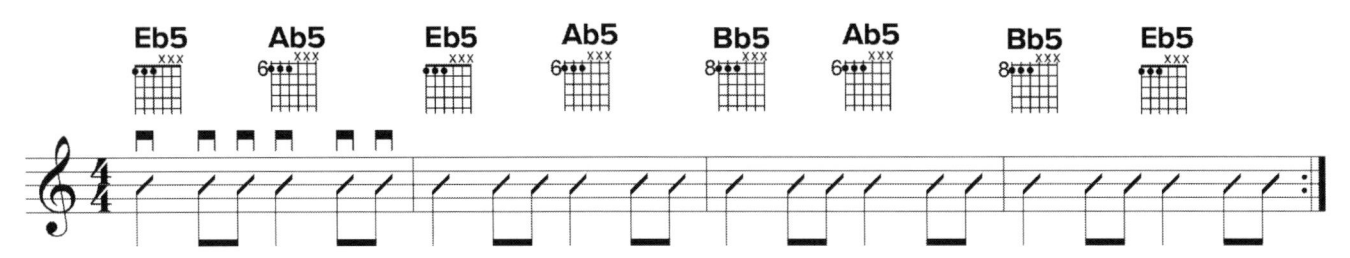

Exercise 8

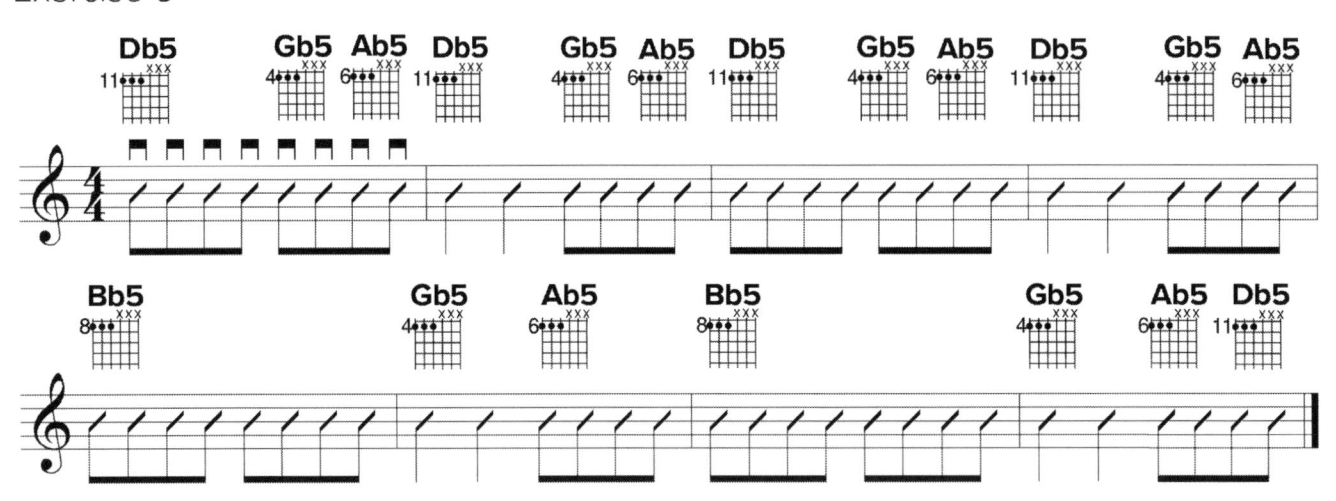

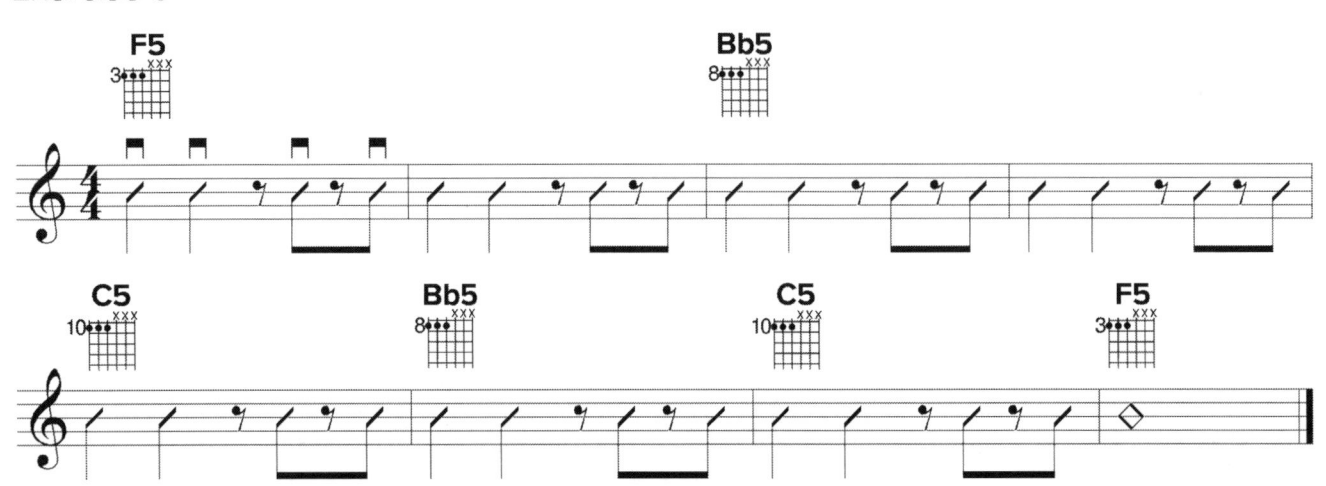

Exercise 9

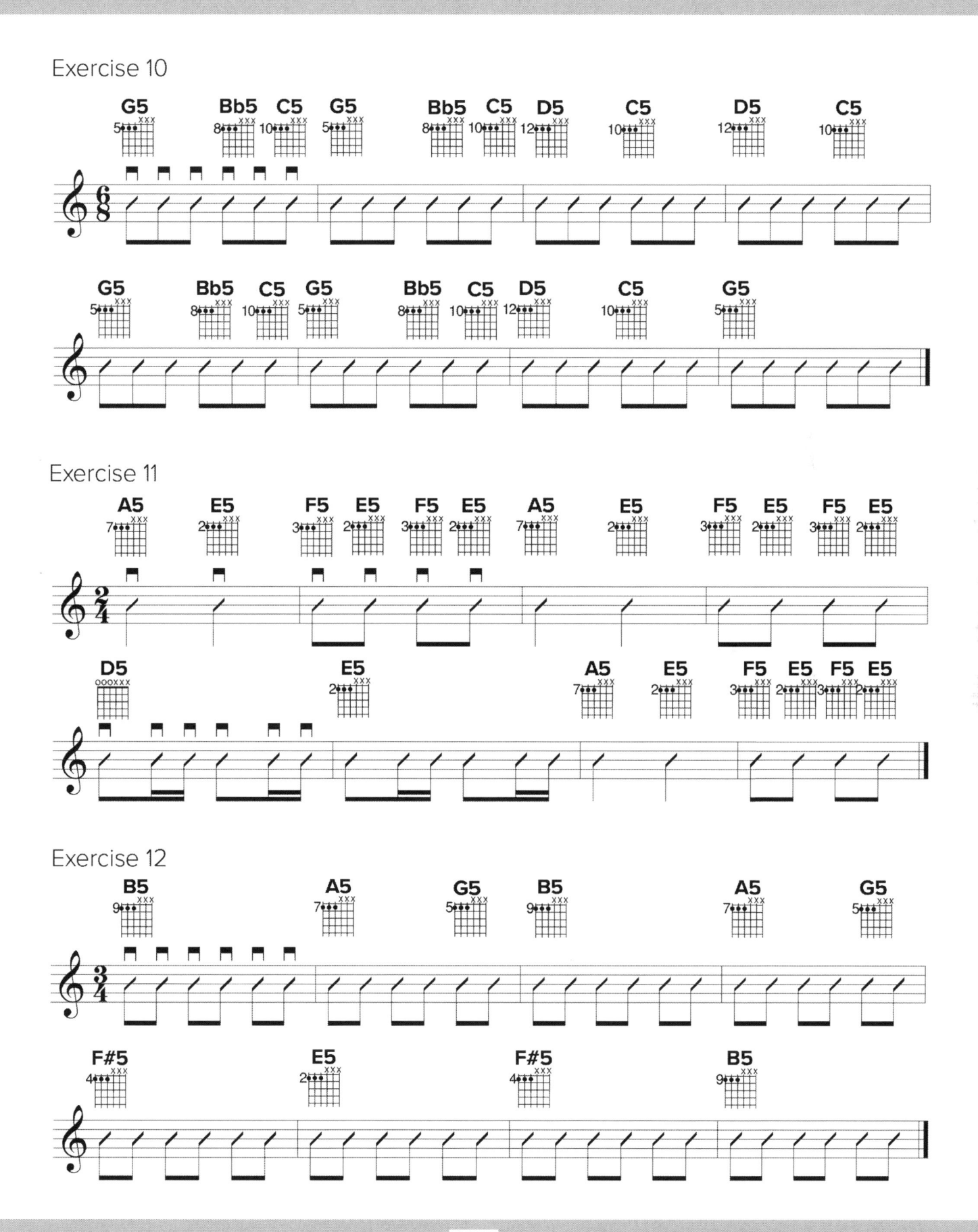

Exercise 10

Exercise 11

Exercise 12

The drop D chord boxes have been omitted in the following exercises to test your memory.

Exercise 13

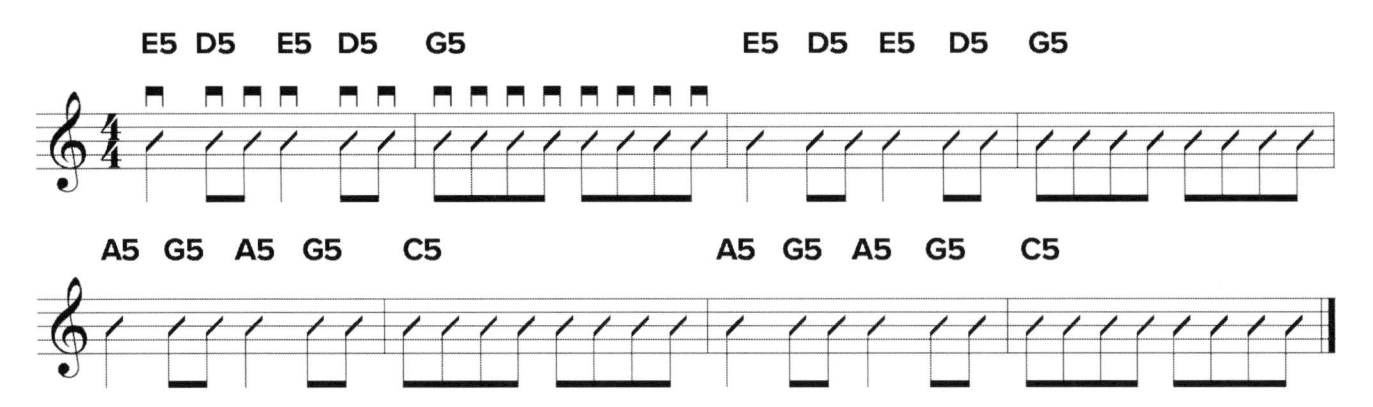

| E5 D5 E5 D5 | G5 | | E5 D5 E5 D5 | G5 |

| A5 G5 A5 G5 | C5 | | A5 G5 A5 G5 | C5 |

Exercise 14

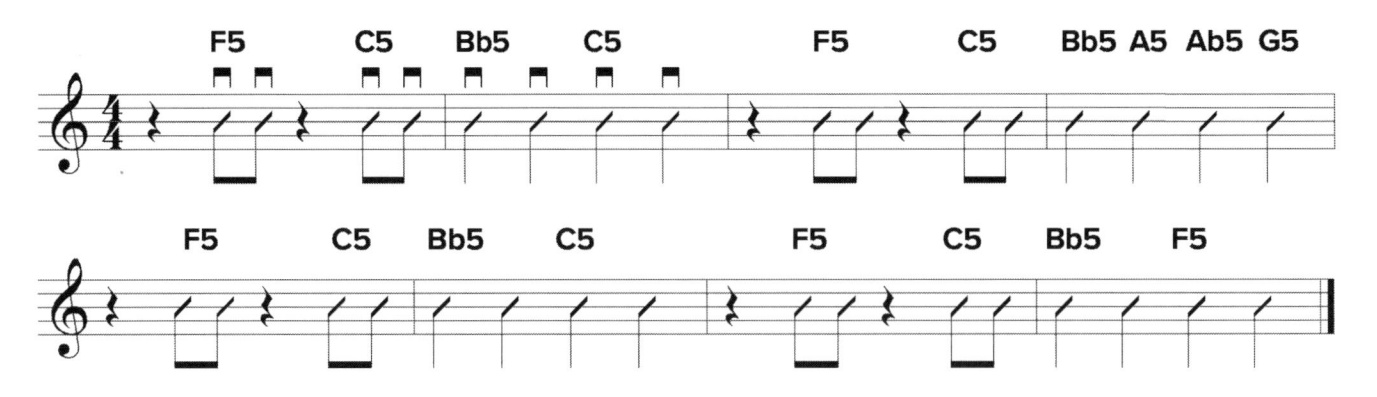

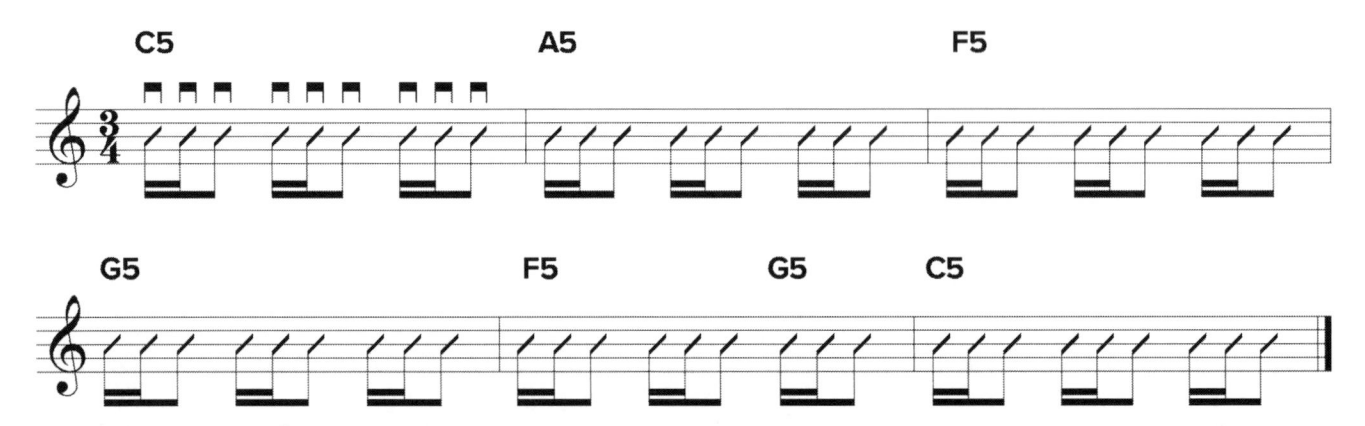

| F5 | C5 | Bb5 | C5 | F5 | C5 | Bb5 A5 Ab5 G5 |

| F5 | C5 | Bb5 | C5 | F5 | C5 | Bb5 | F5 |

Exercise 15

| C5 | A5 | F5 |

| G5 | F5 | G5 | C5 |

In Exercise 16, play the D5 in lines one and two open. Then in measure 9, play the D5 at the 12th fret. Finally, play the D5 open again in the last two measures.

Exercise 16

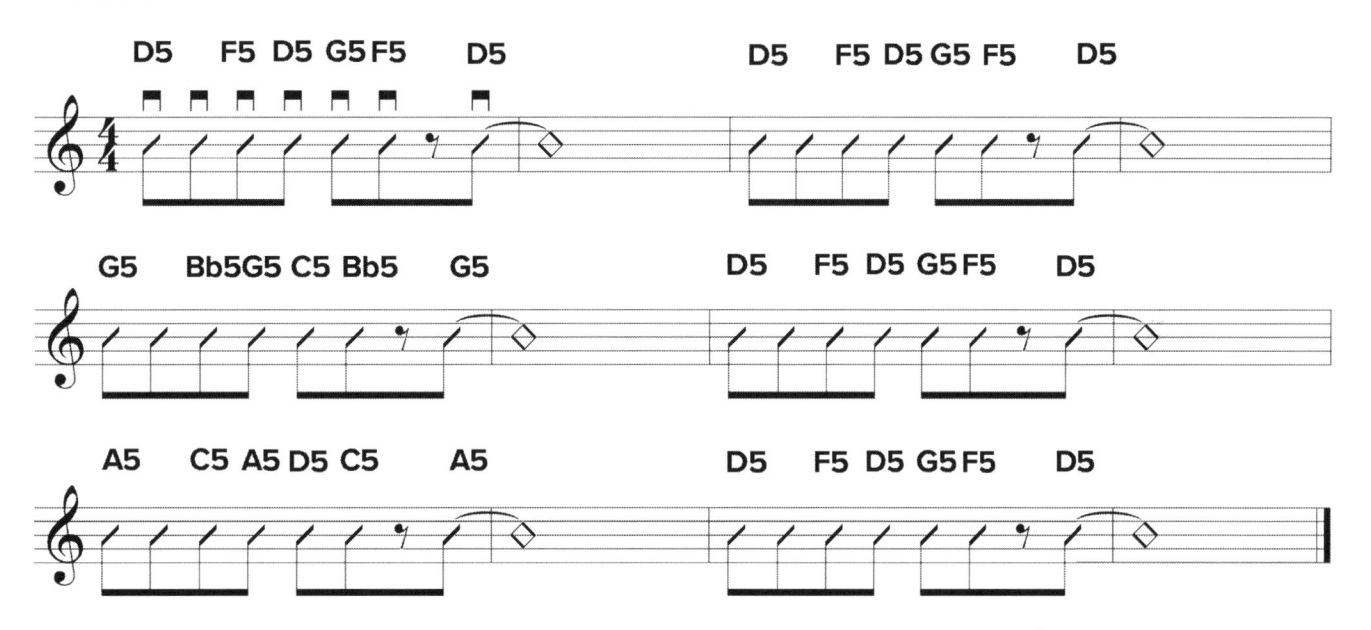

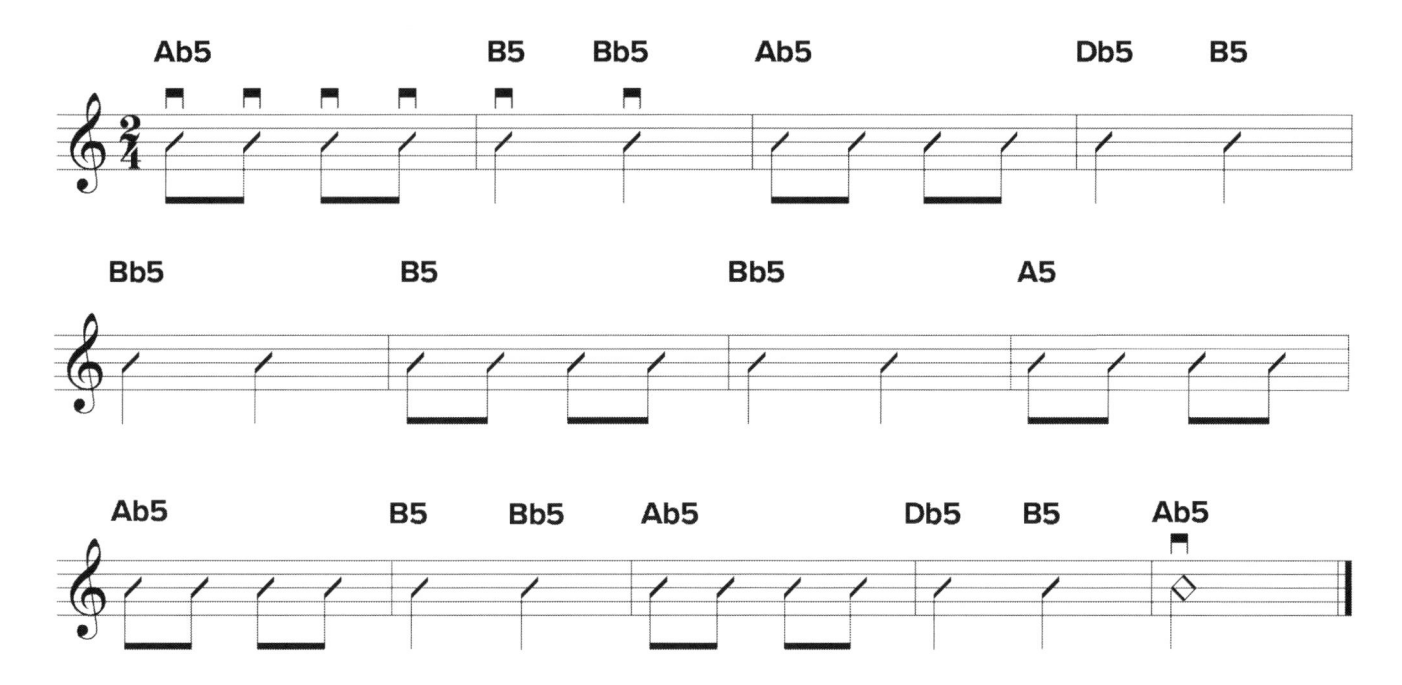

Exercise 17

In this next section, we will now combine drop "D" power chords with some of the other power chords learned in this book. So be sure to read the chord charts carefully.

Review Exercise 1

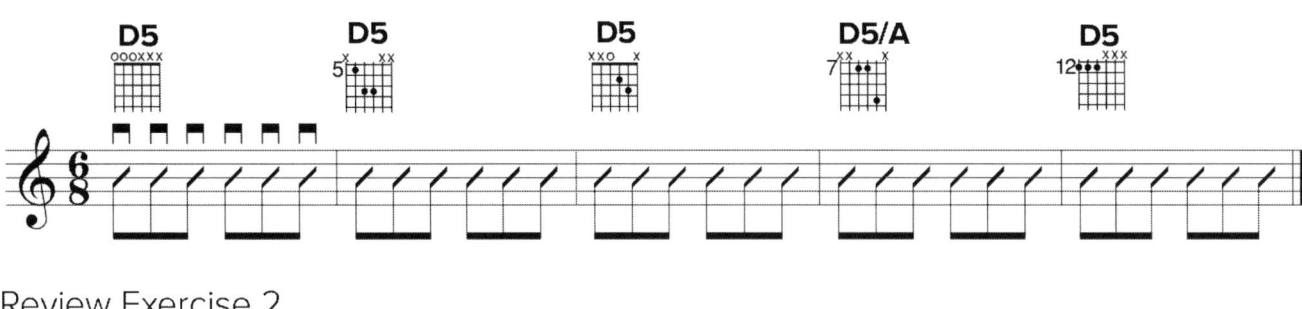

Review Exercise 2

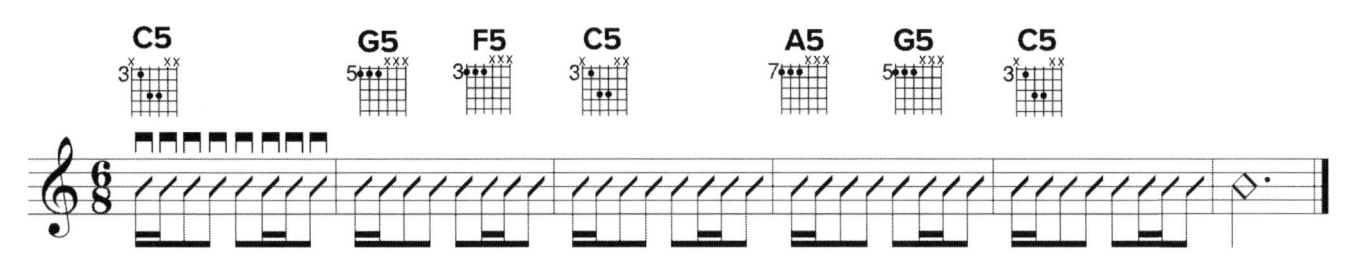

Review Exercise 3

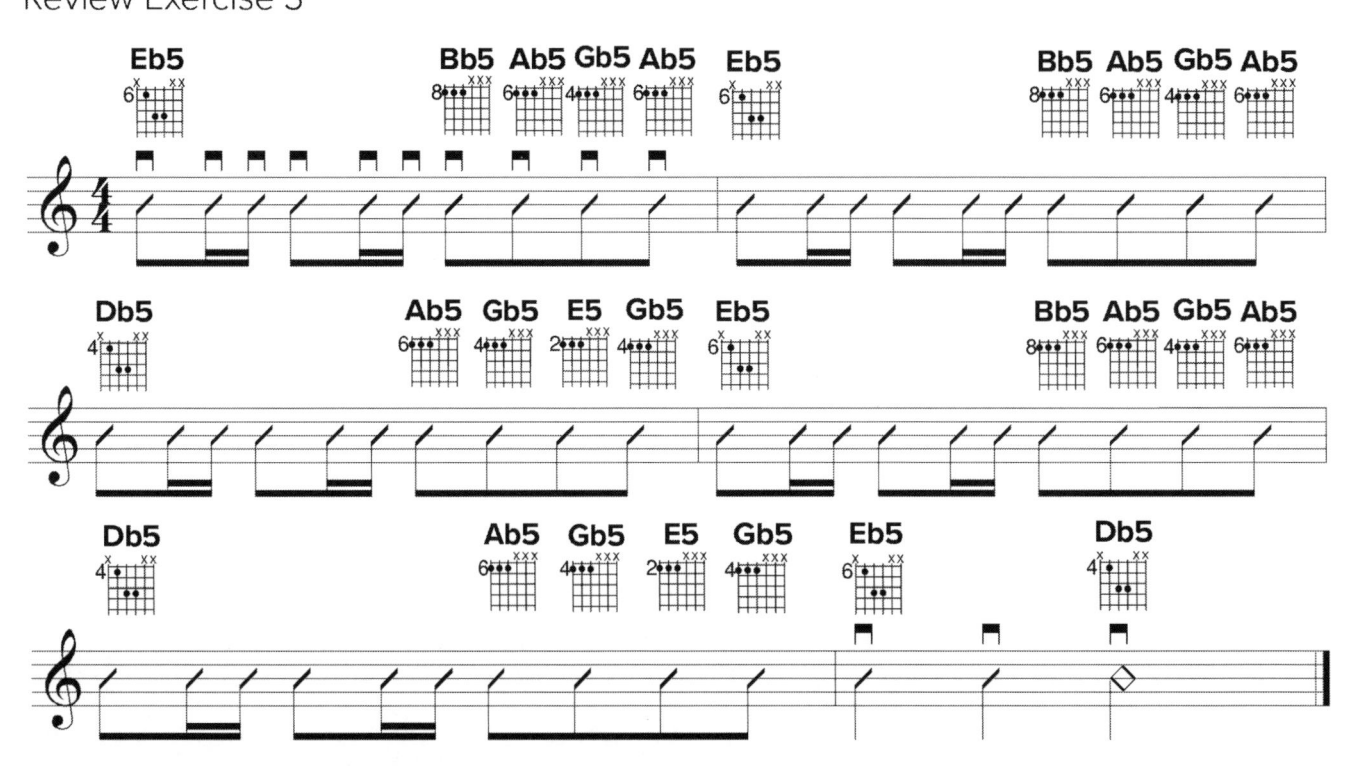

Review Exercise 4

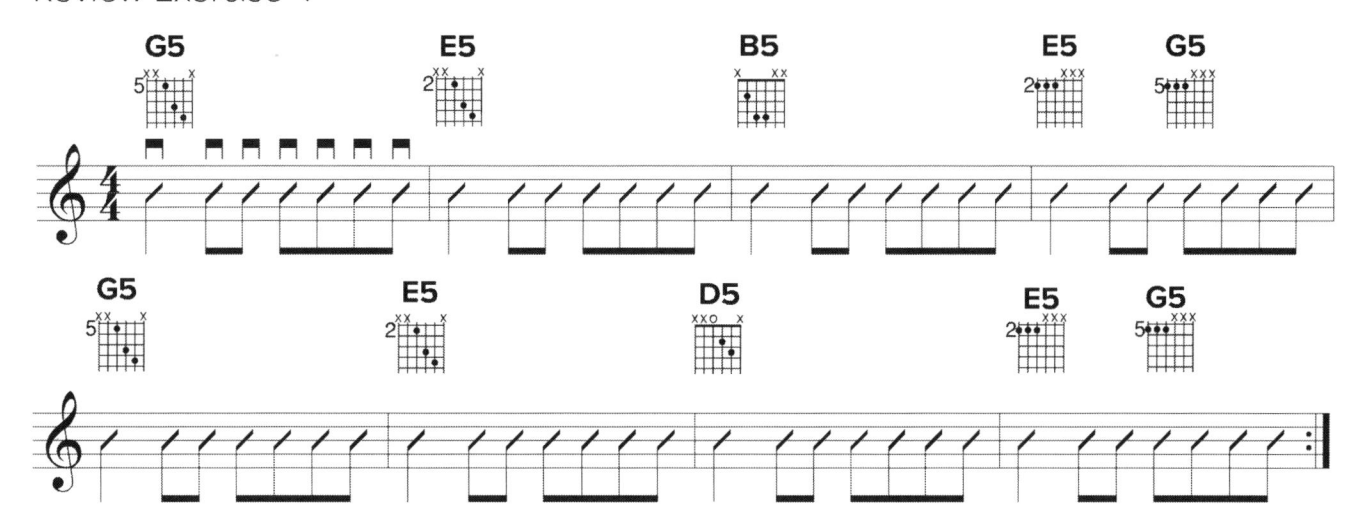

Review Exercise 5

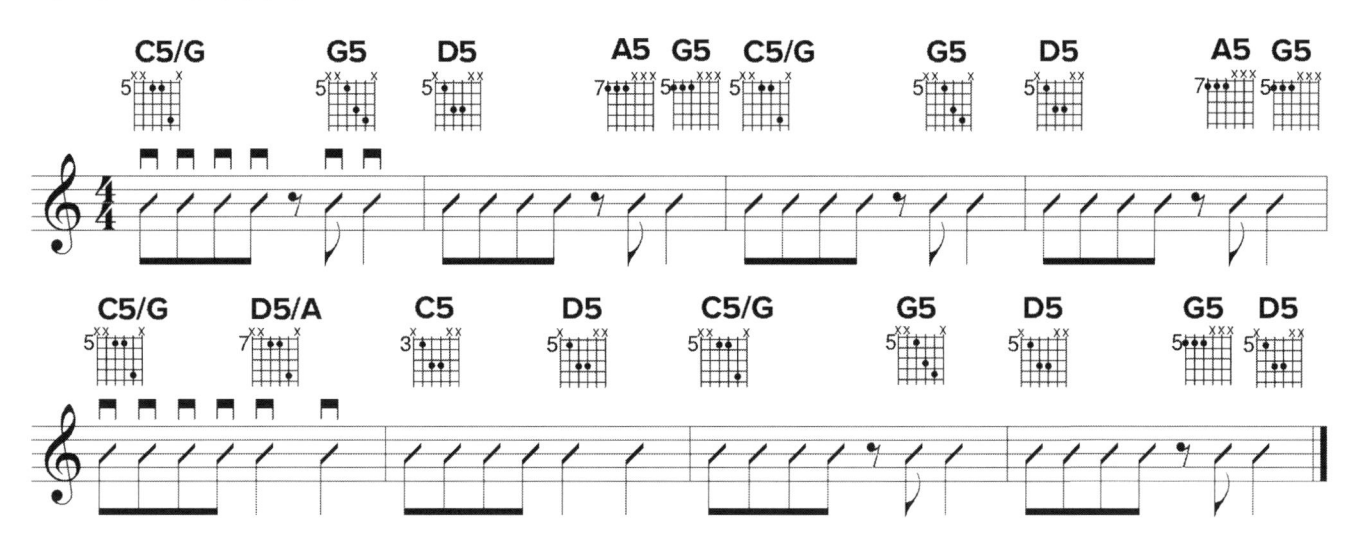

Review Exercise 6

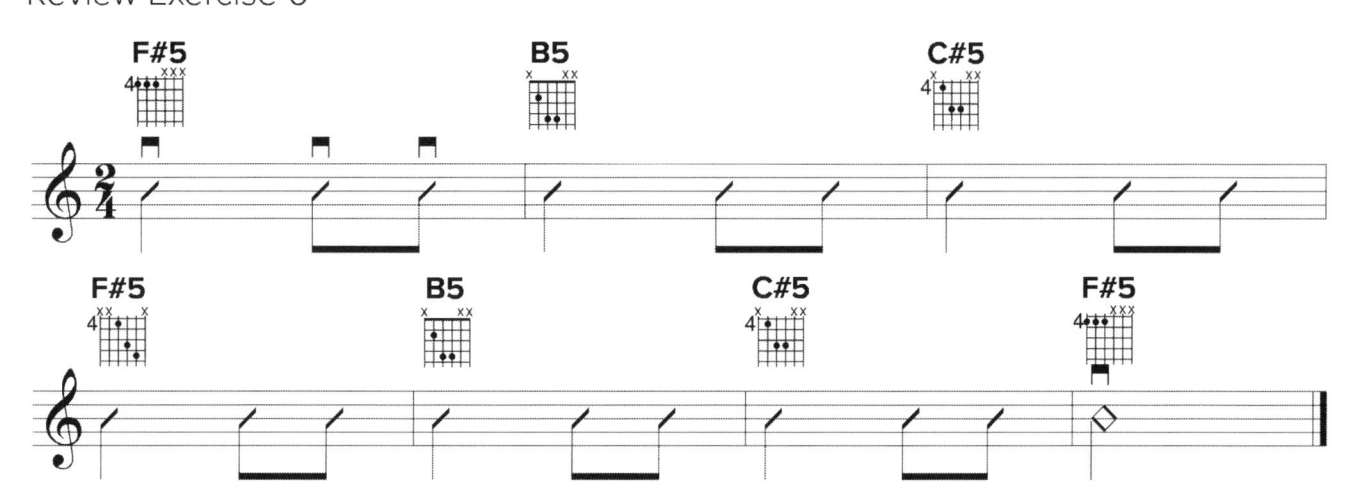

Like all the other power chords in this book, the drop "D" power chords also have a two-note version. These are not as commonly used as their three-note counterparts, but they are still useful to know. Below you can see some examples, followed by a few practice exercises.

Two Note Drop D Power Chord Examples

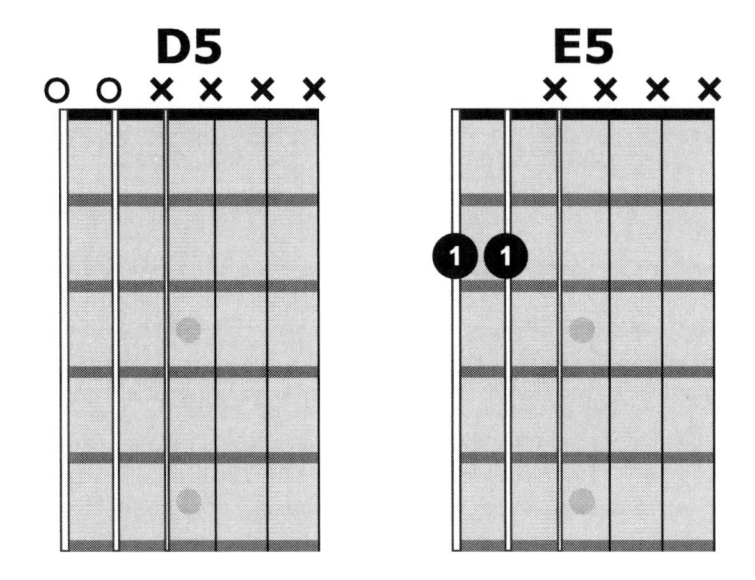

D5

E5

Practice the following Drop D Exercises

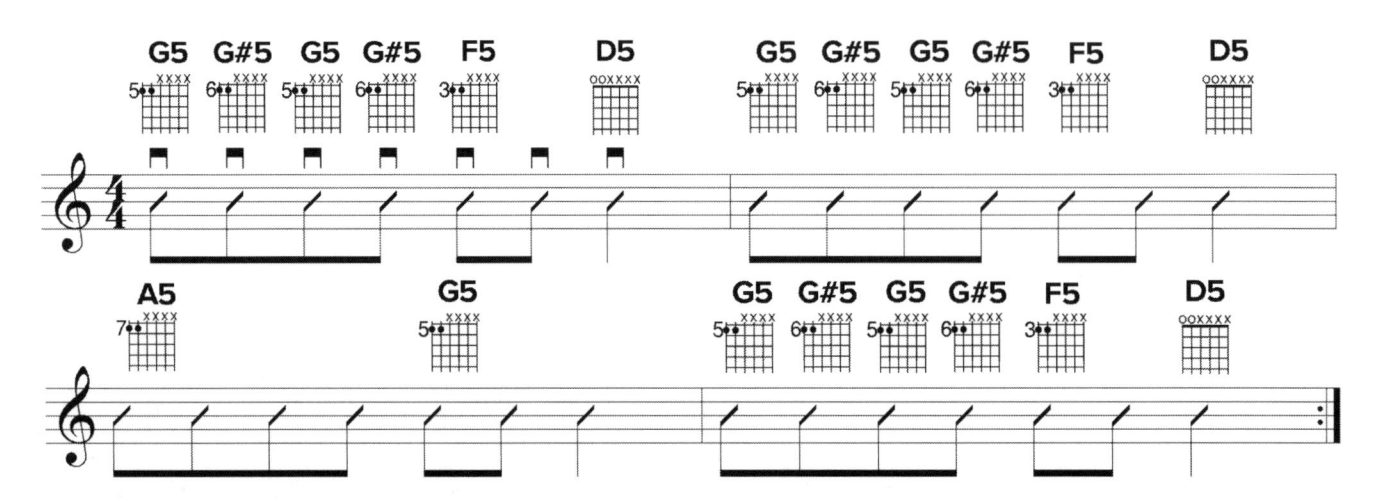

Exercise 1

G5 G#5 G5 G#5 F5   D5   G5 G#5 G5 G#5 F5   D5

A5   G5   G5 G#5 G5 G#5 F5   D5

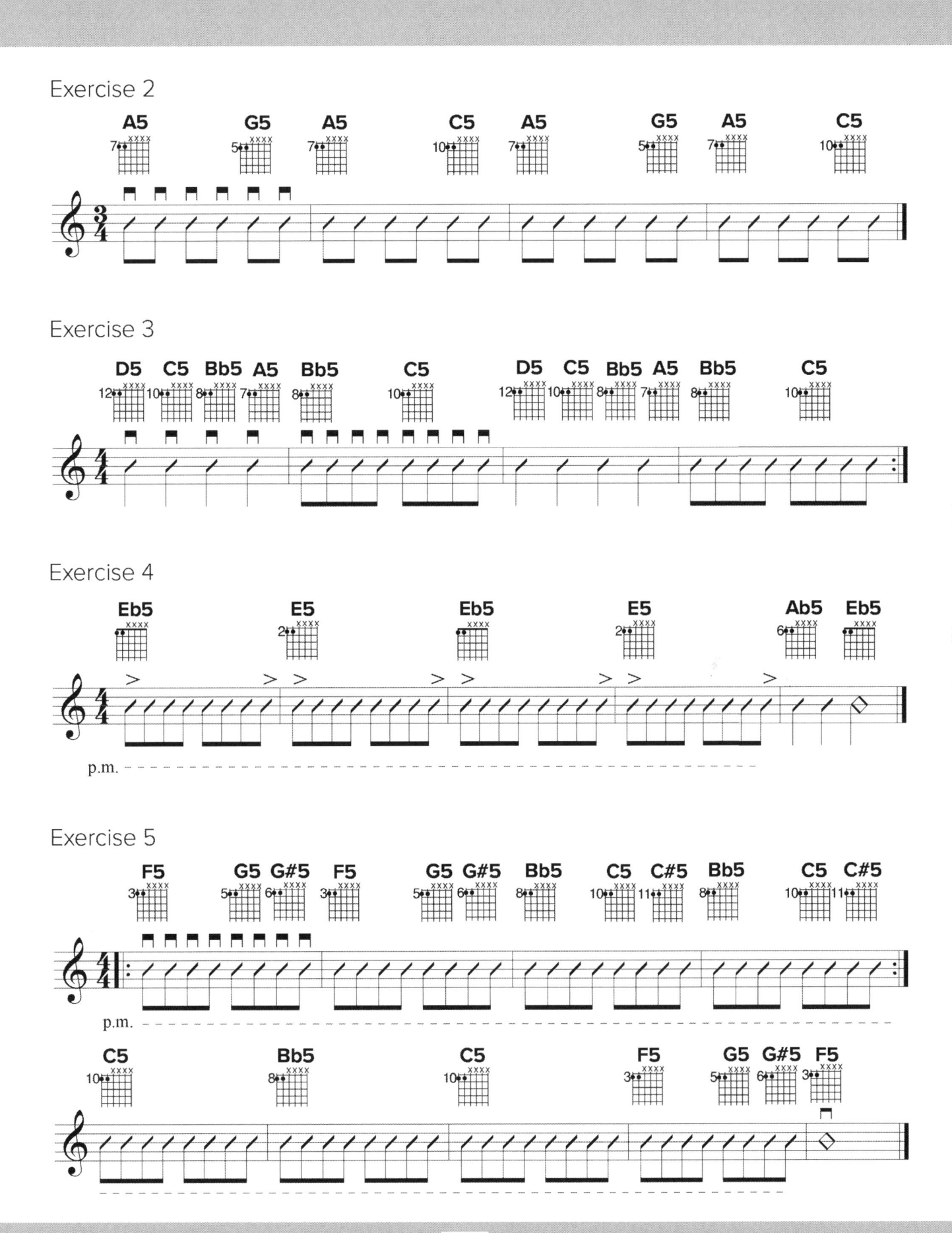

Exercise 2

Exercise 3

Exercise 4

Exercise 5

Lesson 12: Review Songs

I Have The Power

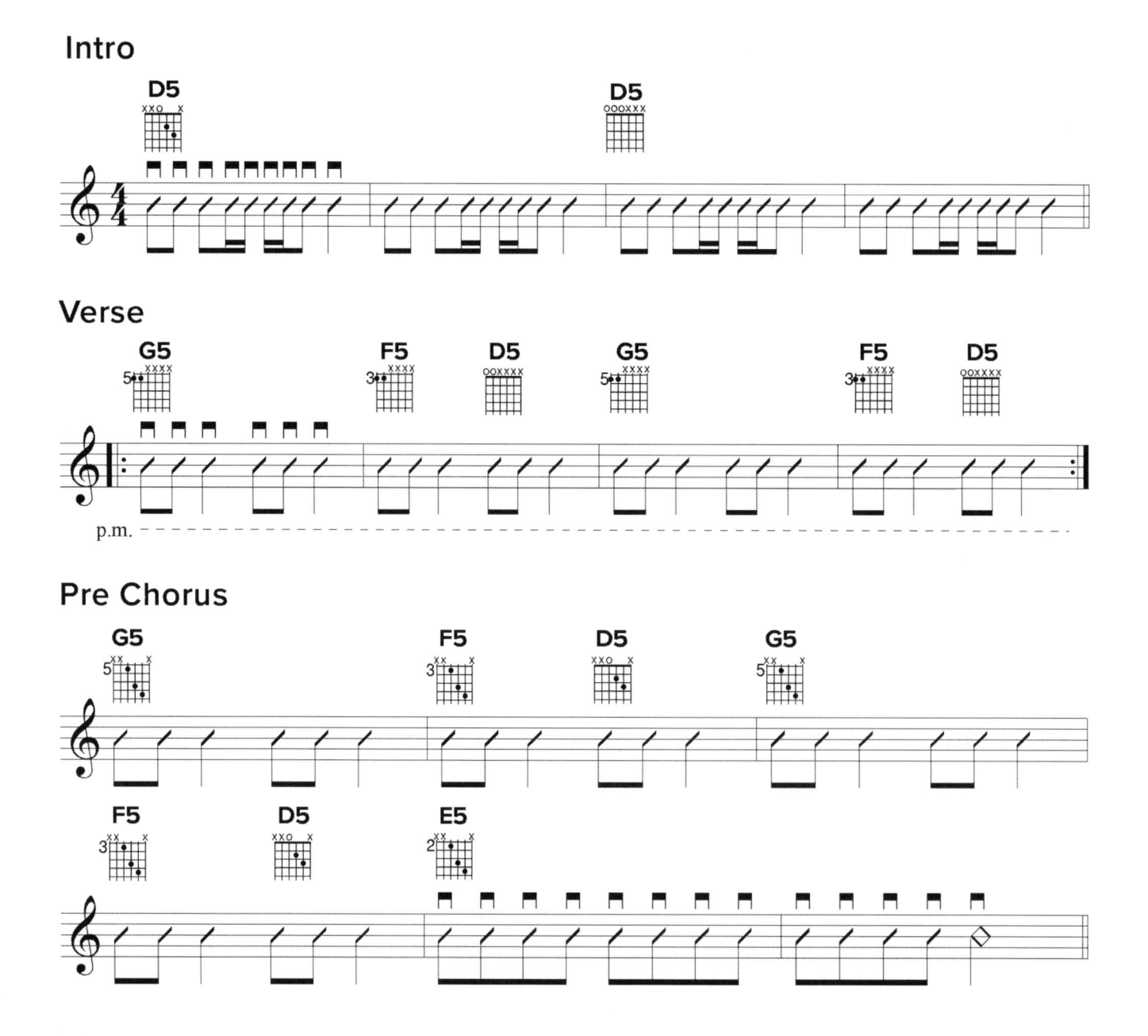

Intro

Verse

Pre Chorus

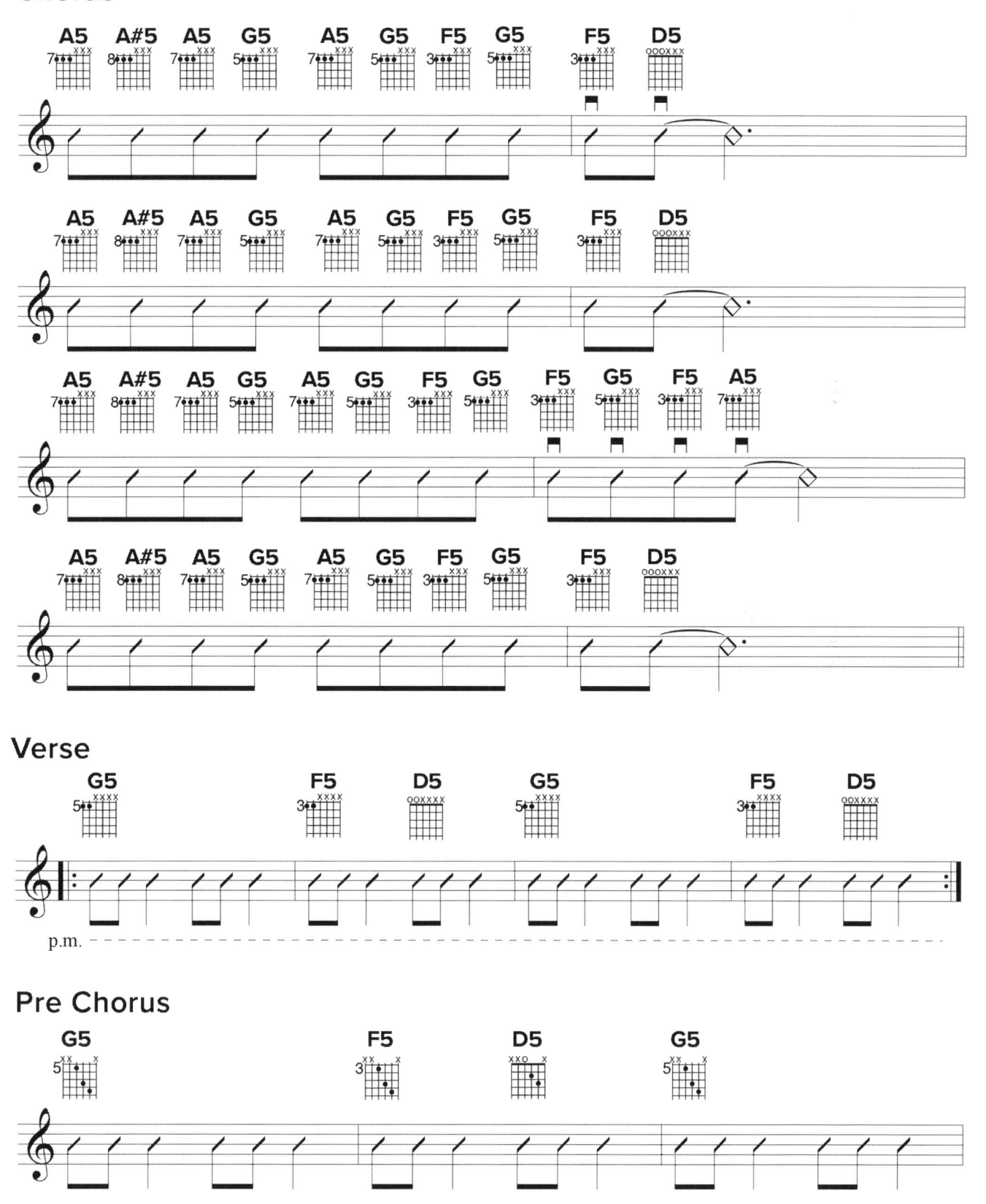

Chorus

Verse

Pre Chorus

Pre Chorus (continued)

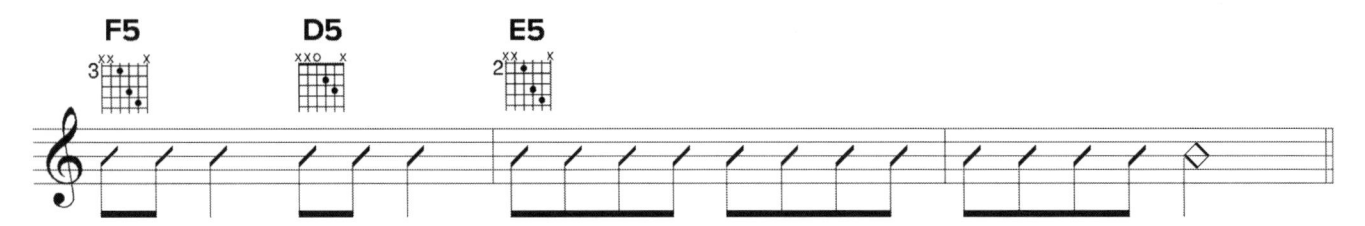

| F5 | D5 | E5 |

Chorus

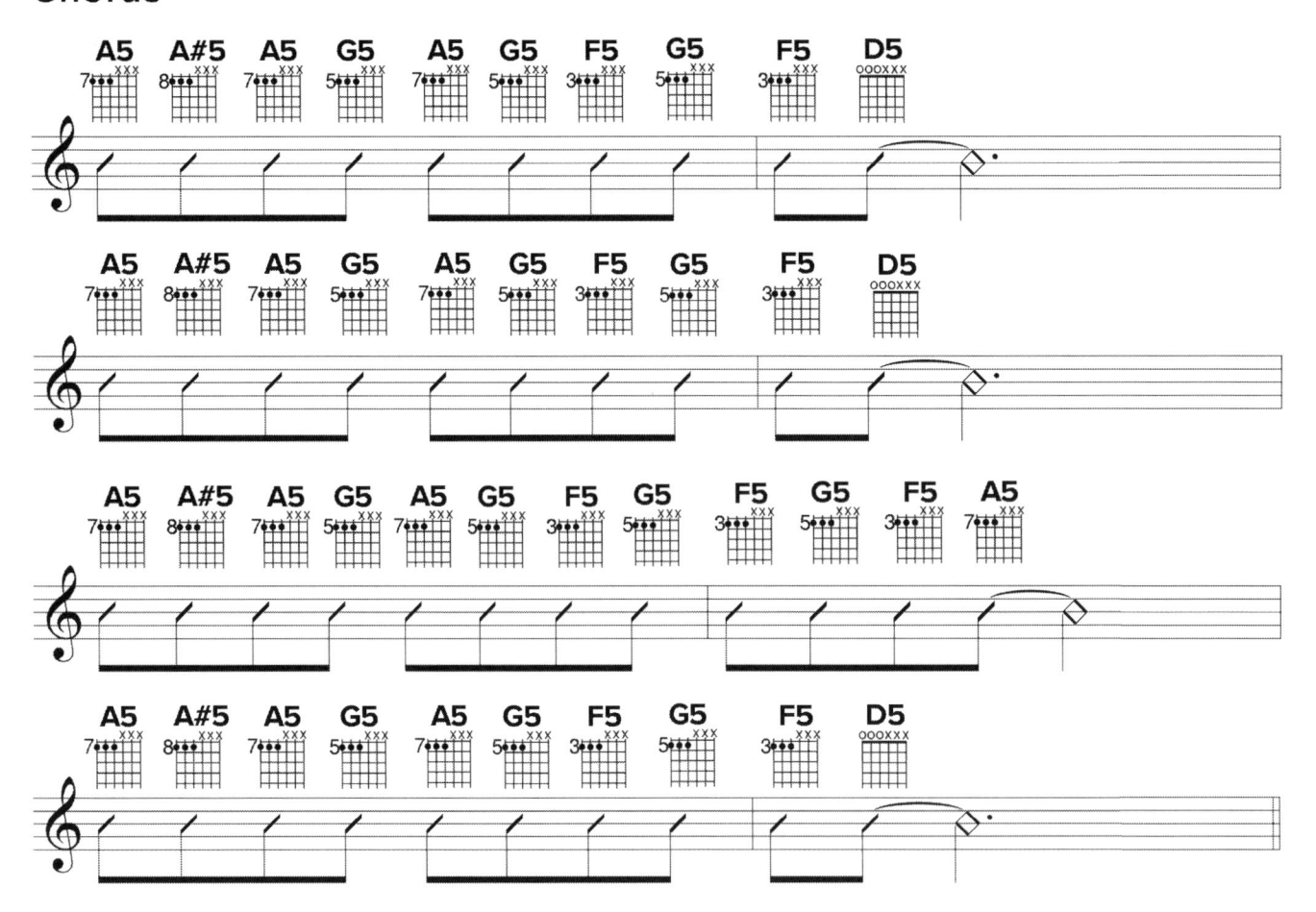

| A5 | A#5 | A5 | G5 | A5 | G5 | F5 | G5 | F5 | D5 |

| A5 | A#5 | A5 | G5 | A5 | G5 | F5 | G5 | F5 | D5 |

| A5 | A#5 | A5 | G5 | A5 | G5 | F5 | G5 | F5 | G5 | F5 | A5 |

| A5 | A#5 | A5 | G5 | A5 | G5 | F5 | G5 | F5 | D5 |

Bridge

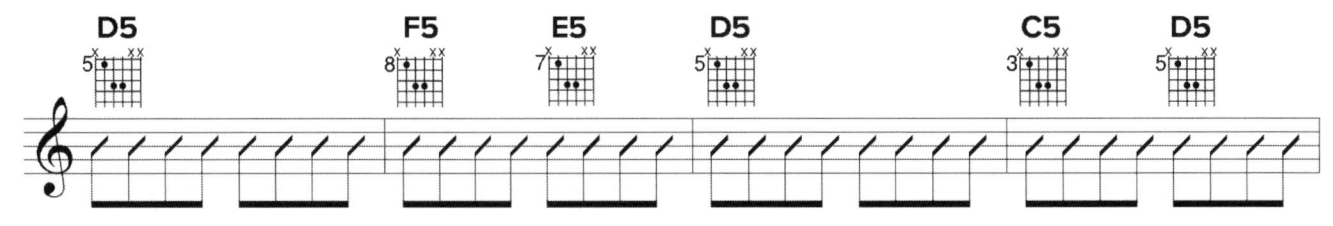

| D5 | F5 | E5 | D5 | C5 | D5 |

Bridge (continued)

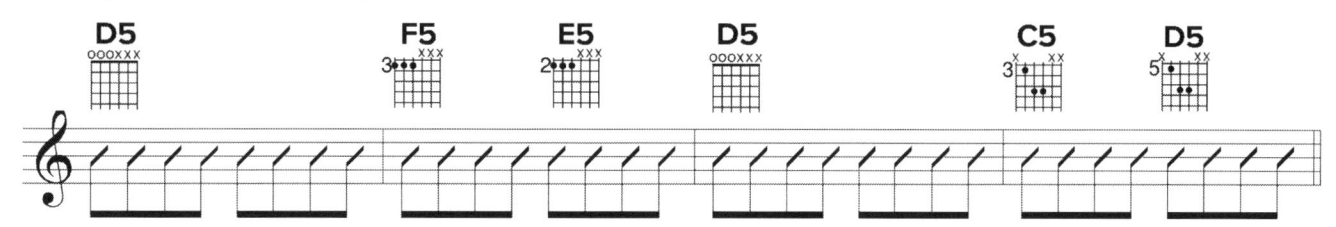

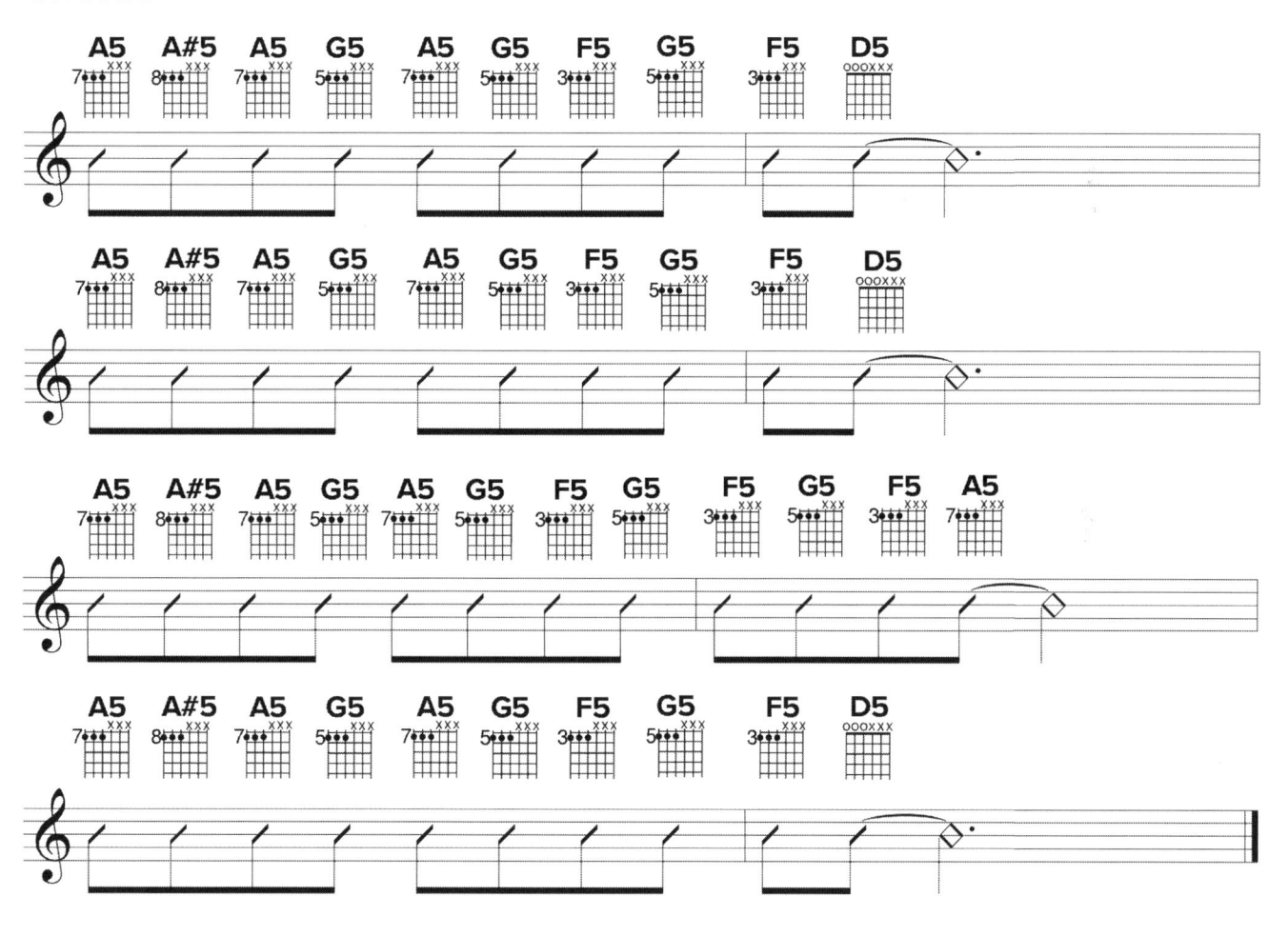

| D5 | F5 | E5 | D5 | C5 | D5 |

Chorus

| A5 | A#5 | A5 | G5 | A5 | G5 | F5 | G5 | F5 | D5 |

| A5 | A#5 | A5 | G5 | A5 | G5 | F5 | G5 | F5 | D5 |

| A5 | A#5 | A5 | G5 | A5 | G5 | F5 | G5 | F5 | G5 | F5 | A5 |

| A5 | A#5 | A5 | G5 | A5 | G5 | F5 | G5 | F5 | D5 |

Blake's Blues

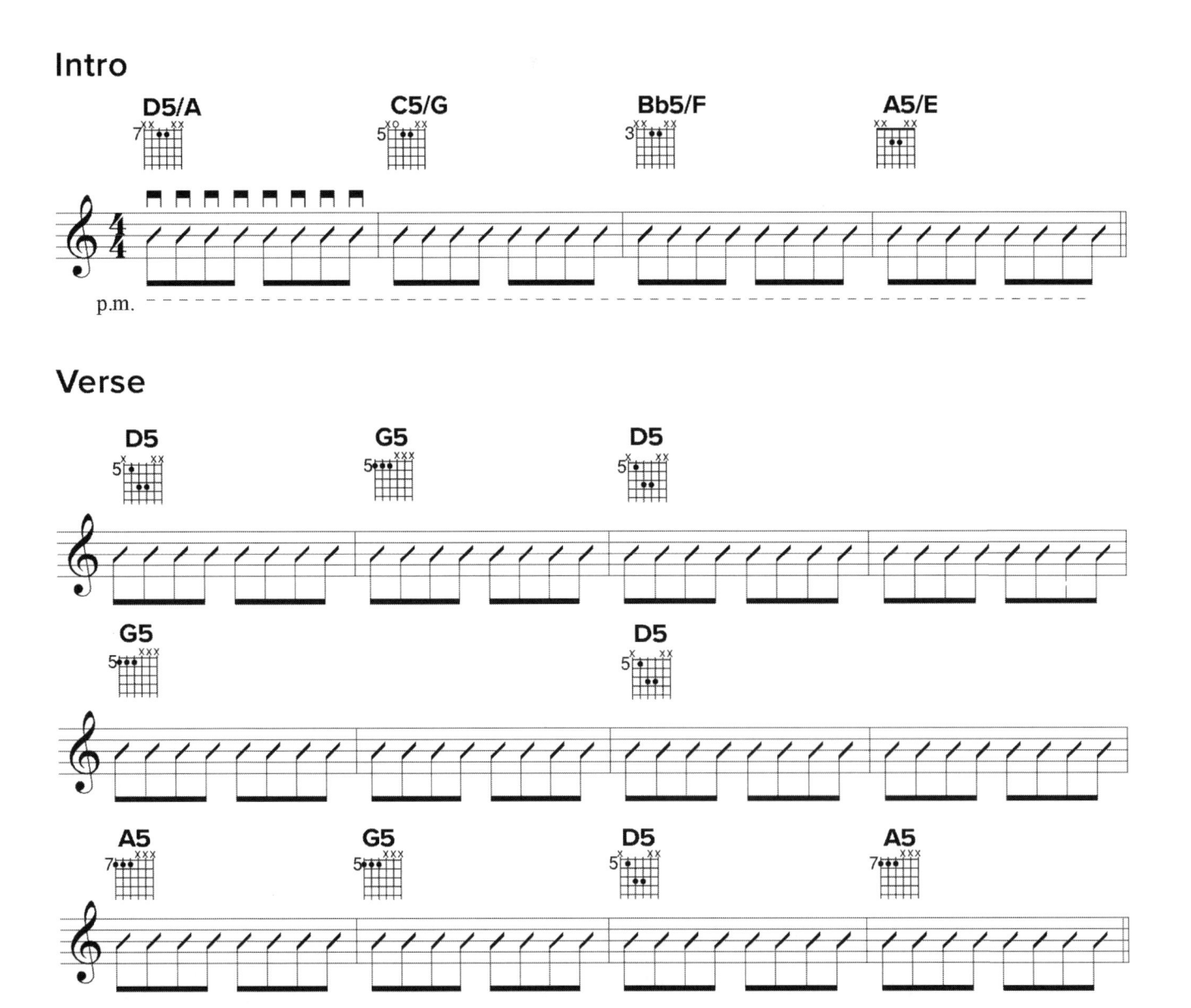

Intro

D5/A   C5/G   Bb5/F   A5/E

p.m.

Verse

D5   G5   D5

G5   D5

A5   G5   D5   A5

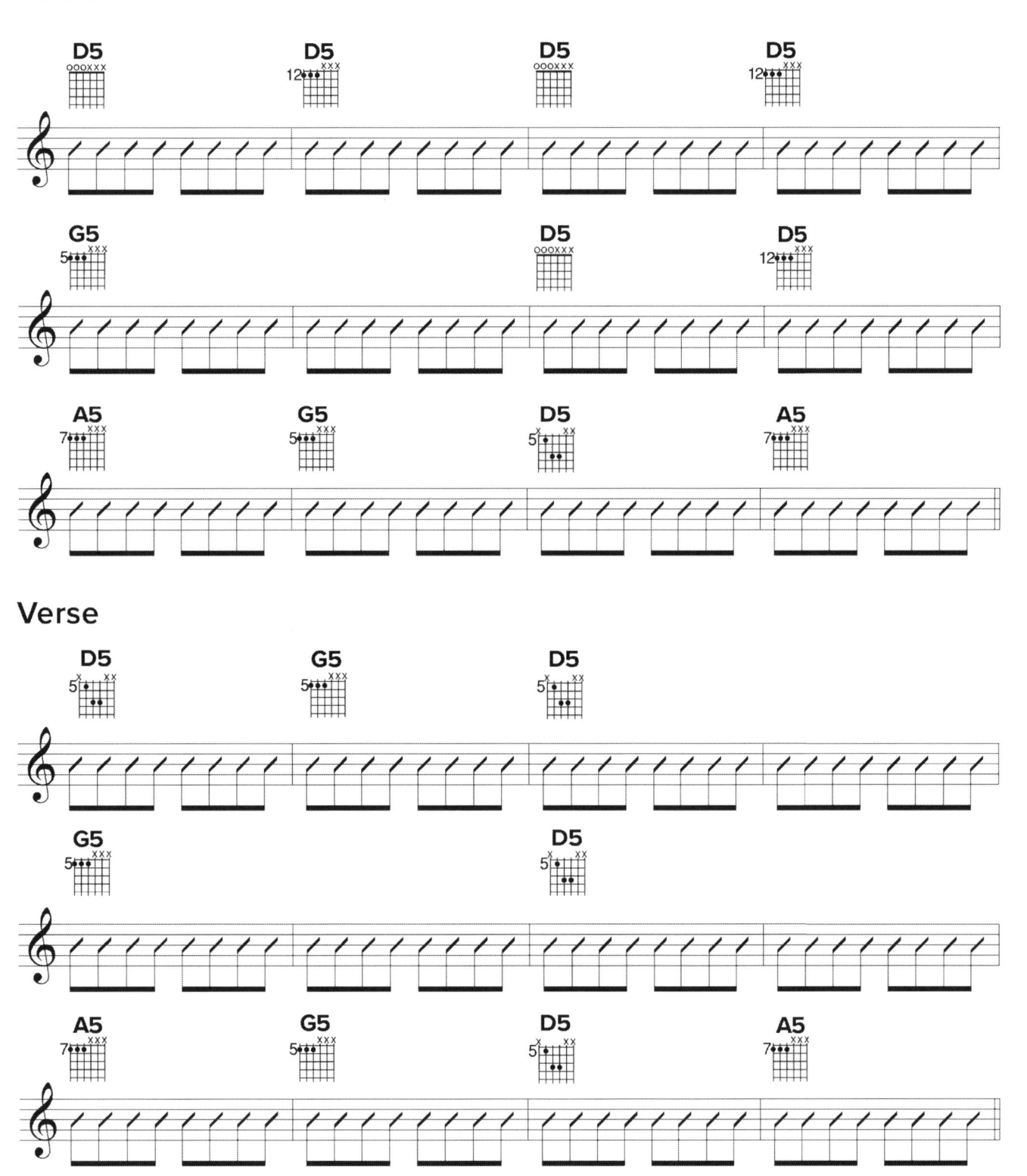

Chorus

D5	D5	D5	D5
G5	D5		D5
A5	G5	D5	A5

Verse

D5	G5	D5	
G5		D5	
A5	G5	D5	A5

Chorus

D5	D5	D5	D5
G5	D5	D5	
A5	G5	D5	A5

Bridge

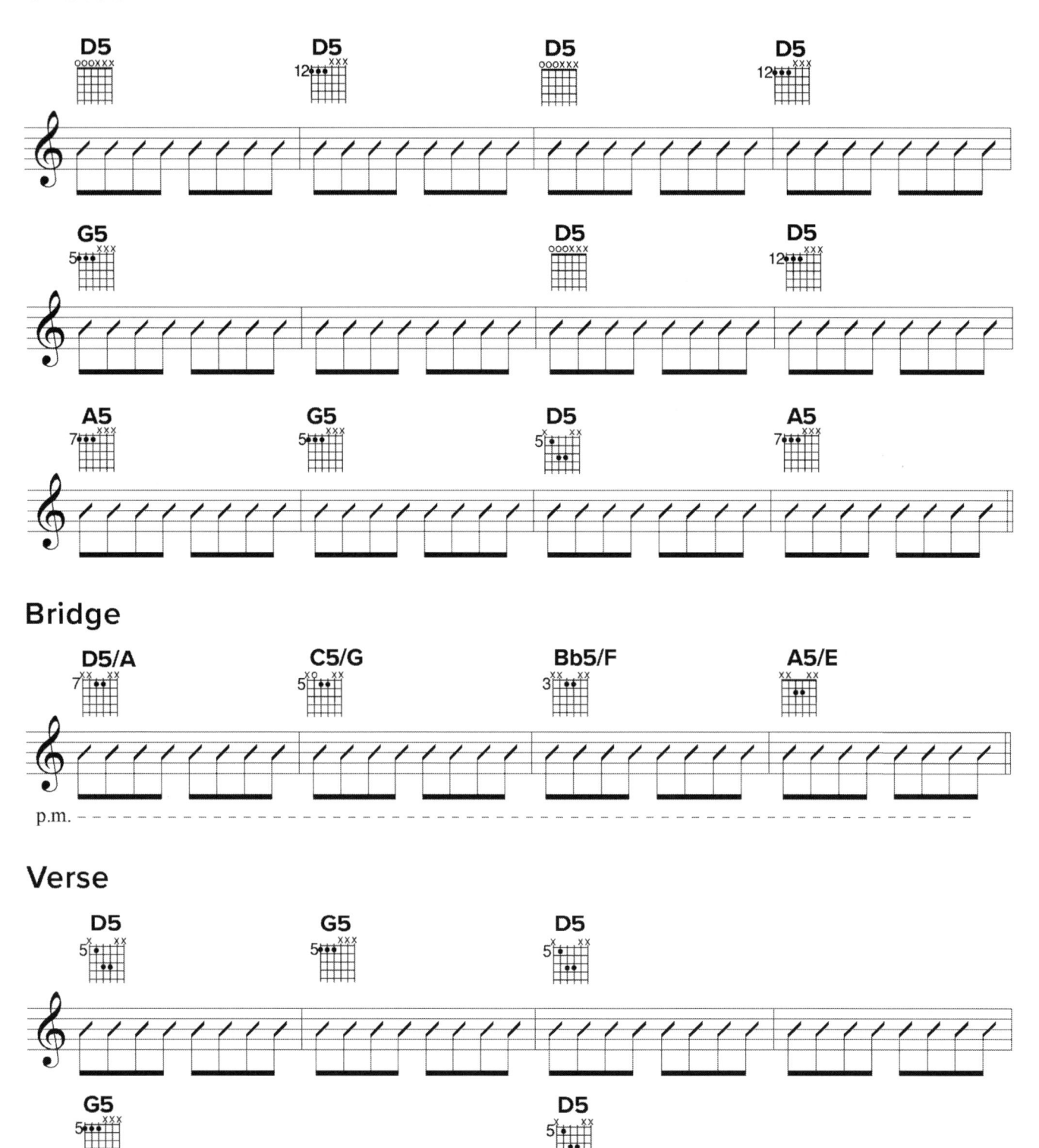

| D5/A | C5/G | Bb5/F | A5/E |

p.m. -

Verse

| D5 | G5 | D5 | |
| G5 | | D5 | |

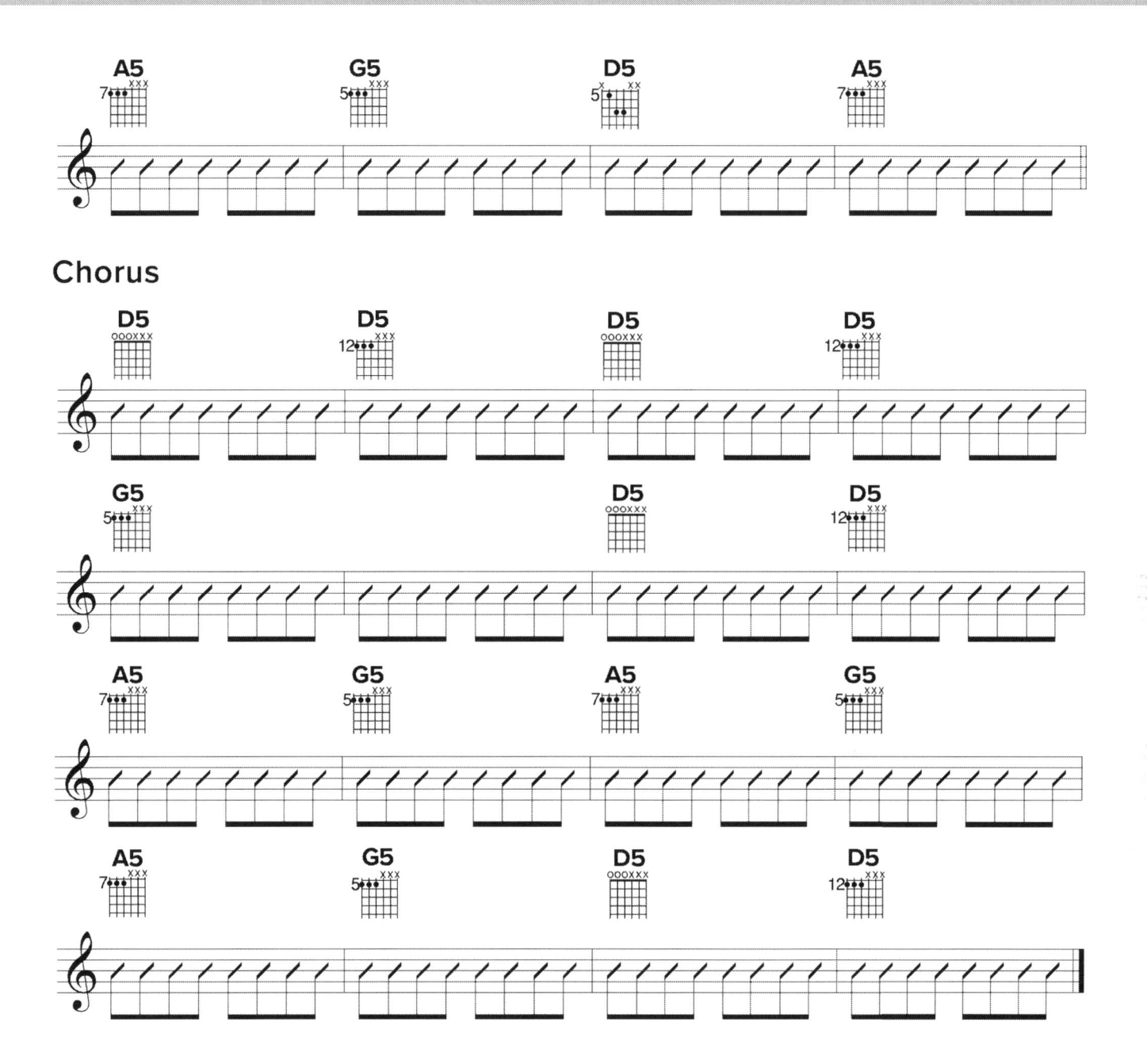

Chorus

The End

Intro

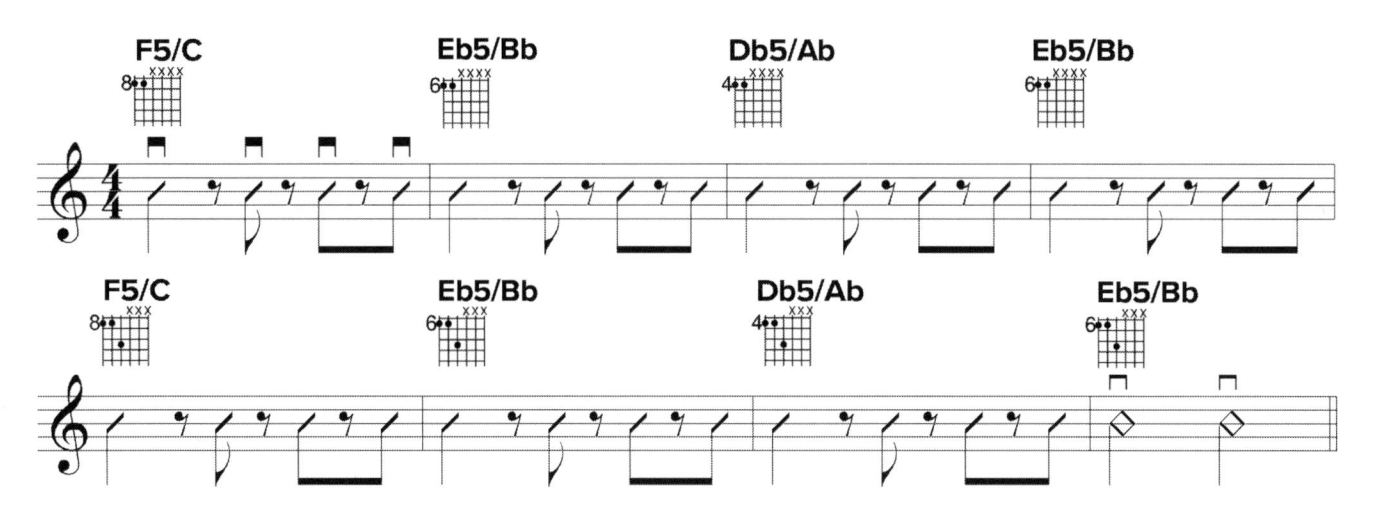

Verse

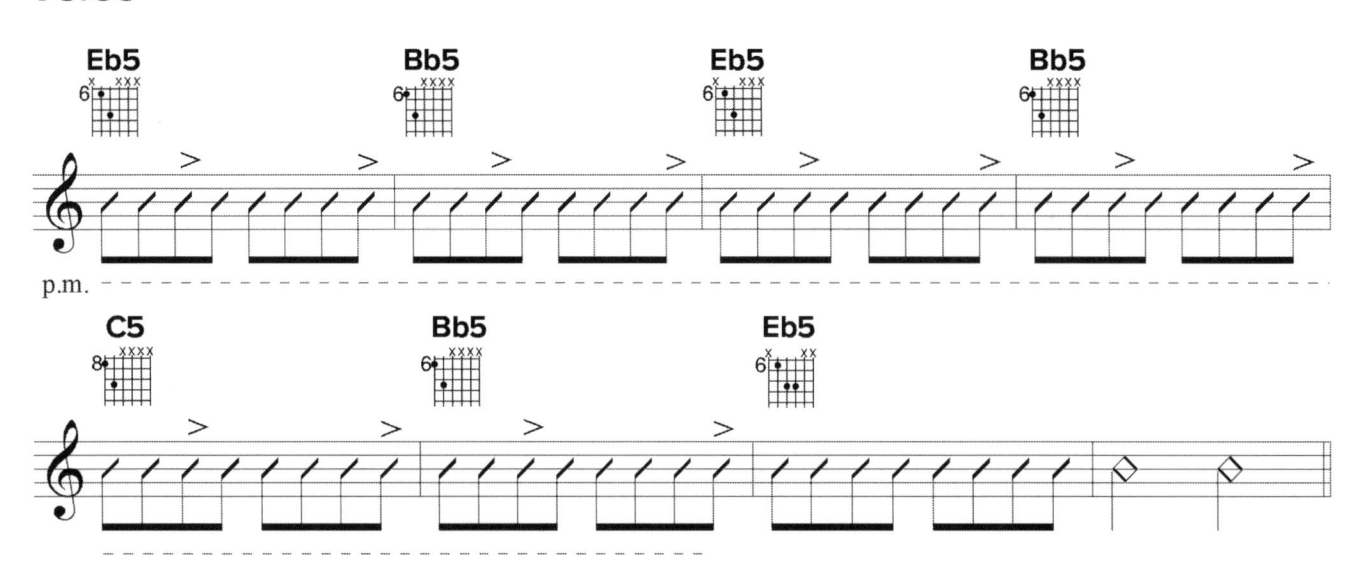

Chorus

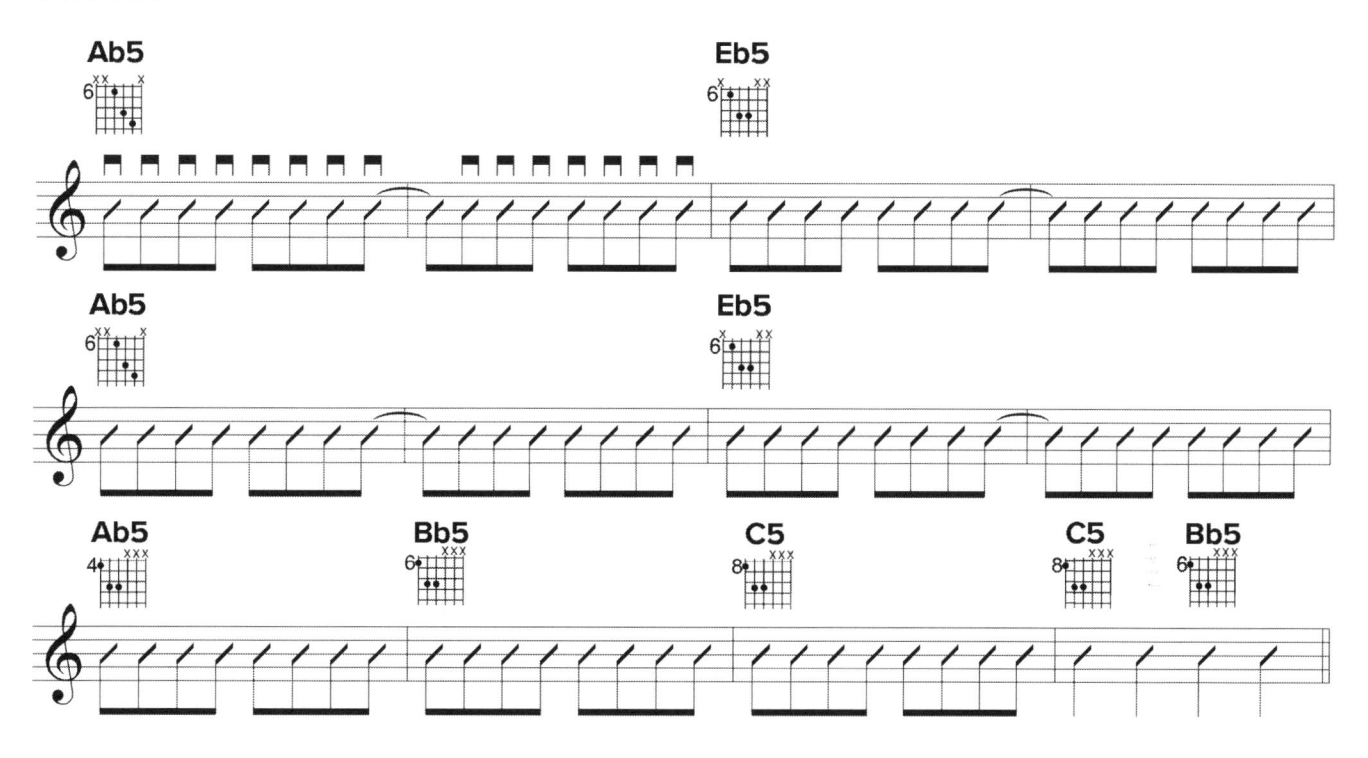

Ab5	Eb5

Ab5	Eb5

Ab5	Bb5	C5	C5	Bb5

Verse

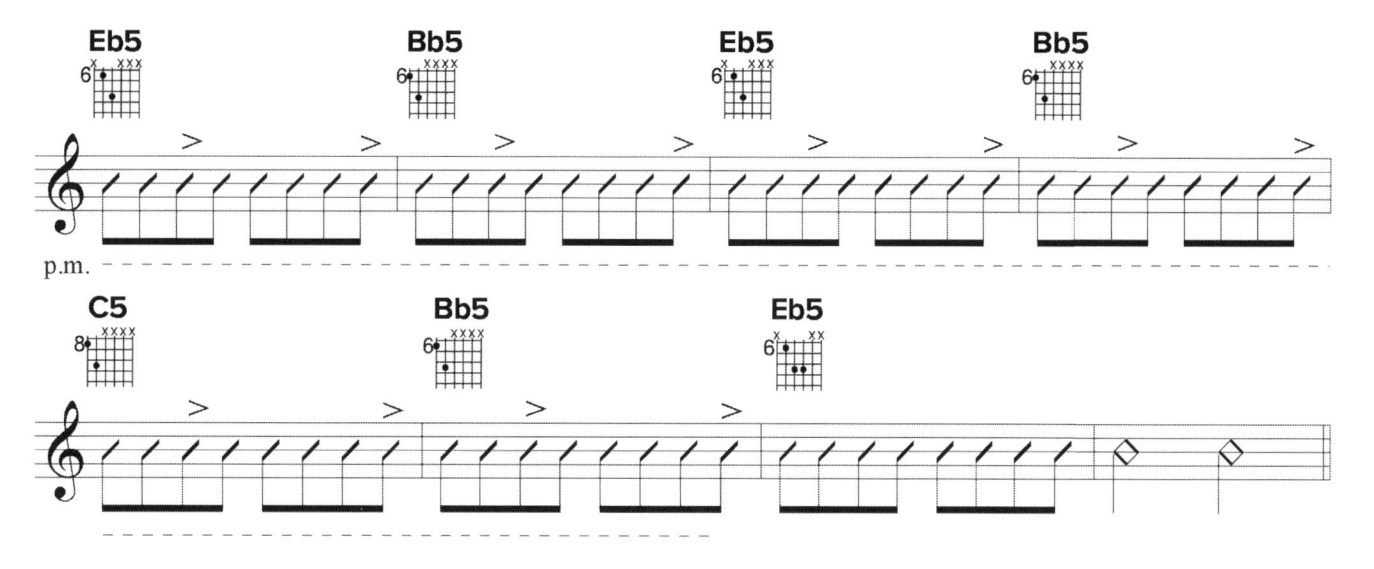

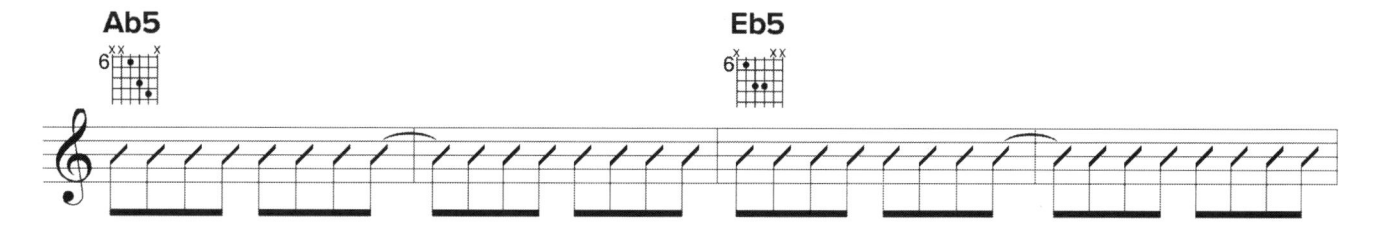

Eb5	Bb5	Eb5	Bb5

p.m.

C5	Bb5	Eb5	

Chorus

Ab5	Eb5

Chorus (continued)

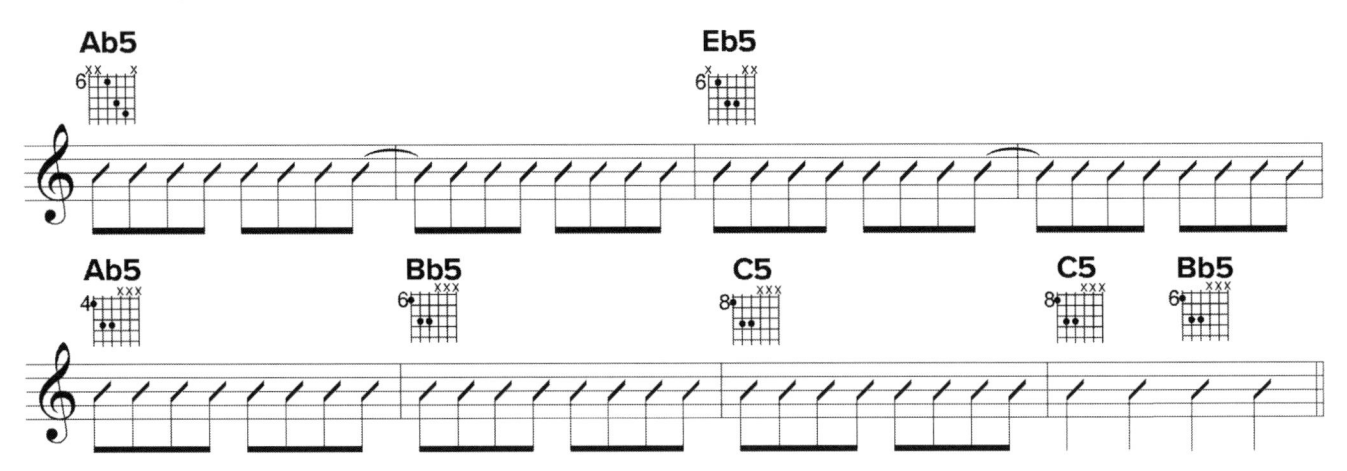

Ab5		Eb5	

Ab5	Bb5	C5	C5	Bb5

Bridge

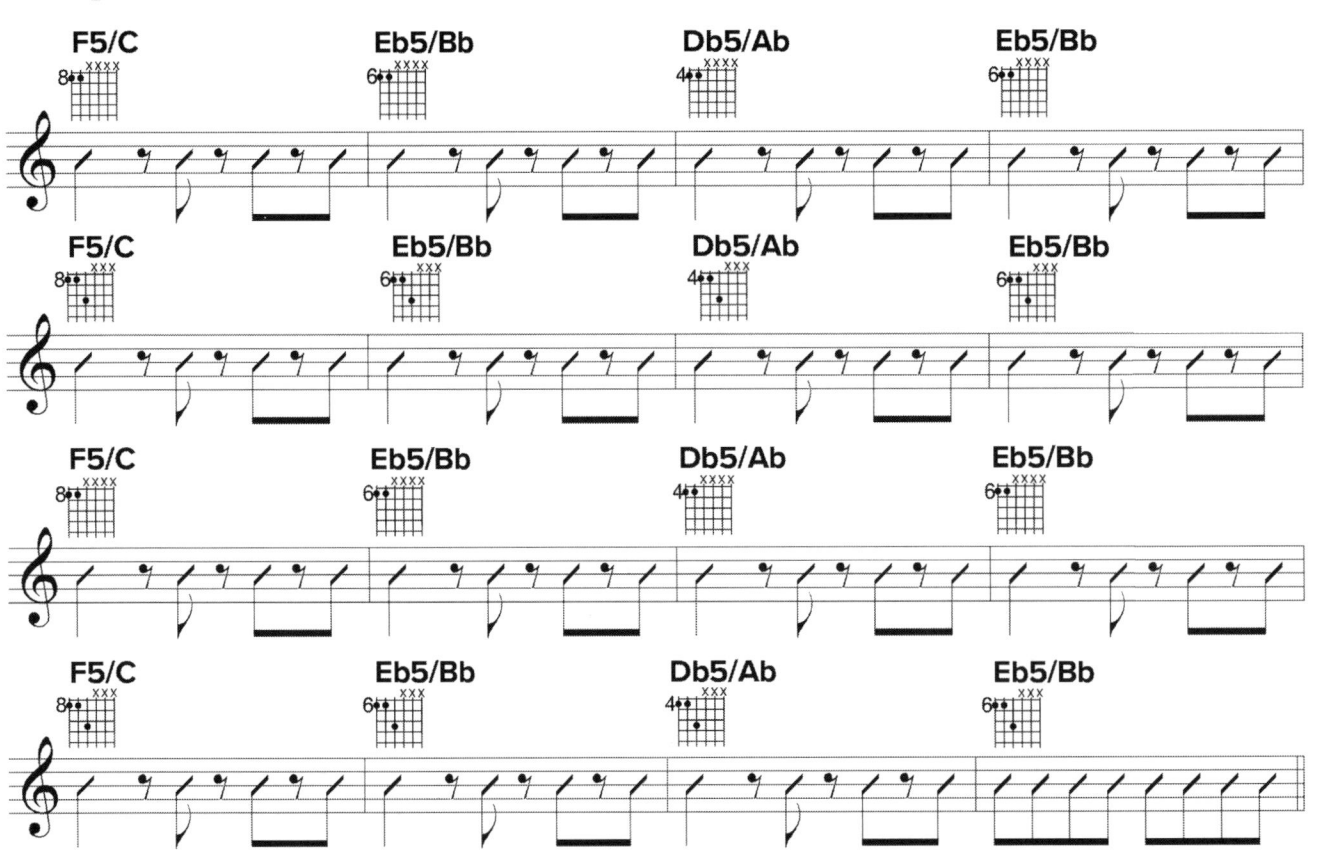

F5/C	Eb5/Bb	Db5/Ab	Eb5/Bb
F5/C	Eb5/Bb	Db5/Ab	Eb5/Bb
F5/C	Eb5/Bb	Db5/Ab	Eb5/Bb
F5/C	Eb5/Bb	Db5/Ab	Eb5/Bb

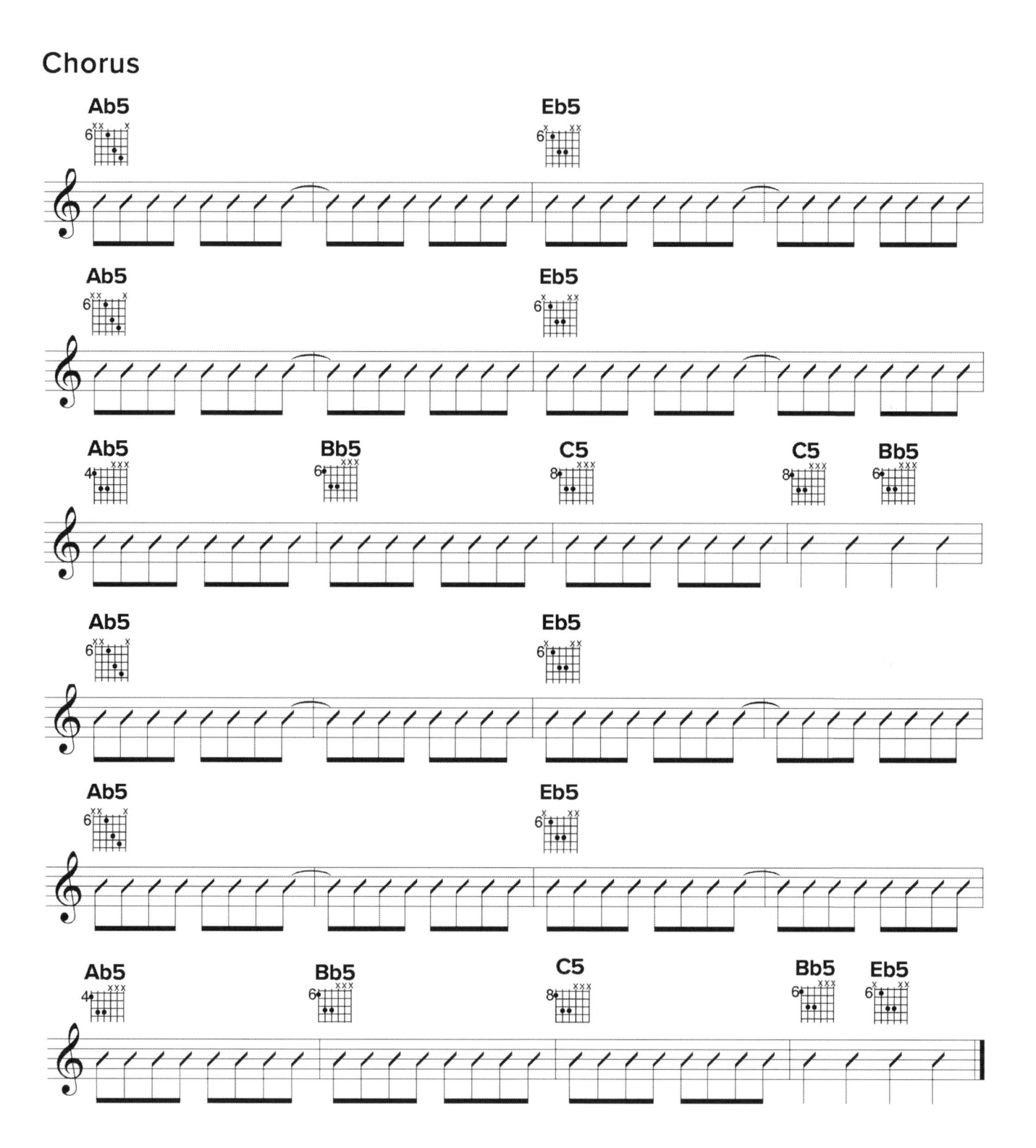

Chorus

Chord Reference

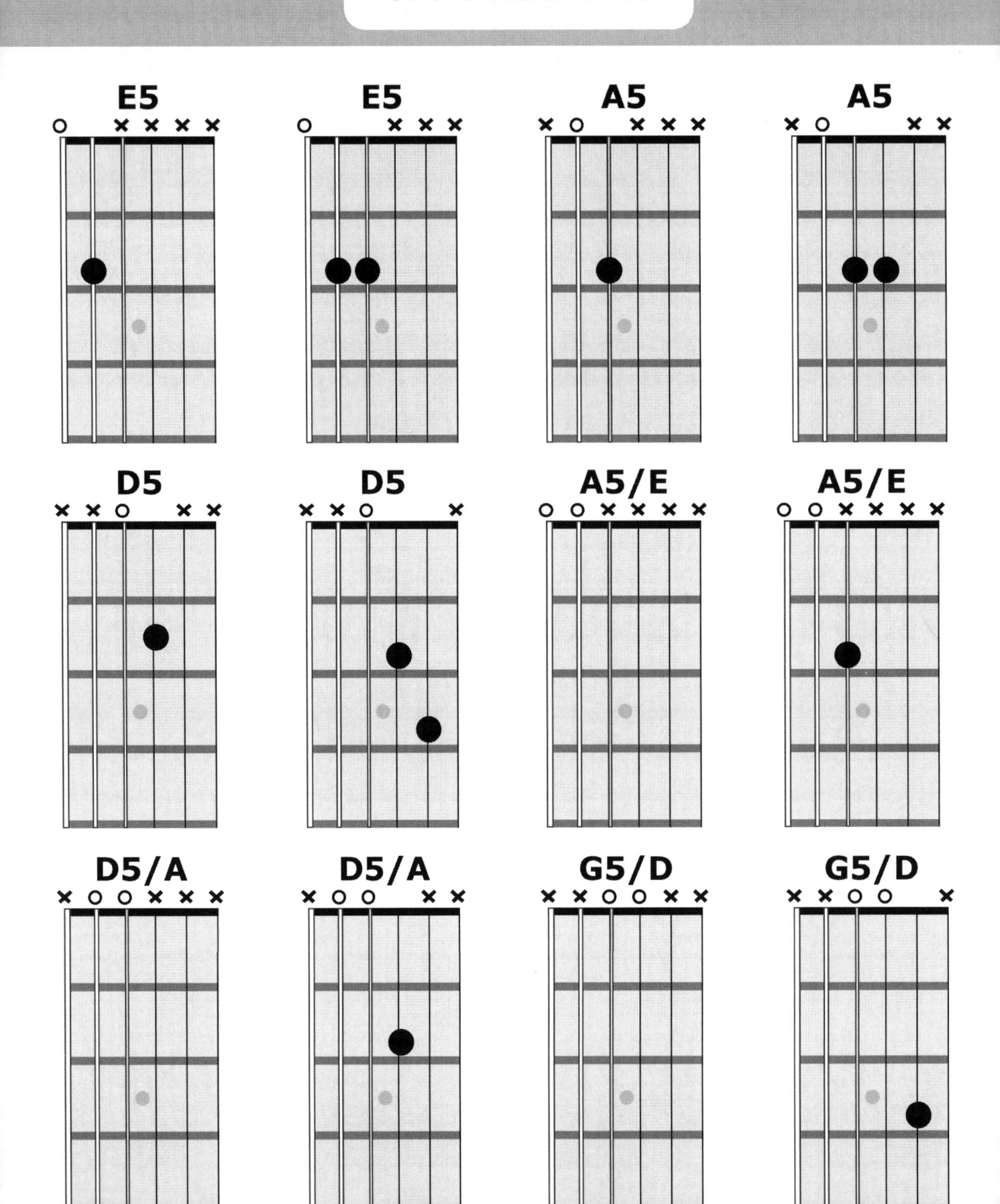

E5	E5	A5	A5
D5	D5	A5/E	A5/E
D5/A	D5/A	G5/D	G5/D

Root 6

Root Location Chart

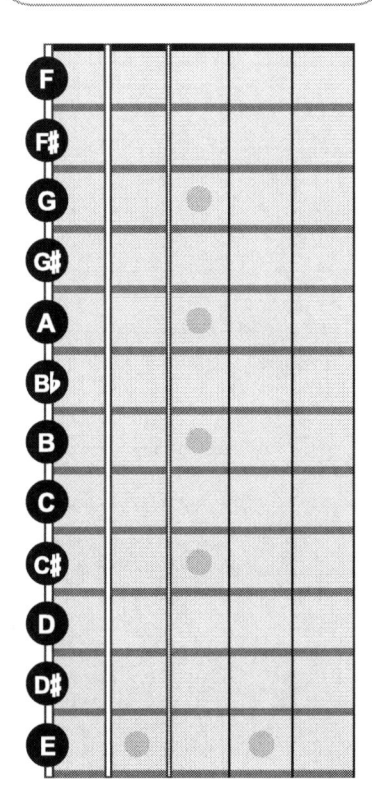

F, F#, G, G#, A, Bb, B, C, C#, D, D#, E

Two-Note
F5

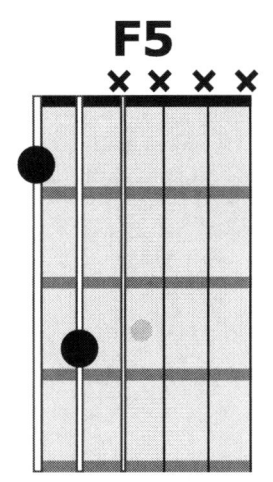

Three-Note
F5

174

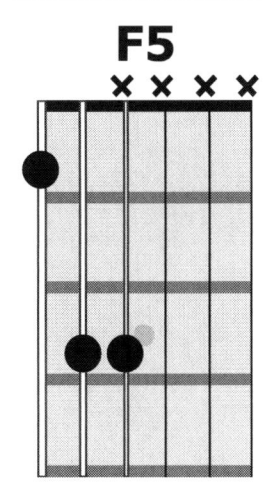

Root 5

Root Location Chart

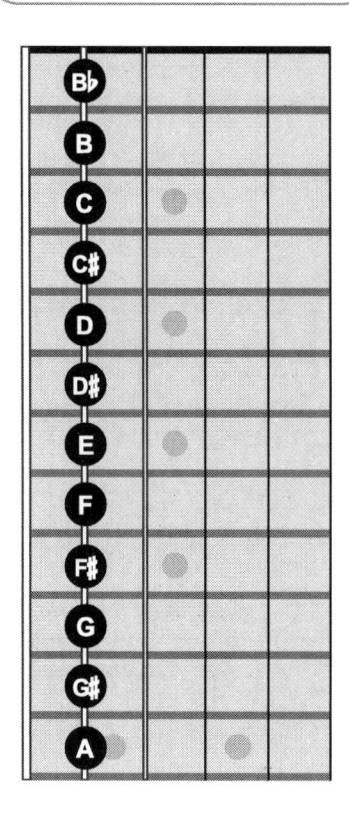

Two-Note	Three-Note	Two-Note	Three-Note
Bb5	**Bb5**	**Bb5/F**	**Bb5/F**

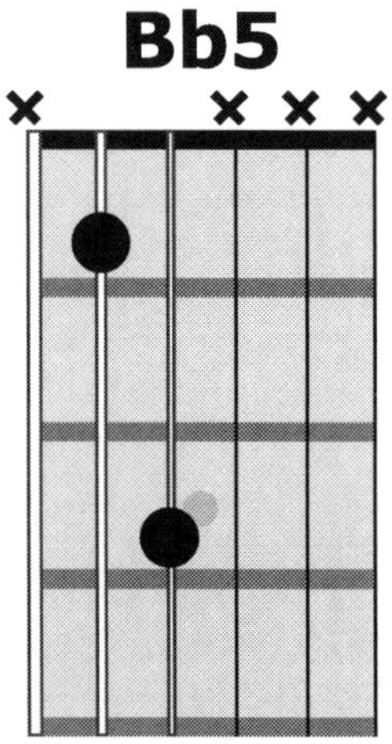

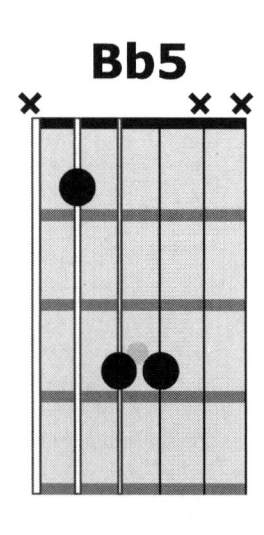

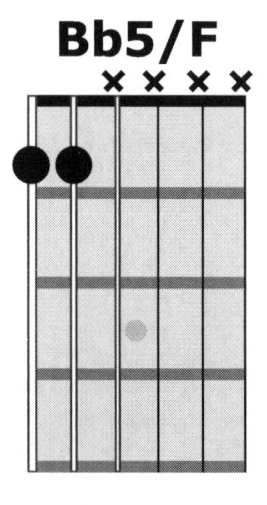

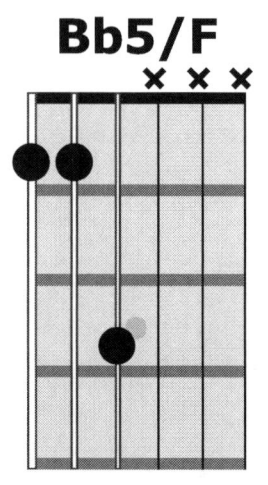

Root 4

Root Location Chart

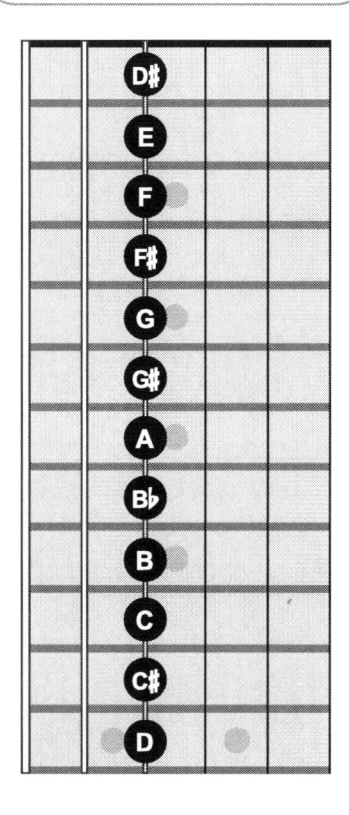

Two-Note	Three-Note	Two-Note	Three-Note
Eb5	**Eb5**	**Eb5/Bb**	**Eb5/Bb**

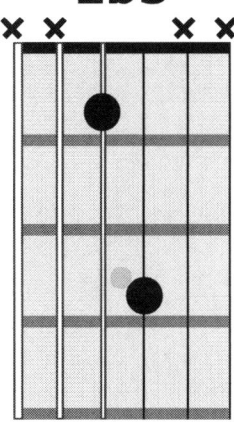

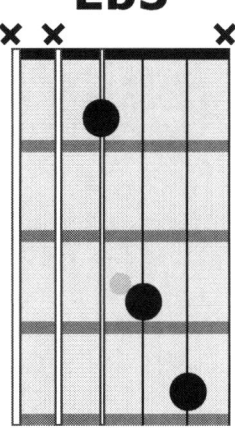

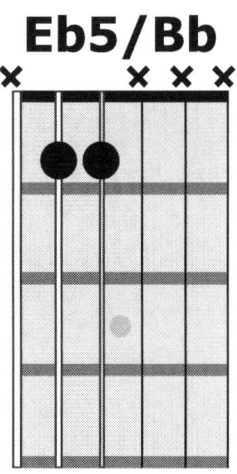

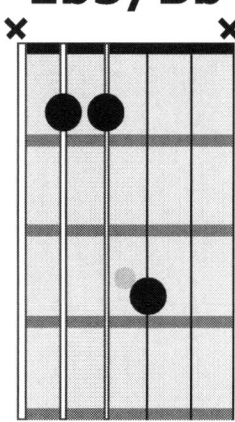

Root 3

Root Location Chart

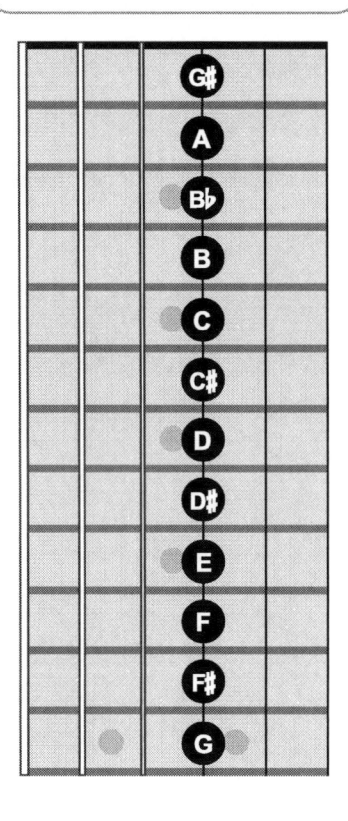

G#, A, Bb, B, C, C#, D, D#, E, F, F#, G

Two-Note

Ab5/Eb

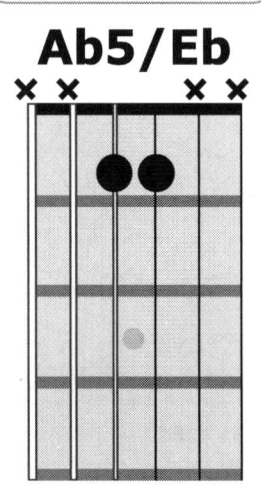

Three-Note

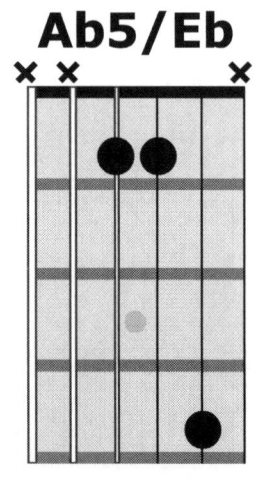

Ab5/Eb

Drop D

Root Location Chart

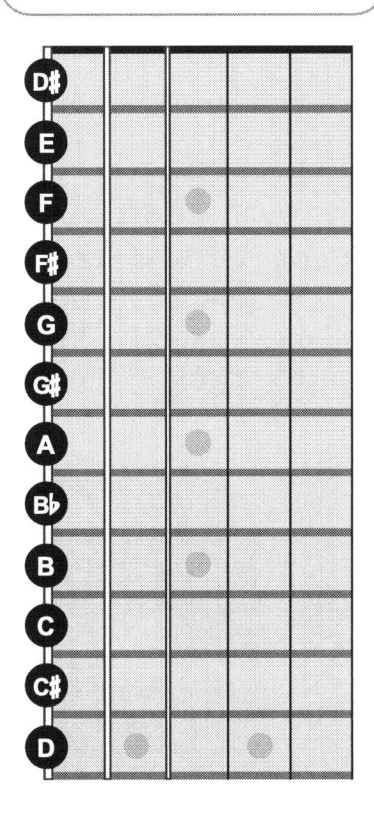

Two-Note — **D5**

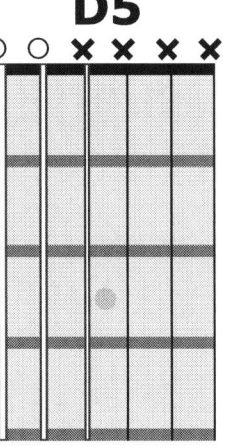

Three-Note — **D5**

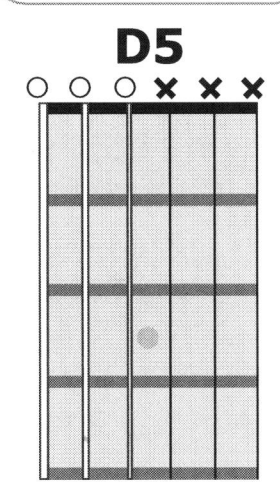

Two-Note — **Eb5**

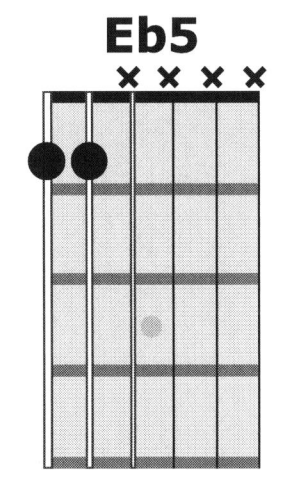

Three-Note — **Eb5**

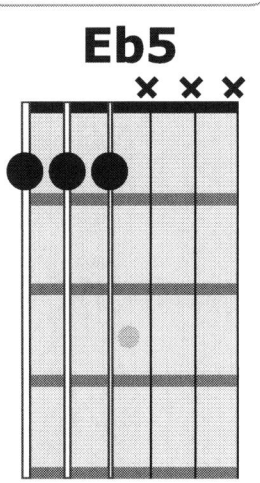

Resources to Take Your Playing Further

Guitar Chord Master™ Beyond Basic Chords

With hundreds of practice exercises and example songs, *Guitar Chord Master: Beyond Basic Chords* takes your rhythm guitar playing to a whole new level. You'll learn how to strum more advanced chords such as maj7, m7, add9, 6s, and more. Not only that, but you'll also learn how to use a capo, play more advanced strum patterns, and start playing in compound time signatures, like 6/8. Available in right and left-handed editions.

The Missing Method for Guitar™ Note Reading Series

Designed with the serious guitar player in mind, The Missing Method for Guitar Note Reading series teaches you how to read every note on the guitar, from the open strings to the 22nd fret. If you are looking to master the fretboard, this is the series for you! Available in right and left-handed editions.

Perfect Practice: How to Zero in on Your Goals and Become a Better Guitar Player Faster

Rethink how you practice. Stop practice burn-out. Learn the secrets to transforming your practice time into time well-spent. This book will help you to figure out how to identify and overcome the obstacles in your way by showing you what to practice and how to structure your time so you see results faster.

Technique Master™ Series

Avoid injury and learn how to play the right way with the Technique Master™ series. Build finger strength, dexterity, and knowledge of the fretboard with warm-up exercises, scales, licks, arpeggios, and more. Discover the difference a good set of warm-ups can make!

Guitar Sheets™ Series

Blank TAB Paper, Chord Chart Paper, Staff Paper, Scale Chart Paper, Songwriting paper and more, bound in paperback to keep your best ideas handy! Need a bit of everything? Check out the first book in the series, the Guitar Sheets Collection, which includes TAB, Staff paper, TAB + Staff, Chord Chart Paper, and Scale Chart Paper. Each book includes useful bonus materials to help you improve.

Find these and more at TheMissingMethod.com.

Printed in Poland
by Amazon Fulfillment
Poland Sp. z o.o., Wrocław